D1527504

Action in
Social Context

Perspectives on Early Development

Perspectives in Developmental Psychology

Series Editor: Michael Lewis
Rutgers Medical School
University of Medicine and Dentistry of New Jersey
New Brunswick, New Jersey

ACTION IN SOCIAL CONTEXT
Perspectives on Early Development
Edited by Jeffrey J. Lockman and Nancy L. Hazen

ASSESSMENT OF YOUNG DEVELOPMENTALLY
DISABLED CHILDREN
Edited by Theodore D. Wachs and Robert Sheehan

COGNITIVE DEVELOPMENT AND CHILD
PSYCHOTHERAPY
Edited by Stephen R. Shirk

THE DIFFERENT FACES OF MOTHERHOOD
Edited by Beverly Birns and Dale F. Hay

FATHERING BEHAVIORS
The Dynamics of the Man–Child Bond
Wade C. Mackey

PSYCHOLOGY OF DEVELOPMENT AND HISTORY
Edited by Klaus F. Riegel

SOCIAL AND PERSONALITY DEVELOPMENT
An Evolutionary Synthesis
Kevin B. MacDonald

Action in Social Context

Perspectives on Early Development

Edited by

JEFFREY J. LOCKMAN

Tulane University
New Orleans, Louisiana

and

NANCY L. HAZEN

University of Texas
Austin, Texas

Plenum Press • New York and London

Library of Congress Cataloging in Publication Data

Action in social context: perspectives on early development / edited by Jeffrey J. Lockman and Nancy L. Hazen.
    p.   cm.—(Perspectives in developmental psychology)
    Includes bibliographies and index.
    ISBN 0-306-43139-4
    1. Ability in infants. 2. Socialization. I. Lockman, Jeffrey J. II. Hazen, Nancy Lynn. III. Series.
BF720.A24A29   1989   89-30873
155.4′22—dc19   CIP

© 1989 Plenum Press, New York
A Division of Plenum Publishing Corporation
233 Spring Street, New York, N.Y. 10013

Printed in the United States of America

Contributors

HEIDELISE ALS, Harvard Medical School and The Children's Hospital, Boston, Massachusetts

MARJORIE J. BEEGHLY, Child Development Unit, Children's Hospital and Harvard Medical School, Boston, Massachusetts

JAY BELSKY, Department of Individual and Family Studies, The Pennsylvania State University, University Park, Pennsylvania

JANETTE B. BENSON, Department of Psychology, University of Denver, Denver, Colorado

INGE BRETHERTON, Department of Child and Family Studies, University of Wisconsin-Madison, Madison, Wisconsin

KURT W. FISCHER, Department of Human Development, Harvard University, Cambridge, Massachusetts

ALAN FOGEL, Department of Psychology, University of Utah, Salt Lake City, Utah

NANCY L. HAZEN, Department of Home Economics, University of Texas at Austin, Austin, Texas

ANNE E. HOGAN, Department of Psychology, University of Miami, Coral Gables, Florida

JAN C. KRUPER, Department of Psychology, Clark University, Worcester, Massachusetts

JEFFREY J. LOCKMAN, Department of Psychology, Tulane University, New Orleans, Louisiana

JAMES P. MCHALE, Department of Psychology, University of California, Berkeley, California

ESTHER THELEN, Department of Psychology, Indiana University, Bloomington, Indiana

INA Č. UŽGIRIS, Department of Psychology, Clark University, Worcester, Massachusetts

MARIE E. VASEK, Department of Psychology, Clark University, Worcester, Massachusetts

JOAN VONDRA, Department of Psychology in Education, University of Pittsburgh, Pittsburgh, Pennsylvania

Preface

This is a book about the development of action and skill in the first years of life. But it differs in an important way from most past treatments of the subject. The present volume explores how the development of action is related to the contexts, especially the social ones, in which actions function. In past work, little attention has focused on this relationship. The prevailing view has been that infants develop skills on their own, independent of contributions from other individuals or the surrounding culture. The present volume is a challenge to that view. It is based on the premise that many early skills are embedded in interpersonal activities or are influenced by the activities of other individuals. It assumes further that by examining how skills function in interpersonal contexts, insights will be gained into their acquisition and structuring. In effect, this volume suggests that the development of cognitive, perceptual, and motor skills needs to be reexamined in relation to the goals and contexts that are inherently associated with these skills. The contributors to the volume have all adopted this general perspective. They seek to understand the development of early action by considering the functioning of action in context.

Our motivation for addressing these issues stemmed in part from a growing sense of dissatisfaction as we surveyed the literature on skill development in early childhood. It often seemed that there was little integration across areas of research concerned with cognitive and perceptual skills on the one hand and with social skills on the other, even though some of the very same actions were being studied. In addition, the types of questions being asked in these research areas seemed very different. In the cognitive and perceptual domains investigators were focusing on structural and processing issues largely independent of context. By contrast, in the social domain, investigators were emphasizing the qualities and characteristics of the contexts in which skills function and not the structures underlying the functioning skills.

A more unified view of skill development requires integrating both structural and functional approaches. We believe that a full explanation of the structure and mechanisms of skill development cannot be achieved without considering the *purposes* skills serve over the course of early development. The implication that follows is obvious. To understand the development of many cognitive and perceptuomotor skills, it is also important to consider how they function in social contexts and how their development is socially influenced.

The idea that context is an integral aspect of development and not some variable to be ignored has been gaining increasing acceptance in developmental circles (Rogoff, 1984). Western psychologists have recently been applying the ideas of the Soviet psychologist Vygotsky to study how children acquire skills through social tutelage. In large measure, though, these efforts have been limited to cognitive abilities appearing in the preschool years and beyond, when children are already capable of symbolic functioning. With the exception of Kaye's (1982) work, there have been few broad attempts to explore how early cognitive and perceptuomotor skills are embedded in social activity. The present volume continues and extends this type of analysis but should not be seen solely or primarily as an attempt to apply Vygotsky's ideas to the infancy period. Rather, it is an effort to understand how actions emerge in context, specifically infant and toddler actions that too often are treated as occurring and developing apart from the contexts in which they naturally reside.

The contributors to this volume initially addressed these issues at a Study Group of the Society for Research in Child Development that was convened at Tulane University. The contributors were selected because their work is representative of research on skilled action from the fields of cognitive, motor, perceptual, and social development and because they have all shown a sensitivity to contextual issues in their efforts to understand the ontogeny of action. At the Study Group meeting, participants were asked to consider how the development of the actions of interest to them could be viewed within a contextual framework. Based on the interchange that occurred during the meeting, Study Group members continued to address this problem and develop their positions. The resulting volume is the product of those efforts. We hope that it captures the excitement and promise that we all felt during the Study Group meeting. More importantly we hope that the present volume promotes a conceptualization of action development that is contextually based but not limited to any one area of development.

Finally, to our contributors, to the Society for Research in Child Development, to the Foundation for Child Development which has generously supported the Study Group program, and to Tulane University, we offer our heartfelt thanks. Without the support of these individuals and organizations, this volume would not have been possible.

Jeffrey J. Lockman
Nancy L. Hazen

REFERENCES

Rogoff, B. (1984). Introduction: Thinking and learning in social context. In B. Rogoff and J. Lave (Eds.), *Everyday cognition: Its development in social context* (pp. 1–8). Cambridge: Harvard University Press.

Kaye, K. (1982). *The mental and social life of babies*. Chicago: University of Chicago Press.

Contents

Part IV. Conclusion

Chapter 9. The Big Picture for Infant Development: Levels and

Kurt W. Fischer and Anne E. Hogan

CHAPTER 1

Skill and Context

NANCY L. HAZEN AND JEFFREY J. LOCKMAN

INTRODUCTION

Few would deny that during the first few years of life, developing humans go through more profound psychological and behavioral changes than they will during the remaining 70 or so years of their lives. In 2 years' time, the helpless newborn becomes a person who can purposely and appropriately explore and manipulate objects and environments, solve practical problems, and represent and communicate information through gesture, speech, and play. Investigators in different areas of early development—perceptual, cognitive, and socioemotional—all describe these achievements in terms of the infant having acquired certain skills. That is, infants become able to perform actions smoothly, without trial and error, to accomplish particular goals.

Classes of skilled action that have been of particular interest to investigators in recent years include motor skills, perceptuomotor coordination, imitation, object play and manipulation, symbolic play and enactment of pretense, nonverbal communication, spatial orientation, and exploration. Very often one particular skill is simultaneously perceived and examined by different investigators as an exemplar of two or more different classes of skilled actions. A baby's action of banging a drum after watching his or her parent do so may be viewed as an example of motor skill development, imitation, object play, or nonverbal communication.

NANCY L. HAZEN • Department of Home Economics, University of Texas at Austin, Austin, Texas 78712.   JEFFREY J. LOCKMAN • Department of Psychology, Tulane University, New Orleans, Louisiana 70118.

1

Despite this common concern with skilled action and even in some instances with the same or similar actions, investigators in different areas have made few attempts to form a shared concept of skill and relate it to the actions that they are studying. The major purpose of this volume is to work toward a more general, integrated conceptualization of skilled action and its development so that we may better understand the ontogenesis of particular action classes. We will argue that this may be accomplished by focusing on how various classes of actions function and develop in social contexts. The contributors to this volume all share an interest in early skill development, although they may study different classes of skilled action or approach them from different theoretical perspectives. However, all in one way or another attempt to understand their particular action class, and more generally, the nature of skill development by considering the purposes that these skills actually serve through the course of early development. We will argue that consideration of how skilled action functions in the social contexts of human development can elucidate the structural nature of skill in general, the functional interrelationships between classes of skilled action, and finally, explanations of skill development.

TOWARD A SHARED CONCEPTION OF SKILL

To achieve these goals, we must first consider what is meant by *skill*. Several investigators (e.g., Bernstein, 1967; Bruner, 1970; Fischer, 1980; Kaye, 1982) have attempted to define skill in terms that cut across different classes of skilled action, recognizing that their formal structure exhibits some common properties. These include the following: (1) skills are intentional and goal-directed; (2) skills develop as the child is progressively able to control sources of variation in using actions to achieve goals; (3) skills are serially and hierarchically organized into constituent subroutines; (4) skills involve the use of feedback to guide their execution; and (5) skills can be generalized and flexibly adapted to different contexts.

In considering these properties, it is important to realize that they can never be completely understood apart from each other or apart from the social contexts in which the actual skills are used. Intentionality or purposefulness, for instance, has been recognized as an integral part of skill since the days of Tolman. Intentionality has been defined in terms of the organism's persistent attempts to overcome obstructions or failures in achieving a goal (Kaye, 1979; Tolman, 1932). Yet intentionality alone does not indicate the presence of skill. Skill also necessarily implies a form of generalization—that the organism can achieve a desired goal by adjusting actions to changing conditions in varied situations. Thus, according to this conception of skill, intentionality is linked to the notions of flexibility and applicability to different contexts and sensitivity to feedback in these different contexts. To determine whether actions possess these properties and hence are skilled requires studying actions in a variety of contexts.

Intentionality, flexibility, and applicability to different contexts are also interrelated in skill acquisition. In acquiring a skill, the organism progressively gains control over the component actions that make up the skill, eventually mastering them and thereby reducing the degrees of freedom involved in performing this system of actions. As this happens, the skill becomes more automatic and falls into a particular spatial-temporal sequential pattern (Bernstein, 1967; Bruner, 1970; Fischer, 1980). However, the outcome of this process should not be viewed as some reflexive or sterotypic form of behavior. Because skills are also defined in terms of intentionality or goal directedness, they are necessarily open systems, not tied to specific situations but flexible and generalizable, adaptive to feedback (Kaye, 1979). Accordingly, they can be applied to new situations to meet new or related goals, capable of being adjusted to deal with relevant sources of variation in these new contexts.

When an old skill is applied to a new situation, the skill will always be modified to some extent. This can be done by (1) adjusting the spatial or temporal configuration of the subroutines; (2) changing the serial ordering of the component subroutines; or (3) substituting, adding, or deleting different subroutines. The latter two cases involve an actual structural change in the skill; in these instances, a new skill may be said to emerge. Then the cycle repeats itself and the components of the new skill become automatic and fall into a smooth spatial-temporal pattern, permitting this new skill to be hierarchically incorporated into still higher order skills.

CONTEXT AND THE STUDY OF SKILLED ACTION

Because skills are intentional or goal directed and are adaptive to feedback, the subroutine structure and emergence of new skills can only be understood in the contexts in which they function. Previous attempts to understand the development of different action classes have often neglected the contextual aspects of skill use, however. Researchers interested in perceptual and motor development have often studied early skilled action to better understand the role of experience in the development of perceptuomotor coordination (e.g., see Lockman & Ashmead, 1983) and the relationship of early biologically determined "units of action" to later skilled activity (Twitchell, 1970). In fact, in work on perceptual development, the Gibsons' (E. J. Gibson, 1982; J. J. Gibson, 1966, 1979) ecological approach has been the only major perspective that has explicitly considered the mutuality of the organism and its environment—in other words, context —in explaining perceptual functioning.

Research on early cognitive development has also focused on early skilled action, largely due to the influence of Piaget (1952, 1954, 1962). Although researchers in cognitive development often dispute Piaget's accounts of skill development, they largely follow Piaget in assuming that the most important questions to ask about early skilled action concern what these actions reveal about the child's developing knowledge of the physical world, particularly the structure of this knowledge.

Thus in most instances, researchers interested in perceptual, motor, and cognitive development have traditionally been concerned with analyzing the nature, operation, and development of the physical and cognitive structures and processes that underlie children's use of skilled actions. As such, they attempt to infer the general principles governing performance of any given skill across situations. They have been much less interested in studying how and when children actually *use* these actions in particular social and affective contexts or in how these uses change with development. In fact, they have made explicit attempts to *decontextualize* experimental procedures and to ensure that their observations will generalize across situations. For this reason, studies of early perceptual and cognitive development have generally been either controlled laboratory experiments or observations made in controlled laboratorylike settings rather than the "everyday" settings in which children actually use their cognitive, perceptual, and motor skills. Although controlled experimental research is clearly essential for determining causal mechanisms, a full explanation of the structure and mechanisms of skill development cannot be obtained without considering the *functions* these skills actually serve during the course of early development. This in turn requires attending to the contexts in which skills function.

The traditional emphasis on *structural* concerns and neglect of *functional* issues has, we believe, impeded an integrated view of early skill development in two general ways. First, investigators of different types of skilled actions typically consider the development of the skills of interest to them in isolation from other, interrelated skills. This may be because they have concentrated on analyzing the nature and development of the structures and principles underlying the development of isolated classes of skills, "unconfounded" by their integration with other classes of skills in everyday contexts. For example, if a mother rolls a ball to a baby and the baby rolls it back, the baby's action involves the interrelation of several social, perceptuomotor, and cognitive skills, including the ability to match or imitate an action, aim and push an object, and take turns in social interaction. Focusing on isolated skills may lead to an overly simlified view of skilled action, neglecting one of its most basic characteristics: the hierarchical integration of component skills within even more complex ones.

Second, the same action classes have often been studied from different theoretical perspectives to understand different areas of development, but these findings have rarely been related to each other. It seems that investigators have seldom recognized that a given action class may serve a variety of goals and thus function in several contexts. Object manipulation, for instance, may function as a means of obtaining information about objects (Lockman & McHale, Chapter 5 this volume) and as a means of establishing a shared format when performed to match a caregiver's activity (Užgiris, Benson, Kruper, & Vasek, Chapter 4 this volume). In general, differences in theoretical frameworks have led to diversity in the types of questions asked and in the types of methods employed. Integration across the domains of perceptuocognitive and socioemotional development has been particularly difficult to achieve.

In contrast to research in perceptual-cognitive development, research in socioemotional development has been directly concerned with the social contexts of skill development, especially mother–infant interaction. Investigators of socioemotional development typically examine how various social contexts affect and are affected by the child's actions and how such effects change with development and vary between individuals. In many of these studies, the same type of event has been observed by researchers from the perceptuocognitive tradition as well. For example, infants unmasking their mothers in a peek-a-boo game have been studied from the perceptuocognitive perspective as an example of covering/uncovering skill and its relation to infants' underlying knowledge of objects (Decarie, 1978; Hodapp, Goldfield, & Boyatzis, 1984) and from the socioemotional perspective as an example of an interactive mother–infant game (Bruner & Sherwood, 1976; Ross & Kay, 1979). The difference, of course, is that investigators interested in perceptuocognitive development have been primarily concerned with the actions themselves rather than their context (mother–child interaction) or their functions in that context, whereas the opposite has generally been true of investigators from the socioemotional tradition. Thus investigators of early adult–child and peer interaction have focused relatively little upon the perceptual and cognitive *structures* underlying the skills involved in early social interaction and more upon the social contexts of interaction.

Because of the focus on the social contexts of interaction, researchers of socioemotional development have generally been careful to insure that their observations occur in settings that permit typical patterns of social interaction. As a consequence, research on early skill development conducted from a socioemotional perspective is typically seen as more "ecologically valid" than research done from the perceptuocognitive perspective. However, the areas of social and emotional development have often been viewed as more descriptive and less explanatory regarding developmental change than the areas of perceptual and cognitive development, perhaps because there is not a clear unifying theory dealing with the structural developments that underlie changes in social behavior.

Clearly, a full understanding of early skill development requires an approach that integrates structural and functional concerns. Because skill does not occur without intentions to achieve goals and because the components, applications, and execution of skill cannot be understood apart from these goals, explanations of structural developments in skill depend upon analyses of skill usage in context. Likewise, developmental changes in the social functions of skills cannot be explained without reference to the structures and processes underlying skill development. Distinctions between perceptuocognitive and socioemotional approaches break down when structural and functional concerns are integrated. For example, to understand fully the development of the infant's skill in covering and uncovering objects, we need to examine the purposes served by this skill in daily life, which will inevitably involve parent–child interactions such as peek-a-boo and hiding/finding games with objects; and to understand fully the development of parent–infant games, we need to examine the underlying cognitive and perceptual competencies that explain how infants actually engage in these games at different points in development. These two lines of inquiry become virtually identical if we acknowledge that the structure of skill is shaped by its function in everyday contexts.

Developmentalists are becoming increasingly aware of the importance of integrating structural and functional issues. This awareness was first manifested in the field of language development. Bruner (1975), in commenting on advances in this field, argued that

> . . . it has become increasingly customary in the past several decades to consider language as a code, a set of rules by which grammatical utterances are produced and in terms of which they are comprehended in order to extract their meaning. . . . It has resulted in the stunning perception of the formal nature of language and has permitted the application of powerful

mathematical techniques to the field of linguistics. But all advances in knowledge have attendant costs. Depth of insight must often be earned at the cost
of breadth of perspective. So, whilst we have in the past decades learned
much about the STRUCTURE of language, we have perhaps over looked
important considerations about its FUNCTIONS. Our oversight has, I think,
turned our attention away from how language is used. And since the uses of
language are, I believe, crucial to an understanding of how language is
acquired, how it is INITIALLY used, the study of language acquisition has
been distorted. . . . Language is acquired as an instrument for regulating
joint activity and joint attention. Indeed, its very structure reflects these
functions and its acquisition is saturated with them. (Bruner, 1975, pp. 1–2)

This paragraph could easily apply to the early development of skilled
action, except that infants typically use actions for nonsocial functions
before social functions. Perhaps because of this, investigators of sensorimotor development generally conduct their research as though infant
action was fundamentally asocial. But even though infants may not
intend that their early vocalizations, gestures, motor movements, and
object manipulations serve communicative functions, caregivers often
interpret them as such, thus influencing the infants' usage of them and
ultimately, infants' interpretations of their meanings (Kaye, 1982; Thelen
& Fogel, Chapter 2 this volume). Because caregivers interpret and structure infants' use of actions, the structure of these actions cannot be
separated from the social contexts in which they occur. Thus, the key to
understanding *why* a given skill has a particular structure at different
developmental periods and *how* children use it during these periods rests
in analyzing the changing social and nonsocial functions of that skill in
the first few years of life.

INTEGRATING SKILL AND CONTEXT

In their endeavors to interface the structural developmental changes
in early skilled action with its changing functions over the course of early
development, the contributors to this volume have largely drawn upon
two types of theoretical approaches that have been sensitive to issues of
how human knowledge and behavior develop in social contexts: biological approaches that emphasize the evolutionary adaptation of organism
to environment and Vygotskian approaches that emphasize the sociocultural origins of human thought.

Biological approaches to early skill development regard developing
humans as holistic, integrated systems. As such, various human behavioral systems can never function independently of each other or out of
context, because evolutionary processes have acted on the organism as a

whole. Its physical and psychological structures are coadapted to each other and to the various environmental contexts encountered over the course of development. As Thelen and Fogel (Chapter 2 this volume) state, "infants never act solely as perception machines or social beings isolated from the matrix of their motor systems or their cognitive capabilities or their emotional responses or out of the contexts of their environments." The biological approach thus explicitly rejects additive, information-processing accounts of skill development in favor of a systems approach in which skill developments appear as emergent properties of the biological system as a whole, adapting to contextual demands.

Because of the view that biological systems cannot be understood apart from the contexts in which they function, biological approaches are also fundamentally ecological. New skills will develop only in response to new environmental pressures, within the constraints of the existing organismic structure. Once new skills emerge, they can be consolidated into the organism's existing structure, altering existing skills and permitting the organism to enter into new types of transactions with the environment—which will introduce new sets of contextual demands and in a sense create new contexts. For example, learning to walk is not simply a maturational program that unfolds independently of the environment but seems to be related to the child's motivation to explore distal objects and places. Evidence for this comes from Fraiberg's (1977) studies of blind infants, which indicate that the onset of locomotion may be delayed to the extent that blind infants are unaware of the existence of distal objects and places. The emergence of walking is thus not only the result of motor abilities and associated constraints but of the entire developing system acting as a unit (see Thelen & Fogel, Chapter 2 this volume). Once children learn to walk, their ecological niche is drastically altered, presenting a variety of new challenges that will lead to the emergence of new skills and the adaptation of old ones to new contextual demands.

The biological approach is most clearly reflected in the chapters by Thelen and Fogel and by Als as well as in chapters that draw upon theories derived from this approach, notably attachment theory and the Gibsons' theory of perceptual development. Attachment theory takes the biological view that attachment between parent and child is a species adaptation, that the infant is predisposed to seek proximity to and derive security from a primary caregiver, and that the primary caregiver is predisposed to respond to and meet the infant's needs. This first relationship is regarded as primary and thus as affecting the infant's later competence in adapting to its environment. Traditionally, attachment researchers have been primarily concerned with the social context of the attachment relationship and less concerned with the structural underpinnings of skills involved in and influenced by the attachment relationship. This is changing as evidence mounts that individual differences in security of early parent–infant attachment affect a wide variety of cognitive and perceptuomotor skills (see Vondra & Belsky, Chapter 6 this volume, and Hazen, Chapter 7 this volume), leading researchers interested in these developments to investigate how the social context of the early parent–child relationship may result in individual differences in these skills. In the chapters by Vondra and Belsky and by Hazen, it is argued that individual differences in security of attachment relate to the parents' ability to modulate the child's affective reactions to the environment, which in turn affect the child's motivation to explore in both infancy (Vondra & Belsky) and early childhood (Hazen). Als (Chapter 3 this volume) also stresses the importance of parents' ability to modulate their offsprings' reactions to the environment, especially for understanding the development of play and problem-solving skills in preterm infants.

The Gibsons' theory represents a biological/ecological perspective dealing primarily with perception and perceptual development. According to E. J. Gibson (1982) and J. J. Gibson (1966, 1979), perceptual systems have evolved to directly pick up environmental features that bear on the organism's daily functioning and survival. In particular, perceptual systems pick up the "affordances" of their environments—the utility of environmental features such as objects, surfaces, or events defined with respect to the organism. Environmental features are thus perceived holistically, in natural units relative to the organism; they do not need to be pieced together bit by bit. Because the Gibsons have asked how perception functions in daily life, their theory is one of the few approaches to perceptuocognitive development that is fundamentally concerned with the ecological contexts in which perception is used over the course of development. As Lockman and McHale (Chapter 5 this volume) point out, the Gibsons' theory is particularly applicable to the study of early action in context because it proposes that perception and action mutually guide one another through and for the purpose of picking up contextual affordances. Work done from a Gibsonian perspective has, however, concentrated almost exclusively on the physical contexts of perception rather than its social ones. Lockman and McHale argue that examination of perceptuomotor development in social context is quite compatible with a Gibsonian perspective, and they offer new research that moves in this direction.

The second major approach reflected in this volume draws upon Vygotsky's theory that the origin of knowledge is fundamentally social.

Vygotsky argued that higher mental abilities appear on an "interpsycho-logical" (social) plane before they appear on an "intrapsychological" (individual) plane (Wertsch, 1979). Vygotsky used the concept of the "zone of proximal development" to describe the role of social context in cognitive development. This is defined as "the distance between the [child's] actual developmental level as determined by independent prob-lem solving and the level of potential development as determined through problem solving under adult guidance or in collaboration with more capable peers" (Vygotsky, 1978, p. 85). Progression from one level of cognitive competence to the next in the zone of proximal develop-ment is accomplished as a result of children's efforts to establish and maintain coherence between their actions and those of adults. But it is the adult or more experienced member of the culture who first sets the higher order goals for the child, by creating a match between the child's current ability level and what he or she may be capable of with as-sistance. The adult and child achieve a shared goal, and the adult then helps the child accomplish this goal by assisting with planning, memo-ry, and direction of attention. In essence, the adult controls several sources of variation *for* the child until the child becomes able, little by little, to control these sources independently.

Several investigators (e.g., Bruner, 1982; Wood, 1980) have used the term *scaffolding* to describe processes by which parents may guide their children in the zone of proximal development. Parents may help young children with certain tasks, such as appropriate object use or problem solving, by using a series of strategies that progressively require the child to take over more sources of variation. At first, the mother simply models the task, controlling all sources of variation. Mothers are then involved in progressive levels of scaffolding, in which they control whichever sources of variation the infant is not yet able to master. For example, they may help the child use a cup by holding his or her hand while he or she drinks or help him or her reconstruct a pyramid correctly by first handing him or her the blocks in the correct sequence (Bruner, 1982; Wood, Bruner, & Ross, 1976). Finally, when the child has mas-tered the task, the mother "raises the ante" by inducing the child to incorporate the task into a more complex routine. Through scaffolded guidance, the child is eventually able to use the skill independently, in nonsocial as well as social contexts. Contributors to this volume have noted that scaffolded guidance in social context plays an important role in the infant's development of several skills, including communication and motor skills (Thelen & Fogel), imitation (Užgiris, Benson, Kruper, & Vasek), object manipulation (Lockman & McHale), and exploration and play (Vondra & Belsky), as well as in the later development of spatial orientation and exploration skills in toddlers and preschoolers (Hazen).

Extending Vygotsky's theory to the very beginnings of life presents a problem: How can the young infant share goals with the parent and thus benefit from guidance in the zone of proximal development, when she or he was born? Because Vygotsky's theory assumes that knowledge is first acquired on an interpsychological level, this implies that the infant must somehow achieve intersubjective understanding with the parent about what's going on between them in order to profit from parental guidance. Indeed Fogel's work indicates that actions incorporated into communicative skills by late infancy, such as crying or pointing, first appear spontaneously in the service of nonsocial functions such as self-regulation of affect or attention (Fogel, 1981; Fogel & Hannan, 1985; Thelen & Fogel, Chapter 2 this volume). At first blush, this evidence appears opposed to a Vygotskian approach, but in fact it can be viewed as supportive evidence when interpreted in light of Kaye's recent extension of the Vygotskian approach to infant development (Kaye, 1982).

According to Kaye, parents interpret their infants' early actions in terms of their own culturally conditioned systems of meanings and supply supportive "frames" to help infants organize their behavior accordingly. Newborn infants are indeed incapable of intersubjective understanding; they are biological organisms who act spontaneously in accordance with their physiological needs, not members of society capable of intentional communication. But parents behave as though their infants are communicating partners and interpret and structure their actions accordingly. Illustratively, parents may often interpret infants' actions as being more intentional than they actually are and respond accordingly, for example, by saying, "Oops!" when babies drop something or by taking an object babies hold and saying, "Thank you." Kaye calls infants at this stage *apprentices* in the social system because, although they may initiate the action and respond to others, they do not yet intend the social interchange attributed to them by their parents. Eventually infants will develop expectations about the social consequences of their actions and will intentionally perform them to get these expected reactions from others. When this happens, for example, when infants purposely drop something to make their parents smile, say "Oops!" and pick it up, infants have become full-fledged *partners* in the social system, capable of true intersubjectivity.

Thus the precursors of communication skills and, followers of Vygotsky would argue, all skills, first appear *in social context*, interpreted by adults as having whatever functions those actions are commonly assumed to have in their culture, even though they actually serve nonsocial functions at first for infants. These early spontaneous actions eventually develop into voluntary skilled actions as a function of parents' interpreting and reacting to them as though they were voluntary to begin with. This implies that accounts of the early development of skilled action must take the functional perspectives of both parents and infants into consideration as well as the motor precursors of skill in young infants.

In this volume, the effects of social contextual factors on a variety of skilled actions are considered at a variety of developmental levels, from the spontaneously occurring precursors of motor and communication skills that appear in early infancy (Thelen & Fogel), to the complexly organized, symbolically mediated actions of pretend play (Bretherton & Beeghly), and spatial skills in preschool children (Hazen). A number of themes recur throughout the chapters. First, children's affective level plays an important role in their early skill development, and the social context is instrumental in modulating children's affect. In particular, scaffolding is not the only way in which parents can influence children in the zone of proximal development. Especially for the youngest children, before shared goals can be established through intersubjective understanding, parental activities that optimally modulate and reflect the infant's affective state may be an important means of facilitating infant competency. Infants cannot take in information or practice actions when they are either too lethargic or too tense.

Als has demonstrated that for the very youngest children—preterm infants—arousal modulation may be especially vital, as their nervous systems are too immature to adapt optimally to the degree of stimulation present in normal parent infant interaction. Užgiris *et al.* suggest that imitative activity between parent and child will occur first in *sharing formats*, in which the goal of participants is to convey mutual interest or emotion, as when the parent matches the emotional facial expressions or vocalizations of the young infant. Vondra and Belsky indicate that parents influence their infants' play and exploration by affecting their mastery motivation. As infants begin to act intentionally and to acquire intersubjective understanding, parents increasingly use scaffolded guidance and direct teaching. But the importance of parental modulation of affect does not disappear as children leave infancy. Hazen describes how children's spatial exploration and orientation skills in the toddler and preschool years are related to their security of attachment, indicating that perhaps insecure children are often either too disinterested or too tense to explore optimally.

A second theme running through these chapters emphasizes the importance of viewing parental scaffolding or direct guidance of skill development as it specifically relates to both developmental and contextual changes. Užgiris *et al.*, Lockman and McHale, Vondra and Belsky, and Hazen all examined parents assisting their children at different developmental levels to investigate how these factors (parental strategy and child's developmental level) influence the outcome of the skill of interest. All note that parents change the focus of their scaffolding as their children develop and as their goals for their children and assessments of their children's capabilities change. Scaffolding techniques also change, becoming more distal, symbolic, and differentiated as children grow older. Joint toy play, for instance, becomes more verbal by the end of the first year, with mothers specifically naming objects to their infants (Užgiris et al., Chapter 4 this volume). In broad terms, children's developing structural capacities and changing goals interact with what their parents consider important at each developmental period.

Because the task context of parent–child interaction affects both child and parent goals, it also exerts important effects on parental guidance and on child outcomes. For example, Užgiris et al. found that parents were more likely to frame imitative interactions with infants in a teaching format when toys were involved, whereas without toys, the goal in matching behavior was more likely to be sharing and reflecting affect or engaging in turn-taking games. Similarly, Hazen found that parents encouraged children to explore a rich environment by simply pointing out interesting objects, but they often encouraged children's exploration of an impoverished environment by engaging in hide-and-seek games.

A third recurrent theme is that examining the social context of early skilled action provides important, even critical, information concerning individual differences in these developments. Fischer (1980; Fischer & Hogan, Chapter 9 this volume) has argued that the range of variation typically found in children's skill level at any given developmental period is largely a function of the social context in which the various skills have been used. Thus, an important task for developmental researchers is to specify the social contextual factors related to optimal or suboptimal performance of various skills. The chapters by Vondra and Belsky and by Hazen directly deal with the issue of how individual differences in skill development are influenced by parental guidance and emotional support, important aspects of social context.

Finally, although most contributors deal primarily with the role of social context on the child's early development, it is generally acknowledged that children affect the social context as well. Each new development allows children to alter their environment at least somewhat. By the time children acquire representational capacities, they become capable of mentally interpreting and transforming their worlds. This theme is most clearly developed in the chapter by Bretherton and Beeghly, who discuss how children represent their knowledge of their social world and transform it according to their own wishes and needs in pretend play. Indeed, pretend play seems to be a set of skills that children can use to achieve social and emotional goals, working out their understanding of social relationships and expressing emotions related to real-world problems by actually creating their own, transformed social contexts.

Our attempt to integrate the diverse skills that develop in the early months and years by examining their development in social context has proved beneficial in several respects. First, adopting this integrative contextual perspective has led to a clearer understanding of *why* skills are structured as they are and, especially, why they follow particular developmental pathways and vary between individuals. In the present volume, the structure and development of such skills as locomotion (Thelen & Fogel), affective interchange and imitation (Thelen & Fogel, Als, Užgiris *et al.*), object exploration and play (Užgiris *et al.*, Lockman & McHale, Vondra & Belsky), environmental exploration (Hazen) and pretense play (Vondra & Belsky, Bretherton & Beeghly) are considered by examining contextual influences on the functioning of these skills. Second, it has helped us see the interrelationships and interdependencies of various action classes and the complexity of skill itself. Locomotor skills, for example, become quickly used for exploratory ventures that are embedded in affective interchanges with the parent (Thelen & Fogel, Hazen). Similarly, object manipulation is used for exploration (Lockman & McHale) but also functions as part of communicative routines, in infancy (Užgiris *et al.*) and early childhood (Bretherton & Beeghly). Attending to such interrelationships and interdependencies reveals the rich structure of many skills. However, the richness of the structure only becomes apparent when skill use is studied in context.

Although the work in this volume has answered many questions, it has no doubt raised many more. One of the most critical is simply, "What is meant by 'social context' "? A more differentiated construct is clearly needed. "Social context" in early development means more than parental influences. In the study of early socioemotional development, influences of siblings, substitute caregivers, and peers are receiving increasing attention; the roles of these individuals in early skill development need to be considered as well. Indeed, parental influences themselves are richly multifaceted and occur at several different levels. The work presented in this volume clearly demonstrates that parents do very different things at different developmental periods and in different immediate task situations. In addition, parental influences vary between individuals and between cultures. Thus social context can vary at the level of the culture, at the level of the individual, at the level of the child's developmental period, and at the level of the immediate situation. We need to examine social context at all these levels in order to understand their unique and interactive effects. In addition, we need to know more about which aspects of social context are universal and whether these contextual universals provide necessary conditions for certain skill developments. Finally, we need to investigate the types of contextual support that are needed for sufficient and optimal skill development as well as the types of skills that will develop with minimal contextual support. We hope this volume will provoke investigators to pursue answers to these difficult but critical questions.

References

Bernstein, N. (1967). *The coordination and regulation of movement.* New York: Pergamon Press.

Bruner, J. S. (1970). The growth and structure of skill. In K. Connolly (Eds.), *Mechanisms of motor skill development* (pp. 63–92). New York: Academic Press.

Bruner, J. S. (1975). The ontogenesis of speech acts. *Journal of Child Language, 2,* 1–11.

Bruner, J. S. (1982). The organization of action and the nature of the adult-infant transaction. In E. Z. Tronick (Ed.), *Social interchange in infancy* (pp. 23–35). Baltimore: University Park Press.

Bruner, J. S., & Sherwood, V. (1976). Peek-a-boo and the learning of rule structures. In J. S. Bruner, A. Jolly, & K. Silva (Eds.), *Play: Its role in evolution and development* (pp. 277–285). Harmondsworth: Penguin.

Decarie, T. G. (1978). Affect development and cognition in a Piagetian context. In M. Lewis & L. A. Rosenblum (Eds.), *The development of affect* (pp. 183–204). New York: Plenum Press.

Fischer, K. W. (1980). A theory of cognitive development: The control and construction of hierarchies of skills. *Psychological Review, 87,* 477–525.

Fogel, A. (1981). The ontogeny of gestural communication: The first six months. In R. Stark (Ed.), *Language behavior in infancy and early childhood* (pp. 17–44). New York: Elsevier.

Fogel, A., & Hannan, T. E. (1985). Manual actions of nine- to fifteen-week old human infants during face-to-face interaction with their mothers. *Child Development, 56,* 1271–1279.

Frailberg, S. (1977). *Insights from the blind.* New York: Basic.

Gibson, E. J. (1982). The concept of affordances in development: The renascence of functionalism. In W. A. Collins (Ed.), *The Minnesota Symposia on Child Psychology: The concept of development* (Vol. 15, pp. 55–81). Hillsdale, NJ: Erlbaum.

Gibson, J. J. (1966). *The senses considered as perceptual systems.* Boston: Houghton Mifflin.

Gibson, J. J. (1979). *The ecological approach to visual perception.* Boston: Houghton Mifflin.

Hodapp, R. M., Goldfield, E. C., & Boyatzis, C. J. (1984). The use and effectiveness of maternal scaffolding in mother–infant games. *Child Development, 55,*772–781.

Kaye, K. (1979). The development of skills. In G. J. Whitehurst & B. J. Zimmerman (Eds.), *The functions of language and cognition* (pp. 23–55). New York: Academic Press.

Kaye, K. (1982). *The mental and social life of babies.* Chicago: University of Chicago Press.

Lockman, J. J., & Ashmead, D. H. (1983). Asynchronies in the development of manual behavior. In L. P. Lipsitt (Ed.), *Advances in infancy research* (Vol. 2, pp. 113–136). Norwood, NJ: Ablex.

Piaget, J. (1952). *The origins of intelligence in children.* New York: International Universities Press.

Piaget, J. (1954). *The construction of reality in the child.* New York: Basic.

Piaget, J. (1962). *Play, dreams and imitation in childhood.* New York: Norton.

Ross, H., & Kay, D. A. (1979). The origins of social games. In K. Rubin (Ed.), *Children's play* (pp. 17–31). San Francisco: Jossey-Bass.

Thelen, E. (1981). Rhythmical behavior in infancy: An ethological perspective. *Developmental Psychology, 17,* 237–257.

Tolman, E. C. (1932). *Purposive behavior in animals and men.* New York: Appleton-Century Crofts.

Vygotsky, L. (1978). *Mind in society.* Cambridge: Harvard University Press.

Wertsch, J. V. (1979). From social interaction to higher psychological proceses. *Human Development, 52* 1–22.

Wood, D. J. (1980). *Teaching the young child: Some relationships between social foundations of language and thought* (pp. 280–298). New York: Norton.

Wood, D. J., Bruner, J. S., & Ross, G. (1976). The role of tutoring in problem solving. *Journal of Child Psychology & Psychiatry, 17,* 89–100.

Part I

Continuity and Change in Infant Motor Development
Effects of Physical and Social Context

Infants engage the world through action. Their cognitive, social, and perceptual skills consist of series of actions structured in space and time. Researchers interested in these skills, however, have focused little attention on the component actions that make up these skills or how these actions become linked together to serve psychological goals. Curiously, these issues have not received much attention in the motor development literature, either. Instead, researchers have often treated motor development in an insular fashion, as if individual motor achievements were unrelated to other developments occurring within or outside the motor domain.

This characterization is especially evident when motor development research is viewed from a historical perspective. Much of the early work involved establishing norms for the onset of many common motor milestones. Although broad maturational principles were derived from these developments, the individual milestones were often treated as separate achievements. Relationships between milestones were obscured because the milestones were not broken down into their component parts. As a consequence, it was not really clear which milestones represented the formation of a new skill, the reorganization of an old one, or the result of some combination of these two processes.

Research on motor development was insular in another sense as well. Because of the prevailing maturational view of the time, little attention was focused on the relationship between behavioral context and behavioral development. Except in extreme cases, the environment was thought to have little influence on motor development. Rather than ask what properties were common across infants' environments and how these commonalities might constrain the development of action, investigators considered motor development to be virtually the sole and universal product of internal biological growth. As a result, motor development was often studied in somewhat artificial and limited contexts.

This state of affairs characterized much of the work on motor development during the 1920s, 1930s, and 1940s (see Benson, in press). By the end of the 1960s, however, work in motor development had taken a new turn. Interest had shifted away from profiling the onset of various milestones to considering the nature of skill and the processes underlying skill formation. More widely, this shift reflected the growing concern in psychology with questions about the *structure* of thought and behavior. In the motor domain, this concern was manifested in discussions about the overall organization of skill, especially how skills could be broken down into component actions that were temporally sequenced.

Developmentally, researchers also became interested in the general structures and processes underlying skill formation. As such, motor achievements were no longer considered in isolation from one another. In principle, motor skills could be related by sharing common elements or at least an overall common structure. According to this new conception, almost all skills were seen as being composed of constituent acts that were temporally sequenced. Reaching, for instance, was no longer viewed as an isolated milestone but as a skill related to earlier and later developing ones by virtue of its common elements and its internal sequential structure (Bruner, 1970).

Still this new conception of motor development remained isolated in a different, perhaps wider sense. Research on motor development continued to be divorced from the contexts in which the skills and component actions under study actually functioned. In effect, the general structure of motor skill was emphasized at the expense of its daily functioning.

In recent years, however, research on motor development has taken a new turn. Investigators have begun to link structural and functional issues in conceptualizing motor development. The chapters by Thelen and Fogel and by Als exemplify this new approach. Thelen and Fogel consider the development of locomotion and communication; Als examines the development of motor skills in premature infants. Despite the different actions of interest to them, Thelen and Fogel, and Als are united in following what generally may be labeled a systems approach. They each seek to understand the development and structure of particular actions in the context of the infant's daily, if not momentary, functioning.

To effect this synthesis, Thelen and Fogel use recent advances in kinesiology and dynamic motor theory. In their ground-breaking chapter, they show how biodynamic concepts that can account for the control of movement in adults can also help explain the development of movement in infants. Thelen and Fogel employ these concepts to examine the ontogenesis of locomotion and communication—two very different action domains that are rarely grouped together in developmental writings. Through this unusual combination, Thelen and Fogel seek to demonstrate the generality of their approach.

In considering locomotion, communication, and more generally action, Thelen and Fogel articulate a fundamental problem that has been neglected in most accounts of behavioral development: How can functioning in real time be integrated with behavioral development in ontogenetic time? Indeed, it is at the intersection of real and ontogenetic time that the integration of functional and structural concerns in motor development, if not development as a whole, becomes possible.

Thelen and Fogel suggest that an integrated view of motor development can be achieved by considering the nature of action across these two time scales. Many previous accounts, including maturational and information-processing ones, suggest that action is the result of series of instructions, of top–down commands. According to these accounts, changes in action—developmental or otherwise, are primarily due to changes in the underlying instructions. The instructions more or less completely specify the accompanying action. In contrast, Thelen and Fogel argue that action is not reducible to prescribed instructions; rather it is emergent, the product of a dynamically changing system. Particular action topographies emerge from a functioning system composed of organismic (especially the organization of muscle coalitions), task, and environmental elements. Although it is possible to identify each of these elements separately, their systemic functioning must be considered to understand how action is structured in real and ontogenetic time. Thelen and Fogel illustrate this approach by examining the development of locomotion and communication.

The systems framework advocated by Thelen and Fogel provides a much more integrated view of motor development than do previous conceptualizations. It explicitly relates action across real and developmental time scales. Further, it directs us to consider how later emerging forms of action are related to earlier ones. And it implies that the structure of action cannot be fully understood apart from the context in which it functions.

Als also adopts a systems approach, although the topic of interest to her is at first glance quite different from Thelen and Fogel's. Als is concerned with self-regulation and motor development in premature infants. Nevertheless, Als, like Thelen and Fogel, seeks to understand the development of skills or subsystems of functioning by viewing them not as isolated abilities but as elements of an unfolding dynamic system. She describes her view of development as "synactive." It implies that at each moment and at each developmental period, the individual subsystems act together and mutually support one another, promoting the overall functioning and development of the infant as well as each subsystem.

To analyze the developmental difficulties associated with prematurity, Als identifies the fundamental subsystems that contribute to the infant's overall functioning, describes in principle how these subsystems interact, and considers how their individual and thus joint operation may be at risk given the mismatch between the premature infant and the extrauterine environment.

Als uses this theoretical analysis as the foundation of her intervention program. In contrast to many medically based interventions that only target the premature infant's autonomic functioning, Als's program is truly systemic in character. It aims to ameliorate the mismatch between the premature infant and the extrauterine environment. Physical, sensory, and social interventions are employed, all designed to reduce stress and promote self-regulation and thus the functioning of the entire system. Als's findings reveal the effectiveness of this approach. Premature infants who were at considerable risk and were given this systems based intervention showed immediate long-term gains relative to controls. Benefits were found across a variety of action and skill domains and behavioral settings.

Despite the applied focus of this work, Als's conceptualization shares a great deal with the theoretical perspective articulated by Thelen and Fogel. Like Thelen and Fogel, Als seeks to understand action across real and developmental time. Her synactive framework relates infants' momentary functioning to their functioning in different developmental periods. Further, Als, like Thelen and Fogel, views the problem of action development from a systems perspective. Broadly speaking, Thelen, Fogel, and Als identify the system's constituent elements and examine how they mutually influence the system's functioning and development.

This common systems perspective points up to some additional similarities in the two approaches. In both approaches, there is a concern with how the elements of the system promote or inhibit the functioning of the entire system. Thelen and Fogel, for instance, discuss the existence of rate-limiting and rate-enhancing elements within functioning systems. Some elements may scale the system to new levels; others may hold it back at present ones; and still others may lead to regression.

Thelen and Fogel give some examples of such scalars in their discussion of the ontogeny of locomotion and communication. Similarly, Als describes how some subsystems may support or constrain premature infants' attempts to function at current levels or more advanced levels of functioning. This idea, in fact, serves as a cornerstone of Als's intervention efforts.

Finally, in both of these approaches, there is a recognition of the integral role that context plays in action development. Thelen and Fogel argue that the ecological context of the child, including its social aspects, is an integral part of the system from which action emerges. Parents' actions, for instance, may play a rate-enhancing role and shift some infant behaviors into new configurations. Similarly, the social context is central to Als's formulation as well. In both her theoretical and applied analyses, Als examines the match between premature infants and the environment provided by caregivers. To the extent that an appropriate match is established, optimal development will be promoted.

Viewed together, then, the chapters by Thelen and Fogel and by Als represent a new and rich way for conceptualizing action development during infancy. In these approaches, action is not divorced from the contexts in which it emerges. Nor are individual actions treated as separate unrelated achievements. With the systems view being advocated here, work in motor development should not be labeled insular any more.

REFERENCES

Benson, J. B. (in press). The significance and development of crawling in human infancy. In J. E. Clark & J. H. Humphrey (Eds.), *Advances in motor development research*, Vol. 3. New York: AMS Press, Inc.

Bruner, J. S. (1970). The growth and structure of skill. In K. Connolly (Ed.), *Mechanisms of motor skill development* (pp. 63–92). New York: Academic Press.

CHAPTER 2

Toward an Action-Based Theory of Infant Development

ESTHER THELEN AND ALAN FOGEL

INTRODUCTION

The purpose of this chapter is to explore a theory of infant development grounded in an analysis of action. This account differs from customary theories of early development in several ways. First, it is preeminently a *movement-based*, "bottom-up" account of behavior in the sensorimotor period. Developmentalists, like other psychologists, have been concerned primarily with the formation of the complex symbolic and affective processes of the "life of the mind" and have paid less attention to the translation of ideas into movement—a "life of the limbs." Infants, however, are born with much movement and few ideas and, for the first year or so, lack symbolic and verbal mediating mechanisms between their mental state and the expressions of their bodies and limbs. At this stage of the life cycle, then, the link between the developing mind and the developing limbs may be especially direct. We see this formulation in no way competing with theories that focus more directly on mental structures but rather as a complement and supplement to understanding the development of cognition.

This perspective is "bottom-up" in another sense as well. Most developmental theories go from long-term evidence—the gradual

ESTHER THELEN • Department of Psychology, Indiana University, Bloomington, Indiana 47405. ALAN FOGEL • Department of Psychology, University of Utah, Salt Lake City, Utah 84112.

growth of competence—and reason back to the real time processes that might account for it. We focus, instead, on the principles organizing real time, everyday behavior, and show how developmental principles can be derived from them. In the sense that both time scales belong to the organism, we seek to unite behavioral processes occurring over both immediate and developmental time domains.

We come to this current perspective, in part, because of persistent puzzles raised by our own studies of infants and left unsolved by existing paradigms. In our individual research programs, we have been studying seemingly different developmental domains—motor skill and communication. Although each area has its specific questions, we discovered that the underlying developmental puzzles were common to both. Thus we seek a theory that will be sufficiently specific to account for the real life phenomena uncovered by our individual research, yet general enough to unite these and other developmental domains in a coherent and biologically relevant fashion.

Puzzles from Motor Development

For Thelen, the puzzles emerged from naturalistic and experimental studies of motor patterns during the first year. When viewed in their everyday settings, infants perform many examples of highly structured and rhythmically repetitive movements of the limbs and body, which appear and disappear in an age-specific progression (Thelen, 1979; 1981a,b). Once initiated, these movements seemed to "play out" in a machinelike fashion, often with little reference to discernible external goals. Yet at some times, elements of these stereotyped movements appeared to be incorporated into more flexible and goal-directed activities. Analysis of the actual kinematic structure of one of these movements, supine leg kicking, revealed some remarkable properties. For example, in very young infants, the topography, or form, of the movements was tightly constrained, with a relatively invariant timing in the phasing of the movement elements (Thelen, Bradshaw, & Ward, 1981; Thelen & Fisher, 1983b). Indeed, aspects of the timing in early infant leg movements were similar to that of adult locomotion in a wide variety of vertebrates. These leg kicks persisted throughout the first year, but their form or elements of coordination changed, sometimes "regressing" into less organized patterns, and later, regaining new forms. During this time, infants increasingly used these movements for intentional tasks, such as locomotion, communication, and exploration. Movements never were performed in isolation. The appearance and specific form of a movement was dependent on the infant's posture, support against gravity, state, and the specific social context. For example, at 7 months of age, infants performed leg movements while supine but not while supported upright.

How could it be that infants of 1 month, with little or no voluntary control of movements, had consistently more highly organized leg movements than 2-, 3-, or 4-month-old infants? Why were these patterns disrupted, leading to instability and asymmetry? What caused new patterns like simultaneous kicking in both legs to suddenly appear at 5 months? Was there a relationship between early coordinations and later skill? Why were these movements at the same time both stable and flexible? How did infants come to use exactly the same topographies as seemingly both spontaneous and intentional actions? At the same time, what allowed infants to recruit a variety of movement forms to attain a goal, such as rolling, rocking, or creeping toward a desired object? What was the relation between the form of the movement, its goal or task, and the context in which it was performed?

Traditionally, motor development has been viewed as being "caused" by neural maturation, especially the development of the motor cortex (McGraw, 1940). For several reasons, neural maturation, although necessary, is an insufficient explanation for these complex and nonlinear developmental changes. First, neural maturation is itself a "black box" explanation that ignores the processes of change. Secondly, as we suggest in a later section, because there is no one-to-one correspondence between events in the nervous system and movement outcome in general, it is unlikely that neural maturation alone "drives" motor development. And what is most important is that there is little concern in maturationist theory over the role of the physical and social context for the ontogeny and performance of movements. Thus the traditional views of motor development were not successful in solving these persistent puzzles.

Puzzles from the Development of Communication

In the early stages of his work, Fogel was struck by the appearance in newborns of all the basic facial expressions of emotion (Oster, 1978) and the descriptive work of Trevarthen (1977, 1979) suggesting that very young infants had nonaffective action patterns of the perioral region resembling later appearing vocal articulatory patterns. Trevarthen also described a variety of hand gestures, including "pointing" (index finger extension) and "waving" (fingers extended and spread).

Observations of mother–infant interaction, under natural and manipulated conditions, both confirmed and extended the findings of other investigators. By documenting the developmental course of facial expressions like smiling and crying and manual expressions like point and finger spread, Fogel discovered that the topography of these movement patterns was relatively invariant over the first year of life (Fogel, 1980, 1981, 1982a,b, 1985; Fogel & Hannan, 1985; Kaye & Fogel, 1980). This suggested that the muscle synergies that produce a smile or a point are both discrete and stable.

One striking and unexpected aspect of these results is that each of these four protocommunicative expressions became linked sequentially with different sets of noncommunicative actions, and the sequences changed systematically during the first year. For example, in the early months, *cry* was associated with head turning, eye closing, squinting, rubbing the face, and with changes in respiration (sighs and gasps). In the later months, cry became associated with sucking on the hand. Earlier instances of hand-in-mouth were fortuitous as when the infant's head turned to meet an upraised arm.

A second important aspect of these findings was that the context often was incorporated directly into the action sequences. During those periods when the infants failed to self-calm using noncry actions, the parent could provide a transitional support, such as a nipple or a hug that helped to reduce distress. Later, as the baby developed the motor control required for self-regulation of distress, the parent played a different role in this process. Thus the provision of contextual supports, both social and nonsocial, could "unmask" a behavior pattern that might not emerge otherwise. The ability of an infant to focus attention on a task, for example, cannot emerge until distress is reduced to tolerable levels.

Why are such motor patterns present at an early age, before they are needed by the infant in communicative encounters? Do these actions remain in the repertoire over the first year of life, or do they drop out and later reappear in intentional form, linked with the appropriate cognitive function? How can we explain the process by which these action patterns become linked into later communicative functions? Do they serve a function for the infant when they first appear, or are they vestigial features of an imperfect ontogeny? How do the same motor patterns become associated with different functions? By what mechanism does the support provided by the parent enhance the capabilities of the infant?

Traditionally, communication has been viewed as an epiphenomenon of the development of sensorimotor and symbolic functions. A considerable body of work has found correlations between measures of sensorimotor substages and corresponding shifts in both vocal and gestural language (Bates, 1979; Bloom, Lifter, & Broughton, 1981). The emergence of intentional pointing as a referential gesture, for example, has been tied to the development of the cognitive differentiation between means and ends. First words have been linked to Piaget's Stage VI, in which infants develop the capacity for symbolization across a number of domains including language and play. These explanations do not do justice to the specific mechanisms by which communicative action becomes interfaced with other infant actions and with actions of the parents in a context. Similarly, pragmatic theories that look at the functional context of communication rather than the structures (Bates, 1979; Bruner, 1975) fail to specify the process by which adult actions lead to the emergence of new forms of communicative actions in the infant.

The Goals of This Chapter

In the task domains of both motor skill and communication, many intriguing questions remain unanswered. Why do infants show age-dependent regularities in the appearance of actions? Why do behaviors arise in a predictable sequence? What, then, accounts for the striking discontinuities in development? What happens to the behaviors that regress, change, or disappear? What are the functions of these developmentally specific activities, both in the immediate world and ontogenetically? How do infants make the shift from spontaneous to intentional activities? What accounts for the individual variability in actions and the multiple pathways to these immediate and developmental goals? What are the mechanisms by which physical and social context facilitate development?

In this chapter, we take a novel approach to these issues by grounding our developmental analysis in an understanding of real-time action. Our central argument is that the questions of structure/function, sequences, transitions, tasks, and contexts are at the heart of the analysis of both *movement and ontogeny* and that *a set of general biological principles can span both time scales*. These principles, in turn, are derived from more general systems theories in biology and physics, which take as a basic tenet the dynamic, relational, and multilevel characteristics of complex cooperative systems.

All of these developmental issues have also been addressed in a similar way by organismic developmental theorists such as Werner (1957) and Piaget (1971), and their attempts to view development holistically as the systemic interaction between multiple levels of organismic action in a context are one basis for the approach we outline in this chapter. We go beyond these theories to the extent that we view development as a dynamic and emergent process embedded in the interface between organism, task, and context, rather than as a set of instructions updated by the environment.

This is a crucial distinction, then, that applies to both the proximate and ontogenetic sources of behavior. As we propose behavior is emergent in context, we place no more causal emphasis on the structural invariants than on the millieu. This, then, allows us to specify mechanisms by which particular parental actions, for example, become translated into developmental changes in the infant, by elaborating on processes described by Bruner (1975) and Kaye (1982), as "framing," "place holding," or "buffering."

To do this, we first review a contemporary theory of action—that is, how motor acts are organized and controlled. In the next section, we use these principles based on motor theory to outline a more general developmental model. Finally, we apply the model to the ontogeny of two skills—locomotion and communication.

UNDERSTANDING REAL-TIME ACTION: DYNAMIC MOTOR THEORY

How does the brain control the muscles of the body to enable individuals to function in their worlds? The question seems to be especially impenetrable. There are approximately 793 separate muscle groups in the human body (each made up of thousands of muscle fibers) that may then be assembled in a nearly infinite number of combinations and sequences. Real-world actions are themselves of nearly infinite variety as the state of the actor and the contexts of the actions are never exactly the same. Yet within this variety, movements retain a recognizable form—there are certain characteristics that make us recognize a kick, a smile, or a tennis swing. At the same time, the motor system is capable of generating novel forms, as even an aging psychologist can learn to tap dance or to ski or to play a musical instrument.

In this section, we review a contemporary theory of action that addresses just these issues in a way quite radically different from more traditional theories of motor control. Unlike older formulations such as motor programming, this new theory, because of its wide generality, can provide a generative model for behavior on a developmental as well as immediate time scale.

The roots of this new theory are twofold: the path-breaking work of the Soviet-movement physiologists of several decades ago, notably N. Bernstein (1967) and other theoretical advances in physical biology, especially the emerging fields of cooperative systems theory in physics and biology (Abraham & Shaw, 1982; Haken, 1977; Iberall, 1972; Prigogine, 1980; Rosen, 1978; Winfree, 1980). Peter Greene, Michael Turvey, Scott Kelso, Peter Kugler, and their colleagues have been largely responsible for the theoretical and empirical elaboration of this integrated *dynamic motor theory* in Western psychology. (The reader is referred to the following for more detailed accounts: Bernstein, 1967; Greene, 1972; Kelso, Holt, Kugler, & Turvey, 1980; Kelso & Tuller, 1984; Kugler, Kelso, & Turvey, 1980; Kugler, Kelso, & Turvey, 1982; Turvey, 1977.)

In our view, the signal contribution of these theories is their explicit rejection of *information-processing analogies* of behavior in favor of explanations based on dynamic and biological principles. Information-processing models essentially view behavior as a series of instructions and the problem of behavior as the formation of the instructions. But what about movement? As Bernstein (1967) first pointed out, when animals move, they are not static recipients of instructions but dynamically changing systems, continually subject to inertial forces, elastic deformations, and gravity. Thus the brain must encode the sequences and trajectories of movements—with all the "degrees of freedom" afforded by the muscles and joints, as the effectors themselves are continually changing. How then, can the central commands ignore the state of the peripheral organs? Yet to continually monitor and correct for the dynamics of the periphery implies nearly infinite central processing and storage capacity as well as processing times incompatible with the rapid, skilled movements of everyday life.

Coordinative Structures: Functional Constraints on Movement

The solution to the "degrees of freedom" problem suggested by these contemporary formulations is to make the periphery—the muscles and joints that receive the commands—part of the solution, not just part of the problem. Let us explain.

As first proposed by Bernstein (1967; see also Whiting, 1984), one way to reduce the control decisions necessary for coordinated movements is to group the individual muscle and joint variables into larger groups or synergies, which would act as a unit. Thus, in locomotion, it is not the individual muscles of the legs that are controlled but the limb as a whole; the time–space behavior of one joint is tied precisely to the

time–space behavior of the other joints, and likely even to the joints of
the opposite leg (Shik & Orlovsky, 1976). Such synergistic organization
has been documented for many actions including locomotion, bimanual
coordination (Kelso, Southard, & Goodman, 1979), posture (Nashner,
1981), skilled markmanship (Arutyunyun, Gurfinkel, & Mirsky, 1969),
facial expressions (Ekman, Friesen, & Ellsworth, 1972), and speech (Kelso, Tuller, Bateson, & Fowler, 1984). In accordance with contemporary
usage in motor control, we shall adopt the term *coordinative structure* to
denote groups of muscles that are recruited to perform functional
actions.

   This notion of distributed control is not unique with this formulation. In and of itself, hierarchical organization is compatible with more
traditional information-processing or top-down models of motor control. What is profoundly different in dynamic motor theory and consequently for our developmental interests is that the coordinative structures—the muscle coalitions themselves—may be *sources of order, not
just recipients of commands.*

   The basis for this conjecture are principles of physical biology and
dynamic pattern formation (see Iberall, 1972; Iberall & Soodak, 1978;
Katchalsky, Rowland, & Blumenthal, 1974). These views, believed to
apply to all living systems, contrast fundamentally with programming
models, which postulate an *a priori* prescription independent of and
antecedent to the actual behavior. Instead, the order of biological systems—from neural networks, to temperature regulation, to diurnal
rhythms, is an *emergent* property—that is, an *a posteriori* phenomenon
that depends upon the dynamical behavior of the system of related
elements. For example, vertebrate temperature regulation has been traditionally pictured as functioning like a home thermostat. The animal
would have a "set point" somewhere in the nervous system. As body
temperature fluctuated with, say, exercise or air temperature, these fluctuations would be detected, compared to the set point, and the necessary adjustments in metabolic rate or blood flow would be made. Recent
models, however, show how the *interactions* of metabolic and heat trans-
port processes alone can account for thermoregulation without the need
for either reference signals or comparators in the nervous system. A
steady temperature is rather a *systems* property uniquely resulting from
the contributing functions (Werner, 1977).

   Similarly, coordinative structures are dynamically assembled systems—assembled in response to tasks—and it is these *systems* attributes
that provide the order and regularity in movement despite the rampant
possible degrees of freedom. Distinctive properties of topography and

timing *emerge* from the unique combination of units. These properties are a function of the relationship and cannot be known from the properties of the units as isolated elements. Thus the assembly of the synergy itself is an *increase in complexity*, as coordinative structures are autonomous and self-organizing. Iconic representations of the trajectories of movements need not exist in the nervous system for movements to be patterned in time and space (Kugler *et al.*, 1980).

A useful physical model of movement that embodies many of these dynamic characteristics is that of a simple spring fixed at one end with a mass attached. When the spring is stretched or compressed and then released and allowed to oscillate, it will do so with a specific cyclical trajectory, and it will finally equilibrate at the same resting length no matter whether the spring was initially pulled or compressed, or how far it was displaced. The details of the trajectory require no coded symbols but depend on the initial stretch of the spring and its intrinsic attributes. The final position of the spring is likewise not encoded as such but rather also depends on attributes of the system—the amount of mass and the tension in the spring. In short, the spring can exhibit fine details of movement trajectory and timing and a predictable final position without central movement commands (Tuller, Turvey, & Fitch, 1982).

This dynamic formulation contains several fundamental insights that are central to our views of development. First is the notion that moving animals are cooperative systems: that movement is determined by gravitational, inertial, and reactive forces that are inherent in the physical properties of the moving segments and of their coalitional linkages as cooperative entities. As a result, the movement outcome is not a one-to-one reflection of programmed muscle firings but a complex interplay of active and passive forces in the contributing components. Equally important, however, is that these biomechanical qualities may themselves be utilized by the system to reduce both the neural processing and the active muscle participation in the movement. Gravity is not just a force to be overcome but, depending on the position and state of the moving system, may also act to facilitate movement. The swing of the leg forward during a step in walking, for example, is accomplished with very little active muscle contraction but results from both passive energy storage first in the stretched muscle as the body is swung forward and later by the effects of gravity, as in an (inverted) pendulum (McMahon, 1984). Natural oscillations of coordinative structures may be a source of movement trajectory and timing, lessening the demands for elaborated neural programs or schematas.

In the preceding section, we have been discussing how predictable sequences or coordination can arise from dynamic, cooperative systems. In the following sections, we address two other consequences of dynamic motor theory: first, the issue of how emergent organization can be both stable and flexible, followed by the crucial question of the processes by which new forms emerge in both real and ontogenetic time.

How Are Emergent Organizations both Stable and Flexible?

We earlier identified a central question in motor theory as how movements can at the same time be both constrained and flexible. Although there is great variability in the moment-to-moment performance of everyday movements to meet the changing nature of tasks and the changing state of the performer, movements do retain a certain stability of form. In the sense that each task is both familiar and novel, each movement adds variability to a stable base. An essential topography or form is thus preserved at the same time that certain components can be flexibly tuned to make fine adjustments of the movement outcome.

How is this accomplished? What are the movement elements that provide a stable *structure*, and what elements adapt that structure to the immediate function? It seems likely that it is the *relative timing* of the muscles in the coordinative structure that provide the stable topography (Kelso & Tuller, 1984; Schmidt, 1982). When the brain recruits a coordinative structure, it is calling upon muscles that relate to each other in a relatively invariant sequence. Speed and force of muscle activity, however, are subject to metrical change and are the means by which the movement is *controlled*. By adjusting the relative tenseness of agonist and antagonist muscles, the individual, in a sense, sets the stiffness of the spring in relation to the demands of the task (Cook, 1980). A fast or powerful movement requires more muscle force and thus a stiffer spring.

Invariant relative timing has been best studied in locomotion and posture. During normal locomotion, the muscles of the legs fire in a fixed sequence. What happens to these muscle-burst patterns during a slow stroll as compared to a brisk walk? When speed (and muscle force) is scaled up, the absolute timing of the phases of the step cycle, especially the stance phase, is decreased. Nonetheless, the muscles involved fired in an invariant relative relationship (Engberg & Lundberg, 1969; Shapiro & Schmidt, 1982; Shapiro, Zernkicke, Gregor, & Distal, 1981). These phase relationships preserve the topography of the movement, even as the force delivered to the muscles changes.

Similar invariant patterns of movement have been observed in facial expressions. Given the large number of facial muscles, only a relatively small number of discrete facial expressions have been observed (Ekman *et al.*, 1972). Facial expressions are invariably composed of synergistically activated muscles in many areas of the face. Within the stability of the configuration of a discrete facial expression, there is flexibility of the activation or force delivered to the muscles. Depending on the context, a person may smile weakly or broadly, for example.

In sum, the coordinative structure notion suggests that in the face of an adaptive task demand, only a limited number of movement topographies can be recruited that serve as constraints on the large number of theoretically available degrees of freedom in the motor system. The topographies result from muscle groups with a relatively invariant timing relationship. Once assembled, coordinative structures, because of their dynamic qualities, assume an autonomy that allows certain movement variables such as timing, trajectory, and goal equifinality to emerge without prior specification. Coordinative structures are flexible, however, to meet varying task demands because performers can set certain scalar dimensions—notably the muscle tension, force, and initial position—in advance of the task.

Coordinative and dynamic properties are not just characteristic of mature or skilled movements but appear to be part of the very fundamental organization of the neuromuscular system even from before birth. We have described the coordinative and self-organizing nature of infant movement in detail elsewhere (Thelen, Kelso, & Fogel, 1986). Briefly, studies of spontaneous leg movements in infants showed that at birth, and even in premature infants, flexions and extensions of the three joints of the legs were highly coordinated, with muscles firing in fixed timing relationship (Heriza, 1985; Thelen & Fisher, 1983b). These early coordinative structures met predictions of a mass-spring model in several ways, including a stable trajectory resulting from viscoelastic rather than active muscle contraction (like the adult step), the ability to adjust to changes in the dynamic load on the limb (Thelen, Fisher, & Ridley-Johnson, 1984; Thelen, Skala, & Kelso, 1987) and the ability to adjust the tension or "stiffness" of the spring in the face of task demands (Thelen & Fisher, 1983a). Even before movements are voluntary, they exhibit properties in agreement with a dynamic model.

In the next section, we address the question of how, in this formulation, do we account for the emergence of *new* forms of movement, including voluntary movement. Although this issue is first discussed in terms of real-time behavior, the developmental implications are profound.

The Process of Emergence in Real Time

As an example, let us consider the locomotion of a common, quadrupedal animal, say a horse. As is commonly known, the gait of the horse (and of other quadrupedal animals) changes with the velocity of locomotion. At low velocities, the gait is asymmetrical (limbs of each girdle are out of phase), but at high speeds, the gait becomes symmetrical. The phase transitions are discontinuous—there is no stable intermediate gait between a walk and a trot, for instance. Thus as the animal increases in speed and thus muscle power, a new topography of movement emerges.

The traditional motor program explanation of this common phenomenon is to assume that somewhere in the nervous system, presumably in the spinal cord, there is a neural "switch" that changes the interlimb firing pattern (Grillner, 1985). In short, that there is an a priori pattern generator for each different gait. In contrast, dynamic motor theory suggests that the new gait behavior can emerge from the scalar changes of energy alone and that it is not necessary to postulate preexisting programs.

The phenomenon of such *discontinuous phase changes* is currently of great interest in thermodynamics and in the physics and mathematics of nonlinear systems (see Haken, 1977; Prigogine, 1980). An everyday example is the flow of water through a faucet. At low levels of water pressure, the flow is not turbulent, and the water molecules follow a random statistical law. As the tap is opened and the water pressure increases, *at a critical point* the form of the flow changes and becomes turbulent, and the molecules are organized into powerful streams. At still higher pressures, other forms like vortexes emerge, as discontinuous events despite continuous increases in pressure.

No one would argue that a program for molecular organization exists in the water stream. These regularies are inherent in the dynamic nature of water molecules under pressure. Such systems—universal in the physical and biological world—exhibit transitions from one state to another that are discontinuous even though the factors controlling the processes are continuous. Thus, as the system is scaled past critical bounds on a sensitive parameter, qualitatively new modes of organization emerge in a stagelike fashion. The intermediate states could conceivably exist—a state somewhere between random and turbulent flow or between walking and trotting—but they do not because the transitional states are, on some dimension, unstable. Within the stable states, fluctuations are tolerated, but when these fluctuations exceed critical limits, the phase shift occurs. In this way, a continuous change in a parameter, say muscle force, is translated into discontinuities of form.

In gait, for example, observations on horses and other ungulates show that they use a restricted range of speeds within each gait that corresponds to a minimum energy expenditure (Hoyt & Taylor, 1981). In horses, the minimum oxygen cost per unit distance is nearly the same for walking, trotting, and galloping, but as speed increases, the "walking" mode becomes inefficient and unstable and "breaks" into the trotting mode. In short, the design of the animal—its inherent geometry— and its organization as a dynamic biological system can constrain movement topography without recourse to preexisting plans.

Similar discontinuities in behavioral organization are apparent in young infants as the well-known *state changes*. When infants shift from one defined state to another (Brazelton, 1973; Prechtl, 1974), they exhibit nonlinear and discrete behavior catagories that appear as a cluster. For example, within quiet sleep, only the topographies of startles and mouthing emerge, whereas the constellation of actions associated with quiet alert states are qualitatively distinct. In fact, what enables observers to reliably make state decisions is that states rarely show a mixture of behaviors. Transitions or mixtures may exist, but they are not stable, just as the transition between a walk and a trot is not seen.

Supine infant kicking offers another example of discontinuity in real-time behavior. In states from quiet sleep through quiet alert, infants act as though there were not enough activation of the system to power the synergy of kicking. Kicking only emerges as the system is "powered up" past a critical value. At the very highest range of activation, which is crying very hard, a new topography may emerge—a rigid, tonic co-activation of all the muscles into a stiff immobility, a new stable state characterized by the maximum muscle tone.

In the remainder of this chapter, we explore the implications of these powerful and provocative insights of movement organization for the development of action in infancy.

FROM REAL-TIME TO ONTOGENETIC TIME: DYNAMIC PRINCIPLES OF DEVELOPMENT

Until this point, we have focused on the organization of movement in real time. Here we propose that the same general biological principles underlying this contemporary perspective of motor behavior can be extended to other time scales, in particular, to the understanding of the emergence of new forms in ontogenetic time.

Readers will recognize this account as in the tradition of *organismic* views of development (Kitchener, 1982; Overton & Reese, 1973; Reese & Overton, 1970; Wapner & Kaplan, 1983). In their holistic theories, Piaget (1971), Werner (1957), and Gesell (1945) drew heavily on embryology as their biological metaphor (e.g., Bertalanffy, 1968; Waddington, 1966). A number of contemporary organismic theorists have also included evolution as a "developmental system" (Sameroff, 1983) or emphasized the intimate role between developmental and evolutionary processes (Alberch, 1982; Bateson, 1984; Goodwin, 1982; Gould, 1977; Webster & Goodwin, 1981). We, in turn, derive the same principles of holism, self-stabilization, self-organization in development from processes on still a third time scale, "real-time" behavior, attesting to the generality and power of these basic systems principles (see also Brent, 1978).

What, then, are the characteristics of biological systems in general that allow us to make this leap from fractions of seconds to days, weeks, and months. First, developing humans, like all other biological systems, are holistic, that is, integrated systems of component *subsystems* and *processes*. Although we may choose to study only a single aspect of the organism—perception, cognition, emotion, motor control, socialization, and so on—any given behavior at any point in time is a function of all these participating subsystems *in dynamic interaction*. That is, infants *never* act solely as perception machines or social beings isolated from the matrix of their motor systems or their cognitive capabilities or their emotional responses or out of the contexts of their environment. To understand the processes of developmental change, ontogeny must be considered as a piece. Just as movement in real time cannot be understood from the activity of the nervous system alone or from the behavior of only one muscle group, so behavior in developmental time must consider the unique systems properties of the cooperating elements.

The lesson from the dynamic systems approach for real-time behavior is that when elements act as cooperative units, certain self-organizing and autonomous properties emerge from the interaction itself. For motor behavior, this means that all the information for movement trajectories and timing need not be encoded somewhere in the central nervous system before the execution of the movement but that this increase in information in the system arose from the dynamic interactions of the participating elements. For development, this suggests that the "instructions" for developmental change also need not be iconically encoded as *a priori* programs or schemata. Here we propose that just as the nervous system can set minimal parameters and generate a rich movement trajectory, developing organisms require only a *minimal* set of instructions *sufficient* to utilize the inherent emergent properties of the system. One consequence is that qualitatively discrete developmental stages may "fall out" of these dynamic interactions without specifically being coded into the organism. Behavioral stages previously interpreted as discrete epochs in the development of the perceptual or cognitive system may be better understood as epiphenomena of such dynamic organization.

A third implication of a dynamic systems approach is an *equifinality of outcome*. In the motor system, self-correcting mechanisms insured that the final goal—a target or phoneme—was reached despite perturbations. Developing organisms also have the ability to reach functional end points from many different initial conditions and through a variety of pathways. The crucial point here is that the outcome rather than the purpose *per se* is what guides development, as it guides real-time behavior.

A fourth principle common to real and developmental time is that of discontinuously *emergent forms*. In real time, movement topographies are stable within a range of activation levels; small fluctuations are tolerated and buffered by the dynamic system. However, when scaled on certain sensitive parameters, the configurations shift to qualitatively new forms—as in the gait of the horse. Development, too, can be conceptualized as a series of stages that appear discrete and stable but then shift quite discontinuously to new forms (Bateson, 1984; Fentress, 1984; Gierer, 1981). In our model, we show how the emergence of new forms can also be explained by the scaling of one sensitive parameter, that is, how a continuous change can lead to discontinuous outcomes.

Because of the systems nature of developing organisms, small fluctuations around a critical dimension can be magnified into a "giant" fluctuation, which, in turn, shifts the entire system. But because development is holistic, the critical parameter may not be immediately manifest. In other words, what appears to be a phase discontinuity in one subsystem—for example, the emergence of a new cognitive stage—may result from the scalar changes in another contributing system—perceptual or motor, for example. We further suggest that many apparently paradoxical regressions and discontinuities in development may be explained when the critical scalar is identified and the systems interactions clarified.

To elaborate our dynamic systems approach to early development, we introduce here two additional biological concepts from embryology and evolution. The first, *heterochronic maturation*, addresses the essential question of the regulators of developmental timing (Anohkin, 1964).

Although development of the organism is of a piece, the *rates* of growth and differentiation of the contributing subsystems may not be synchronous or linear. Particular elements may be comparatively accelerated or retarded in relation to one another, and within each system there may be spurts and times of relative quiescence. In short, development can be envisioned as a series of parallel developmental processes, each with its own timetable. At any point in time, however, the behavior of the organism as a whole cannot be predicted by the developmental status of only one element because it is their interaction that is the crucial determinant.

Nonetheless, any one element can act as a *rate-limiting* factor in the system. Here we borrow from the model proposed by Soll (1979) for morphogenesis in the slime mold, *Dictyostelium*. Let us assume, Soll argues, that to generate a particular morphogenetic Stage B, that some minimal amounts of the products of four separate pathways are needed. If components a, b, and c accumulate to sufficient levels early and component d accumulates later, then d will regulate the timing of Stage B. Component d is no more or less important than a, b, and c, but in a systems sense, Stage B cannot emerge without the accumulation of d. Once this critical level is reached, a new morphogenetic form results. This model also illustrates how the detailed instructions for timing of the developmental structure need not be encoded in the genome—rather, that the instructions need provide only a minimal set of timing regulators for the component processes. Because development is holistic, a small change in one timing dimension can reverberate and result in major consequences for the entire system (Gould, 1977).

In this systems approach, no one subsystem assumes a primary or causal role in developmental change, although one subsystem may indeed limit the performance of the behavior in question. Because we view behavior as emergent rather than driven, we see the role of the context– the social and physical environment—as more than just supportive (as in a maturationist view) or as an aliment feeding the preexisting structures (as in a more Piagetian perspective). Rather, the context itself *is part of the structure of the behavior*. In early infancy, context or task may very intimately interact with the internal state of the infant, but as the infant matures, other persons and objects increase in salience. Thus, at any point in the developmental scale, the impetus to behave is task-directed, whether that task be hunger, temperature regulation, proximity to the caregiver, or exploration (Reed, 1982). Maturational status thus may delimit and constrain possibilities for action, but it is not the *source* of behavior, which is functional and context-specific. This means that within maturational limitations, the infant may use a number of means to obtain functional goals. It is not the level of instructions that guide the task but the demands of the task constrained by the available underlying organization.

Finally, this formulation allows for the emergent behavior to itself be incorporated into the system as a new matrix supporting additional developmental change. Once an infant reaches a new skill level, the context for ongoing behavior has itself been profoundly modified. Because behavioral outcomes are holistic, new skills in one domain can act as a catalyst for emergent change in other, seemingly unrelated domains.

In the final sections of this chapter, we use the theoretical position outlined before to explain development in infancy in two specific functional domains: motor skill and communication. We hope to demonstrate that our holistic, systems approach can help interpret data from these seemingly diverse functions (and collected in two separate research programs) and answer some fundamental developmental puzzles common to both areas.

A DYNAMIC PERSPECTIVE ON LEARNING TO WALK

The traditional explanation of how infants learned to walk is that their nervous systems mature and that their movements became under increasing cortical or voluntary control (McGraw, 1932). More recently, walking has been described as a predominantly cognitive event, coincident with the first use of words and complex play (Zelazo, 1983). Although the acquisition of voluntary control is an essential component of skill development, from our systems perspective, such prescriptive accounts alone are unsatisfactory as explanatory concepts because they do not specify *process* nor do they account for the stagelike appearance of motor forms or, for that matter, their involution.

Here we go beyond neural or cognitive maturation to cast the problem in a more holistic systems model. For the sake of this analysis, we can imagine that the task of learning to walk emerges from the dynamic interaction of a number of components or subsystems. First, infants must learn to both recognize and evaluate the appropriate parameters of the task, that is, they must know that upright locomotion will allow them to reach a desired spatial location. A number of component processes are involved. Infants must have the *perceptual* ability to discriminate and recognize the affordances in the environment. In Gibsonian terms, they must know what surfaces are walkable and be able to identify their goals. In addition, they must acquire the ability to initiate *voluntary* movement toward a goal, be it exploration or proximity to the caregiver. Infants must evaluate and regulate their own emotional and motivational states in relation to the task at hand.

At the same time, subsystems must develop that allow infants to translate their mental states into actual movements. Coordinative structures, or assemblies of muscles, must be available to pattern the legs for forward progress. Additionally, muscle synergies must be available to correct for deviations of the center of gravity and to provide adequate compensatory movements in the torso and arms. The achievement of an erect posture is another essential component, along with necessary muscle strength to support the weight of the body against gravity and the balance mechanisms to shift the weight from foot to foot. Finally, the essential dynamic elements of body size, proportion, composition, and mass must allow for the expression of movement.

What causes a child to be able to walk? Our action-based perspective allows us to ask this question in a new way. Rather than focusing on one element—cognition or pattern generation, for example—we assume that the actual performance of the behavior is a systems function of all the cooperating components. We then may study the *process*, that is, the developmental course of the components and their systems interactions. By identifying the rate-limiting and sensitive parameters among the components (and these will necessarily be changing during the year) we can tease out those that are stable at any point in time and those that are the critical dimensions that may shift the system into new configurations.

We begin with what may be the component providing the element of stability within the matrix of developmental change: the ability of infants at birth (and likely even before birth) to produce highly coordinated and rhythmical movements of the legs. When newborn infants are placed supine or held erect, they move their legs in an alternating fashion, with the hip, knee, and ankle joints flexing and extending in a precisely synchronous manner, as is illustrated in Figure 1 (Thelen & Fisher, 1983b). Not only do the excursions of the joints track each other precisely, but the underlying muscle groups fire simultaneously. Such coordination has also been described for premature infants as early as 28 weeks gestational age (Heriza, 1985). This suggests that the legs are organized in a stable and highly predictable synergy even many weeks before birth.

What is the developmental fate of this intrinsic movement patterning? In supine infants, Thelen (1985) has described a rather uneven ontogenetic course. After the first month, for example, the regular alternating pattern of the newborn period appears to dissolve, and infants will often kick with only one leg. These asymmetries themselves are unstable, with shifts of preference within the same infants and among the sample

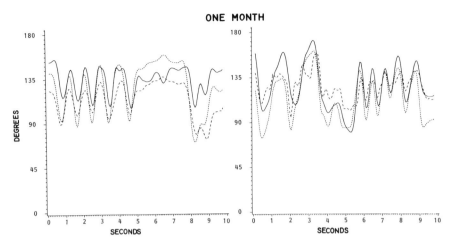

FIGURE 1. Flexions and extensions of the three joints of the leg in two representative 1-month-old infants over a 10-second segment of spontaneous kicking. Solid line = hip joint; short-dashed line = knee joint; long-dashed line = ankle joint. Decreasing joint angles indicate flexion movements; increasing angles indicate extension movements. Note the tight temporal and spatial synchrony of the three joints.

(Thelen, Ridley-Johnson, & Fisher, 1983). At about 5 months, a new level of interlimb coordination appear, with simultaneous kicking added to the repertoire. Also after the first month, the tight coalition between the joints of one legs begins to loosen, so that the ankle excursions are no longer so closely correlated with those of the hip. By about 7 months, supine leg movements may show much less of the interjoint synchrony of the early ages; infants have come to control each joint and can use the legs in a much more flexible and adaptive manner (Thelen, 1985).

The development of patterned leg movements seen when infants are held erect shows a similarly jagged course. Most intriguing is the virtual "disappearance" of these steplike movements during the second month of life, their suppression for many months in middle infancy, and their reappearance only a month or two before supported and independent walking. Does the coordinative pattern of the newborn period underlie later walking? How is the transition accomplished?

First, we must ask what causes the dramatic loss of the well-coordinated steplike movements seen in the newborn period. Traditionally, this has been viewed a single-system result, the inhibition of a primitive reflex by maturing cortical inhibitory centers (McGraw, 1940; Peiper, 1963). Although the inhibition hypothesis has been challenged (Konner, 1977; Super, 1980; Zelazo, Zelazo, & Kolb, 1972), other explanations based on learning or other cognitive functions seem equally *ad hoc*.

The disappearance of neonatal stepping—the transition from one stable state to another—makes more sense when we look at what is happening not only in the pattern-generating mechanisms or their voluntary control, but in the other elements contributing to the movement outcome. In the mass-spring model of motor control, the trajectory of the spring is a function of both the stiffness of the spring and the load. As infants grow and develop, there are naturally occurring changes in these parameters. Limbs and body segments become longer and heavier, and the relative proportions change. Muscle tone and strength develop, and even body composition changes.

The case of the newborn stepping response provides a dramatic example of how such naturally occurring dynamic changes can effect movement outcome. In the first few months, infants gain weight at a very rapid rate. A disproportionate amount of this weight gain is fat rather than muscle tissue. The infant is in effect adding to the load on the spring without increasing the stiffness or strength of the spring. Thelen and Fisher (1982) have proposed that the decline of newborn stepping is a result of the consequences of the increased load. In a sense, the load exceeds the elastic capabilities of the spring, and when infants are in the mechanically demanding upright position, reduced or no movement results. By manipulating the mass of the legs, Thelen, Fisher, and Ridley-Johnson (1984) have simulated these growth-related effects. Adding weights decreased both the amount of stepping (as naturally occurs) and the amplitude of the steps the infants performed. In contrast, submerging infants' legs under water restored high levels of stepping even in 3-month-old infants, who normally show little of the response. Submersion also increased the amplitude of the movement.

Thus, the new stage of *no stepping* may not reflect the actual involution of the pattern-generating ability itself, but a stable topography that falls out of the systems relationships of many elements. Stepping is as dependent on the dynamic elements and the postural context as on the neurological substrate. The spurts and declines of maturation rate in these contributing systems means that the overall behavioral course is not linear. An increase in extensor strength or a particular fat-to-muscle-mass ratio may be the critical dimension to shift the system into these new states (Thelen & Fisher, 1982). Although the growth and development of the contributing elements are presumably continuous, the result is a stagelike sequence. We need not invoke, in short, a command program that inhibits this behavior.

What about the reappearance of steplike movements at the end of the first year and their recruitment as intentional activities? Is there a "switch" somewhere in the central nervous system timed to activate this new skill? A more fruitful analysis is to identify the contributing and rate-limiting components that allow this new stage to emerge. In fact, many of the subsystems appear to be maturationally available long before actual independent walking (Thelen, 1985). For example, infants can use their legs in a voluntary fashion as early as 3 months of age. When reinforced by a moving mobile, infants will increase the rate and the intensity of leg kicks, apparently by controlling both the initiation of kicks and the stiffness of the system (Thelen & Fisher, 1983a). Similarly, the ability to recognize and initiate movement toward a goal matures many months before walking, as infants will use other developmentally available coordinations such as creeping, crawling, or rolling to accomplish these tasks. Note here that it is the task—shaking the mobile or capturing the distant toy—that calls forth the behavior, whereas the specific *form* of the behavior is what is developmentally available.

It is also likely that infants have the ability to generate patterned, steplike movements of the legs long in advance of actual walking and perhaps throughout the first year. We have argued that the apparent disappearance of newborn stepping is indeed only a masking of the coordination by other maturing systems. What then allows the coordination to "return"?

One important clue emerged when infants, who normally show no stepping movements, were allowed to walk on a small, motorized treadmill. Thelen (1986) found that each of her sample of twelve 7-month-old infants performed well-coordinated, alternating steps when held supported on the treadmill. The coordinative structure of stepping appeared at the moment the treadmill was turned on. (The sample averaged 6.3 steps per minute when the treadmill was not activated, compared to 35.7 steps per minute on the "slow"-speed treadmill and 46.8 on the "fast"-speed treadmill.) An analysis of the kinematic structure of such treadmill-elicited stepping revealed that the pattern of joint movements and their relative timing showed more elements of mature locomotion than the steps performed without treadmill assistance. Unlike the more simple newborn stepping, where the hip, knee, and ankle flexed and extended largely in phase, when on the treadmill, infants showed individual but coordinated phasing of these joints similar to adult locomotion, but lacking some of the more refined coordinative elements (Figure 2).

Because it is difficult to argue that a treadmill hastens neurological or cognitive maturation, this manipulation must substitute for a subsystem that normally is rate-limiting for independent walking. That is, the treadmill kicks the system into a new topography. Several explanations are possible. Clearly, the treadmill mechanically stretches the legs backward, a mechanical effect normally accomplished for the stance leg

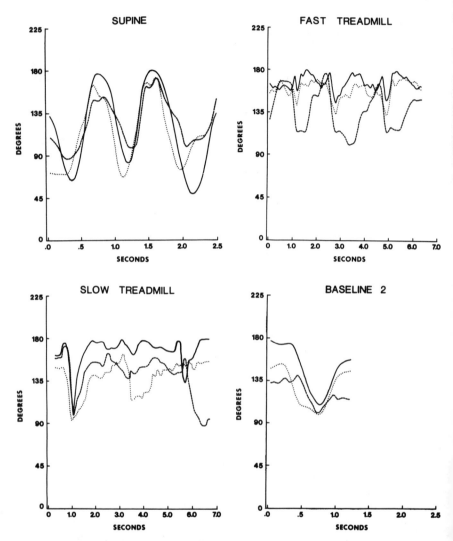

Figure 2. Joint angle excursions of a 7-month-old male infant during spontaneous supine kicking and stepping on a nonmoving treadmill and a treadmill moving at two speeds. Smaller joint angles indicate a flexion of the joint; larger angles an extension. Note the smooth and nearly synchronous excursions of the hip, knee, and ankle in the supine and baseline conditions and the more elaborated and complex phasings with the treadmill. Key: ——— = hip; ⋯⋯ = knee; ----- = ankle.

when the opposite leg is swung up and forward. Experiments with treadmill locomotion on spinalized cats suggested that the forward swing of the limb was initiated by a reflex trigger of the hip extended back and/or the release of load on the extended ankle (Pearson & Duysens, 1976).

Throughout the middle part of the first year and until the onset of independent locomotion, infants do not appear to have the muscle strength to support the weight on one leg sufficiently to allow the other leg to swing forward for the step (Sutherland, Olshen, Cooper, & Woo, 1980). Even as infants begin to walk, their unstable support is reflected in hyperflexion during stance, increased cadence, decreased step length, lack of arm swing, and the characteristically rotated "Charlie-Chaplin" stance (Statham & Murray, 1971). Because infants are unable to hold one leg steady while the opposite is in the air, they may be unable, on their own, to stretch the stance leg sufficiently to initiate swing. In addition, in adult locomotion, much of the force needed to swing the leg forward is not active muscle contraction but the passive, stored energy of the stretched leg (McMahon, 1984). Infants, in contrast, are unable to "stretch the spring," so to speak, in order to fuel the propulsive forward movement. This can be done passively by the treadmill. In our systems terminology, we can envision simple muscle strength as the rate-limiting component. When muscle strength reaches some critical dimension, the system shifts into a new phase—independent walking. Neither the phase timing of the joints nor a locomotor "timetable" need be encoded beforehand. The coordinative structure of walking truly emerged under the facilitating dynamic conditions—provided experimentally by the treadmill and developmentally by the gradual accretion of strength.

This view is in contrast to accounts of human locomotion that propose a "locomotor program" that directs the coordination of the joints and their relative timing in a highly specific way (Forssberg, 1985). Rather, the data from new walkers suggests that the underlying pattern-generating mechanisms only provide the most general outline of the movement topography and that the specific details are context-emergent. This allows the system the flexibility to respond to nearly infinitely varying contextual demands without the need to call forth special neurological structures to meet them. Thus the biodynamic requirements of roller skating, for example, are sufficient to change the coordination of the legs when the child is actually faced for the first time with roller skates, although practice will certainly improve the outcome. Understanding the nature of this task-specificity and flexibility is one of the most important challenges in studying the motor system (Bernstein, 1967).

A Dynamic Perspective on the Ontogeny of Communication

The application of dynamic action theory to motor development is a logical extension down to the infant of a theory developed with adults. The methods of kinematic analysis are common to both age domains, and there is a large overlap in the terminology.

We think that our developmental theory is more general in the sense that all behavior partakes of movement, and all movement is regulated in part by perceptual affordances, cognitive conceptualizations, and motivational states. The same general principles—of systems properties, coordinative structures, stable states, emergent forms, and asynchronous parallel developmental processes—can apply to all domains of early development, and in particular, to the development of communicative behavior.

Traditional theories of language development implicate brain and cognitive development as the primary causal factor in the emergence of language and intentional communication, much like the neural-cognitive explanations of motor development. Because linguistic functions have been related to the left hemisphere of the brain, psycholinguists have placed much weight on the evidence that specific stages of language development are tied to changes in hand preference during manual tasks at different ages (Bates, O'Connell, Vaid, Sledge, & Oakes, 1985; Ramsay, 1984). On the other hand, conventional words, imitation, symbolic play, tool use, and deictic gestures all emerge about the same time, suggesting a cognitive structural change underlying language (Bates, 1979; Bloom et al., 1981).

From our perspective, these explanations are inadequate because they do not take into account the appearance of communicative expressions in the first weeks and months of life, long before the infant has control over these expressions. Although cognitive structural stage theory describes the stage changes that occur across many domains of the infant's functioning, it does not account for the process of change from one stage to the next nor for the unique properties of each stage.

How do infants progress from simple, almost reflexive facial, manual, and vocal expressions in the newborn period, to become intentional communicators, aware of their role in the communication process? As in the development of task-motivated locomotion, intentional communication requires the infant to recognize and evaluate the parameters of the task. This means the infant must recognize that other people are the senders and receivers of communicative signals and must have the cognitive ability to differentiate self from other. Emotional and state control is required because communication involves indirect, and sometimes delayed, action toward a goal.

Muscle synergies are required both within and outside the expressive system. Expressive movements must be developed that carry illocutionary force and have conventional meaning. Nonexpressive action patterns allow for the smooth execution of expressive movements within instrumental contexts, and postural controls are needed to assure mutual coorientation with the partner.

Infants must also develop integrative subsystems that establish the relationship between self, other, and object, or between action and meaning (Bakeman & Adamson, 1984). Idiosyncratic action must be fashioned into conventionalized action and grammatical structures. In addition, the infant must learn to adjust to maturational changes in communicative morphology and to exploit those changes in the service of communicative goals.

Because the cognitive and motivational skills implicit in linguistic communication are more sophisticated than those required for learning to walk, it is not surprising that language has been viewed primarily as a cognitive function. We propose that a good deal of the explanation of the development of communicative action in the first year is based on an overreliance on cognitive changes and an overattribution of meaning and purpose to the early forms of expression.

In the rest of this section, we will review briefly the evidence for the development of two expressive action systems during the first year of life: cry and point. In each case, we will show that these systems develop in relation to functions that do not in themselves imply progression toward intentional communication for the infant. In the case of cry, we will look at the development of self-calming, and for point, the development of pointing to a specific object.

For each of these expressions we will show that their development is consistent with the predictions of dynamic action theory. First of all, both expressions are coordinative structures that are topographically stable over a range of ages and contextual conditions. These expressive configurations are recruited as a whole for certain task demands and thus represent constraints on the available degree of freedom. Second, new action patterns emerge spontaneously later in the first year—self-calming and intentional pointing—by the combination of the existing expressive coordinative structures with nonexpressive actions (in particular, arm movement control) that have been developing continuously in other instrumental functional contexts.

Cry

As a Coordinative Structure

As a coordinative structure, crying exhibits two important and related dynamic systems properties: a stable and "tunable" configuration and, later, a series of discrete phase topographies from continuously varying parameters. At birth, the cry is a synergistically organized sequence of expiration, rest, and inspiration periods. The rhythmical sound topography is preserved over a crying bout. At the same time, variations in the cry reflecting the intensity and quality of the eliciting stimulus—pain, hunger, or even general risk status of the newborn—can be obtained by the infant "tuning" the duration of the cry phases and the rests between them, as well as the pitch and intensity of the sound (Wolff, 1967; Zeskind & Lester, 1978).

By the age of 1 year, infants command a variety of vocalic skills that can be used to produce a number of distinct cry patterns. A set of stable cry synergies were identified by Thompson and Lamb (1984) in 12-month-old infants, including intermittent brief distress vocalizations, arrhythmic fussy crying, high intensity rhythmic crying (sobbing), arrythmic high intensity and high pitch crying (screaming), and hyperventilated crying in which respirations were audible. In crying, as in newborn state and gait patterns, continuous variations in particular scalars, in this case rhythm, intensity, pitch, and respiration rates, leads to a stable and finite set of cry patterns.

Crying and Parallel Processes

The dynamic, emergent nature of the development of the cry system is apparent in two domains. First is the interdependence of the articulatory features of crying, like those of other vocal behaviors, on the anatomic and neurological structures of the vocal apparatus itself. Although the developmental processes are poorly understood, there is evidence that the same articulatory features appear in both cry and noncry sounds over the first year. Some have suggested that the anatomical changes in the speech motor control system develop as a result of the large forces generated during feeding and oral exploration (Bosma, 1975) and that speech and cry sounds use these motor structures opportunistically. Thus developments in the cry expressive system can occur when the coordinative structures of cry become associated with other motor and anatomical structures that have been developing independently in instrumental, rather than expressive, contexts.

The stable and discrete states in both cry and noncry sounds produced by the articulatory apparatus are believed to be an emergent property of the anatomical and motor structures of the system (Kelso & Tuller, 1984; Kent, 1981; Lindblom & Sundberg, 1969; Netsell, 1981). It would appear that developmental changes in speech motor control and anatomical features of the orofacial region are more closely tied to changes in vocal production than might be suggested by a strict cognitive or neurological explanation.

Second, a systems approach emphasizing parallel developmental processes helps explain crying as part of the infant's overall distress system. In Fogel's research, two infants were videotaped weekly during social interaction with their mothers from 1 to 12 months of age (Fogel, 1981, 1985). Although the frequency of all cries taken together did not increase or decrease systematically with age, the relationship of crying to other behavior of the infant did show a nonlinear developmental course.

For example, when cry occurred in the first few months, it was preceded or followed by frown expressions. Closer examination of these associated frown expressions showed that they were always accompanied by nonexpressive action patterns that seemed to be involved in the regulation and alleviation of the distress. During frowning in the early months, the following related actions were observed: head turning, eye closing and squinting, rubbing the face, eyes, and head with the hands (or into a blanket if prone or into the mother's clothing when cradled), and changes in respiration patterns such as deep breaths, sighs, and gasps.

Beginning at about 9 months of age for both infants, both cry and frown were likely to be associated sequentially with hand-to-mouth activity (Fogel, 1985). Both crying and frowning terminated rapidly once the hand entered the mouth. Nonnutritive sucking has a calming effect on newborns (Kessen, Haith, & Salapatek, 1970), and one would expect sucking on the hand to calm babies at any age.

At younger ages, both of the infants in our study calmed down when they were sucking on the mother's or their own hands. If the actions of squinting, head turning, and deep breathing did not serve to calm the baby in the early months, however, the introduction of the infant's own hand into the mouth required that the head be turned to the side in order for the mouth to contact a hand that happened to be raised to the mouth's level, either by spontaneous activity or because the infant's arm was "caught" in that position during cradling against the mother. Not only does this method rely on chance proximity of the mouth to the hand, it requires the infant to turn away from the midline and thus lose the attentional focus that might make calming adaptive in that situation (see Figure 3).

By 9 months of age, however, the infants had gained a degree of control over the arms such that they could both manipulate objects with one hand and freely move the other hand in and out of the mouth as needed (Figure 3). Thus, when levels of internal distress increased, infants could self-calm with more than fortuitous success at the same time they maintained their attention to social and nonsocial objects. The continous maturation of arm control, combined with the already existing synergy between calming and sucking led to a discontinous shift in outcome—to the ability to self-calm in a context of ongoing activity. (During the second year, other, even less cumbersome nonaffective actions are recruited for self-calming. These include sucking on the lips, making a "lip funnel," or biting the lower lip (Demos, 1982). Apparently, increasing control over muscles in the perioral region makes it less necessary to use the hand.)

One explanation for the change in control of distress at 9 months might be a cognitive shift to object permanence and a change in the infant's ability to evaluate events related to affective state (Sroufe, 1979). Qualitative changes occur about this time not only in distress expressions but in the expressions of enjoyment and fear. Although there is not enough research detailing the emergence of affective expressive behavior to allow us to decide unequivocally between a single-process cognitive-structural model of development and the more multicausal model we propose here, our formulation focuses attention on the interaction of contributing subsystems and allows us to ask about the rate-limiting components. Motor control of the arm and the ability to fractionate the activities of both arms, rather than a cognitive structural change, may limit the emergence of reliable self-calming. This motor control develops in instrumental contexts such as locomotion and exploration.

At the same time, a certain degree of distress control is essential for instrumental actions that facilitate acquisition of motor control, as highly distressed infants do not engage in manipulation and exploration. At early ages, parents may give the infant external support for distress regulation such as holding, rocking, and provision of nipples on which to suck, which then affords the infant the calm state necessary for interaction with objects in the external world. When a sufficient degree of arm control is acquired, the task of calming can become more infant-initiated.

Action theory predicts that processes occurring at the effector level may be sources of order and catalysts for developmental change and not

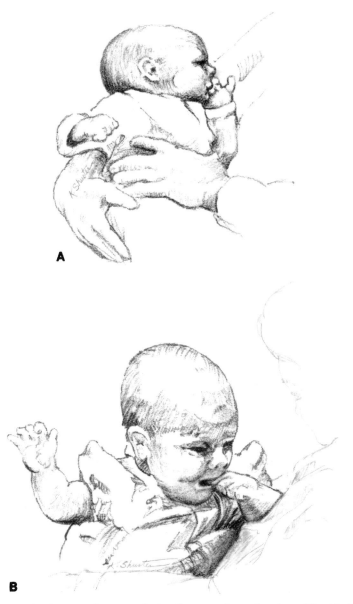

FIGURE 3. (A) Hand-to-mouth contact during distress at 2 months of age. Hand is "found by accident" when baby turns head to the side. Hand cannot be pulled to midline for sucking. (B) Hand-to-mouth contact during play at 9 months. Baby mouths object, her own hand, and mother's hand. Baby can keep her finger in her mouth as she turns and changes posture.

mere recipients of central commands. The dynamic interaction of sub-systems developing in parallel like suck/calm and arm control can lead, at any point, to the emergence of new patterns not available without the synergism. In the development of the crying system, both the coordinative structure and the state dependency of cry are well established in the newborn period. This coordinative structure serves the function of alerting the mother to the infant's internal state and serves a tension-releasing function for the baby. Further developments in the cry system include the articulation of a wider range of internal states and the ability to calm the self easily, without losing control of other action systems such as attention to the environment. These new developments are emergent combinations of already existing cry coordinative structures with parallel processes developing in other contexts at a different rate.

Point

As a Coordinative Structure

The ontogeny of gestural communication has been studied in more detail than the ontogeny of affective communication. Index finger extensions in 2-month-olds were first reported in 1977 (Trevarthen, 1977, 1979) and have been verified and traced ontogenetically by Fogel and his students (Fogel, 1980, 1981, 1985; Hannan, 1981, 1982; Platzman, 1983). Those interested in pointing as an intentional communication have begun their observations at the end of the first year of life (Bates, 1979; Leung & Rheingold, 1981; Murphy & Messer, 1977).

Similar to discrete facial expressions, there appear to be a small number of discrete coordinative structures involving the muscles of the hand. All possible combinations of joint angles and muscle contractions do not appear. A more complete analysis of interdigit coordinations and their developmental changes is yet to be done for young infants; however, Connolly and Elliot (1972) have documented discrete hand morphologies and digit coordination in adults across primate species and have traced the development of hand control in young infants in a tool-using situation. In addition, Ruff (1984) has catagorized instrumental coordinative structures of 1-year-old infants in exploratory play, and Kiennapple (1983) has conducted an analysis of sequences between discrete hand actions during exploratory play at 7 and 12 months.

Pointing, like other early movement configurations, does not appear regularly or randomly in the infant's repertoire but is linked to specific contexts, likely associated with internal state. In 3-month-old infants, the gesture point occurs just before or just after a vocalization or mouth movement such as sucking, mouthing, or chewing. When babies point, they are neither smiling nor crying but are in a neutral and attentive affective state and not concurrently vocalizing (Figure 4) (Fogel & Hannan, 1985; Hannan, 1981; Platzman, 1983).

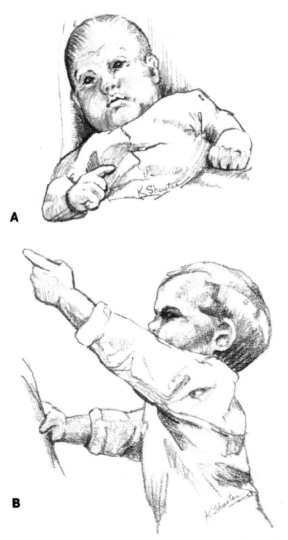

FIGURE 4. (A) Point at 2 months during face-to-face interaction with mother. Index finger extends while arms are flexed and does not indicate direction of gaze. (B) Point at 9 months during free play with mother. Both arm and finger are extended in direction of object of interest.

From its first appearance, therefore, point appears to be part of the orienting response (Lempert & Kinsbourne, 1985). This hypothesis is particularly appealing because pointing is used in later illocutionary actions to direct the attention of both the mother and infant, suggesting a continuity of function from the early noninstrumental association with attention and alertness to the more focused orientation later in the first year.

Point and Parallel Processes

Changes in arm and postural control influence the way in which point is displayed and the function that it serves for the infant. At 3 months, point rarely occurs when the arm is extended. More often, one or both arms are in a moderate state of flexion. Furthermore, early pointing does not seem to be directed to the focus of attention. Indeed, index finger extension is perhaps a more accurate descriptive term at this age (see Figure 4).

At 9 months, the point occurs when the infant is sitting, usually with a flexed arm, and is used to touch objects that the infant is exploring. Infants also use many other hand actions for the purpose of exploration; thus the task, not the structure, guides the action. By 11 months, point occurs directionally to an object from a sitting or standing posture and with an extended arm. At this age, the point is intentional, but it is not a speech act, because the baby uses it as an extension of the orienting response and does not systematically look between the object of interest and the adult nearby. The orienting goal is also served by first words themselves, which function more as attentional "place holders" than as names (Lempert & Kinsbourne, 1985).

It has been assumed in previous research that this emergence of intentional pointing is a manifestation of the three-way cognitive integration between self, adult, and object and the awareness of infants of their roles in communicative exchanges (Bates, Camaioni, & Volterra, 1975; Masur, 1983). An alternative view, however, is that pointing is an emergent action that results when slowly developing cognitive structures combine with the orienting response, present since the first weeks of life and with the motor skill of holding the arm outstretched with respect to the body and against gravity.

The ontogeny of the gesture point is consistent with our dynamic action-based accounts of other emergent behaviors such as walking and the cry system. First, point is a state-dependent coordinative structure available from the first weeks of life. Unlike crying, which serves a signal function to the mother and a tension release function for the infant, there is no clear purpose to the early appearing point expression. (The function of early coordinated leg movements is likewise not apparent.) As an epiphenomenon of the orienting response, however, pointing becomes readily available to the infant later in the first year, just as leg movements become appropriated for a variety of communicative and instrumental tasks (Thelen, 1981a). In the act of exploring the object world, the infant develops arm control and articulation over the fingers in manipulative tasks. Pointing, already associated with orienting and object attention, becomes available for further use and elaboration: first to tap and explore objects and later as a highly salient index of the direction of attention.

Thus because the first intentional points are egocentric expressions of interest, the emergence of intentional pointing must be a dynamic, multicausal phenomenon in which advances in cognitive understanding of self and other is only one factor. Intentional pointing, like other action systems, emerges only after arm and hand control develop and when infants combine action subsystems developing in parallel into new coordinated action patterns in the service of a goal.

CONCLUSIONS: THE ROLE OF THE CONTEXT IN THE ONTOGENY OF COMMUNICATION AND MOTOR SKILL

We have emphasized in our action-based account that behavior in real time as well as in developmental time is *task* rather than instruction driven and that the functional demands and ecological contexts of actions must be part of the dynamic system. Although this review does not allow for a full exposition of the parent's role in the development of communication and skill in infancy, we wish to acknowledge the central role of the social environment in our scheme.

Central to our formulation is the notion that one developing subsystem may either be rate-limiting for the emergence of behavior or serve to shift the system into new configurations. There is indeed a good deal of evidence to suggest that parents—the social ecology of infants—may function in the latter role, that is, to supply "missing" or "incomplete" elements of more mature behavior patterns and thus allow performance of behaviors not available without this contribution. Because the parent can intuit some of the infant's needs and predict the approximate direction of developmental change, she or he can supply supportive "frames" by which the infant can organize existing behavior patterns (Kaye, 1982).

Take the example used before related to distress regulation. When the infant shows signs of distress and searches for a nipple, the parent can provide it, thus leading to the emergence of a quieter state. Long before the infant develops the arm control to accomplish this task alone, the parental "frame" can fill the gaps in this incomplete skill. As shown in Figure 5, the simple provision of a pacifier leads to the spontaneous reorganization of the infant's state because pacifier-induced sucking incorporated into the already existing linkages between sucking and distress reduction creates an emergent distress control state previously unavailable. This is indicated by the change from a broken to a solid line between the left and right sides of Figure 5.

Although the development of early motor skills is rarely considered as a social process, it is clear that in walking, as well as in other tasks, the parent can similarly substitute for immature components. Clark and Phillips (1985) discovered that new walkers who were supported by the hands by an adult showed more mature stepping patterns than they did while walking alone. Here the parent accelerates the rate-limiting strength and balance component to allow the child to show more skilled locomotion, exactly analogous to role of the experimental treadmill for nonambulatory infants.

In both systems, external support of an immature component allowed the system to shift into new topographies or emergent forms. The social context—a parent who adjusts posture, brings a toy into reach,

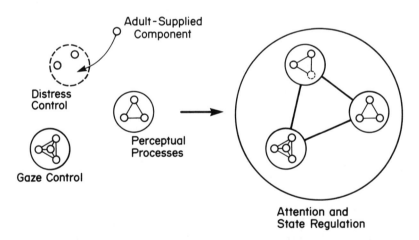

FIGURE 5. Schematic representation of adult's role in the development of new action patterns. Solid lines indicate already functioning subsystems; broken lines are subsystems that have not fully formed. Straight lines between the circles represent systemic integrations between the connected elements.

demonstrates the properties of the environment—is as much a determinant of the infant's performance as the instructions "within" the child. In dynamic action theory, there is no formal difference between these adult-supported shifts into controlled attentional behavior or more skilled motor actions and similar shifts that occur in development. In each case, the behavior spontaneously emerges when the missing piece is supplied. In the early months, when the parent withdraws the pacifier or does not support the walking child, the new coordination disappears. When the infant acquires arm or balance control developmentally, the shift into the new topography is stable, and it becomes part of the infant's repertoire.

This *socially constructed* emergent state is then free to combine with other existing subsystems to form more complex emergent systems. In the communication example, when arm control is combined with gaze control (composed of eye-scanning movements, the ability to hold the head upright and turn it freely from left to right and the ability to shift the focus of attention) and perceptual processes (such as innate preferences for contours and high contrast)—many aspects of attention and state regulation, including attention span, task performance, information-processing capabilities, and optimal muscle tone, may emerge spontaneously. In a similar manner, when parents provide mechanical walkers or other means of postural support, infants may shift into new levels of achievement in other domains, including perceptual, cognitive, and social activities (Gustafson, 1984). The new behavioral abilities, in turn, influence adults' behaviors toward their infants, and a spiraling, supporting matrix for development is built.

ACKNOWLEDGMENTS. We would like to thank Lauren Adamson, Pat Bateson, Tom Hannan, Nancy Hazen, Kim Kienapple, and Jeffrey Lockman for their detailed and thoughtful comments on the manuscript. Research discussed in this chapter was supported by NSF Grant BNS 8200434 and NICHD RCDA HD-00492 to E. T. and NSF Grant BNS-77-14524 and a grant from the Purdue University Agriculture Experiment Station to A. F.

REFERENCES

Abraham, R. H., & Shaw, C. D. (1982). *Dynamics—The geometry of behavior*. Santa Cruz, CA: Aerial Press.
Alberch, P. (1982). The generative and regulatory roles of development in evolution. In C. Roth (Ed.), *Environmental adaptation and evolution* (pp. 19–36). New York: Springer-Verlag.

Anokhin, P. K. (1964). Systemogenesis as a general regulator of brain development. *Progress in Brain Research, 9,* 54–86.

Arutyunyan, G. H., Gurfinkel, V. S., & Mirksy, M. L. (1969). Investigation of aiming at a target. *Biophysics, 13,* 536–538.

Bakeman, R., & Adamson, L. B. (1984). Coordinating attention to people and objects in mother-infant and peer-infant interaction. *Child Development, 55,* 1278–1289.

Bates, E. (1979). *The emergence of symbols: Cognition and communication in infancy.* New York: Academic Press.

Bates, E., Camaioni, L., & Volterra, V. (1975). The acquisition of performatives prior to speech. *Merrill-Palmer Quarterly, 21,* 205–226.

Bates, E., O'Connell, B., Vaid, J., Sledge, P., & Oakes, L. (1985). *Language and hand preference in early development.* Paper presented at the Society for Research in Child Development, Toronto.

Bateson, P. (1984). Sudden changes in ontogeny and phylogeny. In G. Greenberg & E. Tobach (Eds.), *Behavioral evolution and integrative levels* (pp. 155–166). Hillsdale, NJ: Lawrence Erlbaum.

Bernstein, N. (1967). *Co-ordination and regulation of movements.* New York: Pergamon Press.

Bertalanffy, L. von. (1986). *General system theory.* New York: George Braziller.

Bloom, L., Lifter, K., & Broughton, J. (1981). What children say and what they know: Exploring the relations between product and process in the development of early words and early concepts. In R. Stark (Ed.), *Language behavior in infancy and early childhood* (pp. 301–326). New York: Elsevier.

Bosma, J. F. (1975). Anatomic and physiologic development in the speech apparatus. In D. B. Tower (Ed.), *The Nervous System, Vol. 3: Human Communication and its disorders* (pp. 469–481). New York: Raven Press.

Brazelton, T. B. (1973). *Neonatal behavioral assessment scale.* London: S.I.M.P. and Heinemann Medical Books.

Brent, S. B. (1978). Prigogine's model for self-organization in nonequilibrium systems: Its relevance for developmental psychology. *Human Development, 21* 374–387.

Bruner, J. (1975). The ontogenesis of speech acts. *Journal of Child Language, 2,* 1–19.

Clark, J. E., & Phillips, S. J. (1985). *The organization of upright locomotion.* Paper presented at the Biannual Meeting of the Society for Research in Child Development, Toronto.

Connolly, K., & Elliott, J. (1972). The evolution and ontogeny of hand function. In N. Blurton Jones (Ed.), *Ethological studies of child behavior* (pp. 329–384). Cambridge: Cambridge University Press.

Cooke, J. D. (1980). The organization of simple, skilled movements. In G. E. Stelmach and J. Requin (Eds.), *Tutorials in Motor Behavior* (pp. 199–212). New York: North-Holland.

Demos, V. (1982). Facial expressions of infants and toddlers: A descriptive analysis. In T. Field & A. Fogel (Eds.), *Emotion and early interaction* (pp. 127–160). Hillsdale, NJ: Erlbaum.

Ekman, P., Friessen, W., & Ellsworth, P. (1972). *Emotion in the human face.* New York: Pergamon.

Engberg, I., & Lundberg, A. (1969). An electromyographic analysis of muscular activity in the hindlimb of the cat during unrestrained locomotion. *Acta Physiologica Scandinavica, 75,* 614–630.

Fentress, J. C. (1984). The development of coordination. *Journal of Motor Behavior, 16,* 99–134.

Fogel, A. (1980). The effect of brief separations on two-month-old infants. *Infant Behavior and Development, 3,* 315–330.

Fogel, A. (1981). The ontogeny of gestural communication: The first six months. In R. E.

Stark (Ed.), *Language behavior in infancy and early childhood* (pp. 17–44). New York: Elsevier.

Fogel, A. (1982a). Affect dynamics in early infancy: Affective tolerance. In T. Field & A. Fogel (Eds.), *Emotion and early interaction* (pp. 25–26). Hillsdale, NJ: Erlbaum.

Fogel, A. (1982b). Social play, positive affect and coping skills in the first six months of life. *Topics in Early Childhood Special Education, 2*, 53–65.

Fogel, A. (1985). Coordinative structures in the development of expressive behavior in early infancy. In G. Zivin (Ed.), *The development of expressive behavior: Biology-environment interaction* (pp. 249–267). New York: Academic Press.

Fogel, A., & Hannan, T. E. (1985). Manual actions of two- to three-month-old human infants during social interaction. *Child Development, 56*, 1271–1279.

Forssberg, H. (1985). Ontogeny of human locomotor control. I. Infant stepping, supported locomotion, and transition to independent locomotion. *Experimental Brain Research, 57*, 480–493.

Gesell, A. (1945). *The embryology of behavior.* New York: Harper.

Gierer, A. (1981). Generation of biological patterns and form: Some physical, mathematical, and logical aspects. *Progress in Biophysics and Molecular Biology, 37*, 1–47.

Goodwin, B. C. (1982). Development and evolution. *Journal of Theoretical Biology, 97*, 43–55.

Gould, S. J. (1977). *Ontogeny and phylogeny.* Cambridge: Harvard University Press.

Greene, P. H. (1972). Problems of organization of motor systems. In R. Rosen & F. Snell (Eds.), *Progress in theoretical biology* (pp. 303–338). New York: Academic Press.

Grillner, S. (1985). Neurobiological bases of rhythmic motor acts in vertebrates. *Science, 228*, 143–149.

Gustafson, G. E. (1984). Effects of the ability to locomote on infants' social and exploratory behaviors: An experimental study. *Developmental Psychology, 20*, 397–405.

Haken, H. (1977). *Synergetics: An introduction.* Heidelberg: Springer-Verlag.

Hannan, T. E. (1981). *Infant "pointing" behavior in the first three months of life.* Unpublished doctoral dissertation, Purdue University.

Hannan, T. E. (1982). Young infant's hand and finger movements: An analysis of category reliability. In T. Field and A. Fogel (Eds.), *Emotion and early interaction* (pp. 253–266). Hillsdale, NJ: Erlbaum.

Heriza, C. (1985). *The organization of spontaneous leg movements in premature infants.* Paper presented at Bienniel Meeting, Society for Research in Child Development, Toronto.

Hoyt, D. F., & Taylor, C. R. (1981). Gait and the energetics of locomotion in horses. *Nature, 292*, 239–240.

Iberall, A. S. (1972). *Toward a general science of viable systems.* New York: McGraw-Hill.

Iberall, A. S., & Soodak, H. (1978). Physical basis for complex systems —Some propositions relating levels of organization. *Collecting Phenomena, 3*, 9–24.

Katchalsky, A. K., Rowland, V., & Blumenthal, R. (Eds.) (1974). *Dynamic patterns of brain cell assemblies.* Cambridge: MIT Press.

Kaye, K. (1982). *The mental and social life of babies.* Chicago: University of Chicago Press.

Kaye, K., & Fogel, A. (1980). The temporal structure of face-to-face communication between mothers and infants. *Developmental Psychology, 16*, 454–464.

Kelso, J. A. S., & Tuller, B. (1984). A dynamical basis for action systems. In M. S. Gazzaniga (Ed.), *Handbook of cognitive neuroscience* (pp. 321–356). New York: Plenum Press.

Kelso, J. A. S., Tuller, B., Bateson, E. V., & Fowler, C. A. (1984). Functionally specific articulatory cooperation adaptation to jaw perturbations during speech: Evidence for coordinative structures. *Journal of Experimental Psychology: Human Perception and Performance, 10*, 812–832.

Kelso, J. A. S., Holt, K. G., Kugler, P. N., & Turvey, M. T. (1980). On the concept of coordinative structures as dissipative structures: II. Empirical lines of convergence. In G. E. Stelmach & J. Requin (Eds.), *Tutorials in motor behavior.* (pp. 49–70). New York: North-Holland

Kelso, J. A. S., Southard, D. l., & Goodman, D. (1979). On the nature of human interlimb coordination. *Science, 203,* 1029–1031.

Kent, R. D. (1981). Articulatory-acoustic perspective on speech development. In R. Stark (Ed.), *Language development in infancy and early childhood* (pp. 105–126). New York: Elsevier.

Kessen, W., Haith, M., & Salapatek, P. (1970). Infancy. In P. Mussen (Ed.), *Carmichael's manual of child psychology* (3rd ed., pp. 287–445). New York: Wiley.

Kienapple, K. G. P. (1983). *From recognition to categorization; The development of conceptual knowledge in 7- and 10-month-old infants.* Unpublished doctoral dissertation, Purdue University.

Kitchener, R. F. (1982). Holism and the organismic model in developmental psychgology. *Human Development, 25,* 233–249.

Konner, M. (1977). Maternal care, infant behavior and development among the Kalahari Desert San. In R. B. Lee & I. DeVore (Eds.), *Kalahari hunter gatherers* (pp. 218–245). Cambridge: Harvard University Press.

Kugler, P. N., Kelso, J. A. S., & Turvey, M. T. (1980). On the concept of coordinative structures as dissipative structures. I. Theoretical lines of convergence. In G. E. Stelmach & J. Requin (Eds.), *Tutorials in motor behavior* (pp. 3–47). New York; North-Holland.

Kugler, P., Kelso, J. A. S., & Turvey, M. T. (1982). On the control and co-ordination of naturally developing systems. In J. A. S. Kelso & J. E. Clark (Eds.), *The development of movement control and co-ordination* (pp. 5–78). New York: John Wiley.

Lempert, H., & Kinsbourne, M. (1985). Possible origin of speech in selective orienting. *Psychological Bulletin, 97,* 62–73.

Leung, E., & Rheingold, H. (1981). The development of pointing as a social gesture. *Developmental Psychology, 17,* 215–236.

Lindblom, B., & Sundberg, J. (1969). A quantitative model of vowel production and the distinctive features of Swedish vowels. *Quarterly Progress Status Report, Speech Transmission Laboratory, Royal Institute of Technology* (Stockholm, Sweden), *1,* 14–32.

Masur, E. F. (1983). Gestural development, dual directional signalling, and the transition to words. *Journal of Psycho-linguistic Research, 12,* 93–109.

McGraw, M. B. (1932). From reflex to muscular control in the assumption of an erect posture and ambulation in the human infant. *Child Development, 3,* 291–297.

McGraw, M. B. (1940). Neuromuscular development of the human infant as exemplified in the achievement of erect locomotion. *Journal of Pediatrics, 17,* 747–771.

McMahon, T. A. (1984). *Muscles, reflexes, and locomotion.* Princeton, NJ: Princeton University Press.

Murphy, C. M., & Messer, D. J. (1977). Mothers, infants, and pointing; A study of gesture. In H. R. Schaffer (Ed.), *Studies in mother-infant interaction* (pp. 325–354). New York: Academic Press.

Nashner, L. M. (1981). Analysis of stance posture in humans. In A. L. Towe & E. S. Luschei (Eds.), *Handbook of behavioral neurobiology, Vol. 5: Motor coordination* (pp. 527–565). New York; Plenum Press.

Netsell, R. (1981). The acquisition of speech motor control. In R. Stark (Ed.), *Language behavior in infancy and early childhood* (pp. 127–156). New York: Elsevier.

Oster, H. (1978). Facial expression and affect development. In M. Lewis & L. A. Rosenblum (Eds.), *The development of affect* (pp. 43–75). New York: Plenum Press.

Overton, W., Reese, H. (1973). Models of development: Methodological implications. In J. Nesselroade & H. Reese (Eds.), *Life-span developmental psychology: Methodological Issues* (pp. 65–86). New York: Academic Press.

Pearson, K. G., & Duysens, J. (1976). Function of segmental reflexes in the control of stepping in cockroaches and cats. In R. M. Herman, S. Grillner, P. S. G. Stein, & D. G. Stuart (Eds.), *Neural control of locomotion* (pp. 519–537). New York; Plenum Press.

Peiper, A. (1963). *Cerebral function in infancy and childhood*. New York: Consultants Bureau.

Piaget, J. (1971). *Biology and knowledge*. Chicago: University of Chicago Press.

Platzman, K. (1983). *The ontogeny of pointing in the first ten months of life*. Unpublished doctoral dissertation, University of Chicago.

Prechtl, H. F. R. (1974). The behavioural states of the newborn infant (a review). *Brain Research, 76*, 185–212.

Prigogine, I. (1980). *From being to becoming*. San Francisco: W. H. Freeman.

Ramsay, D. S. (1984). Onset of duplicated syllable babbling and unimanual handedness in infancy: Evidence for developmental change in hemispheric specialization? *Developmental Psychology, 20*, 64–71.

Reed, E. S. (1982). An outline of a theory of action systems. *Journal of Motor Behavior, 14*, 98–134.

Reese, H. W., & Overton, W. F. (1970). Models of development and theories of development. In L. R. Goulet & P. B. Baltes (Eds.), *Life-span development psychology: Research and theory* (pp. 115–145). New York: Academic Press.

Rosen, R. (1978). *Fundamentals of measurement and representation of natural systems*. New York: North-Holland.

Ruff, H. (1984). Infants' manipulative exploration of objects: Effects of age and object characteristics. *Developmental Psychology, 20*, 9–20.

Sameroff, A. J. (1983). Developmental systems: Contexts and evolution. In P. H. Mussen (Ed.), *Handbook of child psychology. History, theory, and methods* (4th ed., Vol. I, pp. 237–294). New York: Wiley.

Schmidt, R. A. (1982). *Motor control and learning: A behavioral emphasis*. Champaign, IL: Human Kinetics Publishers.

Shapiro, D. C., & Schmidt, R. A. (1982). The schema theory: Recent evidence and developmental implications. In J. A. S. Kelso and J. E. Clark (Eds.), *The development of movement control and co-ordination* (pp. 113–150). New York: John Wiley.

Shapiro, D. C., Zernicke, R. F., Gregor, R. J., & Diestel, J. D. (1981). Evidence for generalized motor program using gait pattern analysis. *Journal of Motor Behavior, 13*, 33–47.

Shik, M. L., & Orlovsky, G. N. (1976). Neurophysiology of locomotor automatism. *Physiological Reviews, 56*, 465–501.

Soll, D. R. (1979). Timers in developing systems. *Science, 203*, 841–849.

Sroufe, L. A. (1979). Socioemotional development. In J. Osofsky (Ed.), *Handbook of infant development* (pp. 462–518). New York: Wiley.

Statham, L., & Murray, M. P. (1971). Early walking patterns of normal children. *Clinical Orthopaedics, 79*, 8–24.

Super, C. M. (1980). Behavioral development in infancy. In R. H. Monroe, R. L. Monroe, & B. B. Whiting (Eds.), *Handbook of cross-cultural human development* (pp. 181–270). New York: Garland STPM.

Sutherland, D. H., Olshen, R., Cooper, L., & Woo, S. L.-Y. (1980). The development of mature gait. *The Journal of Bone and Joint Surgery, 62*, 336–353.

Thelen, E. (1979). Rhythmical stereotypies in normal human infants. *Animal Behaviour, 27*, 699–715.

Thelen, E. (1981a). Kicking, rocking, and waving: Contextual analysis of rhythmical stereotypies in normal human infants. *Animal Behaviour, 29*, 3–11.

Thelen, E. (1981b). Rhythmical behavior in infancy: An ethological perspective. *Developmental Psychology*, 17, 237–257.

Thelen, E. (1985). Developmental origins of motor coordination: leg movements in human infants. *Developmental Psychology*, 18, 1–22.

Thelen, E. (1986). Treadmill-elicited stepping in seven-month-old infants. *Child Development*, 57, 1498–1506.

Thelen, E., & Fisher, D. M. (1982). Newborn stepping: An explanation for a "disappearing reflex." *Developmental Psychology*, 18, 760–775.

Thelen, E., & Fisher, D. M. (1983a). From spontaneous to instrumental behavior: Kinematic analysis of movement changes during very early learning. *Child Development*, 54, 129–140.

Thelen, E., & Fisher, D. M. (1983b). The organization of spontaneous leg movements in newborn infants. *Journal of Motor Behavior*, 15, 353–377.

Thelen, E., Bradshaw, G., & Ward, J. A. (1981). Spontaneous kicking in month-old infants: manifestations of a human central locomotor program. *Behavioral and Neural Biology*, 32, 45–53.

Thelen, E., Ridley-Johnson, R., & Fisher, D. M. (1983). Shifting patterns of bilateral coordination and lateral dominance in the leg movements of young infants. *Developmental Psychobiology*, 16, 29–46.

Thelen, E., Fisher, D. M., & Ridley-Johnson, R. (1984). The relationship between physical growth and a newborn reflex. *Infant Behavior and Development*, 7, 479–493.

Thelen, E., Kelso, J. A. S., and Fogel, A. (1986). Self-organizing systems and infant motor development. *Developmental Review*, 7, 39–65.

Thelen, E., Skala, K., & Kelso, J. A. S. (1987). The dynamic nature of early coordination: Evidence from bilateral leg movements in young infants. *Developmental Psychology*, 23, 179–186.

Trevarthen, C. (1977). Descriptive analyses of infant communication behaviour. In H. R. Schaffer (Ed.), *Studies in mother-infant interaction* (pp. 227–270). New York: Academic Press.

Trevarthen, C. (1979). Communication and cooperation in primary inter-subjectivity. In M. Bullowa (Ed.), *Before speech* (pp. 321–348). New York: Cambridge University Press.

Tuller, B., Turvey, M. T., & Fitch, H. (1982). The Bernstein perspective. II. The concept of muscle linkage or coordinative structure. In J. A. S. Kelso (Ed.), *Human motor behavior: An Introduction* (pp. 252–270). Hillsdale, NJ: Lawrence Erlbaum.

Turvey, M. T. (1977). Preliminaries to a theory of action with a reference to vision. In R. Shaw & J. Bransford (Eds.), *Perceiving, acting, and knowing: Toward an ecological psychology* (pp. 211–265). Hillsdale, NJ: Lawrence Erlbaum.

Waddington, C. H. (1966). *Principles of development and differentiation*. New York: Macmillan.

Wapner, S., & Kaplan, B. (1983). *Toward a holistic developmental psychology*. Hillsdale, NJ: Lawrence Erlbaum.

Webster, G., & Goodwin, B. (1981). History and structure in biology. *Perspectives in Biology and Medicine*, 25, 39–62.

Werner, H. (1957). The concept of development from a comparative and organismic point of view. In D. B. Harris (Ed.). *The concept of development* (pp. 125–148). Minneapolis: University of Minnesota Press.

Werner, J. (1977). Mathematical treatment of structure and function of human thermoregulatory system. *Biology Cybernetics*, 25, 93–101.

Whiting, H. T. A. (1984). *Human motor actions: Bernstein reassessed*. Amsterdam: North-Holland.

Winfree, A. T. (1980). *The geometry of biological time.* New York: Springer-Verlag.

Wolff, P. H. (1967). The role of biological rhythms in early psychological development. *Bulletin of the Menninger Clinic, 31,* 197–218.

Zelazo, P. R. (1983). The development of walking: New findings and old assumptions. *Journal of Motor Behavior, 15,* 99–137.

Zelazo, P. R., Zelazo, N. A., & Kolb, S. (1972). "Walking" in the newborn. *Science, 177,* 1058–1059.

Zeskind, P. S., & Lester, B. M. (1978). Acoustic features of auditory perceptions of the cries of newborns with prenatal and perinatal complications. *Child Development, 49,* 580–589.

CHAPTER 3

Self-Regulation and Motor Development in Preterm Infants

HEIDELISE ALS

INTRODUCTION

The preterm human infant is a product of mankind's advances in neonatal medical technology and medicine. Today, many more preterms survive than ever before, and infants of 24 to 25 weeks' gestation have extended the lower limit of extrauterine viability. Coincident with such medical advances is the necessity of equally vigorous advances in creating a nurturing extrauterine environment and support system in order to ameliorate the mismatch between the environment for which the preterm organism is biologically prepared and the highly demanding and stress-producing environment into which the preterm is thrust.

A preterm infant, depending on postconceptional age at birth, may biologically be expecting up to 16 more weeks of *in utero* existence with the maternal blood flow and the placenta providing aid in the respiratory, cardiac, digestive, and temperature control functions. The infant is still fully reliant on cutaneous somasthetic input from the amniotic fluid, on motoric kinesthetic input within the amniotic sac wall, on maternal diurnal rhythms, and, in general, on a protective environment that attenuates sensory inputs to the primary sense organs. The preterm infant must not be thought of as a deficient full-term organism but, rather, as a well-equipped, competently adapted fetus, functioning appropriately

HEIDELISE ALS • Harvard Medical School and The Children's Hospital, Boston, Massachusetts 02115.

for stage within the natural environment, the womb, yet being outside of that womb.

The preterm infant in the neonatal intensive care unit (NICU), who is, in essence, a displaced fetus, appears as keenly sensitive to all parameters of environmental impingement, hyperresponsive, because higher cortical systems, especially association cortical systems that provide buffering and differential inhibitory controls, have not yet developed. This sensitivity of the very young nervous system provides a unique opportunity for the caregiver to make it an organism-appropriate, developmentally supportive environment, rather than a hazardous place of increased stress. To improve the environmental structure and timing, the input and experiences provided by the caregiver need to be based on better understanding of the functioning of the "transitional newborn" (Desmond, Rudolf, & Phitaksphraiwan, 1966; Thurber & Armstrong, 1982), who biologically is on the way to become a full-term infant.

Because the brain of the transitional newborn is the critical organ in orchestrating all aspects of development, it is the protection and support of the immature, but rapidly evolving brain that must be a primary consideration for those providing care for preterm infants in our NICU environments. All parts of the brain are complexly interdependent. Areas that are neuroarchitectonically and temporally remote from the focus of insult or scar formation can show damage or malfunction much later, when certain connections become important in the course of the ontogenesis and evolution of complex integrative motor, cognitive, and affective functions. All areas of development are intimately interrelated, and damage in one area may have ripple effects into other areas. Yet compensatory strategies can also be developed, with appropriate developmental support, especially in the very young brain, as has been demonstrated with animal models (Goldman, 1976; Goldman-Rakic, 1981). The burden and opportunity, then, are on the identification and provision of brain developmentally appropriate and supportive environments to ensure normal developmental functioning and progression.

The synactive model of development, which I will elaborate on in the following chapter, provides a meaningful paradigm for understanding emergent brain function via observation of current infant behaviors. Autonomic, motoric, state organizational, attentional, and self-regulatory capabilities of an infant can be observed and characterized so as to identify functional thresholds and responses to stress. The caregiver(s) can evaluate the current ability levels of the individual infant in coping with evolving, increasingly differentiated agenda and can thus establish a developmentally supportive environment without overtaxing or overstressing the child.

In the following discussion, I will first provide a review of development of the full-term infant, emphasizing the important role of the social
environment for normal, healthy development of newborns. Based on
the insights gained from the exploration of "normal" development, I
will then examine the issues confronting and challenging the preterm
infant. The Assessment of Preterm Infants' Behavior (APIB), a means of
identifying the preterm infant's current functional levels, is described,
and our current research based on application of the APIB is presented.
The objective of our research is to synthesize an evolutionarily appropriate environment to support normal development in preterm infants,
characterizing appropriate environmental and social interventions. The
remainder of this chapter will address these issues.

THE FULL-TERM INFANT IN DEVELOPMENTAL PERSPECTIVE

It becomes the task of the NICU to provide a nurturing yet stimulating milieu which simulates, to the extent possible, the intrauterine functions which the fetus would have normally experienced. The observation of the fullterm may aid us in understanding the differences of
preterm and fullterm functioning.

The Developmental Task of the Full-Term Newborn

From our work with healthy full-term newborns examined with the
Brazelton Neonatal Behavioral Assessment Scale (Brazelton, 1973) and
in direct observation of newborns with their mothers over the first 3
months (Als, 1976, 1977), we learned that the differentiation of the attentional system is the most salient, most rapidly changing, and apparently
newly emerging agendum of the human full-term (Als, 1978, 1979).
Autonomic stability in terms of respiratory control, temperature regulation, and digestive visceral functioning is relatively quickly restabilized
after the birth process, as are smoothness of movements and adaptation
of well-regulated, smooth balance between flexor and extensor posture
(Casaer, 1979). The same holds true for state organization in terms of the
range of states available and their transitions (Sander, 1962, 1964). Most
healthy full-term newborns have no difficulty achieving a robust, lusty
crying state and can return to a sleep state relatively readily. The issue
most full-term newborns seem to attempt to get under control in the first
several weeks after birth is the increasing stabilization of the alert state
in their movement from sleep to aroused crying states and back down to

sleep state. Although in the 2-day-old full-term infant the alert periods are still somewhat difficult to come by and are embedded in long stretches of sleep and episodes of crying. By 2 and 3 weeks these periods of alertness have become increasingly reliable and solidified, and by 1 month to 6 weeks many infants easily spend an hour and more at a time in an alert, socially, and cognitively available state.

The Social Environment of the Full-Term Human Newborn

It appears that the full-term newborn is not the only one grappling to solidify these periods of alert availability. The infant's social partners from the very first postnatal contact on tend to be keen and sensitive in aiding the infant in stabilizing these periods (Als, 1977; Grossman, 1978). On the very first contact, mothers and, presumably, fathers will prod their newborn vocally and tactilely to open the eyes, even at the cost of eliciting crying. Even if the newborn then opens only one eye, the mother will typically acknowledge this initial connection and mutual recognition by an affectively positive, heightened vocal pattern for his or her accomplishment: "Hi!," she may say, over and over again, in a drawn-out, loving manner. "There you are! That's right. I knew you were in there!" (Als, 1975). Her behavior, in turn, appears to facilitate and support the infant's alertness. From a brief, initial glance, the infant may go on to widen the eyes, raise the eyebrows, soften and raise the cheeks, and shape the mouth into an "ooh" configuration. The partners mutually support and drive each other to prolong this episode. One of them will then reset or break the intensity. The infant may, for instance, avert the gaze, and may move into a yawn or a sneeze, thus resetting the intensity at a lower level by utilizing subtle attentional regulation strategies. Or the infant may avert and move into a fussy, crying, or drowsy state, thus utilizing state shifts to reset the interaction. Or the infant may not avert but may stay locked on the mother's face, become tense, and perhaps spit up or move into hiccoughs, gags, or even the strain of bowel movement, thus reacting at an autonomic visceral level in resetting the interaction. Or the infant may begin to extend and flail the arms and start to squirm, thus utilizing motoric shifts in the resetting of the interaction. If the infant is able to sustain alertness for a substantial period, keeping the respective subsystems of functioning in balance, the mother may be the one resetting the intensity of the interaction by pulling the baby close and nuzzling and kissing or stroking and patting the infant, thus changing the cyclic attentional interchange (Als, 1975). Thus, there appears to exist a predictably ordered patterning of interaction of the full-term newborn on the first contact after delivery with the mother, emphasizing the connnection of the newborn alertness supported by parental affection. Figure 1 shows a schematic presentation of the results from a study of 40 full terms in initial interaction with their primiparous mothers.

It is curious that such emphasis appears to be placed on these early attentional episodes of the infant that are embedded in affectively supportive and highly positive inputs from the parent, given that later on this alertness will be much more easily available. From an evolutionary species perspective, this early valuing of the interactive attentional connection gains an added dimension. Phylogenetically, it appears that humans are at the apex of evolution for the combination of cognitive attention and affective engagement with another individual. This may be gleaned from a study of this connection in the progression through the order primate from the nocturnal prosimians via the Old and New World monkeys to the great apes and man (Bolwig, 1959a,b; Buettner-Janusch, 1966; Huber, 1931). As we move through the phylogenetic scale, we find an increasingly complex and simultaneously increasingly flexible social system. The essence of humanness and, in fact, of human species' survival appears to be in man's enormously complex capacity for social and emotional interaction, which is the prerequisite for the virtual supersystem of material culture, that is, technology we have constructed and are dependent on for our survival as humans (Vygot-

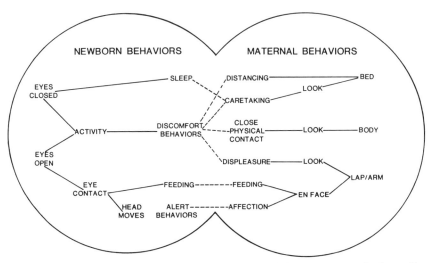

FIGURE 1. Full-term newborn and maternal behaviors and their interactive fit (from Als, 1975; reproduced with permission).

sky, 1978). Highly differentiated capacities for collaboration and cooperation of species' members are necessary to make such a complex adaptation workable. It appears that from the very beginning of extrauterine life, the full-term, well-developing newborn organism is already launched onto the species' specific, interactive, collaborative communicative track and is in turn supported and affectively rewarded by the caregivers in this capacity as a social interactor. The interactive attentional capacity of the newborn and young infant therefore becomes a salient parameter of newborn functioning. It appears to be in current ascendancy and is highly valued and supported by those around the infant (Als & Duffy, 1982).

The Full-Term Newborn's Attentional/Interactive Capacity

Not all full-term newborns are equally able to increase their interactive attentional capacity. For some, as we learned in a study of thin-for-height full-term newborns (Als, Tronick, Adamson, & Brazelton, 1976), this is a very difficult task, which impinges on the infant's other functional systems. These thin infants showed great reluctance to come into alertness, moving into hypertonic, flexed, high-guard arm position with fisted hands, while becoming pale, showing tachypneic and irregular respiration with pained and drawn facial expressions. With slow, calm support, they would eventually gradually open their eyes, but then the hypertonic high-guard fisted defendedness shifted abruptly into motoric flaccidity and tuning out, the color paled further, and breathing became slow and irregular. The mustered attention was of a glassy-eyed, strained, barely focused kind that came at great cost to the autonomic and motor regulation. The identification of this pattern of subsystem syncresis with relatively poor subsystem differentiation, in which, as one system attempts to accomplish a task, the other systems are drawn into the reaction in a generalized manner, exemplifying the relative cost to the total system on many levels, is of interest. It is one avenue toward understanding the current standing of the infant on the developmental lines of subsystem differentiation.

Parameters to Be Considered in Assessing the Infant's Functioning

On the basis of our observations of this subsystem interaction, we have, therefore, formulated the following parameters to be described when assessing an individual infant's functioning (Als, 1982b):

1. The infant's current, newly emerging developmental agendum and the degree of ascendancy of this agendum.
2. The infant's current level of subsystem balance and smooth integrated subsystem functioning regardless of the agendum identified as in ascendancy.
3. The threshold of disorganization indicated in behaviors of defense and avoidance, at varying subsystem levels of functioning as the developmental agendum in ascendancy is tested.
4. The degree of relative modulation and regulation of the various subsystems in accomplishing the new skill.
5. The degree of differentiation and effectiveness in rebalancing the subsystems in the accomplishment of the skill.
6. The degree of environmental structuring, support, and facilitative aid necessary to bring about optimal implementation of the new skill.
7. The degree of environmental structuring, support, and facilitative aid necessary to bring about organization at a smooth, well-integrated and ideally more differentiated new level of functioning.

This approach to the assessment of organism functioning is thought to be appropriate throughout the life span of the organism. At each stage of development, newly salient agenda are being negotiated on the backdrop of previously accomplished subsystem differentiation and modulation. Figure 2 (Als, 1982b) is a schematic attempt to visualize this conceptualization of the perspective of development applied to the fetal and neonatal stages.

Looked at from above, four concentric circles or cones are seen, represented from the innermost going outward. The first is the autonomic system in its basic position, assuring the organism's baseline functioning. Around it, as it were, is seen the motor system, unfolding from very early embryonic stages with recognizable flexor posture, limb, and trunk movements and becoming increasingly differentiated in its explication. Around it, as a third cone, lies the state organizational system, the unfolding of distinct states of consciousness from diffuse quasi-sleep states to increasingly differentiated sleep, wake, and aroused bands of consciousness. And around this cone lies the gradual differentiation of the awake state into more and more elaborated, subtly branched, and finely tuned nuances of affective and cognitive receptivity and activity, shaping the social and inanimate world, and negotiating one's own developmental progression in the process. These cones are continuously in contiguity if not interacting with one another, influencing and supporting one another or infringing on one another's relative stability. The

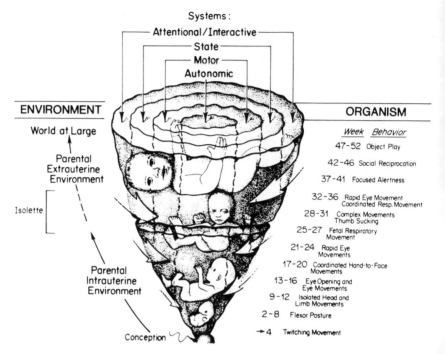

FIGURE 2. Model of the synactive organization of behavioral development (from Als, 1982b; reproduced with permission).

within-subsystem differentiation each system is striving for depends on the other subsystems' support and relative intactness. The whole organism with its intraorganism subsystem interaction is at all stages surrounded and embedded in an environment it has evolved to expect for its species-*appropriate* ontogenesis. The organism is actively shaping and selecting from this environment as it is constantly challenged and impinged upon by this environment (Hunt, 1961; Piaget, 1963, 1971).

THE PRETERM INFANT IN DEVELOPMENTAL PERSPECTIVE

A substantial body of research indicates that a broad array of physiological and emotional abnormalities are disproportionately represented in the population of children born preterm. These studies also tend to indicate that these problems are neurological in origin. Developmental impairment is due to direct insult to the brain, as in hemorrhage, or indirect insult, as in anoxic and hypoxemic events and metabolic imbalances, all of which are the consequences of mismatch of extrauterine environment and the capacity of the central nervous system of the fetal newborn adapted for an intrauterine existence. The fact that developmental impairment is also present in those infants spared the more massive insults of hemorrhage or hypoxemic anoxic events forces one to consider that the environment influences the development of the brain in additional ways, namely through the various senses of the organism— the visual, auditory, cutaneous, tactile, somatesthetic, kinesthetic, olfactory, and gustatory senses. The interplay of sensory information and experience is thought to form species-appropriate ontogenetic integration patterns, on the one hand, and deleterious adaptation patterns leading to malfunction or distortion of functioning, on the other hand (Piaget, 1971). Given the rapid development of the brain from the twenty-fourth to the fourtieth week of fetal life and the emergence and differentiation, especially of association cortical areas in this period, the impact of biologically, ontogenetically unexpected experience should not be surprising. Animal models have given substantial evidence of the fine-tuned specificity of environmental inputs necessary in the course of sensitive periods of brain development to support normal cortical ontogenesis (Duffy, Burchfiel, & Snodgrass, 1978; Mower, Burchfiel, & Duffy, 1982; Spinelli, Jensen, & Deprisco, 1980; for a review, see Duffy, Mower, Jensen, & Als, 1984). The mechanisms leading to developmental distortions implicated by this work are largely active inhibition or suppression of normal pathways through overactivation of currently functional pathways, thus leading to less differentiated and less modulated overall later functioning. The suppressions appear to be mediated by endorphin mechanisms inferred from the successful experimental reactivation by morphine antagonists. This hypothesis is particularly appealing, given the hierarchical ordering of endorphin receptor sites in primates, with substantial increase in evolutionarily and ontogenetically later structures, that is, more recent, association cortical areas, culminating in frontal cortex (Lewis, Mishkin, Bragin, Brown, Pert, & Pert, 1981), which is one of the areas strongly implicated in attentional learning and behavior deficits in the school-age population (Denckla, 1978).

   In trying to understand the preterm infant's functioning, our first question, then, must be: What is the species-appropriate adaptation that the organism is equipped with, and what from the central nervous system and other systems' perspective is he or she adapted for? The preterm infant is biologically expecting 13 to 16 more weeks of *in utero* existence, with respiratory, cardiac, digestive, and temperature control aided by the maternal blood flow and placental functioning. The infant is expecting total cutaneous somatesthetic input from the amniotic fluid. The infant is expecting motoric kinesthetic input from the contingently reactive amniotic sac, preventing full extensor patterns and assuring flexor inhibition and flexor maintenance for the typical head–trunk extremity adjustments and movements of soft modulated limbs, trunk, and head movement, so vividly described by Birnholz, Stephens, and Faria (1978) and Milani-Comparetti (1980). The infant is expecting maternal diurnal rhythms presumably entraining the gradually differentiating states of consciousness; and the infant is expecting presumably muted sensory inputs to the primary senses of vision and audition, being readied for the experience of the extrauterine world. The preterm infant is not an inadequate or deficient full-term organism, but is, rather, a well-equipped, competently adapted fetus appropriately functioning at this stage and in the natural environment.

Suddenly the infant is in a vastly different environment, the passage to which has irreversibly triggered subsystem functioning in an environment only poorly matched to the infant's expectations. Instead of the maternal organism, medical technology attempts to take care of respiratory, cardiac, digestive, and temperature control functions. The motor system, the state organizational system, and sensory functioning intimately dependent on an adaptive environment are largely left to their own devices. The center in our schematic model of Figure 2, the autonomic functioning, is currently largely the primary focus of medical care. When a preterm infant reactivates body movement and state organization after a period of virtual shock, what Bottos (1985) calls the "apostural-akinetic phase," we hypothesize that the infant is trying to reestablish a level of developmental activity that the infant was capable of before the shutdown. In this context, we need to ask with what supports and in what situations is the infant already able to bring about the smooth and balanced functioning that will be critical for the realization of new pathways. The freeing-up of the small strands of the next developmental agenda in the offing must occur on the background of well-integrated functioning in order to set and maintain the path of development in a positive direction. This is necessary to avoid the unwitting reinforcement of only the disturbing, distorted defense behaviors that are all too readily concommitant of a discrepant organism–environment fit. All too easily, this poor fit can lead to a vicious cycle of increasing and reverberating distortion and disorganization (Herzog, 1979), possibly mediated neurosynaptically (Duffy & Als, 1983). From this perspective, it is not surprising that the number of autistic children and children with organizational, visual motor integration, spatial, impulsivity, emotional, and attentional deficits (OAID) (Denckla, 1978; Hertzig, 1981; Hunt, Tooley, & Harvin, 1982; Siegel, 1982) is made up of a disproportionately high number of prematurely born infants. The developmental agendum that we have identified for the full-term newborn, namely to increasingly free-up the ability to maintain an alert state, may not as yet be the appropriate issue for the preterm infant. The mutual regulation of autonomic functioning with motoric balance and equilibrium in a well-defined sleep state may well be the salient agendum for a while, before further state differentiation becomes possible.

Subsystems of Functioning

The model of development we propose (Als, 1979, 1982b) here specifies the degree of differentiation of behavior and the ability of the infant at a given moment in time to modulate and organize behavior. The level of differentiation and ability to modulate behavior are the dominant parameters of an infant's individuality and personal uniqueness, recognizable over time. The conceptualization of development presented here focuses on the way the individual infant appears to handle the experience of the world, rather than on the assessment of skills *per se*. The infant's functioning is seen in a model of continuous intraorganism subsystem interaction, and the organism, in turn, is seen in continuous interaction with its environment. We have termed this view of development *synactive*, because at each stage in development and each moment of functioning, the various subsystems of functioning discussed are existing side by side, often truly interactive, but often in a relative supporting holding pattern, as if providing a steady substratum for one of the system's current differentiation (synaction).

The systems we are speaking of include, as seen in Figure 2, the autonomic system, the motor system, the state organizational system, the attention and interaction system, and a self-regulatory balancing system. The functioning of all these systems is reliably observable without technical instrumentation. The autonomic system is behaviorally observable in the pattern of respiration, color changes, and visceral signals such as bowel movements, gagging, hiccoughing, and the like. The motor system is behaviorally observable in the range of states of consciousness available to the organism, from sleeping to alert to aroused states, in the pattern of state transitions exhibited and in the clarity, robustness, and definedness of the states. The attention and interaction system is exemplified in the organism's ability to come to an alert, atten-

tive state and to utilize this state in order to take in cognitive and socioemotional information from the environment and in turn elicit and
modify these inputs from the world. The regulatory system is behaviorally exemplified in the observable strategies the organism utilizes to
maintain a balanced, relatively stable and relaxed state of subsystem
integration or to return to such a state of balance and relaxation. If the
infant's own regulatory capacity is exceeded momentarily and the infant
is unable to return to an integrated balanced subsystem state, a further
parameter of functioning is identifiable in the kind and amount of facilitation from the environment that is useful to the infant in aiding the
infant's return to balance.

The question posed to the organism in this synactive model of development is consequently: How well differentiated and how well modulated are the various subsystems in their functioning and their mutual
balance, given varying demands placed on the organisms and given
varying developmental tasks the organism attempts to master driven by
intrinsic biological developmental motivation? Where are the thresholds
of functioning beyond which smoothness and balance become strained
or coping behaviors become stressed and eventually behavioral organization becomes so costly that only bare subsistence protections remain
and finally even counterproductive maladaptations set in? Which subsystem is differentially vulnerable at which level of environmental and
endogenous demand? How severe is its kindling of other systems' im-
balance by virtue of its own current disorganization? How much or how
little does it take in terms of environmental modification to reinstitute a
more balanced integrated state?

Description of the Assessment of Preterm Infants' Behavior (APIB)

In an attempt to systematically identify the infant's relative standing
in terms of differentiation and modulation of behavioral subsystems, we
have formulated the Assessment of Preterm Infants' Behavior (APIB)
(Als, Lester, Tronick, & Brazelton, 1982). This instrument is appropriate
not only for preterm infants but also for otherwise at-risk infants and for
healthy full-term infants. It is a substantial refinement and extension of
Brazelton Neonatal Behavioral Assessment Scale (NBAS) (Brazelton,
1973), in that it provides an integrated subsystem profile of the infant,
identifying the current level of smooth, well-balanced functioning in the
face of varying developmental demands. In the APIB, the maneuvers of
the NBAS are used as graded sequences of increasingly vigorous en-

vironmental inputs or packages, moving from distal stimulation presented during sleep to mild tactile stimulation, to medium stimulation paired with vestibular stimulation to vigorous tactile and vestibular stimulation. The social interactive attentional package is administered at

ASSESSMENT OF PRETERM INFANT BEHAVIOR (APIB)

H. Als, Ph.D.
B.M. Lester, Ph.D., E. Tronick, Ph.D., T.B. Brazelton, M.D.
©February 1979

INFANT'S NAME	MED. REC. NO.	DATE OF BIRTH	AGE (Post-conception)
TIME – LAST FEEDING	TYPE OF FEEDING	CURRENT INTERVAL BETWEEN FEEDS	

INITIAL CIRCUMSTANCES OF INFANT

POSITION:	☐ SUPINE	☐ PRONE	☐ SIDE	
HEAD:	☐ RIGHT	☐ LEFT	☐ MIDLINE	
COVERING:	☐ DIAPER	☐ SHIRT	☐ CLOTHES	☐ BLANKET(S)

INFANT'S INITIAL STATE		INFANT'S PREDOMINANT STATE	
WEIGHT ____ LBS ____ OZS ____ GMS	HEIGHT ____ INCHES ____ CM	HEAD CIRCUMFERENCE ____ INCHES ____ CM	PONDERAL INDEX
DATE OF EXAM	TIME OF EXAM	PLACE OF EXAM	PERSONS PRESENT ☐ MOTHER ☐ FATHER ☐ SIBLING(S) ☐ OTHER ____
INTERFERING VARIABLES	EXAMINER	VIDEO	DURATION OF EXAM

SCORE SHEET I – SYSTEMS

LEGEND: B = Baseline R = Reaction P = Post-package Status

	ORDER OF PKG.	PHYSIOLOGY			MOTOR			STATE			ATTN/INTERACT			REGULATORY			EXAM FACIL
		B	R	P	B	R	P	B	R	P	B	R	P	B	R	P	
PACKAGE I SLEEP/DISTAL																	
PACKAGE II UNCOVER/SUPINE																	
PACKAGE III LOW TACTILE																	
PACKAGE IV MEDIUM TACTILE/VESTIBULAR																	
PACKAGE V HIGH TACTILE/VESTIBULAR																	
PACKAGE VI ATTENTION/INTERACTION																	

COMMENTS:

FIGURE 3. APIB Systems Sheet (from Als *et al.*, 1982; reproduced with permission).

any time in the course of the examination that the infant's behavior
organization indicates availability for this sequence. It receives priority
in the examiner's attempts to facilitate the infant's organization. The
systems sheet (see Figure 3) of the assessment permits one to then read
off which tasks are already handled with ease by the infant in terms of
maintaining well-regulated, balanced functioning of all subsystems;
which tasks begin to stress the infant and trespass the balance and
modulation of various subsystems yet can be handled with enough environmental facilitation; and which tasks are clearly as yet inappropriate
for the infant. In this fashion, developmentally appropriate supportive
facilitations can be instituted so that the infant is not continuously over-
taxed or, less likely, underchallenged.

Aside from the systems sheet, the APIB provides detailed information on each individual item of the tasks presented in documenting the
behavior of the immature, the dysmature, as well as the mature full-
term organism. Particular attention has been given, moreover, to the
reliable body language of the developing organism, and a catalog of
specific regulation behaviors has been established that can be helpful in
understanding the infant's current functioning. The signals can be classified as signals of stress and signals of stability. Table 1 gives a list of
stress and defense behaviors; Table 2 gives a list of self-regulatory and
approach behaviors readily observed in the preterm, at-risk full-term,
and/or healthy full-term, respectively (Als, 1982a, 1984). They are
grouped into autonomic/visceral stress signals, motoric stress signals,
and state-regulation stress signals, on the one hand, and signals of
autonomic/visceral stability, signals of motoric stability, and signals of
state organizational stability, on the other hand (Als, 1982b). The conceptualization underlying this approach is that the organism will defend
itself against stimulation if it is inappropriately timed or inappropriate in
its complexity or intensity. If properly timed and appropriate in its complexity and intensity, stimulation will cause the organism to seek it out
and move toward it, while maintaining itself at a balanced level (Denny-
Brown, 1962, 1972; Schneirla, 1959, 1965).

The formulation of this dual antagonist integration of avoidance
and approach as applied to the newborn infant (Als, 1982b; Als & Brazelton, 1981; Als & Duffy, 1983) can be helpful in identifying the infant's
current thresholds of balanced, well-modulated functioning. In turn, it
can facilitate the individualization of caregiving and interaction with
such an infant. Figure 4a (Als, 1983) shows an example of a poorly
integrated, withdrawn, and flaccid infant at 1-month postterm during
optimal interaction with a social partner. Figure 4b (Als, 1983) shows an
example of a well-integrated, robust, and animated infant at the same

TABLE 1
Stress and Defense Behaviors (APIB)[a]

1. Autonomic and visceral stress signals:
   a. Seizures
   b. Respiratory pauses, irregular respirations, breath holding
   c. Color changes to mottled, webbed, cyanotic, or gray
   d. Gagging, choking
   e. Spitting up
   f. Hiccoughing
   g. Straining as if or actually producing a bowel movement
   h. Gasping
   i. Tremoring and startling
   j. Coughing
   k. Sneezing
   l. Yawning
   m. Sighing
2. Motoric stress signals:
   a. Motoric flaccidity, or "tuning out"
      (1) trunkal flaccidity
      (2) extremity flaccidity
      (3) facial flaccidity (gape face)
   b. Motoric hypertonicity
      (1) With hyperextensions of legs: sitting on air; leg bracing of arms: airplaning; saluting of trunk: arching; opisthotonus fingerplays; facial grimaces; tongue extensions; and high guard arm position
      (2) With hyperflexions of trunk and extremities: fetal tuck; fisting
   c. Frantic, diffuse activity; squirming
   d. Frequent twitching
3. State-related stress signals:
   a. Diffuse sleep or awake states with whimpering sounds, facial twitches and discharge smiling
   b. Eye floating; roving eye movements
   c. Strained fussing or crying; silent crying
   d. Staring
   e. Frequent active averting
   f. Panicked or worried alertness; hyperalertness
   g. Glassy-eyed, strained alertness; lidded, drowsy alertness
   h. Rapid state oscillations; frequent buildup to arousal
   i. Irritability and prolonged diffuse arousal
   j. Crying
   k. Frenzy and inconsolability
   l. Sleeplessness and restlessness

[a]Als, 1982b.

FIGURE 4. (a) Optimal alerting during social interaction (1-month postterm): poorly integrated infant (withdrawn and flaccid) (from Als, 1983; reproduced with permission).

age in social interaction. The difference of flexibility and modulation is quite apparent.

The APIB requires extensive training in developmental psychology, a working knowledge of developmental neurology and neonatology, and extensive experience and training in the observation and handling

TABLE 2
Self-Regulatory and Approach Behaviors (APIB)[a]

1. Autonomic stability:
   a. Smooth respiration
   b. Pink, stable color
   c. Stable viscera
2. Motoric stability:
   a. Smooth, well-modulated posture
   b. Well-regulated tone
   c. Synchronous, smooth movements with efficient motoric strategies: hand clasping, foot clasping, finger folding, hand-to-mouth maneuvers, grasping, suck searching and sucking, hand-holding, and tucking
3. State stability and attentional regulation:
   a. Clear, robust sleep states
   b. Rhythmical robust crying
   c. Effective self-quieting
   d. Reliable consolability
   e. Robust, focused, shiny-eyed alertness with intent and/or animated facial expression: frowning, cheek softening, mouth pursing to ooh-face, cooing, attentional smiling

[a]Als, 1982b.

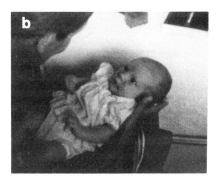

(b) Optimal alerting during social interaction (1-month postterm): well-integrated infant (animated and motorically modulated (from Als, 1983; reproduced with permission).

of preterm and full-term newborns in order to identify and modulate their integrative capacities and to know when systematic examination is inappropriate or even dangerous. The continuous identification of the thresholds of balance and stress is the key feature of this examination. Scoring and administration require extensive training,[1] and reliability needs to be achieved before the assessment can be safely used.

Research with the APIB

The validity of the APIB has been recently documented in the identification of stable, reproducible behavioral patterns in a group of 98 preterm and full-term newborns at 2 weeks after expected due date (Als, Duffy, & McAnulty, 1988a,b) and in the identification of orderly electrophysiological (BEAM) correlates to those behavioral patterns implicating differential vulnerability of the right hemisphere and the frontal lobe (Duffy, Als, & McAnulty, in press). Furthermore, predictive validity to 9 months (Als, Duffy, & McAnulty, in press) and to 5 years has been shown (Als, Duffy, McAnulty, & Badian, in press) in a subsample, identifying the low-threshold, easily disorganized newborn as at greater risk for later organizational difficulties than the well-modu-

[1]Training is available on an individual basis in Boston by writing to the author or in Tucson, Arizona, by writing to Dr. Elsa Sell, Associate Professor of Pediatrics, University Medical Center, Tucson, Arizona 85724.

lated stable newborn and again differentially implicating right hemi-spheric and frontal lobe functioning.

ENVIRONMENTAL AND SOCIAL INTERVENTION IN SUPPORT OF PRETERM INFANT DEVELOPMENT

If the synactive model of development improves our understanding of the immature infant, it should provide a testable formulation for the amelioration if not prevention of some of the neuro-organizational se-quelae associated with prematurity. We hypothesize that attention to the individual infant's behavioral cues with the goal of environmental and behavioral modification in order to bring about reduction in specific stress behaviors and increase in specific self-regulatory behaviors will improve the medical and developmental outcome of the infant. To test this hypothesis, we focused on the most vulnerable preterms in our NICU, the <1250-g respirator-dependent infant at high risk for bronchopulmonary dysplasia (Als, Lawhon, Brown, Gibes, Duffy, McAnulty, & Blickman, 1986). These are the infants with highest mor-tality and morbidity. The study was conducted in two phases: Phase I, the control phase, and Phase II, the experimental phase. Because the infants were initially too sick to be manipulated in a systematic way to administer the APIB, a behavioral observation method was devised based on the conceptualizations of the APIB. Each infant was observed on Days 10, 20, 30, and so forth throughout nursery stay. The behavioral observations conducted were based on the assumption that the behavior of infants is their primary route of communicating their thresholds to stress or their relative functional stability. An observation began with the recording of a minimum of 20 minutes of baseline observation before the infant under study received any medical or nursing caregiving ma-nipulations, continued throughout a caregiving manipulation (e.g., IV line placement, suctioning, spinal tap, vital sign taking, feeding, bathing, diaper changing, etc., or any combination of these) and was followed by an additional 20 minutes of postmanipulation observation in order to assess the infant's return to baseline or continued stress. An observation typically lasted from approximately 90 minutes up to 3 hours. The behavioral observation sheet used, based on the concep-tualization of the Assessment of Preterm Infants' Behavior, focuses on behaviors thought to indicate stress and behaviors thought to indicate self-regulatory efforts and maintenance (see Tables 1 and 2). Each obser-vation sheet is segmented into five 2-minute time-sampling columns, covering a total of 10 minutes. Digital readouts of the transcutaneous oxygen level ($TcPO_2$) and heart rate monitors were also sampled and recorded every 2 minutes. Ongoing respiratory rate was collected by counting chest wall expansions every 2 minutes for 30 seconds and multiplying the figure by 2. Behavioral categories were checked as to their presence in the course of any given 2-minute epoch. A manual of definitions of all behavioral categories is available (Als, 1981).

For the intervention group infants, the observation record formed the basis for a narrative description of the infant's behavior before, during, and after the respective caregiving procedure observed, with interpretation of behavioral signals as stress versus self-regulatory behaviors, as outlined in Tables 1 and 2. On the basis of this description, we developed strategies for the reduction of stress behaviors and the increase of self-regulatory behaviors, yielding specific inputs for an individualized developmental care plan. This care plan was executed by the nurse and the parent caregiver, with the hypothesis that their social regulation of the individual infant's behavioral organization would result in the enhancement of overall development.

Three major areas of caregiving were attended to: the physical distal and proximal environment of the infant, direct caregiving to the infant, and discharge planning.

Considerations regarding the *physical environment* included (1) location of the infant's crib or isolette (e.g., avoidance of proximity to X-ray screen, faucets and sinks; reduction in telephone and radio-noise level, lighting, traffic, and activity levels); (2) bedding and clothing (e.g., provision of water mattress, sheepskin, boundaries, "nesting," shielding of isolette or crib; clothing, hat, swaddling, bunting, hammock); (3) specific aids to self-regulation (e.g., opportunity to suck during and between feedings [gavage feedings]; opportunity to hold on during manipulations; finger rolls to grasp, foot rolls, hammock); (4) reduction of stress on the treatment table (e.g., by covering and shielding); and (5) consideration of optimal position of infant (e.g., prone, side lying; supports to maintain position ["nesting," back rolls, bunting, etc.]).

Considerations regarding *direct caregiving* to the infant included (1) timing and sequencing of manipulations (e.g., bathing and feeding in one or two separate sessions; reduction of unnecessary vital sign taking, weighing, chest physical therapy, suctioning; adjustment of timing of blood drawing, X rays, ultrasound, spinal taps; with supported positioning of infant for such procedures); (2) feeding (e.g., gavage inside the shielded isolette; supported by holding on and with opportunity to suck; bottle or breast feeding in quiet, shielded corner or parent room; feeding without simultaneously talking to or looking at infant; positioning with shoulder and trunkal support, foot bracing; provision of hand holding, use of bunting; timing of feeding with natural sleep cycle, without periods of exhaustive crying preceding feeding); (3) bathing (e.g., immersion, due to its soothing effect, instead of sponge bathing; increased temperature of water; contained position during bathing); (4) transition facilitation (e.g., preparation of the infant's state and calmness in situations definitionally painful and stressful but necessary, such as spinal tap, suctioning, etc., plus support to flexor positioning, with a facilitator present to give inhibition to hands and feet; efficient and quick execution of the necessary manipulation; opportunity for holding onto caregiver's finger and for sucking; encasement of trunk and back of head in caregiver's hand; inhibition provided to soles of feet; unhurried reorganization and stabilization of the infant's regulation with provision of prone placement; removal of all extraneous stimulation such as stroking, talking, position shifts, etc., in order to institute calm restabilization securely; gradual removal of one aid at a time to assure continued maintenance of stabilization); (5) sleep organization (e.g., attention to the sleep cycle of the infant, with prevention of interruption, especially of deep sleep; structuring of transitions into sleep and structuring of sleep maintenance by avoidance of peaks of frenzy and overexhaustion; continuous maintenance of a calm, regular environment and schedule; establishing a reliable, repeatable pattern of gradual transition into sleep in prone or side lying in the isolette or crib; use of the caregiver's body initially and gradual transfer to the crib; use of the isolette with provision of steady boundaries and encasing without any additional stimulation; use of soothing, gentle instrumental music); (6) organization of alertness (e.g., prevention of bright light, shielding of eyes and of isolette or crib; prevention of overstimulation by a cluttered visual environment in the isolette and when outside of the isolette; careful titration of social input modalities: looking, talking, touching; low animated facial expression with quiet looking without movement while providing firm containment to limbs and trunk for optimal maintenance of alertness; prevention of talking while looking; prevention of patting, stroking, rocking, etc.; provision of quiet containment; tactile vestibular inputs while removing visual and auditory inputs; prone position with provision of steady, firm extremity and mouth containment; careful titration of social inputs during and after other activities such as feeding, to avoid hiccoughing, gagging, spitting, aspiration, etc.); and (7) social contact (e.g., involvement of parent and other family members; provision of continuous containment by soothing, quiet inhibition by the parent's steady hands and/or body for the hands, feet, and mouth of the baby; avoidance of unnecessary touching, stroking, taking out of the isolette, holding and talking to the infant to avoid frenzy, apnea, and/or other withdrawal behaviors; individualized careful timing of inputs in support of increasing self-regulatory stability and differentiation of the infant).

Considerations regarding *discharge planning* to the infant included taking into account the behavioral stability and reactivity of the infant, sleep and wake cycle organization and internal regulatory capacities; avoidance of discharge during persistence of volatile, poorly regulated, hypersensitive, and overreactive behavior patterns; and implementation of discharge after establishment of self-regulatory ability. It was considered to role of the primary caregiver to support behavioral stability by developing a carefully structured, systematic care plan for the experimental infants that would be adhered to by all caregivers. Results of the study showed that the experimental infants showed significantly briefer stays on the respirator (18 days vs. 43 days; $p<.01$) and in increased levels of oxygen (32 days vs. 66 days; $p<.05$). Their feeding behavior was normalized significantly earlier (50 days vs. 79 days; $p<.01$).

Developmental outcome after discharge from the NICU was assessed at 1, 3, 6, and 9 months post-EDC.[2] All observations were performed at the Neurobehavioral Observation Laboratory at The Children's Hospital. Assessments included, at 1 month, the APIB (Als *et al.*, 1982) described earlier; and at 3, 6, and 9 months, assessments with the Bayley Scales of Infant Development (Bayley, 1969). In addition, at 9 months post-EDC, the infants were observed and videotaped in a 15-minute play observation with one of their parents (Kangaroo Box Paradigm) (Als, 1983, 1985b; Als & Brazelton, 1981).

The kangaroo box paradigm was developed from the theoretical basis of the APIB (Als *et al.*, 1982) to provide better documentation and quantification of dimensions of functioning, such as the differentiation and modulation of various subsystems of performance. These include autonomic modulation, gross and fine motor modulation, affective expressive and social interactive modulation as well as self-regulatory capacity, among others. The paradigm consists of a clear plexiglas box in which there sits a windup kangaroo that can be obtained via various access routes: a porthole with a swinging latch door, the top lid, or the two open sides of the box. The box is placed in the center of an otherwise completely empty yet carpeted play-observation room. Mother and child are instructed to play with the toy and box in whichever way they would like, so that both of them have a good time. Six minutes of play ("Play Episode") are videotaped by a two-camera remote control color

---

[2]Estimated date of confinement.

recording system. After 6 minutes, the mother is instructed to now sit at the edge of the room, facing the child, but no longer smiling, talking, or in any other way reacting to the child. The child is observed in the 6-minute "Still-Face Episode" in efforts to attempt to obtain the windup toy on his or her own and/or solicit the nonreactive parent's reaction and help. Three minutes of reunion in play of parent and child are then videotaped. The videotapes are analyzed using a behaviorally specified manual (Als & Berger, 1979), yielding 20 scores for the infant's performance in the play episode, 19 scores for his or her performance in the still-face episode, 12 scores for the parent's performance in play, 1 still-face and 1 reunion score, and 3 interactive measures, Degree of Turntaking Ability, Synchrony of Interaction, and Overall Quality of Interaction. All scales range from 1 (poorly organized performance) to 5 (well-organized performance).

All assessments were performed by trained examiners not familiar with the goals of the study nor the group membership of the infants nor their performance at previous assessment points. This was easily accomplished, because, in the course of the 2 years of subject intake and the 2 years thereafter, over 120 preterm and full-term infants from other projects were examined at the same data points, allowing for complete blindness of the examiners to a given infant's group and study status.

Developmental outcome after discharge from the NICU showed significantly better behavioral regulation scores at 1 month post-EDC, as measured with the APIB, significantly better Mental and Psychomotor Developmental Indices at 3, 6, and 9 months post-EDC, as measured with the Bayley Scales of Infant Development, and significantly better behavioral regulation scores at 9 months post-EDC, as measured in the videotaped play observation.

APIB: One Month Post-EDC

As Figure 5a shows, of the six APIB System Scores, four are significant at greater than the .1 level; of these, one at better than the .05 level and one at better than the .02 level, all favoring the experimental infants. The parameters involved describe the experimental infants as more well-modulated with higher thresholds to disorganization in terms of motor system (MOTOR, $p<.05$),[3] state maintenance (STATE, $p<.1$), attentional competence (ATTENT, $p<.1$), and self-regulation ability (SREGU, $p<.02$). Figure 5b supports the results shown in 5a. Of the 18 summary

[3]Acronyms for summary variables of the APIB are briefly defined in the test. For a more complete description, see Als (1981).

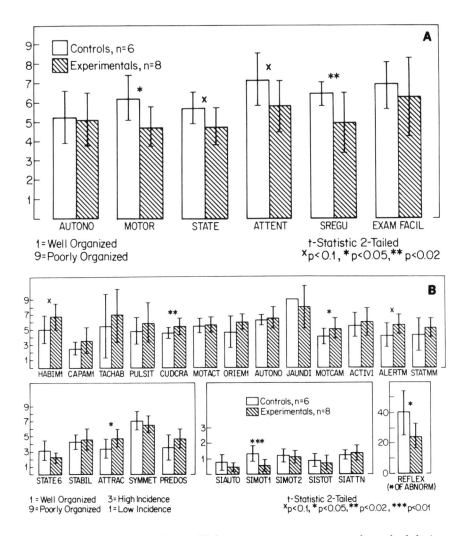

FIGURE 5. (A) APIB at 1-month post-EDC—systems scores, means, and standard deviations. (B) APIB at 1-month post-EDC—summary scores, means, and standard deviations.

variables presented, again 4, more than expected by chance, show significant differences between control and intervention group, favoring the intervention group. These include the ability to cuddle and to inhibit crawling motion when placed in supine (CUDCRA, $p<.02$), a motor capacity measure including the assessment of tone, motor maturity, and balance of postures (MOTCAM, $p<.05$), a measure of alertness (ALERTM, $p<.1$), and of overall behavioral organization and interactive

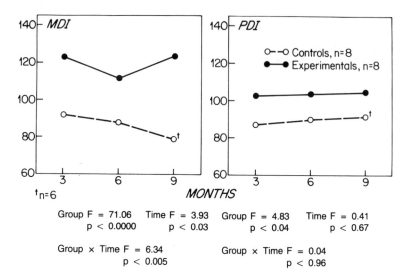

FIGURE 6. Bayley Scale Scores at 3, 6, and 9 months post-EDC—Mental Developmental Index (MDI) and Psychomotor Developmental Index (PDI).

attractiveness (ATTRAC, $p<.05$). Of the five body signal parameters measured, the intervention group shows a significantly lower incidence of motoric extension behaviors such as grimacing, arching, and so forth, considered indicators of stress (SIMOTO, $p<.02$). They also show a higher number of normal reflexes (REFLEX, $p<.05$). Thus, at 1-month post-expected due date, the intervention infants appear to be significantly more well organized along several dimensions of functioning than the control infants.

Bayley Scales of Infant Development: Three, Six, and Nine Months Post-EDC

Figure 6 shows the results of a repeated measures analysis of variance of the Mental Developmental Index (MDI) and the Psychomotor Developmental Index (PDI) of the Bayley Scales.[4] The MDI shows a highly significant group difference at all three age points favoring the experimental infants ($p<.00001$). The experimental infants show mean

[4]One control infant was discharged from the NICU after 45 weeks. This infant was, therefore, not included in the 1-month post-EDC assessment described. One control infant died at 7 months post-EDC of SIDS by autopsy report and was lost to the 9-month study. Another control infant moved out of town at 8 months and was not studied at the 9-month data point.

scores between 110 and 124, the control infants between 91 and 78; the difference between the two groups ranged from 1½ to 2 standard deviations. Moreover, there is a significant time effect, with the control infants declining significantly over time ($p<.03$); and there is a significant group by time interaction effect with the experimental infants, showing a relative dip in performance at 6 months and improvement at 9 months, whereas the control infants steadily decline from 3 to 6 to 9 months to below 1 standard deviation below the mean ($p<.005$). The Psychomotor Developmental Index (PDI) shows a significant group effect, again favoring the experimental infants at all three age points ($p<.04$), yet the difference between the two groups is not as pronounced (slightly less than 1 standard deviation). There is no significant time nor group by time interaction effect as regards the PDI. Thus the intervention infants perform better at 3, 6, and 9 months post-EDC in terms of mental performance and motor performance.

Kangaroo Box Paradigm: Nine Months Post-EDC

Figure 7a shows the *t*-test results for the 20 parameters measured by videotape analysis involving the 6-minute play episode of parent and child focused on the kangaroo box. Six parameters show group differences favoring the intervention infants and ranging in significance level from .1 to .001. They involve fine motor fluidity and modulation (FMOTOP, $p<.05$),[5] degree of differentiation, range and appropriateness of affective functioning (AFFECP, $p<.001$), highest affective phase achieved in the course of the interaction (HIPOTP, $p<.05$), social interactive competence (SOCIAP, $p<.1$), modulation and speed of movement (TEMPOP, $p<.02$), and overall summary rating of performance (SUMMAP, $p<.05$). In the Still-Face Episode (see Figure 7b), in which the parent is instructed to no longer help and/or interact with the child in any way; 9 parameters out of 19 show significant differences, ranging in significance level from $<.05$ to $<.01$, and again favoring the experimental infants over the control infants. The parameters involve again fine motor modulation (FMOTOS, $p<.01$), apparent understanding of the task without the mother's help (COGNIS, $p<.02$), highest affective level achieved in the Still-Face Episode (HIPOS, $p<.05$), ability to elicit the parent by socially positive measures in order to resume play with the child (SOCIAS, $p<.01$), ability to combine object play with social elicitation (OBSOCS, $p<.01$), ability to stay engaged in the task and break it down into manageable components (ATTENS, $p<.01$),

---

[5]Acronyms for selected subtests of the Kangaroo Box Paradigm are briefly defined in the text. For a more complete description of this measure, see Als and Berger, 1979.

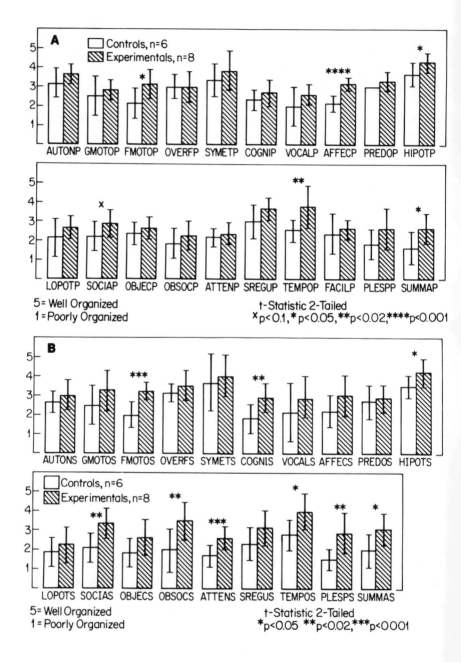

modulation of speed of movement (TEMPOS, $p<.05$), the ability to show pleasure and pride in an accomplishment (PLESPS, $p<.01$), and the overall Summary Competence Rating (SUMMAS, $p<.05$). It is of interest that the control infants show poorer performance than the experimental infants on many more parameters when studied under increased stress, that is, the Still-Face Episode, when their parent no longer can be of assistance, than when they are helped by the parent. The results reinforce the importance of social context in facilitation of skill development and self-regulation of preterms.

Figure 7c shows the 12 parent parameters in play, the parent's ability to maintain the still face (PSTILF), and the parent's ability to reengage the infant during the reunion episode (REPLAY). Only 1 parent parameter shows a significant group difference, namely Degree of Parent's Facilitation of Play (DPFACL, $p<.05$), indicating that control and experimental infants' parents are overall equally adept and invested in making the play successful and enjoyable to the infant, yet the intervention parents may be more sensitive to the specific needs of their

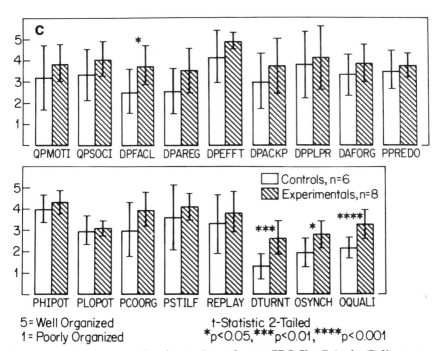

FIGURE 7. (A) Kangaroo Box Paradigm at 9 months post-EDC: Play Episode. (B) Kangaroo Box Paradigm at 9 months post-EDC: Still-Face Episode. (C) Kangaroo Box Paradigm at 9 months post-EDC: Parent and Interaction Parameters.

babies, although this may be a chance finding. The last three parameters graphed involve interaction parameters, and all three show significant group differences. The parameters measured are Degree of Turn-Taking Ability (DTURNT, $p<.01$), Degree of Overall Synchrony of the Interaction (OSYNCH, $p<.05$), and Overall Quality of the Interaction (OQUALI, $p<.001$). Again, the experimental parent–infant pairs show the better scores in free play at 9 months. The experimental infants appear, again, significantly more well organized, well differentiated, and well modulated than the intervention infants. These results support the hypothesis that the synactive formulation of development provides a specific framework for the design of appropriate social and sensory contexts for the high-risk preterm infant in the NICU, from which the infant profits significantly not only medically but also developmentally.

Spinoffs of the study have since affected overall caregiving in the NICU, especially the care of the long-term hospitalized, chronically ill newborns with severe lung disease who typically suffer from extreme hypersensitivity to stimulation often accompanied by increasingly distorted motor system development with shoulder retraction, head and trunkal arching and extension, poor trunkal tone, and increased leg extensor tone (Als, 1986). Position of flexor tone and calm relaxation together with structuring of a developmentally supportive environment in order to maximally facilitate normal socioemotional, cognitive, and motor development in the face of chronic severe illness and prolonged hospitalization is the goal. Humanization of the hospital environment with the integration of the infant's care by his or her own parents, affording space, privacy, and the ongoing opportunity for increasing developmental differentiation is aimed for. The context provided by caregivers in general and the parents, in particular, reinforces and supports the preterm infant in his or her ongoing confrontation of an otherwise stressful environment.

A training course in the observation of the behavioral signals of the infant and in the individualized caregiving based on these behaviors is available.[6]

SUMMARY

The preterm infant is a product of our advances in neonatal medical technology. Now that survival even of very early born and very small infants is increasingly assured, our attention can shift to the quality of

[6]For information regarding the individually scheduled training course, write to H. Als, Enders Research Building, Room M-29, The Children's Hospital, Boston, Massachusetts 02115.

this survival. The brain of the immature fetal infant is the critical organ that orchestrates and influences all aspects of development. The protection and support of the immature yet rapidly differentiating brain in our NICU environments has to become a foremost priority for all those giving care to the infant. The synactive model of development outlines access avenues for the observation of that brain's function via the behavior displayed by the infant. Autonomic, motoric, state organizational, attentional, and self-regulatory capacities of the infant can be observed productively in order to identify succinctly and specifically where an individual infant's thresholds to stress and ability for self-maintenance and increasing self-regulation and self-differentiation lie. Stress is always a necessary concomitant of all development. In order to take the next step to differentiation, previously integrated and synchronized connections have to be opened up which necessitates the disorganization and dyssynchronization of subsystems in their interplay. When the newly in-reach agendum becomes gradually mastered, that is, stress diminishes, then the subsystems realign and support each other again, now at a higher level of more differentiated functioning. If stress is too massive, more differentiated new alignment of subsystems is not possible; then a maladaptive, costly realignment occurs at a more rigid, canalized level of functioning, forcing the infant over time to practice and fall back onto maladaptive strategies and precluding flexible differentiation. The synactive framework of development provides an approach for the caregiver to identify on an individual basis for each child the opportunities currently available with the infant in the quest to support optimal differentiation and modulation without overtaxing and overstressing the child. Respect for the child's behavioral communications as meaningful will engender in the caregiver confidence in the child and her or his own ability to jointly negotiate the next step in the developmental process.

The social context that evolved over thousands of generations of human phylogenesis in surprisingly fine-tuned specificity provides the good-enough environment for the normal full-term nervous system to unfold initially intrauterinely, then extrauterinely, adequate to assure the continuation of human evolution. With the advances in medical technology, that is, material culture, even the very immature nervous system can exist and survive outside the womb. However, the social context of the traditional special care nursery brings with it less than adequate support for that immature nervous system, leading to maladaptations, disability, and even at times death. Is the human mind and emotional makeup good enough to pair instrumentation and technology with appropriately tailored social context in order to support adequately the threatened immature nervous system? In the NICU, detailed observation of the behavior of the fetus displaced from the womb as it reacts to the onslaught of sensory experiences is necessary. Such observation provides the opportunity to estimate and infer how appropriate social context can be provided sufficiently to support that highly sensitive and highly vulnerable being's developmental progression. We are evolved as adults to be attuned biologically to the full term, just as the full term is evolved to be attuned to us, a mutual developmental fueling system established and tuned over time. We have to become differently conscious of our reaction to and interaction with the displaced fetus we are confronting *ex utero*. In this challenge lies our opportunity.

ACKNOWLEDGMENTS. The work reported here was supported by grant 1 RO1 HD 1 5482 from NICHD, grant GO 08435063 from NIDRR, and a grant from the Merck Family Fund. Special thanks go to my research assistants, Sharon Gillis and Sarah Phillips, and to my secretary, Christine Murray, for their unflagging support, and to David McAnulty for his sensitive yet decisive editing. Further deep-felt thanks go to the nurses and medical staff in our NICU, the parents of our study infants for their generous openness in permitting us to observe their babies and themselves in interaction with their babies, and last but not least, to our study babies, who are helping us become more astute in understanding their amazing complexity and competence.

REFERENCES

Als, H. (1975). The human newborn and his mother: An ethological study of their interactions (Doctoral dissertation, University of Pennsylvania, 1975). *Dissertation Abstracts International, 36,* No. 5.

Als, H. (1976). *Autonomous state control: The first stage in successful negotiation of parent-infant Interaction.* Paper presented at the Meetings of the American Academy of Child Psychiatry, Toronto.

Als, H. (1977). The newborn communicates. *Journal of Communication, 27,* 66–73.

Als, H. (1978). Assessing an assessment: Conceptual considerations, methodological issues, and a perspective on the future of the Neonatal Behavioral Assessment Scale. In A. J. Sameroff (Ed.), Organization and stability of newborn behavior: A commentary on the Brazelton Neonatal Behavioral Assessment Scale. *Monographs of the Society for Research in Child Development, 43,* 14–28.

Als, H. (1979). Social interaction: Dynamic matrix for developing behavioral organization. In I. C. Uzgiris (Ed.), *Social interaction and communication in infancy: New Directions for child development* pp. 21–41. San Francisco: Jossey-Bass.

Als, H. (1981). *Manual for the naturalistic observation of newborn behavior (preterm and fullterm).* Revised edition (1984). The Children's Hospital, Boston.

Als, H. (1981). *APIB features: Summary variables* (Rev. ed., 1984). Manuscript available from the author.

Als, H. (1982a). The unfolding of behavioral organization in the face of a biological violation. In E. Tronick (Ed.), *Human communication and the joint regulation of behavior* (pp. 125–160). Baltimore: University Park Press.

Als, H. (1982b). Towards a synactive theory of development: Promise for the assessment of infant individualtiy. *Infant Mental Health Journal, 3,* 229–243.

Als, H. (1983). Infant individuality: Assessing patterns of very early development. In J. Call & R. L. Tyson (Eds.), *Frontiers of infant psychiatry* (pp. 363–378). New York: Basic Books.

Als, H. (1985b). Patterns of infant behavior: Analogs of later organizational difficulties? In F. H. Duffy & N. Geschwind (Eds.), *Dyslexia: Current status and future directions* (pp. 67–92). Boston: Little, Brown & Co.

Als, H. (1986). A synactive model of neonatal behavioral organization: Framework for the assessment and support of the neurobehavioral development of the premature infant and his parents in the environment of the neonatal intensive care unit. *Physical & Occupational Therapy in Pediatrics, 6,* 3–55.

Als, H., & Berger, A. (1979). *Manual, Kangaroo Box Paradigm. Infant & Toddler version.* Manuscript available from the first author, at Neurobehavioral Infant & Child Studies, Enders Pediatric Research Laboratories, The Children's Hospital, Boston, MA 02115.

Als, H., & Brazelton, T. B. (1981). A new model for assessing the behavioral organization in preterm and fulterm infants: Two case studies. *Journal of the American Academy of Child Psychiatry, 20,* 239–263.

Als, H., & Duffy, F. H. (1982). Behavior of the fetal newborn: Theoretical considerations and practical suggestions for the use of the A.P.I.B. In *Issues in neonatal care.* Western States Technical Assistance Resource (WESTAR) (pp. 21–60). TADS, 500 NCNB Plaza, Chapel Hill, NC 27514.

Als, H., & Duffy, F. H. (1983). The behavior of the premature infant: A theoretical framework for a systematic assessment. In T. B. Brazelton & B. M. Lester (Eds.), *New approaches to developmental screening of infants* (pp. 153–174). New York: Elsevier North-Holland.

Als, H., Duffy, F. H., & McAnulty, G. B. (1988a). Behavioral differences between preterm and full-term newborns as measured with the APIB system scores: I. *Infant Behavior Development, 11,* 305–318.

Als, H., Duffy, F. H., & McAnulty, G. B. (1988b). The APIB, an assessment of functional competence in preterm and fullterm newborns regardless of gestational age at birth: II. *Infant Behavior Development, 11,* 319–331.

Als, H., Duffy, F. H., & McAnulty, G. B. (in press). Neurobehavioral competence in healthy preterm and fullterm infants: Newborn period to 9 months. *Developmental Psychology.*

Als, H., Duffy, F. H., McAnulty, G. B., & Badian, N. (in press). Assessment of neurobehavioral functioning in preterm and fullterm newborns and the question of predictability of later development. In N. Krasnegor & M. Bornstein (Eds.), *Continuity in Development.* Hillsdale, NJ: Lawrence Erlbaum.

Als, H., Lawhon, G., Brown, E., Gibes, R., Duffy, F. H., McAnulty, G., & Blickman, J. G. (1986). Individualized behavioral and environmental care for the VLBW infant at high risk for bronchopulmonary dysplasia: NICU and developmental outcome. *Pediatrics, 78,* 1123–1132.

Als, H., Lester, B. M., Tronick, E., & Brazelton, T. B. (1982). Towards a research instrument for the assessment of preterm infants' behavior (APIB), and Manual for the assessment of preterm infants' behavior (APIB). In H. E. Fitzgerald, B. M. Lester, & M. W. Yogman (Eds.), *Theory and research in behavioral pediatrics* (Vol. 1, pp. 35–63, 65–132). New York: Plenum Press.

Als, H., Tronick, E., Adamson, L., & Brazelton, T. B. (1976). The behavior of the full-term yet underweight newborn infant. *Developmental Medicine and Child Neurology, 18,* 590–602.

Bayley, N. (1969). *Manual for the Bayley Scales of Infant Development.* New York: The Psychological Corporation

Birnholz, J. C., Stephens, J. C., & Faria, H. (1978). Fetal movement patterns: A possible means of defining neurologic developmental milestones in utero. *American Journal of Roentgenology, 130,* 536–540.

Bolwig, N. (1959a). Observations and thoughts on the evolution of facial mimic. *Koedoe, 2,* 60–69.

Bolwig, N. (1959b). A study of the behavior of the chacma baboon, Papio Ursinis. *Behavior, 14,* 136–163.

Bottos, M. (1985). Strategy of neuromotor development in the premature. *Clinica Pediatrica,* University of Padua, Italy, unpublished manuscript.

Brazelton, T. B. (1973). *Neonatal Behavioral Assessment Scale.* Clinics in Developmental Medicine, No. 50. Philadelphia: J. B. Lippincott.

Buettner-Janusch, J. (1966). *Origins of man.* New York: John Wiley.

Casaer, P. (1979). *Postural behavior in newborn infants.* Clinics in Developmental Medicine, No. 72. Philadelphia: J. B. Lippincott.

Denckla, M. B. (1978). Minimal brain dysfunction. In J. Chall & A. Mirsky (Eds.), *Education and the brain.* 77th Yearbook of the National Society for the Study of Education (pp. 223–268). Chicago: University of Chicago Press.

Denny-Brown, D. (1972). *The basal ganglia and their relation to disorders of movement.* Oxford: Oxford University Press.

Denny-Brown, D. (1972). *The cerebral control of movement.* Springfield, IL: Charles C Thomas.

Desmond, M. M., Rudolph, A. J., & Phitaksphraiwan, P. (1966). The transitional care nursery. A mechanism for preventive medicine in the newborn. *Pediatric Clinics of North America, 13,* 651–668.

Duffy, F. H., & Als, H. (1983). Neurophysiological assessment of the neonate: An approach combining brain electrical activity mapping (BEAM) with behavioral assessment (APIB). In T. B. Brazelton & B. M. Lester (Eds.), *New approaches to developmental screening of infants* (pp. 175–196). New York: Elsevier North-Holland, Inc.

Duffy, F. H., Als, H., & McAnulty, G. B. (in press). Behavioral and electrophysiological evidence for gestational age effects in healthy preterm and fullterm infants studied two weeks after expected due date. *Child Development.*

Duffy, F. H., Burchfiel, J. L., & Snodgrass, S. R. (1978). The pharmacology of amblyopia. *Archives of Ophthalmology, 85,* 489–495.

Duffy, F. H., Mower, G. D., Jensen, F., & Als, H. (1984). Neural plasticity: A new frontier for infant development. In H. E. Fitzgerald, B. M. Lester, & M. W. Yogman (Eds.), *Theory and research in behavioral pediatrics* (Vol. II, pp. 67–96). New York: Plenum Press.

Goldman, P. S. (1976). The role of experience in recovery of function following orbital prefrontal lesions in infant monkeys. *Neuropsychologia, 14,* 401–412.

Goldman-Rakic, P. S. (1981). Development and plasticity of primate frontal association cortex. In F. O. Schmitt & E. G. Worden (Eds.), *Organization of the cerebral cortex* (pp. 69–97). Cambridge, MA: MIT Press.

Grossman, K. (1978). Die Wirkung des Augenoffnens von Neugeborenen auf das Verhalten ihrer Mutter. *Geburtsh. u. Frauenheilk. 38,* 629–635.

Hertzig, M. E. (1981). Neurological "Soft" signs in low birthweight children. *Developmental Medicine and Child Neurology, 23,* 778–791.

Herzog, J. M. (1979). *Attachment, attunement, and abuse, and occurrence in certain premature infant-parent dyads and triads*. Paper presented at the American Academy of Child Psychiatry Meeting, Atlanta.

Huber, E. (1931). *Evolution of facial musculature and facial expression.* Baltimore: Johns Hopkins Press.

Hunt, J. McV. (1961). *Intelligence and experience.* New York: Ronald Press.

Hunt, J. V., Tooley, W. H., & Harvin, D. (1982). Learning disabilities in children with birthweights <1500 g. *Seminars in Perinatology, 6,* 280–287.

Lewis, M. E., Mishkin, M., Bragin, E., Brown, R. M., Pert, C. B., & Pert, A. (1981). Opiate receptor gradients in monkey cerebral cortex: Correspondence with sensory processing hierarchies. *Science, 211,* 1166–1169.

Milani-Comparetti, A. (1980). *Fetal movement.* First E. Zausmer Lecture, The Children's Hospital Medical Center, Boston.

Mower, G. D., Burchfiel, J. L., & Duffy, F. H. (1982). Animal models of strabismic amblyopia: Physiological studies of visual cortex and the lateral geniculate nucleus. *Develomental Brain Research, 5,* 311–327.

Piaget, J. (1963). *The origins of intelligence in children.* New York: W. W. Norton Company

Piaget, J. (1971). *Biology and knowledge: An essay on the relations between organic regulation and cognitive processes.* Chicago: University of Chicago Press.

Sander, L. W. (1962). Issues in early mother-child interaction. *Journal of the American Academy of Child Psychiatry, 1,* 141–166.

Sander, L. W. (1964). Adaptive relationships in early mother-child interaction. *Journal of the American Academy of Child Psychiatry, 3,* 232–264.

Schneirla, T. C. (1959). An evolutionary and developmental theory of biphasic processes underlying approach and withdrawal. In M. R. Jones (Ed.), *Nebraska symposium on motivation* (pp. 1–42). Lincoln: University of Nebraska Press.

Schneirla, T. C. (1965). Aspects of stimulation and organization in approach and withdrawal processes underlying vertebrate development. *Advances in Study Behavior, 1,* 1–74.

Siegel, L. S. (1982). Reproductive, perinatal and environmental variables as predictors of development of preterms (<1501 g) and fullterm children at 5 years. *Seminars in Perinatology, 6,* 274–279.

Spinelli, D. N., Jensen, F. E., & DePrisco, G. V. (1980). Early experience effect on dentritic branchings in normally reared kittens. *Experimental Neurology, 68*(1), 1–11.

Thurber, S. D. & Armstrong, L. B. (1982). *Developmental support of low birthweight infants: Nurses' guide.* Texas Children's Hospital, Houston, TX.

Vygotsky, L. S. (1978). *Mind in Society.* M. Cole, V. John-Steiner, S. Sorilner & E. Sauberman (Trans.). Cambridge, MA: Harvard University Press.

PART II

Establishing Action–Environment Correspondences
Contextual Influences on Infant Imitation and Manipulation

In the course of their daily activities, infants often attempt to establish correspondences between themselves and their environments. They relate their actions to what the environment has offered in the past, what it offers in the present, and what it may offer in the future. This ability is evident, for example, during imitation when infants relate their actions to past or present environmental events. It is also evident during object exploration when infants relate their actions to the present or anticipated positions of objects. The attempts of infants to bring their actions and the environment into correspondence appear basic and cut across psychological domains and behavioral settings.

In the present part, the development of this general ability is considered through examination of two seemingly diverse infant skills. Užgiris, Benson, Kruper, and Vasek examine the development of imitative interaction or matching ability, whereas Lockman and McHale examine the development of object manipulation. In previous work, these two skills have been treated as somewhat distinct, although both skills have been analyzed within a cognitive-structural framework. In the present part, however, the authors seek to understand the development of each of these skills by considering the contexts in which they function and hence the functions that these skills serve.

In the chapter that follows, Užgiris, Benson, Kruper, and Vasek consider the development of imitative interaction by examining its functioning in different contexts. Užgiris and her colleagues note that in previous work, imitation has been principally viewed as an unidirectional process, one in which a model influences an observer. In contrast, these authors argue that imitation is best conceptualized as an interpersonal process, one in which the roles of model and observer may shift. They prefer the terms *imitative interaction* or *matching* because these terms capture the bidirectional nature of this activity. Moreover, they point out that viewing imitative interaction as an interpersonal process directs us to consider the perspectives of both partners involved in the interaction. In many ways, then, this conception shares much with the general systems view that Thelen, Fogel, and Als presented in the previous part. In both formulations, there is an emphasis on the overall context in which the activity or activities of interest function.

By focusing on the interpersonal nature and relatedly the contexts in which matching occurs, Užgiris, Benson, Kruper, and Vasek illuminate some of the important social, cognitive, and communicative functions of this activity. According to these authors, matching may be used to establish and express a shared experience, to promote learning, or to maintain and to continue an interaction. Their research shows that these functions are present in different degrees depending on the context of the exchange (e.g., face-to-face interaction or toy play) and the developmental level of the infant. For example, these investigators found that mothers were more likely to match their infants' activities during face-to-face interaction than during toy play, indicating that mothers used the former situation more as a format for establishing mutuality and the latter situation more as a format for teaching.

Additionally, Užgiris, Benson, Kruper, and Vasek propose that an important function of matching activity may be structural. By only matching certain actions, more experienced partners like mothers may help infants to segment the continuous flow of activity around them into discrete units of action. Once infants have apprehended these discrete units, they may be able to combine them to form more complex action sequences. More generally, this proposal suggests that by studying action in context, investigators may be better able to understand how changes come about in the structure of action.

This theme is echoed in Lockman and McHale's chapter on the development of object manipulation. These authors argue that a complete understanding of object manipulation requires that it be studied in the contexts in which it functions and develops. In their chapter, they review past theory and research on the development of object manipulation and note that the role of context has largely been ignored. In fact, in previous work, object manipulation has often been treated as a skill that develops apart from the contexts in which it functions. In this respect, there is a parallel in the past treatment accorded object manipulation and the general field of motor development—as was discussed in the previous part. In both cases, development has been divorced from context.

To describe the influence of context on object manipulation, Lockman and McHale report a study on how infants manipulate objects individually and jointly with their mothers. Their results indicate that infants show more appropriate manual behaviors when manipulating objects with their mothers than when doing so alone. Additionally, in the context of this joint activity, mothers demonstrate highly appropriate manual behaviors and actively engage their infants in these behaviors. Lockman and McHale suggest that mothers and other experienced partners may contribute to the development of infant object manipulation by demonstrating appropriate actions and by providing opportunities to practice these actions.

These results and conclusions are similar to those of Užgiris and her colleagues. Taken together, the findings from both sets of investigators suggest that the development of object manipulation and imitative interaction are more interrelated than the available literature implies. In fact, these authors end up examining the development of some of the same actions. They both consider infants' manual behaviors and suggest that mothers use the context of joint exploration to teach infants about the properties and conventional uses of objects.

Additionally, Užgiris and her coauthors point out that such teaching situations can also foster a sense of mutuality between mothers and infants. For instance, when infants match the manual movements of their mothers, infants externalize a type of shared understanding about objects and the actions that can be performed on them. It seems then that at least two general correspondences are established in the context of joint object exploration: one between the individual and the object and the other between the participants involved in the exchange. The establishment of these two general correspondences may fuel object exploration even further, both immediately and developmentally.

More generally, the idea that object manipulation develops within social contexts can be viewed in light of the systems perspective put forth by Thelen, Fogel, and Als in the previous part. From this perspective, mothers or other experienced partners can be seen as an element in the overall system from which infant manipulation emerges. In this system, mothers may play a rate-enhancing role by enabling infants to perform actions that they would not yet be able to produce on their own.

To conclude, the functioning and development of imitative interaction and object manipulation are linked through the context of interpersonal activity. Matching and manipulation are connected formally and functionally. Formally, both activities involve the establishment of corre-

spondences. Functionally, both activities occur simultaneously and appear to influence the operation and development of each activity individually. The following chapters thus show how studying action in context can lead to insights about the relationships between activities that have been considered separately in the developmental literature.

CHAPTER 4

Contextual Influences on Imitative Interactions between Mothers and Infants

Ina Č. Užgiris, Janette B. Benson, Jan C. Kruper, and Marie E. Vasek

INTRODUCTION

It is a challenge for developmental psychology to understand how an individual's experience is interlaced in the construction of competence, for experience is at once constrained by existing competence and a means for enhancing competence. As competence is utilized in different contexts, some features of experience are retained and influence future deployment of competence. Moreover, it is through experience that the lines of cultural and personal distinctiveness are introduced into the universal patterns of human development. Our purpose here is not to discuss the different ways that the role of experience may be understood nor the biological and social contexts within which experience takes shape, but to examine the structure of one kind of experience common during the first year of life—imitative interaction.

Experience is linked to actions in the world, which depend on avail-

Ina Č. Užgiris • Department of Psychology, Clark University, Worcester, Massachusetts 01610. Janette B. Benson • Department of Psychology, University of Denver, Denver, Colorado 80208. Jan C. Kruper and Marie E. Vasek • Department of Psychology, Clark University, Worcester, Massachusetts 01610.

able opportunities as well as on the individual's construal of those opportunities. For infants, the world is significantly shaped by their caregivers. The caregivers provide infants opportunities for action by
arranging their environments with respect to both objects and events as
well as by interpreting those objects and events in accord with their own
culturally accented understanding (Kruper & Užgiris, 1987; Newson,
1974). This interpretation of the world is initially conveyed to infants
through interaction with them. Therefore, the study of interactions between infants and their parents assumes a central place in studies of
human development.

Interpersonal Experience

Theorists concerned with development have analyzed experience
linked to different types of activities. Piaget (1970) included experience,
together with maturation, social transmission, and equilibration, among
the factors that account for development. He distinguished experience
that results in knowledge of the characteristics of the world from experience that allows knowledge of one's own actions, that is, of the relations
created by acting in the world. Although Piaget was primarily concerned
with the child's actions on physical reality, the distinction that he made
with respect to experience might be worth keeping in mind when considering the child's interactions with people as well. In time, children
come to appreciate not only the characteristics of different people but
also the different forms that their relations with others take during purely interpersonal exchanges and when acting jointly on objects in the
world.

Furthermore, in discussing the development of reflection as "the
grasp of consciousness," Piaget (1976) noted that children seem to focus
on the effects of action before starting to analyze the structure of action
in relation to its effects. For example, in the game of tiddlywinks, Piaget
found that young children relate the action of pressing one counter with
another to the first counter's jump into a box, but they fail to relate the
trajectory taken by the counter to its final destination. With age, however, they come to appreciate that such factors as the positioning of the
second counter and the nature of the surface affect the first counter's
trajectory and thereby determine where it comes to rest. If a similar
progression may be extrapolated to children's understanding of interactions with people, it suggests that children first note the responses of
others to their actions and only gradually come to understand the different patterns of exchange that constitute interpersonal interactions. This

implies that a child's level of competence for coordinating, analyzing, and deriving knowledge from actions will circumscribe the experience that can be gained from social interaction.

Vygotsky (1978) also considered the role of experience in development. He placed particular emphasis on sociocultural experience derived from introduction to various cultural products and to language. He pointed out that cultural artifacts have forms of activities linked to them and that the appropriate use of those artifacts involves a grasp of the activities that led to their production. Experience with cultural objects may be said to result in knowledge of the construals of physical and social reality prominent in a specific culture. He attributed particular significance to children's joint activities with others, who already are more competent in the language and ways of the culture. "The path from object to child and from child to object passes through another person. This complex human structure is the product of a developmental process deeply rooted in the links between individual and social history" (Vygotsky, 1978, p. 30).

Vygotsky's point regarding the role of cultural artifacts is important because of the prevalence of human-made objects in our children's worlds. From houses and furnishings to utensils and toys, the objects that children constantly encounter have been designed in accord with the cultural conception of human needs and interests. Even the town and country landscapes have been fashioned to suit human activity. Therefore, to the extent that the object world encountered by a child carries a sociocultural imprint, the child's experience when interacting with it can be considered social as well.

More importantly, Vygotsky suggested that with the guidance of a more competent person, children can engage in actions that go beyond those of which they are capable when acting alone and can gain from that experience. The range of competence that can be realized only in the context of supportive joint activity has come to be known as the "zone of proximal development." This notion not only emphasizes the importance of social experience but also expands the unit of analysis to include both partners in a social interaction.

The importance of joint activity for the development of human competence has been highlighted in Bruner's work as well. His concept of "scaffolding" (Bruner, 1978) refers to adult actions that enable an infant to successfully participate in an activity by steering the infant's efforts and by eliminating unproductive paths until each constituent part of the activity is mastered and can be carried out by the infant alone. Observed during such culturally meaningful activities as playing games (Bruner & Sherwood, 1976; Ratner & Bruner, 1978) or labeling pictures in books

(Ninio & Bruner, 1978), scaffolding may be regarded as a more detailed specification of the supportive social interaction envisioned by
Vygotsky as enabling a child to function within the zone of proximal
development.

In relation to development during infancy, Kaye (1982) has elaborated the significance of joint activities between parents and infants for
the evolution of shared meanings and of shared ways for expressing
those meanings. His description of development in symbolization illustrates the role that jointly structured activities have in allowing infants to
experience the effects of their actions on others, to observe others acting
in the same context, and thereby to grasp more fully the social meaning
of their own acts at each successive phase of development. As Kaye
emphatically states, infants become able to interact by means of symbols
because parents engage their infants in specific patterns of interaction in
which the mutual significance of acts and intentions can be learned.

Joint activity may be important not only for its tutorial function but
also for revealing new motives for engagement in an activity. Leont'ev
(1981) has written explicitly about the acquisition of new motives in the
course of participating in an activity. He discussed the example of a first-
grader, who is persuaded to sit down and do her homework by being
told that she can not go out to play until the homework is finished. In
this instance, the child's motive for doing the homework is the desire to
play, although she may understand that praise from the teacher can be
expected only if homework assignments are carried out. In time, however, the girl may start doing homework without even considering the
rule about play. At such a time, the motive for doing homework would
have become the desire to be a good student rather than the desire to
play.

Leont'ev suggested that as individuals engage in goal-directed activities, they learn more about the components of those activities and the
various means for carrying them out; in the process, they may come to
see the activity as a whole in a different light. To return to the previous
example, trying to be a good student may involve memorizing information, finding answers in reference books, making drawings to illustrate
assignments, writing about community events, and so forth. The opportunity to use, for instance, drawing and construction skills in various
assignments may affect how a child experiences the activity of studying.
Although Leont'ev did not specifically speak about infants, his formulations may apply to infant development as well. Participation in joint
activities with a more experienced member of a culture may lead infants
to appreciate goals for the activity that they did not initially grasp and
thereby to gain new motives for engaging in that activity. For example,

toy play that is initially engaged in for the sake of fun may acquire distinct rules and specific ends.

Various aspects of infants' interactions with others have been observed and studied by numerous investigators in recent years (e.g, Bruner, 1978, 1983; Kaye, 1982; Newson, 1979; Papoušek & Papoušek, 1979; Richards, 1974; Stern, 1977, 1985; Trevarthen, 1980; Tronick, 1982; Užgiris, 1979). Although their views differ in a number of respects, several common themes stand out in their writings: (1) Adults treat even young infants as persons and impute meaning to infant actions; (2) adults convey their own interpretation of the world, including their view of the infant–adult relationship, to infants through interactions with them; and (3) adults support infants' developing competencies by providing both challenges and help in appropriately scaled tasks. These themes highlight that achievement of shared interests, shared goals, and shared knowledge is central to the development of competence. They also point to the need for research on the realization of such achievements in the context of infant–adult interaction.

Imitative Interactions

The production of similar acts in close temporal sequence by the two interacting partners has been observed in a number of the fine-grained studies of mother–infant face-to-face exchanges. The fact that it is the mother who usually "mirrors" or "shadows" the facial expressions or vocalizations of her young infant has been noted in informal comments (Kaye, 1979; Malatesta & Haviland, 1982; Papoušek & Papoušek, 1977; Trevarthen, 1977). However, these instances of behavioral congruence have not received express attention from most investigators, possibly because they were viewed as instances of imitation conceived as a unidirectional process of influence from model to observer. But imitation basically is a social process; it needs to be considered in the interpersonal context in which it usually takes place (Užgiris, 1981, 1984). Imitation can then be appreciated as one process that contributes to mutual understanding during early infant–adult interactions as well as to progress toward the more conventional modes of communication achieved later in development.

A discussion of imitation in the context of infant–adult interaction has been presented by Kaye (1982). Although he views imitation more from the standpoint of the infant than of the dyad, Kaye does attribute importance to mutual imitation for the initial attainment of shared meanings in the course of developing communicative competence. The parent is a model but also an interpreter of the infant's imitation attempts. To make progress, the infant has to arrive at an understanding of his or her own acts that matches the interpretation given them by the parent. Because he is primarily concerned with the construction of symbols, Kaye focuses more on the role of imitation in the achievement of true symbols than on its role in the process of parent–infant interaction. We are more concerned with imitation as a form of interpersonal exchange at different levels of development, but our position is close to Kaye's in giving imitation an important place in the development of communication.

We think that an act of imitation captures the juncture of the individual and the world with which the individual interacts. It reflects both the model and the imitator's understanding of the model and externalizes that understanding. This externalization through action has the potential for extending the initial understanding. In addition, because imitation is overt, it also has the potential for being shared by those involved in the interaction.

Although imitation usually takes place in an interpersonal context, it has been studied largely as individual behavior. Viewing imitation as interpersonal activity suggests a number of different emphases. First, it becomes clear that imitation can be a reciprocal activity. Following an act of imitation, the roles can shift, the model can become the imitator, and the sequence can continue. Or the model can become the imitator at a different time during the course of the interaction. Thus imitative activity can be a means of social exchange. Second, it suggests that the meaning of an imitative act must be considered from the perspective of both participants. An imitative act can be noted by the model and can affect the subsequent activity of the model as well as of the imitator. The term *matching activity* may be preferable to imitation when the form of interaction is being emphasized because, from the perspective of interaction, the most salient factor is the establishment of behavioral congruence. The specific act or the participant responsible for establishing the congruence seems less central. Third, it suggests that a unit of analysis that encompasses the acts of both participants, such as a round, might be better suited for studying matching activity. And, clearly, matching must be observed during interaction if its interpersonal significance is to be understood.

Stern (1985) has recognized that imitation may serve as a way to regulate interpersonal exchanges, but because he is most concerned with affective regulation, he suggests that typically a more global process is involved, which he calls *affect attunement*. Affect attunement is "the performance of behaviors that express the quality of feeling of a shared affect state without imitating the exact behavioral expression of the inner state" (1985, p. 142). He judges imitation inadequate for conveying feeling states because he considers imitation only in its behavioral aspect. However, he does mention that imitative exchanges often have a theme-and-variations quality, especially as infants reach higher levels of competence. Such imitative exchanges with variations seem to come close to instances of affect attunement when the focus of the exchange is the sharing of affect.

But sharing of affect is only one aspect of interpersonal interaction; setting mutual goals, sharing information as well as tutoring and learning are also often aspects of interaction. We think imitative or matching exchanges deserve attention because they carry a double function: They can reflect the state of ongoing interaction, but also, as emphasized by Kaye, they have the potential for teaching the infant new ways for interacting. It is this double function that makes imitative exchanges an important part of the supportive infant–adult engagements that foster the development of competence.

We studied matching activity as an aspect of mother–infant interaction during the infant's first year of life. Our first goal was to document the occurrence of matching activity as a frequent and regular aspect of such interactions in a larger sample of mother–infant dyads. Matching activity was defined to include instances where the mother replicates an act of the infant as well as instances where the infant replicates an act of the mother. We expected the incidence of matching activity to be higher among dyads with older infants because of the older infants' greater facility for imitation. Our second goal was to examine the differences in matching activity between dyads with infants of different ages. We expected that matching exchanges would be more reciprocal and more complex in dyads with older infants. Our final goal was to compare the form of matching activity in two contexts: face-to-face interaction and interaction with toys. We expected the two contexts to highlight different facets of matching exchanges. Some of our findings on matching activity have been reported in previous papers (Užgiris, 1983; Užgiris, Benson, & Vasek, 1983; Užgiris, Vasek, & Benson, 1984).

MATCHING IN THE FIRST YEAR OF LIFE

The findings reported in this chapter are derived from a study of 80 mother–infant dyads. The infants comprised four age groups: 2 to 3 months, 5 to 6 months, 8 to 9 months, and 11 to 12 months. There were 20 infants in each age group, equally divided by sex. About half of the

infants were firstborns, whereas the others had from 1 to 4 older siblings. The families represented a stable lower-middle to upper-middle-
class population.

The families were contacted by letter and a telephone call on the
basis of birth announcements in the local newspaper. Those who agreed
to participate were asked to bring their infants to a university child study
laboratory for two sessions, spaced about a week apart. During the first
session, a period of face-to-face interaction was videotaped, followed by
a period of interaction with toys. During the second session, the mothers were interviewed about interaction with their infants, and the infants were given some additional tasks. The findings reported here are
based on the interactions videotaped during the first session. The interaction with toys always followed the face-to-face interaction because
infants were found to fuss much more if the face-to-face interaction was
attempted after a period of play with toys.

The interactions took place in a small room containing a table, seats
for the mother and infant, and two cameras mounted on the walls. Once
the mother and infant were comfortable, the experimenter left the room
and observed the interaction on a TV monitor in an adjacent control
room. The seating arrangements were adjusted for the different age
groups, but in all cases the mother faced her infant and their eyes were
at about the same level. The same seating arrangement was used during
both periods of interaction. The split-image videotape provided a three-
quarters view of the face and shoulders of the mother and a full view of
the face and upper body of the infant and contained a continuous time
record. The face-to-face interaction was coded second by second, whereas the interaction with toys was coded as a sequence of acts by the two
partners.

Matching during Face-to-Face Interaction

In the face-to-face interaction, mothers were instructed to play with
their infants the way they usually did but to try to maintain the seating
arrangement as much as possible. A period of 12 minutes was scheduled
for this interaction, and dyads that completed at least 9 minutes of
interaction were retained in the sample. Breaks in recording were permitted but were rarely needed.

The videotapes of these interactions were first coded for periods of
interpersonal involvement, which were defined as episodes during
which the mother and infant established eye contact and at least one
member attempted to engage the other in interaction or episodes during

which the pair became mutually involved through the tactual or auditory modalities prior to eye contact. Two independent judges coded interpersonal involvement episodes with 93% agreement.

Interpersonal involvement was considered to be a state of active engagement during which matching activity might occur. The proportion of interaction time spent in interpersonal involvement by the different age groups is shown in Table 1. There was no significant difference across age in the proportion of interaction time spent in interpersonal involvement. On average, the dyads spent about 7 minutes in interpersonal involvement or 65% of total interaction time. However, with age, the number of separate interpersonal involvement episodes increased and their duration decreased, most notably between the 2½- and 5½-month groups.

Within periods of involvement, all episodes of matching activity were identified. A matching episode was defined as extending from the beginning of the act that was then replicated by the partner to the last production of this act by one of the partners. Both exact and approximate replications of an act occurring within 2 seconds and without other intervening activity were counted. Coding was done in terms of behavioral acts such as banging, pointing, or frowning rather than in terms of specific features such as the degree of arm extension or of forehead elevation. Similarly, vocalizations were judged as a totality, not on the basis of specific aspects such as pitch. Reciprocal smiles were excluded from the category of matched acts because they occur so routinely during greeting exchanges. For each matching episode, the partner whose act was initially matched, the sequence of turns taken by the partners, the accuracy of matching, and the content of the acts being matched were noted. Independent judges averaged 85% agreement in coding different aspects of matching episodes.

The increase in the overall frequency of matching episodes with age is shown in Table 2. The number of episodes increased from a mean of

TABLE 1
Characteristics of Interpersonal Involvement in the First Year of Life

	Age group (months)			
	2½	5½	8½	11½
Mean proportion of time in interaction	0.71	0.59	0.60	0.68
Mean number of interaction episodes	14.85	24.20	25.35	25.60
Mean duration of interaction episodes (in seconds)	46.92	25.38	17.11	20.43

TABLE 2
Mean Number of Matching Episodes during Interpersonal Interaction

Age group (months)	Infant's act matched by mother	Mother's act matched by infant	All episodes
2½	4.85	0.90	5.75
5½	5.20	0.60	5.80
8½	8.20	2.45	10.65
11½	11.70	3.50	15.20

5.75 episodes in the 2½-month group to a mean of 15.20 episodes in the 11½-month group. When adjacent age groups were considered, the increase was found to be significant between the 5½- and the 8½-month groups (Mann-Whitney $U=42$, $p<.01$) and again between the 8½- and the 11½-month groups ($U=121$, $p<.05$). There were no sex differences in the frequency of matching episodes. However, individual pairs differed markedly in the frequency of matching activity.

Matching episodes can be divided according to the partner who first matches the immediately preceding act of the other. In a sense, the partner matching the other's act is directly establishing the behavioral congruence between them, although once established, it can be experienced by both participants. At all ages, we found that mothers matched infant acts more often than infants matched their mothers' acts. A significant increase in both mother-initiated and infant-initiated episodes was found between the 5½- and 8½-month groups ($U=70$, $p<.01$ and $U=120$, $p<.05$, respectively). This result shows that with age, matching became a more reciprocal activity, more likely to be initiated by either partner.

The increasing participation in matching activity by both partners is also revealed by the occurrence of longer matching episodes among the older age groups. We examined the length of matching episodes in terms of rounds of matching. The performance of the same act once by each partner was defined as one round. For an episode to be counted as two rounds in length, each partner had to perform the act at least twice. Thus, if a mother matched her infant's act, the infant reciprocated, and the mother matched a second time, the episode was counted as two rounds in length. Similarly, if an infant matched the mother's act, the mother reciprocated, and the infant matched again, the episode was also counted as two rounds in length.

As shown in Table 3, most of the episodes were one round in length for all age groups studied. None of the infants in the youngest age group

TABLE 3

Mean Number and Mean Percentage (in Parentheses)
of Matching Episodes of Different Lengths
during Interpersonal Interaction

Age group (months)	Episode length		
	1 round	2 rounds	3+ rounds
2½	5.15 (90%)	0.60 (10%)	0.00 (0%)
5½	4.80 (83%)	0.65 (11%)	0.35 (6%)
8½	8.00 (75%)	2.00 (19%)	0.65 (6%)
11½	11.65 (77%)	2.45 (16%)	1.10 (7%)

participated in episodes exceeding two rounds in length. Episodes three rounds in length and longer were seen only in the older age groups. These data also show that matching activity becomes more reciprocal with age. Moreover, it seems that greater matching of mothers' acts by infants was most responsible for the increased reciprocity seen in the 8½-month group; at that age, there was a significant increase in one round episodes in which the mother's act is matched by the infant (U =83, $p<.01$) as well as in two-round episodes in which the infant's act is initially matched by the mother, but the infant reciprocates, and the mother can match the infant's act a second time ($U=114.5$, $p<.05$). These data support findings from more controlled studies (e.g., Killen & Užgiris, 1981; Rodgon & Kurdek, 1977) showing greater facility in imitation by infants toward the end of the first year of life.

The content of the acts constituting the matching episodes also changed with age. Overall, more than half of the episodes involved motoric acts. Vocal matching accounted for over a third of the episodes, whereas the remainder consisted of a combination of both vocal and facial or vocal and manual acts. For the youngest age group, the most frequently matched acts were various vocalizations and mouth movements, especially opening the mouth wide. For the 5½-month-olds, following of the partner's gaze was added to vocalizations and mouth openings as a frequently matched act. In most cases, it was the mother who matched one of these acts of her infant. In the 8½-month group, vocalizations and motoric acts such as following of the partner's gaze and hand banging constituted the frequently matched acts. In this age group, the mother's hand action, vocalization, or head turn was much more likely to be matched by her infant. In the oldest age group, words were sometimes matched as well as sounds, and, in addition to hand banging, more conventional acts such as clapping, waving, shaking, or nodding the head were among the frequently matched acts. Thus in the 11½-month group, many of the acts making up the matching exchanges had meaning in the wider sociocultural context.

In sum, during face-to-face interaction, we observed matching by both mother and infant throughout the first year of life. In the youngest age groups, matching activity consisted of short episodes in which the mother matched a facial expression or vocalization of her infant, establishing an affective congruence with the infant. In the older age groups, matching activity became elaborated into longer episodes, in which both the mother and infant matched each other's previous acts and attained a practiced quality, suggesting through the matching a commonality of interests or goals for the interaction. Thus, as the episodes of matching activity became more frequent and more reciprocal, they became a format for interpersonal exchange.

Matching during Toy Interaction

For the interaction with toys, the mothers were asked to use each of four toys in turn. Three of the toys were meant to be new to the infant, and one was a familiar toy that the mother had been asked to bring from home. The three standard toys were a wooden dog on wheels, a squeeze toy shaped like a clothespin with a painted-on face, and a wooden string puppet; substitute toys were used if an infant had any of the standard toys at home. The order of the toys was counterbalanced across mother–infant pairs. Only the results for play with the three standard toys are reported here.

The interaction with toys was scheduled for 8 minutes, with 2 minutes allowed for play with each of the toys. The mothers were told the order in which to play with the toys and were signaled by a knock on the wall when it was time to switch from one toy to the next. They were instructed to "introduce each of the toys" to their infants and to play together with the toy until signaled to switch to the next one.

The frequency of matching activity during interaction with toys was considerably lower than during face-to-face interaction. Even when the shorter time for interaction with toys is taken into account (6 minutes of play with the three standard toys as against an average of 7 minutes of interpersonal involvement), the average number of matching episodes turns out to be smaller during toy interaction. However, as shown in Table 4, there was an age-related increase in matching episodes during toy interaction also. The number of such episodes was significantly higher in the 11½-month group when compared to the 8½-month group

TABLE 4
Mean Number of Matching Episodes during Toy Interaction

Age group (months)	Infant's act matched by mother	Mother's act matched by infant	All episodes
2½	0.75	0.00	0.75
5½	1.35	0.45	1.80
8½	2.60	0.55	3.15
11½	1.90	2.85	4.75

($U=138$, $p<.05$, corrected for ties), and in the 8½-month group when compared to the 5½-month group ($U=131.5$, $p<.05$, corrected for ties).

The lower overall frequency of matching was due primarily to less frequent matching of infant acts by the mothers. Although mothers in the 8½-month group did match their infants' acts more often than mothers in the 5½-month group ($U=137.5$, $p<.05$, corrected for ties), mothers in the 11½-month group did not engage in more matching activity than mothers in the two younger groups. Moreover, most of the infants' acts matched by the mothers were unrelated to the toys. In contrast, most of the matching by infants was related to actions on toys. The oldest infants matched their mothers' acts significantly more often than the 8½-month-olds ($U=48.5$, $p<.01$). We speculate that the instruction given to the mothers to interest their infants in playing with the different toys led the mothers to assume a different, less symmetrical role in relation to their infants during toy interaction.

In general, the toy interactions consisted of one partner, usually the mother, performing some act with a toy, eliciting some response from the other partner, and then either acting again or giving the toy to the other partner. In the youngest age group, mothers held the toys practically all of the time and acted on them most of the time. In the 5½-month group, mothers held the toys less than half the time but often held the toys jointly with their infants. In the two oldest groups, infants held the toys over half the time, but the mothers also held the toys some of the time, suggesting some turn taking with the infants.

Toy interactions were analyzed in terms of initiations, types of actions on toys, responses to these actions by the partner, and verbalizations. Acts that engaged the attention of the partner, differed from the immediately preceding activity, and allowed for a response by the partner were called *initiations*. Agreement in coding initiations was 94%. Play actions with toys were classified into a number of categories, including simple, differentiated, and conventional actions. These categories were coded with an average agreement of 88%. Responses to the

partner's actions or initiations were coded into five categories: nonat-
tending, observing, commenting/vocalizing, matching, and reciprocal.
The response categories were coded with 96% agreement. In addition,
verbalizations by the two partners were transcribed and the specific
naming of a toy for the partner as well as the use of a toy's name in a
sentence was recorded. Verbalizations were coded with 86% agreement.

That toy interactions became more reciprocal with age is indicated
by several findings. As shown in Table 5, although the average number
of initiations was greater in the older age groups, the proportion of
initiations by mothers declined, whereas the proportion of initiations by
infants increased, so that in the two oldest groups, infants initiated just
slightly less than half of the play episodes.

Similarly, the distribution of toy actions between mothers and infants demonstrates a greater reciprocity in the older age groups. As
shown in Table 6, although the overall number of play actions was fairly

TABLE 5
Mean Number and Mean Percentage (in Parentheses)
of Initiations by Each of the Partners
during Toy Interaction

Age group (months)	Mothers' initiations	Infants' initiations	Total
2½	3.00 (100%)	0.00 (0%)	3.00
5½	4.60 (78%)	2.10 (22%)	6.70
8½	6.20 (57%)	4.80 (43%)	11.00
11½	7.45 (58%)	5.70 (42%)	13.15

TABLE 6
Mean Number and Mean Percentage (in Parentheses)
of Play Actions by Each of the Partners
during Toy Interaction

Age group (months)	Mothers' actions	Infants' actions	Total
2½	40.60 (100%)	0.00 (0%)	40.60
5½	26.35 (75%)	8.80 (25%)	35.15
8½	21.45 (52%)	18.15 (48%)	39.60
11½	24.75 (55%)	20.60 (45%)	45.35

similar in all four age groups, the proportion of actions performed by infants increased substantially, so that in the oldest group they performed almost half of all the play actions.

We also considered the nature of the acts comprising the toy interactions. Because toys are cultural artifacts, it is to be expected that there would be culturally accepted ways for using different toys. Acts constrained by the social definition of objects were considered to be conventional. We designated one action as conventional for each of the toys. They were squeaking the clothespin, rolling the toy dog on its wheels, and moving the puppet by pulling on the string. In all age groups, all of the mothers performed these conventional acts; they made up a large proportion of the mothers' acts on toys. In contrast, only infants in the older age groups performed the conventional acts with any frequency.

As shown in Table 7, over half of the initiations by mothers involved conventional acts. In the remaining instances, they showed the toy or commented on it, which could be considered different kinds of conventional acts. Initiations by infants usually involved some simple action; conventional acts were seen only in the oldest age group. Similarly, a high proportion of the mothers' actions with toys involved these conventional acts. As shown in Table 8, infants also performed some of these conventional acts when they played with the toys, but quite rarely, except in the oldest age group. Only toward the end of the first year did the infants begin to treat these toys as objects having a meaning that could be shared through a distinct set of acts.

Because the mothers performed the conventional acts quite frequently for infants in all age groups, it seems plausible to think that infants learned these acts through observing their mothers and trying to act in a similar way themselves. When mothers performed a conven-

TABLE 7

Mean Number and Mean Percentage
(in Parentheses) of Initiations
by Conventional Acts during Toy Interaction

Age group (months)	Mothers' initiations	Infants' initiations
2½	1.65 (55%)	0.00 (0%)
5½	3.10 (70%)	0.00 (0%)
8½	3.40 (55%)	0.00 (0%)
11½	4.05 (57%)	0.60 (13%)

TABLE 8
Mean Number and Mean Percentage
(in Parentheses) of Play Actions
Involving Conventional Acts
during Toy Interaction

Age group (months)	Mothers' actions	Infants' actions
2½	11.65 (29%)	0.00 (0%)
5½	11.40 (45%)	0.65 (7%)
8½	9.45 (46%)	0.95 (6%)
11½	11.15 (46%)	4.70 (24%)

tional act, infants in the younger age groups typically observed the act, appeared interested in the toy, but upon getting the toy, usually did something different with it. Infants in the older age groups occasionally responded to their mothers' conventional initiations and conventional play actions by matching those acts. Moreover, as shown in Table 9, of all instances where infants matched their mother's acts, a very high proportion involved the matching of mothers' conventional actions. This suggests that matching for infants served to demonstrate their understanding of the socially given meaning of the toys and allowed them to participate in a common play pattern with the mother.

The data on mothers' verbalizations also illustrate their attempts to teach their infants more conventional forms of communication. Mothers of infants in all age groups talked about the toys and used a name for each of the toys when referring to them. However, we distinguished the use of a name embedded in a sentence when commenting on a toy and the specific naming of a toy for the infant. As shown in Table 10, a much

TABLE 9
Mean Number and Mean Percentage (in Parentheses) of Different
Types of Mothers' Acts Matched by Infants during Toy Interaction[a]

Age group (months)	Mothers' acts matched by infants		
	Conventional	Nonconventional	Total
2½	0.00 (0%)	0.00 (0%)	0.00
5½	0.05 (11%)	0.35 (78%)	0.45
8½	0.30 (55%)	0.15 (27%)	0.55
11½	2.10 (74%)	0.65 (23%)	2.85

[a]Matching of mothers' vocalizations and actions unrelated to the toys has been added into the total.

TABLE 10
*Number and Percentage (in Parentheses) of Mothers
Referring to at Least One Toy by Name
during Toy Interaction*

Age group (months)	Uses toy's name	Names toy
2½	20 (100%)	3 (15%)
5½	20 (100%)	4 (20%)
8½	15 (75%)	4 (20%)
11½	18 (90%)	10 (50%)

higher proportion of mothers of infants in the oldest age group specifi-cally named the toys for their infants. This suggests that with slightly older infants, naming may constitute a pattern of exchange during toy play similar to the labeling routines studied by Ninio and Bruner (1978) during looking at picture books. This change illustrates how maternal actions are adjusted to the developmental level of the infant.

In sum, mother–infant interaction with toys showed age-related changes in the direction of greater reciprocity and conventionalization. In the older age groups, mothers and infants shared more equally the performance of specific play actions and the initiation of new directions in play. However, matching was a less important means for establishing mutuality, at least for the mothers. The mothers very rarely matched their infants' acts with the toys; instead, they performed conventional play actions. In contrast, infants in the older age groups did match their mothers' actions, especially their conventional actions. This suggests that in the context of toy interaction, matching helps the infant to learn culturally defined forms of activity.

Matching Activity and Development

Although the frequency of matching activity was lower during toy interaction than during face-to-face interaction, the age trends were sim-ilar in both contexts. These age differences in matching can be related to the cognitive and action abilities of the infants and to the mothers' perception of their infants' participation in the interaction.

In the youngest age group, almost all of the matching episodes were due to the mother matching an act of her infant. This "mirroring" by the mother has been usually related to affective sharing (Stern, 1985;

Tronick, 1982), which regulates the intensity of interaction and helps to maintain a comfortable level of involvement for the two participants. Such overt expression of congruence may facilitate smooth regulation of the interaction at this level of development, when other means for communicating about the state of the interaction are not available.

The mother's matching activity may also contribute to the delineation of action units for the infant. The mother's matching is not continuous; it is responsive to the mother's experience of the flow of the interaction, but it is also responsive to the specifics of the infant's actions. By matching only certain acts, the mother highlights those acts and helps to segregate them into distinct units for the infant. They are lifted out from the flow of experience and can become familiar tokens in their interpersonal exchanges. Thus a more symmetrical exchange becomes eventually possible.

The mother's matching is also selective in a different sense. She brings her cultural orientation to the interaction and selectively matches those infant acts that have some meaning for her. Although there is need for more cross-cultural studies of mother–infant interaction, even the scant existing evidence suggests that levels of visual co-orientation, vocalization, and inclusion of objects in play varies between cultures (e.g., Mundy-Castle, 1980; Strydom, 1985). Interest in the inanimate environment and its exploration is expected in our culture. Therefore, the tendency by the mother to join her infant in looking at specific features of the surround even at 5½ months of age may be seen as a selective response to highlight a culturally meaningful action. But by matching her infant's orientation, the mother also establishes a coordinated exchange with the infant, at a time when the infant is functioning at the level of only single unit actions. When looked at from the interpersonal perspective, this "matching of orientation" exchange can be viewed as an initiation to share an interest and an acknowledgment of that interest, even though at first it may be only an individual expression of interest for the infant. But, to paraphrase Vygotsky, by participating in this interpersonally constructed exchange pattern, the infant can come to know it and, eventually, to understand it.

The higher frequency of matching episodes in the 8½-month group, particularly the higher number of episodes in which the infant matched some act of the mother, may be linked to cognitive progress of the infant. Most accounts of cognitive development during infancy postulate a transition to a new level of functioning at around 8 months of age (e.g., Case, 1985; Fischer, 1980; McCall, Eichorn, & Hogarty, 1977; Piaget, 1952; Užgiris, 1976). Infants are described as capable of more differentiated understanding of events in the environment, more complex coordination of means in problem solving, more intentional expression of interests and wants. The ability to coordinate action sequences consisting of several components also permits the infant to relate the acts of the two participants in interaction. For example, alternating vocalizations or alternating hand bangs can come to be understood as sequentially related and evolve into "follow-the-leader" games. Once a match as a second component in a sequential action can be distinguished, it can come to identify a specific type of exchange.

Although Trevarthen (Trevarthen & Hubley, 1978) has described this period as a time of waning interest in interpersonal activity on the part of the infant, because of heightened interest in objects, other studies suggest that infants eagerly extend their new cognitive skills to interactions with people. Infants become more active in playing social games (Gustafson, Green, & West, 1979), begin to use vocal and manual gestures for communication (Bates, Benigni, Bretherton, Camaioni, & Volterra, 1979; Harding & Golinkoff, 1979), and become more adept at imitating others (Killen & Užgiris, 1981; Pawlby, 1977). The observed increase in matching activity during interaction may be viewed as another indication of the extension of cognitive skills to interpersonal contexts.

As infants become capable of constructing multicomponent actions, matching can be recognized as a specific form of exchange. Hence, when the mother matches her infant's action, the infant can respond in kind, thus extending the activity to two rounds, or the infant can initiate this form of exchange by matching the mother's act. This ability to coordinate a unit of exchange that includes the acts of the two participants as components may account for the increase in reciprocity seen in the older age groups both in the face-to-face and toy interactions.

In our oldest age group, matching exchanges also contained a greater number of conventional acts in both the face-to-face and the toy interaction contexts. Although a specific category of conventional acts was not coded during face-to-face interaction, the most frequently matched acts for the oldest group included many game actions, gestures, and conventionalized sounds. An increase in the incidence of conventionalized acts toward the end of the first year of life during play with mothers has been also reported by Bakeman and Adamson (1985). During toy interaction, matching by the oldest infants consisted largely of conventional acts with toys. Infants of this age have been found to imitate conventional acts on toys in controlled settings also (Killen & Užgiris, 1981).

This increase in matching of conventional acts toward the end of the infant's first year may be due to selective matching of infant acts by the mother, to modeling by the mother, as well as to selective response to infant matching by the mother. As infants begin to regulate sequences of action in terms of a differentiated analysis of their effects (Užgiris, 1976), maternal reactions may direct matching activity toward the use of more set, conventionally meaningful acts, especially when the exchange revolves around such culturally well-defined objects as toys. While participating in play with their infants, mothers may be more inclined to join in an activity with, for example, blocks, if it involves a culturally recognized action such as stacking, and to follow the lead of the infant rather than trying to introduce a different action. A better grasp by the infant of the social definition of toys may also lead to the smoother collaboration during play with toys that has been observed in other studies (Hubley & Trevarthen, 1979).

Clearly, a matching exchange is not the only coordinated, two-component exchange that can be seen during interaction. The matching exchange may be important, however, in establishing a shared meaning for acts and in delineating specific acts as components with a fairly set meaning. These components then become available for inclusion into longer interaction sequences and scenarios (Bretherton, O'Connell, Shore, & Bates, 1984; Bretherton, Chapter 8 this volume), in which mutual understanding is largely presumed or is supplemented by verbal means. The greater reciprocity, complexity, and conventionality of matching activity seen toward the end of the infant's first year reflect the infant's greater understanding both of specific actions and of the process of interpersonal interaction.

THE CONTEXTS FOR MATCHING ACTIVITY

Our study showed that matching activity is part of mother–infant interaction during the first year of life in both face-to-face and toy play situations. Similar age-related trends in the two situations suggested that changes in matching activity are related to development of the infant's general cognitive abilities. There were, however, some clear differences in matching activity between the two situations. These differences lead us to propose that matching might be a part of three different interaction formats.

We think of an interaction format in much the same way as it has been recently discussed by Bruner (1983), except that we do not attempt to specify the regularized forms that various formats might take. Bruner defines a format as "a contingent interaction between at least two acting parties, contingent in the sense that the responses of *each* member can be shown to be dependent on a prior response of the *other*" (1983, p. 132). He focuses on the routine moves that make up specific formats. We are interested in delineating broader classes of formats within which matching may be a regularized interaction unit.

One type of interaction in which matching activity occurs may be called the *sharing format*. The function of matching in this format is to establish mutuality, to convey a similarity of interest or feeling. To accomplish this, a recognition of the similarity established through matching is required, but a grasp of the means by which this similarity was brought about is less necessary. Matching of the facial expressions or vocalizations of the youngest infants by the mothers may be viewed as an example of matching in this format. The affective matching that takes place at the conclusion of somewhat difficult tasks or game routines may be another example. This format serves to establish accord and equality between the participants in the interaction. Thus it may be considered a regulator of the cohesiveness and flow of the interaction as experienced by the participants.

Another type of format in which matching activity occurs is the *teaching/learning format*, in which the roles of the participants are clearly not symmetrical but are complementary. Acts are performed as demonstrations, and matching is an attempt to learn what is being demonstrated. This format was most evident in our study during the interaction with toys, when the mother often acted to demonstrate the conventional way of using a toy for the infant. In this format, the continuation of a matching sequence may depend most on the accuracy of matching by the learner and have little to do with reciprocity. Attainment of accurate matching may equalize the relation of the participants, but it is also likely to terminate the matching sequence. In this format, although there is a common goal, the focus is mostly on the means for reaching the goal. The use of identical means for attaining congruence is important. Therefore, the ability to analyze means in relation to end states may be a prerequisite for matching in this format. This format permits the exchange of information about what has been mastered in relation to what is yet to be mastered. It may be considered a regulator of the pace and direction of interactions.

Matching activity also occurs in what might be called a *structural format*, in that the matching of the partner's act functions as a turn and thereby continues the interaction. The focus in this format is on the larger structure of the interaction and on the necessity for successive contributions by both participants in order to maintain mutual involvement. The matching of conventional acts by infants in the oldest age group may be a beginning toward matching in this format. The use of routine repetitions in order to take a turn in games or, later, in conversations may be better examples. Researchers studying linguistic development in children have noted that repetition of the previous utterance is sometimes used by children to fill a turn in conversation (Ramer, 1976). In studying imitation in children around 2 years of age, we have observed instances of both matching and modeling by the child that seem to be directed toward extending the interaction (McCabe & Užgiris, 1983). Here matching does equalize the contributions of the two participants, but neither the similarity achieved through matching nor the exactness of matching seems to be particularly central. Matching basically functions as a unit of exchange in the interaction and is inserted to maintain the interactive structure.

Although matching in each of these formats may become evident at different times during infancy, we do not wish to suggest that they form some system of developmental levels. Matching in each of these formats presupposes an ongoing interaction within which the formats serve as orientations or frames. The mother clearly has the ability to assume each of these formats and to focus both on goals and on means, to establish symmetrical and complementary relations, and to understand the interaction process itself. Infants' abilities may constrain their participation in these formats of interaction, but the opportunities offered them by adults are important in eventually helping them to master these and other formats of interaction.

Culturally specified interaction modes may influence the prevalence of matching in each of these formats and not just during infancy. We think that matching in these formats is evident to some extent throughout life. Matching in the sharing format is most evident in empathic exchanges. Matching in the teaching/learning format occurs in apprenticeship situations, in demonstrations of skilled actions, the use of instruments, or working styles, with both children and other adults. Matching in the structural format can be observed in many polite conversations between not particularly well-acquainted individuals. However, these formats are not very salient when both participants are quite skilled in interpersonal interaction.

In conclusion, we are proposing that in the context of interaction, matching may function to establish accord, to continue the interaction, and to mold interpersonal acts toward mutually understood and culturally meaningful forms throughout life. The beginnings of these three formats are already evident during the infant's first year of life during interaction with the mother, but the incidence of the formats is influenced by the context in which the interaction takes place.

ACKNOWLEDGMENTS. The research reported in this chapter was supported by a grant from the Spencer Foundation to the senior author. We gratefully acknowledge the generous cooperation of the families that participated in the research and the help of Elaine Cooney in coding some of the data.

REFERENCES

Bakeman, R., & Adamson, L. B. (1985, April). *Infants' conventionalized acts: Gestures and words with mothers and peers.* Paper presented at the meetings of the Society for Research in Child Development, Toronto, Canada.

Bates, E., Benigni, L., Bretherton, I., Camaioni, L., & Volterra, V. (1979). *The emergence of symbols: Cognition and communication in infancy.* New York: Academic Press.

Bretherton, I., O'Connell, B., Shore, C., & Bates, E. (1984). The effect of contextual variation on symbolic play development from 20 to 28 months. In I. Bretherton (Ed.), *Symbolic play* (pp. 271–298). New York: Academic Press.

Bruner, J. S. (1978). Learning how to do things with words. In J. S. Bruner & A. Garton (Eds.), *Human growth and development* (pp. 62–84). Oxford: Clarendon Press.

Bruner, J. (1983). *Child's talk.* New York: Norton.

Bruner, J. S., & Sherwood, V. (1976). Peek-a-boo and the learning of rule structures. In J. Bruner, A. Jolly, & K. Sylva (Eds.), *Play—Its role in development and evolution* (pp. 277–285). New York: Basic Books.

Case, R. (1985). *Intellectual development: Birth to adulthood.* Orlando, FL: Academic Press.

Fischer, K. W. (1980). A theory of cognitive development: The control and construction of hierarchies of skills. *Psychological Review, 87,* 477–531.

Gustafson, G. E., Green, J. A., & West, M. J. (1979). The infant's changing role in mother-infant games: The growth of social skills. *Infant Behavior and Development, 2,* 301–308.

Harding, C. G., & Golinkoff, R. M. (1979). The origins of intentional vocalizations in prelinguistic infants. *Child Development, 50,* 33–40.

Hubley, P., & Trevarthen, C. (1979). Sharing a task in infancy. In I. Č. Užgiris (Ed.), *New Directions for Child Development* (Vol. 4), *Social interaction and communication during infancy* (pp. 57–80). San Francisco: Jossey-Bass.

Kaye, K. (1979). Thickening thin data: The maternal role in developing communication and language. In M. Bullowa (Ed.), *Before speech* (pp. 191–206). New York: Cambridge University Press.

Kaye, K. (1982). *The mental and social life of babies.* Chicago: University of Chicago Press.

Killen, M., & Užgiris, I. Č. (1981). Imitation of actions with objects: The role of social meaning. *Journal of Genetic Psychology, 138,* 219–229.

Kruper, J. C., & Užgiris, I. Č. (1987). Fathers' and mothers' speech to young infants. *Journal of Psycholinguistic Research, 16,* 597–614.

Leont'ev, A. N. (1981). The problem of activity in psychology. In J. V. Wertsch (Ed.), *The concept of activity in Soviet psychology* (pp. 37–71). Armonk, NY: Sharpe.

Malatesta, C. Z., & Haviland, J. M. (1982). Learning display rules: The socialization of emotion expression in infancy. *Child Development, 53,* 991–1003.

McCabe, M., & Užgiris, I. Č. (1983). Effects of model and action on imitation in infancy. *Merrill-Palmer Quarterly, 29,* 69–82.

McCall, R. B., Eichorn, D. H., & Hogarty, P. S. (1977). Transitions in early mental development. *Monographs of the Society for Research in Child Development, 42*, 3, (Serial No. 171).

Mundy-Castle, A. (1980). Perception and communication in infancy: A cross-cultural study. In D. R. Olson (Ed.), *The social foundations of language and thought* (pp. 231–253). New York: Norton.

Newson, J. (1974). Towards a theory of infant understanding. *Bulletin of the British Psychological Society, 27*, 251–257.

Newson, J. (1979). The growth of shared understandings between infant and caregiver. In M. Bullowa (Ed.), *Before speech* (pp. 207–222). New York: Cambridge University Press.

Ninio, A., & Bruner, J. S. (1978). The achievement and antecedents of labelling. *Journal of Child Language, 5*, 1–15.

Papoušek, H., & Papoušek, M. (1977). Mothering and the cognitive head-start: Psychobiological considerations. In H. R. Schaffer (Ed.), *Studies in mother-infant interaction* (pp. 63–85). New York: Academic Press.

Papoušek, H., & Papoušek, M. (1979). Early ontogeny of human social interaction: Its biological and social dimensions. In M. von Cranach, K. Foppa, W. Lepenies, & D. Ploog (Eds.), *Human ethology: Claims and limits of a new discipline* (pp. 456–478). Cambridge: Cambridge University Press.

Pawlby, S. J. (1977). Imitative interaction. In H. R. Schaffer (Ed.), *Studies in mother-infant interaction* (pp. 203–224). New York: Academic Press.

Piaget, J. (1952). *The origins of intelligence in children* (M. Cook, Trans.). New York: International Universities Press. (Original work published in 1936)

Piaget, J. (1970). Piaget's theory. In P. H. Mussen (Ed.), *Carmichael's manual of child psychology* (Vol. 1, pp. 703–732). New York: Wiley.

Piaget, J. (1976). *The grasp of consciousness* (S. Wedgwood, Trans.). Cambridge, MA: Harvard University Press. (Original work published in 1974)

Ramer, A. L. H. (1976). The function of imitation in child language. *Journal of Speech and Hearing Research, 19*, 700–717.

Ratner, N., & Bruner, J. S. (1978). Games, social exchange, and the acquisition of language. *Journal of Child Language, 5*, 391–401.

Richards, M. P. M. (Ed.). (1974). *The integration of a child into a social world.* Cambridge: Cambridge University Press.

Rodgon, M. M., & Kurdek, L. A. (1977). Vocal and gestural imitation in 8-, 14-, and 20-month-old children. *Journal of Genetic Psychology, 131*, 115–123.

Stern, D. N. (1977). *The first relationship.* Cambridge: Harvard University Press.

Stern, D. N. (1985). *The interpersonal world of the infant.* New York: Basic Books.

Strydom, L. M. (1985, April). *Development of communication between African mothers and their infants in the first year of life.* Paper presented at the meetings of the Society for Research in Child Development, Toronto, Canada.

Trevarthen, C. (1977). Descriptive analyses of infant communicative behaviour. In H. R. Schaffer (Ed.), *Studies in mother-infant interaction* (pp. 227–289). New York: Academic Press.

Trevarthen, C. (1980). The foundations of intersubjectivity: Development of interpersonal and cooperative understanding in infants. In D. R. Olson (Ed.), *The social foundations of language and thought* (pp. 316–342). New York: W. W. Norton.

Trevarthen, C., & Hubley, P. (1978). Secondary intersubjectivity: Confidence, confiding, and acts of meaning in the first year. In A. Lock (Ed.), *Action, gesture and symbol* (pp. 183–229). New York: Academic Press.

Tronick, E. Z. (Ed.). (1982). *Social interchange in infancy.* Baltimore: University Park Press.

Užgiris, I. Č. (1976). Organization of sensorimotor intelligence. In M. Lewis (Ed.), *Origins of intelligence* (pp. 123–163). New York: Plenum Press.

Užgiris, I. Č. (Ed.). (1979). *New directions for child development*, Vol. 4: *Social interaction and communication during infancy.* San Francisco: Jossey-Bass.

Užgiris, I. Č. (1981). Two functions of imitation during infancy. *International Journal of Behavioral Development, 4,* 1–12.

Užgiris, I. Č. (1983, August). *Mother-infant communication during the first year of life.* Paper presented at the meetings of the International Society for the Study of Behavioral Development, Munich, F. R. Germany.

Užgiris, I. Č. (1984). Imitation in infancy: Its interpersonal aspects. In M. Perlmutter (Ed.), *The Minnesota Symposia on Child Psychology,* Vol. 17: *Parent-child interactions and parent-child relations in child development* (pp. 1–32). Hillsdale, NJ: L. Erlbaum.

Užgiris, I. Č., Benson, J. B., & Vasek, M. (1983, April). *Matching behavior in mother-infant interaction.* Paper presented at the meetings of the Society for Research in Child Development, Detroit, MI.

Užgiris, I. C., Vasek, M. E., & Benson, J. B. (1984). *A longitudinal study of matching activity in mother-infant interaction.* Paper presented at the meetings of the International Conference on Infant Studies, New York, NY.

Vygotsky, L. S. (1978). *Mind in society.* Cambridge: Harvard University Press.

Chapter 5

Object Manipulation in Infancy
Developmental and Contextual Determinants

Jeffrey J. Lockman and James P. McHale

Introduction

Soon after infants begin to reach, they devote an increasing amount of time to manipulating objects. They finger, bang, and rotate objects often with great interest and delight. They do so in a variety of situations, whether it be in the context of solitary play or social interaction. Most parents, in fact, recognize this proclivity and tolerate it even in situations where similar behaviors by adults would be considered inappropriate. (Just imagine an adult banging a spoon on a table in a restaurant—even if service is slow!)

Researchers have also recognized infants' proclivity to manipulate objects and have viewed it with great interest. By examining manipulative activity, investigators have hoped to uncover the cognitive and perceptual structures and processes that characterize early development. Thus object manipulation has been studied to gain insights into infants' knowledge of the physical world (Piaget, 1954) and cultural conventions (Fenson, Kagan, Kearsley, & Zelazo, 1976) as well as the underlying organization of this knowledge (Langer, 1980; Piaget, 1952; Užgiris, 1983). In addition, object manipulation has been investigated to

Jeffrey J. Lockman • Department of Psychology, Tulane University, New Orleans, Louisiana 70118. James P. McHale • Department of Psychology, University of California, Berkeley, California 94720.

assess various perceptual and cognitive processes including cross-modal recognition (Rose, Gottfried, & Bridger, 1981), categorization (Riccuiti, 1965), attention (McCall, 1974) and sensitivity to novelty (Rubenstein, 1974; Schaffer & Parry, 1969, 1970).

In almost all of these endeavors, the key question has been whether infants' manipulatory behaviors are *appropriately* varied as a function of some object property or property shared by a set of objects. The presence of such manipulation has been taken to indicate that infants possess the particular capacity or process under investigation. Yet if we were to ask how does object appropriate manipulation develop—that is, how do infants come to relate their manual behaviors to the properties of a given object that they are handling—the existing literature would not provide a clear answer. Because object manipulation has often been used to index some other cognitive or perceptual capacity, basic questions remain about the ontogenesis of this skill. We suggest that in order to understand the development of object-appropriate manipulation, attention needs to be given to the component actions that make up manipulation, how they become used appropriately, and how they operate or function.

In this chapter, we examine these issues by reviewing previous work on the development of object manipulation. Based on our review, we identify three general problems that limit conclusions about early manipulation. One centers on the stimuli employed in previous investigations. Objects have varied markedly and unsystematically across studies and sometimes within them, largely as a function of the particular cognitive domain under scrutiny. As a result, definitions of "appropriateness" have varied too, a practice that precludes easy developmental comparisons.

A second limitation involves the responses that have been measured in past research. Little attention has been given to the motor components of manipulation—that is, the motor behaviors that make up the act of manipulation. Instead investigators have been interested in other research questions, quite often whether infants use manipulation in detecting novelty (Schaffer & Parry, 1969, 1970; Steele & Pederson, 1977). As such, measurements have been made of the *amount* rather than the *kind* of manipulation that infants display, a practice that also restricts developmental accounts.

A final limitation centers on the contexts that have been investigated in past object-manipulation research. There has been little work directly concerned with the influence of situational factors on the functioning or execution of different manipulation skills. Neglect of contextual variables can be traced to certain research traditions in the object manipulation literature. Many investigators have been concerned with cognitive or perceptual issues that do not emphasize the role of context in the performance of these actions. As a result, manipulation has primarily been studied by having infants explore objects by themselves. However, as other contributors to this volume have argued, understanding the performance and development of an action class requires that it be studied in the social and nonsocial contexts in which it functions. In this chapter, we discuss how a functional perspective that considers contextual or situational variables will enhance our understanding of manipulation performance and development.

The goals, then, of this chapter are to examine the early development of object-appropriate manipulation and address the limitations of previous work. In doing so, we first review theoretical approaches on the development of object manipulation and look at how these approaches have shaped the current literature. Next, we examine empirical findings on the development of object manipulation to determine when and how infants relate their manual behaviors to specific object features. In reviewing these findings, we consider not only developmental changes in manipulatory behaviors but also the contexts in which these behaviors have been studied. Finally, we present new work on the development of object manipulation that addresses some of the limitations of the previously reviewed findings. In this research we examine directly (1) the actions that infants and mothers display while they manipulate objects that vary systematically along salient dimensions, and (2) the effects of social and nonsocial contexts on infants' manipulatory behaviors. The chapter concludes by considering how a functional perspective, one that investigates the influence of situational or contextual variables, can improve our understanding of manipulation performance and development.

THEORETICAL POSITIONS ON OBJECT MANIPULATION

How do infants come to relate their hand and finger movements to the features of an object while they are manipulating it? When do infants adjust these movements so that they are suited to an object's particular characteristics? Answers to these questions have important implications for accounts of perceptuomotor and cognitive development and ultimately for discussions about the relationship between the infant and objective reality. Two quite different theories have guided most contemporary thinking on these matters—one put forth by Piaget (1952, 1954) and the other by the Gibsons (E. J. Gibson, 1982; J. J. Gibson, 1966, 1979).

Piaget's Theory

Piaget argued that infants *construct* their notions of objective reality by acting on the external environment and observing the consequences of their actions. In Piaget's observations of sensorimotor development, emphasis is given to actions that involve manual behaviors—at first prehensile movements and later manipulatory ones. In a general sense, these behaviors can be taken to indicate whether infants have differentiated themselves from the world of objects that surround them and whether they have constructed basic notions about time, space, causality, and the permanence of objects. But even more directly, these behaviors indicate whether infants act on objects in an appropriate manner. In this section, we consider Piaget's observations and their implications for understanding the development of object-appropriate manipulation.

Piaget claimed that infants initially show little differentiation between themselves and the objects they contact. During Stage 2 of sensorimotor development (roughly from the second until the fourth or fifth month when vision and prehension have become coordinated), infants often exercise a limited number of manual schemes simply for the sake of exercising them. As a consequence, when applied to objects (including parts of the infant's body), these schemes are employed rather indiscriminately regardless of the objects' features.

Piaget argued that these behaviors reflect a more general characteristic of Stage 2. Actions are centered on themselves rather than designed to produce a result in the external environment. For example, when infants evidence a primary circular reaction by trying to repeat an interesting or pleasurable event, they are attempting to reinstate the action rather than the *result* of that action in the environment. According to this view, infants do not yet have the capacity to intentionally manipulate objects appropriately.

With the onset of visually coordinated prehension, usually around 4 or 5 months, infants have entered into Stage 3 of sensorimotor development. In contrast to the previous stage, infants are now directly concerned with the results of their actions in the environment. This shift is reflected in a variety of changes, all of which have important implications for the development of object-appropriate manipulation.

Perhaps the most characteristic behavioral pattern of this period is the secondary circular reaction. This reaction, a form of reproductive assimilation, refers to infants' attempts to repeat or rediscover an action of theirs that initially by chance caused an interesting event to occur in the environment. Unlike the primary circular reaction, infants here are attempting to reinstate the result in the environment, not the sensations associated with the action.

For our purposes, the secondary circular reaction is of interest because it indicates how new, sometimes appropriate manual schemes, evolve from well-practiced ones. Piaget (1952) reports, for example, how the act of swinging a hanging doll arises accidentally from attempts to grasp the doll. Nevertheless, it would be incorrect to suggest that infants manipulate all objects appropriately at this point. Infants are still treating novel objects alike in that they do not *initially* attempt to relate their actions to the objects' characteristics.

When novel objects are confronted, infants of this period often treat them in an habitual manner, trying to assimilate them to familiar (practiced) schemes with little intentional accommodation to the novel features of the object. The following observation illustrates this pattern:

> At 0;6 (7) I offer [Laurent] various new objects to see if he will resume his attempts at spatial exploration which seemed to appear in connection with the last object. This does not occur; the child utilizes the new object as aliment for his habitual schemata. So it is that a penguin with long feet and a wagging head is only looked at briefly: at first Laurent strikes it, then rubs it against the side of the bassinet, etc., without paying attention to the end by which he grasped it. Several knick-knacks receive the same treatment: he grasps them with one hand and strikes them with the other. (Piaget, 1952, p. 198)

Piaget labeled this habitual treatment of novel objects, *generalizing assimilation*. Although it suggests little differentiation of novel objects, some appropriate manipulation might emerge. To the extent that the well-practiced schemes are suited to the properties of the novel object, manipulation that appears appropriate would be displayed.

Despite the limitations associated with novel stimuli, Piaget's observations suggest that infants treat at least some *familiar* objects appropriately. This typically occurs through the mechanism of recognitory assimilation. In recognitory assimilation, infants will display a motor scheme that has previously been applied to a stimulus as if to indicate that recognition (albeit in a motor form) has occurred. Appropriate manual behaviors could conceivably arise in the following manner. Through repeated encounters with objects that have given rise to secondary circular reactions that entail some appropriate form of action, infants may display manual behaviors that are suited to the features of the object. In some instances, infants may indicate that they recognize an object by demonstrating appropriate actions but in an abbreviated form—for example, outlining the movement of striking upon seeing a hanging rattle. Although Piaget's observations of this type of recognitory assimilation involve instances in which his children see rather than handle a familiar stimulus, the children nevertheless evidence recognition through appropriate manual behaviors.

Taken together, these Stage 3 phenomena suggest that in certain circumstances, manual behaviors appear to be tailored to the objects' characteristics. But in a larger sense, appropriate manipulation is restricted. When it does occur, it is limited to objects, familiar or unfamiliar, in which appropriate behaviors were initially discovered by chance.

During the fourth period of sensorimotor development, roughly from 8 to 12 months, object exploration changes in an important way. Infants are no longer using novel objects as "aliments" for familiar schemes; rather, they try to determine which of their familiar schemes is most suited to the object that they are exploring. Piaget describes this change in the following way:

> Not only does he look at such objects for a much longer time than the 4- to 5-month-old child before proceeding to acts, but furthermore, he engages in an ensemble of exploratory movements relating to the object and not to himself. He feels, explores the surface, the edges, turns over and slowly displaces, etc., and the last behavior patterns are very significant of a new attitude. The unfamiliar obviously represents to the child an external reality, to which he must adapt himself and no longer a substance which is pliable at will or a simple aliment for the activity itself. Finally comes the application of habitual schemata to this reality. But in trying out each of his schemata in turn, the child at this stage gives more the impression of making an experiment than of generalizing his behavior patterns: He tries to "understand." (Piaget, 1952, pp. 258–259)

Although infants are not intentionally inventing new schemes to deal with novel objects at this point, the advances that have occurred increase the likelihood of infants manipulating objects in an appropriate fashion.

During this period as well, infants begin to combine two familiar schemes together in a means-end fashion. This advance is usually discussed in terms of the onset of truly intentional behavior. But it also results in instances in which infants begin to *relate* objects appropriately in a truly intentional manner. The following observation illustrates this development:

> By manipulating a tin of shaving cream he [Laurent] learned, at 0;10 (2) to let this object fall intentionally. Now, at 0;10 (3) I give it to him again. He at once begins to open his hand to make it fall and repeats this behavior a certain number of times. I then place, 15 cm. from Laurent, a large wash basin and strike the interior of it with the tin in order to make Laurent hear the sound of the metal against this object. It is noteworthy that Laurent, already at 0;9 (0), had, while being washed, by chance struck a small pot against such a basin and immediately played at reproducing this sound by a simple circular reaction. I therefore wanted to see if Laurent was going to use the tin to repeat the phenomenon and how he was going to go about it.

> Now, at once, Laurent takes possession of the tin, holds out his arm and drops it over the basin. I moved the latter, as a check. He nevertheless succeeded, several times in succession, in making the object fall on the basin. Hence this is a fine example of the coordination of two schemata of which the first serves as "means" whereas the second assigns an end to the action: the schema of "relinquishing the object" and that of "striking one object against another." (Piaget, 1952, p. 225)

Thus even though infants in this period are not intentionally inventing novel schemes to deal with novel objects or situations, they do combine familiar schemes in a novel manner. And in doing so, they begin relating objects appropriately.

Viewed together, Piaget's observations suggest that by the end of the first year, infants manipulate objects with greater frequency and diversity. Even more importantly, infants attempt to discover which of their available schemes are most suited to the object that they are handling. Infants also begin to relate objects together, sometimes appropriately, with the limitation that these relations are based on the novel combination of familiar schemes.

Research on Object Manipulation Using a Piagetian Perspective

Research on object manipulation that has emanated from a Piagetian perspective has been primarily concerned with examining three related claims—namely (1) the age-related increase in the diversity and specificity of manual schemes, (2) the sequential progression of developments within the somewhat wider domain of schemes for relating to objects, and (3) the stagelike nature of sensorimotor development. Additionally, researchers have also investigated the role of environmental experience in the development of many Piagetian achievements involving object manipulation.

Many of these concerns are reflected in the research underlying attempts to formulate developmental scales from Piaget's original observations. Within the domain of schemes for relating to objects, Užgiris (1967) reported an age-related increase both in the diversity of available manual schemes and the specificity with which they are applied. Some of these schemes are present early in development and go through a period of indiscriminate use before they are applied selectively. Others do not go through an initial period of indiscriminate use but emerge later out of attempts to adapt to the features of the particular object being handled. Overall, infants move from treating all objects similarly to treating objects in a selective manner based on objects' physical characteristics and somewhat later, their social significance (Užgiris, 1967).

An important question that arises from Piaget's work concerns whether the sequence of developments in the domain of object manipulation is an invariant one. This question is difficult to answer for a number of reasons. First, there is no single scale derived from Piaget's sensorimotor observations that encompasses all of his observations on object manipulation. His observations on object manipulation are often divided amongst several scales that assess this capacity in one form or another (e.g., see Kopp, Sigman, & Parmelee, 1974; Užgiris & Hunt, 1975). Perhaps the closest assessment of object manipulation as conceptualized in this chapter can be found in Užgiris and Hunt's (1975) scale of schemes for relating to objects. But even here the match is not perfect as some nonmanual schemes are included in the scale and some involving relating objects are not.

A second difficulty concerns the developmental distance between items on various sensorimotor scales. Adjacent steps within some of these scales sometimes correspond to achievements within the same stage. In light of this fact, failure to find perfect evidence for certain expected sequences must be interpreted with caution.

A final difficulty concerns the level at which such invariance is assessed. As Užgiris (1983) has emphasized, Piaget has claimed an invariant order for the sensorimotor stages, not for the individual tasks that are selected to index a given stage. Performance on individual tasks may vary from day to day before stage consolidation has been achieved.

Despite these problems, researchers have investigated whether achievements within a given sensorimotor domain (however defined) are acquired in an invariant order. For the domain of object manipulation, perhaps the most relevant findings involve Užgiris and Hunt's (1975) series concerning schemes for relating to objects. Užgiris and Hunt reported that items in this series constitute an ordinal scale (Green's Index of Consistency = .80), although this scale relative to their six other sensorimotor scales had the lowest consistency index. Additionally, they found that scores on the scheme scale increased as infants progressed through the sensorimotor stages. However, it should be noted that these findings are not based on observations of the same infants during the entire period spanned by the scale. Somewhat different results might emerge with longitudinal observations. Nevertheless, the existing evidence suggests that items composing Užgiris and Hunt's schemes series, many of which involve object manipulation, satisfy the statistical requirements for an ordinal scale. However, some minor variations in this sequence are possible in individual infants, perhaps as a function of achievements within a stage becoming consolidated.

More generally, investigators have also asked whether developments in the sensorimotor period emerge in a stagelike manner. Despite unresolved issues concerning the definition of a sensorimotor domain and the points at which congruence should be expected, investigators have looked for evidence of developmental synchrony during the sensorimotor period. With reference to the domain of object manipulation, the most relevant evidence can again be found in Užgiris and Hunt's (1975) work. When scale scores on the schemes series were related to scale scores on each of their other series (with age partialled out), only low to moderate correlations were obtained (.12 to .61). These lower than expected correlations might be due in part to the unequal distances between steps on the different scales (Užgiris & Hunt, 1975). Whatever the reasons, it seems clear that the previously noted definitional and conceptual problems need to be overcome before the issue can be resolved.

Research on various sensorimotor skills including object manipulation has also been concerned with the role of experience in the ontogenesis of these skills, especially how different environmental characteristics influence their rate of development. Although the rationale for this research is often discussed within a Piagetian framework, in one sense it does not directly follow. Questions of rate are of secondary importance for Piaget. Yet as some have argued, to the extent that sensorimotor achievements are constructed from appropriate environmental experiences, the rate of sensorimotor development should vary as a function of such experiences.

To investigate this possibility, researchers have studied the impact of the physical and social environment on the rate of acquisition of various sensorimotor skills. Before selective research regarding environmental effects on the development of object manipulation is examined, several points are worth noting. In this work, object manipulation is typically assessed in the context of the infant's solitary activity, possibly because of the Piagetian framework that has implicitly guided many of these investigations. Piaget's descriptions of course primarily deal with his infants manipulating objects on their own, although Piaget was an active participant during many of these observations. Additionally, Piaget emphasized structural change in the activity of the infant rather than in the joint activity of parent and child. Nor was he directly concerned with the influence of situational or contextual variables on the execution of various sensorimotor behaviors. Even when contemporary researchers have looked at the impact of the social environment on object manipulation as well as other sensorimotor skills, these biases are still evident. Direct comparisons, for example, of how these skills develop and are executed in social and nonsocial contexts, as would be expected from a Vygotskyian perspective, are rare.

Nevertheless, research using a Piagetian conceptualization of object manipulation (as indexed by Užgiris and Hunt's scale of scheme development) has indicated that characteristics of the physical and social environments are related to the development of this skill. With regard to the impact of the physical environment on scheme development, research by Wachs (1979) and findings reviewed by Wachs and Gruen (1982) indicate that in the second year of life, scheme development is positively related to the addition of new toys, the richness of the environment (as indexed by the audiovisual responsivity of available toys), the regularity of the environment (as indexed by the scheduling of meals), and negatively related to the amount of noise confusion in the home. Some of these findings pertain to particular periods during the second year and vary according to the sex of the child.

During the first year, there is also evidence that scheme development is related to characteristics of the physical environment. Hunt, Mohandessi, Ghodssi, and Akiyama (1976), working with orphaned infants in an institution, found that enriching the physical environment (through audiovisual stimulation and opportunities to manipulate materials) as compared to reducing the ratio between infants and untrained caregivers led to improved performance on the intermediate steps of the schemes scale—that is, on those items dealing primarily with object manipulation. These findings are in agreement with those of Yarrow, Rubenstein, and Pedersen (1975) who found that at 6 months of age, performance on measures that included assessments of object manipulation was correlated with the responsivity, complexity, and variety of inanimate toys in the environment.

Research on the influence of the social environment on the rate of development of object manipulation skills (using Piagetian indexes) also indicates some significant relationships. As was the case before, this evidence is somewhat indirect in that the most relevant measures that are employed do not simply involve object manipulation but rather items that assess scheme development in general. Nevertheless, work by Wachs (1984) indicates that during parts of the second year, the level of scheme development in males was related to some rather specific aspects of the language environment; for females the pattern was somewhat different and less clear. The finding that aspects of the linguistic environment predict scheme development in the second year, however, may reflect the fact that some of the higher level items on the schemes scale involve the naming of objects. When more direct measures of object manipulation have been employed, positive correlations have been found between level of scheme development between the first and second years and a factor identified as optimal maternal care (Clarke-Stewart, 1973).

During the first year, there is also some suggestive evidence that progress in object manipulation is related to characteristics of the social environment. Hunt *et al.* (1976), in their work with institutionalized infants, found that when the infant–caregiver ratio was reduced *and* training was provided for these caregivers, infants showed gains in achieving the intermediate and top steps on the Užgiris and Hunt schemes scale. Additionally during the first half year of life, level and variety of social stimulation and physical contact stimulation, especially kinesthetic-vestibular stimulation, appear related to progress on several developmental indexes, some of which include measures of object manipulation (Wachs & Gruen, 1982; Yarrow *et al.*, 1975). Although these findings suggest that scheme development and possibly more specifically, object manipulation, are influenced by characteristics of the social environment, the mechanism(s) by which these factors exert their influence is by no means clear.

Together, these findings suggest that certain characteristics of the physical and social environment are related to the rate of development of object manipulation skills. However, it should be borne in mind that the demonstrated relationships are primarily correlational in nature. All the caveats about inferring causation from correlation apply. Even when research designs have involved the experimental manipulation of environmental conditions (Hunt *et al.*, 1976), it is difficult to determine which features of the intervention program either in isolation or combination resulted in the reported gains. A further difficulty compounding the interpretation of these early experience studies involves the assessment of object manipulation skills. Rather than assessing object manipulation in its own right, investigators have typically used composite measures that assess the more general domain of scheme development. And even when more direct measures of object manipulation have been obtained, contextual variables have not always been taken into account. Either assessment has occurred in the context of the infant's solitary activity, or little distinction has been made between object manipulation that occurs in social and nonsocial contexts. Not surprisingly, changes in the nature of parent–child object manipulation during the first year have not been described in detail. These practices may in part stem from a Piagetian perspective of sensorimotor development that emphasizes structural changes in the infant's solitary activities rather than the actual functioning and operation of these activities.

The Gibsons' Theory

A quite different perspective on the development of object manipulation can be found in the work of the Gibsons on perception and perceptual development (E. J. Gibson, 1982, 1984; J. J. Gibson, 1966, 1979). Unlike other theories that suggest that perception is indirect— that is, constructed from impoverished sensory inputs, the Gibsons' ecological approach holds that perception is based on picking up invariant information that *directly* specifies environmentally relevant features. Organisms actively seek this information through perceptual systems that have evolved for this purpose.

A key aspect of the Gibsons' ecological approach is that it stresses the mutuality of the perceiving animal and its environment. This mutuality is embodied in the notion that perception involves registering the affordances of an environment. Affordances refer to what the environment "offers the animal, what it provides or furnishes, either for good or ill" (J. J. Gibson, 1979, p. 127). As such, they concern the utility of environmental features like layout, objects, or events—but importantly, in relation to the animal.

The affordance notion links perception and action in a way that is different from other theories of perception and perceptual development. As a result, it has important implications for discussions of object manipulation. Other accounts, notably Piaget's, suggest that perceptual knowing is somehow constructed from the results of actions, often manipulative activity. The Gibsonian view, however, holds that perception and action mutually guide one another; neither is "prior" to the other (E. J. Gibson, 1984, 1985). Perception involves picking up affordances for action, but this in turn requires actively searching for information in the environment. Developmentally, even very young infants probably possess this coordinated ability through certain preadapted systems. With age, however, children become increasingly able to differentiate information for affordances in the environment, partly as the result of more developed exploratory skills (E. J. Gibson, 1984; Gibson & Spelke, 1983).

From this perspective, manipulation may be viewed as an important means of seeking information about affordances in the environment. As such, the *development* of manipulation is of interest for a number of reasons. Object-*appropriate* manipulation can indicate whether affordances have been perceived and relatedly, whether affordances have been differentiated by specific manual behaviors. Generally speaking, the presence of appropriate behaviors implies the perception of affordances (E. J. Gibson, 1982).

The development of manipulation can also be studied to examine more general questions about the relationship between the maturation of action modes and the perception of affordances. As new modes of action develop, new ways of obtaining information for affordances become available (E. J. Gibson, 1982). In some instances, the availability of an action mode may influence whether certain affordances are perceived. For example, the locomotor status (crawling or walking) of infants appears to determine whether some surfaces of support are perceived as being traversable (Gibson, Riccio, Schmuckler, Stoffregen, Rosenberg, & Taormina, 1987). In other instances, new modes of action may entail some new affordances. Manipulation, for example, may enable objects to function in some hitherto novel ways. In general, then, newly emerging modes of action may be studied to examine how they come to be used to detect affordances, how they influence which affordances are detected, and, possibly, how new affordances are learned. Manipulatory behaviors are ideal for studying these developmental issues because they mature relatively late, becoming skilled during the second half year of life.

There has been a considerable amount of recent research on the early perception of affordances, some of it directly concerned with object manipulation. In addition, many previous investigations of object manipulation have been reevaluated within the affordance framework (E. J. Gibson 1982, 1984; Gibson & Spelke, 1983). In the more recent investigations that have been directly concerned with the perception of affordances, two general research strategies may be discerned. One involves presenting infants with some ecologically meaningful display (usually an object, surface, or event) and determining whether infants act appropriately in relation to it. As noted, appropriate behaviors can indicate which affordances have been differentiated by which behaviors (E. J. Gibson, 1982). This strategy is illustrated in a recent report by Gibson and Walker (1984) in which infants' perception of the affordance of substance was studied. In one experiment, they found that 12-month-olds displayed more striking with rigid objects and more pressing and squeezing with spongy ones. In other words, manipulation was appropriate, suggesting that the affordance of substance was perceived.

The other strategy for investigating the perception of affordances is less direct and involves examining infants' appreciation of intermodal relations in events that imply the perception of affordances. Infants are presented an object or event in one modality, and their ability to recognize this object or event in another modality is then tested. To the extent that intermodal correspondences are detected, meaningful perception is indicated, implying the perception of affordances. Gibson and Walker (1984) also employed this method to investigate the perception of the affordance of substance. Using otherwise identical objects that were either hard or soft, they found that 1-month-olds preferred to look at the novel substance (specified by differentiating motions) following oral haptic familiarization with the other substance. Related designs have been used to demonstrate that older infants can detect intermodal invariants by manipulating and observing objects (Gibson & Walker, 1984).

In experiments like these that have been directly concerned with the perception of affordances, infants are typically studied in the context of their own exploratory and perceptual activities. Even when the affordances of social stimuli or situations have been investigated (Walker, 1982), the focus of the work has been on how infants alone explore and perceive the social world. Yet if we were to examine how infants obtain information about their environments outside the laboratory setting, it would become clear that they often do so in the context of joint activity with their caregivers. Parents frequently guide infants' activities and highlight information that is available in the environment. Examining the role that parents play in helping infants seek information should not be viewed as being inconsistent with a Gibsonian perspective—especially given its ecological approach. To date, however, most investigations of perceptual development, including ones on object manipulation that have employed a Gibsonian perspective, have not examined these kinds of contextual variables.

In trying to relate parents' activities to those of their infants within a Gibsonian framework, it would be a mistake to think that parents add something to the environmental stimulation that enables infants to perceive the affordance in question. Rather, parents by virtue of their actions may highlight information *already available* in the environment, by focusing or guiding their infants' activity or demonstrating appropriate behaviors. For example, when parents help infants manipulate objects by guiding their infants' fingers over a surface, information about that object is being made more accessible. In many such instances, the parents' activities reflect selectivity, economy, and specificity—just those characteristics that describe a mature perceiver. Investigating the role that parents play in the development of infants' skills for perceiving affordances may provide insights into how these skills are perfected and perhaps how some new affordances are learned.

Although the Piagetian and Gibsonian approaches have not emphasized the role of the social context in the development of sensorimotor skills, there already exists a body of work that has considered this issue (Bruner, 1982; Kaye, 1982; Rogoff & Werstch, 1984; Werstch, 1979). In many respects, this work represents an extension of ideas put forth by Soviet psychologists on the ontogenesis of higher mental functions. According to this Soviet view, the origins of these abilities can be found in social life, especially in the interactions of children with adults and peers. Vygotsky (1978) maintained that children master many cognitive abilities by initially exercising them in the context of social interaction. Joint cognitive activity with more experienced members of the culture enables less experienced members to carry out processes that they otherwise would be unable to complete on their own. Gradually, the regulation supplied by these more experienced members is internalized, enabling the children to exercise these activities individually.

Vygotsky did not directly concern himself with the social origins of skills in the infancy period; his analysis of cognitive growth extends down to the preschool years. However, a number of Western investigators have recently applied this perspective to the sensorimotor period. Like Vygotsky, these investigators have also stressed the social origins of many sensorimotor skills, detailing the strategies that parents employ that gradually enable infants to exercise a skill independently from start to finish. Kaye (1982), for example, has described the "frames" or interactional modes that parents adopt while their infants are learning and consolidating a skill. As learning progresses, parents relinquish more and more control of the skill to their infants. Relatedly, Bruner (1982) has suggested that infants master many object skills during the course of interaction with their caregivers. Caregivers often promote skill development by "scaffolding" their infants' activities, adjusting their own contribution to the task, depending upon their infants' skill level. Mastery of these skills, however, should not be simply viewed as the result of parental tutelage but also as the result of infants' preparedness to be responsive to such efforts.

Despite the increased interest in questions concerning the social origins of many sensorimotor skills, this issue has only been investigated for a limited number of perceptuomotor abilities with infants under a year of age. Researchers have looked at how skills like detour reaching (Kaye, 1982) and uncovering an object (Hodapp, Goldfield, & Boyatzis, 1984) emerge and are exercised during the course of joint activity with the caregiver. In some instances, infants may perform certain skills (returning or uncovering an object in games with the mother) before performing comparable skills alone (Hodapp et al., 1984). Yet for a skill as basic as object manipulation, little is known about its social origins. Although it is clear that parents often help infants while they manipulate objects, little attention has been given to what transpires during such joint activity or even how much time infants spend manipulating objects alone or with their caregivers. Work with infants over a year of age indicates that parents who have been encouraged to direct their children's attention to objects have children who demonstrate more advanced levels of object play during the second year (Belsky, Goode, & Most, 1980; Vondra & Belsky, Chapter 6 this volume). Such findings, however, highlight the need for careful descriptions of object exploration during the course of social interaction, especially in the first year. They also suggest that greater attention be given to the actual functioning and execution of manipulation across different situations.

Before we consider this issue by presenting some new evidence on the social origins of object manipulation, it is necessary to review what is currently known about the development of this skill. In surveying the existing literature on object manipulation in the first year, we have been guided by the following question: *When do infants begin to show differential and appropriate manual behaviors with an object that they are handling?* To answer this question, we have organized the literature along the following four dimensions: (1) the stimulus or object property under investigation, (2) the ages of the infants under investigation, (3) the context (social or nonsocial) in which infants manipulated objects, and (4) the types of manual behaviors that infants demonstrated. The review that we present is necessarily selective. We focus on objects in terms of what traditionally has been called their perceptual dimensions (e.g., shape, color, texture, etc.) rather than their conventional uses. Because of this focus on stimulus dimensions rather than sociocultural conventions, our definitions of appropriateness vary somewhat from previous investigations of object play (Fenson *et al.*, 1976). But as a result, we will be able to search for instances of appropriate behavior where previously they were likely to be overlooked. Additionally, we restrict our review to published findings at the time that this chapter was being written. There have been some recent and exciting reports suggesting that well before the end of the first year, infants manipulate objects differentially, relating their hand movements to an object's particular properties. Palmer (1985) has elegantly documented the diversity of infants' manipulatory behaviors even at 6 months, and Rochat (1985) has presented some preliminary evidence suggesting that newborns may differentially handle hard and soft objects. Undoubtedly, these reports and the review and research we subsequently present indicate that early in the second half year of life, if not before, infants are capable of manipulating objects appropriately.

Object-Appropriate Manipulation in the First Year

As we have already noted, although there are many good theoretical reasons to study the development of object-appropriate manipulation, or perhaps because of this, object manipulation has seldom been investigated as a topic in its own right. This has led to studies in which object characteristics and behavioral contexts have not been systematically varied, with manipulation described in terms of amount rather than type of activity. As a result, even though object manipulation has served as a dependent variable in many investigations, little can be clearly said about the variation of specific manual behaviors as a function of specific object properties or behavioral contexts during the first year.

The following review of research on early object manipulation is organized primarily with reference to those object properties that have been the focus of most empirical attention. It is important to recognize that in many of these investigations, the goal has not been to study how infants explore a specific object characteristic but rather whether infants detect novelty—that is, a change along a particular stimulus dimension. For our purposes, this practice limits the conclusions that can be drawn about the development of object appropriate manipulation in two important ways. First, because the emphasis in this work has been on the detection of novelty, investigators have typically measured changes in the *amount* rather than the *type* of manipulation that infants display. Second, in these novelty studies, variation along a dimension has typically occurred *between*, rather than *within* trials and hence across objects, not within objects. Variation occurring between trials may not be the most sensitive means for investigating how infants gather information about a dimension or different values of it. Besides the obvious drawback of a memory component in many novelty paradigms, the presence of only one dimensional value within an object may lead to reduced and somewhat limited forms of exploration. However, using single objects that vary along different values of a given dimension (for example, an object with different colored sides) may provide a more sensitive means of investigating manual exploration of that dimension.

With these precautions in mind, we now examine evidence on the development of object-appropriate manipulation, focusing on those dimensions that have been the subject of most empirical attention.

Color

At first glance, we might wonder whether infants should vary any of their manipulatory behaviors to gain information about an object's color. Color, after all, is a visual characteristic. If color evokes any type of exploratory behavior, it should be primarily visual in nature. However, some have suggested that to the extent that the visual and manipulatory exploratory systems are linked, visual modes of exploration should give rise to manual ones as well (Bushnell, 1981). Although the exact nature of these manual behaviors has not often been specified, researchers have investigated whether manipulation and visual inspection are linked as infants gather information about an object's color.

Representative studies on infants' manual exploration of an object's color are presented in Table 1. The table highlights several important aspects of these investigations: (1) the age range of the subjects, (2) the relevant behaviors that serve as dependent variables, (3) the context in which these behaviors were studied, and (4) the findings that pertain to the development of object-appropriate manipulation.

Most of the studies in Table 1 have been concerned with questions about the linkage between the visual and manual exploratory systems, especially with the point in development when infants first manifest such coordinated activity (Pederson, Steele, & Klein, 1980; Schaffer & Parry, 1969, 1970; Steele & Pederson, 1977). In these investigations, a novelty detection paradigm has often been employed. Infants explore an object during a familiarization period; a dimension (color) of the object is then changed, and infants' subsequent exploratory attempts are noted. These studies tend to show that in response to a color change, infants younger than 8 months exhibit only an increase in looking. By contrast, infants older than 8 months behave concordantly, showing an increase in both looking and manipulation (see also Bushnell, 1981, for a review of this work).

In the subsequent experimental work, investigators have gone beyond recording global measures of manipulation (amount or latency to) and have examined *how* infants use the manipulatory system to respond to a color change. Pederson *et al.* (1980) employed this strategy to investigate the types of manual behaviors that infants use to explore a color change. In the most relevant condition, 6-month-olds were familiarized with a singly colored object over the course of seven trials. On the eighth and ninth trials, infants were exposed to a novel object that differed from the previous one only in color. Both looking and types of manual behaviors were measured (see Table 1). Pederson *et al.* (1980) reported that in response to a color change, 6-month-olds increased their looking time but none of their manual behaviors, a finding consistent with previous results on the lack of concordance between visual and manual exploration at this age.

In summary, the preceding findings suggest that infants do not use the manipulatory system to explore color changes before 8 months. After 8 months, when infants do use the visual and manipulatory systems concordantly for this purpose, the findings only indicate that infants increase their manipulative activity, not *how* they do so. Additional work is needed to describe the manual actions that infants actually em-

TABLE 1
Representative Studies on Infant Manual Exploration of Color

Study	Age range	Behaviors	Context	Findings
Schaffer & Parry (1969)	6 and 12 months	Looking, manipulation	Infant-object	Color change—greater looking and no increase in latency to manipulate (6 mo.)—nonsignificant increase in latency to manipulate (12 mos.)
Schaffer & Parry (1970)	5–7, 8–10, and 11–13 months	Looking, manipulation	Infant-object	Color change—only greater looking (5–7 mos.)—greater looking and manipulation (8–10, 11–13 mos.)
Steele & Pederson (1977)	6 months	Looking, manipulation	Infant-object	Color change—greater looking, no change in manipulation
Pederson, Steele, & Klein (1980)	6 months	Looking, touching, pulling, banging, mouthing, turning, circular reactions, holding	Infant-object	Color change—greater looking, no significant increase in active manual behaviors (significant decrease)

ploy to explore the color of an object. Further, our knowledge of this manual ability needs to be supplemented in other important ways. One limitation of previous work concerns how color variation has been operationalized. Because investigators have employed a detection of novelty paradigm, color has been varied *between* trials and hence across objects, not within objects. Even when objects with simple colored patterns (e.g., a red object with two yellow stripes) have been used (Steele & Pederson, 1977), the colored pattern was apparently distributed uniformly across the object, possibly leading to reduced levels of manipulation. Object surfaces that are characterized by different color values distributed in a nonuniform fashion across the object (e.g., an object with different colored sides) might lead to manipulation that is greater in degree and kind, even in infants younger than 8 months.

Another limitation of this previous research has been the context in which manipulation has been studied. In virtually all of the controlled work on manual exploration of color changes, infants have explored objects by themselves. It is not clear how the presence of caregivers, supporting their infants' activities, would influence exploration by infants.

Until these limitations are addressed, conclusions about the early use of the manipulatory system to gather information about color should be viewed with caution.

Shape/Texture

Shape and texture are object characteristics that may be specified through vision and/or touch. Because information about shape and texture can be gained by looking and by manipulating an object, some investigators have asked when do infants begin to use both exploratory systems for this purpose in a concordant manner (Pederson *et al.*, 1980; Schaffer & Parry, 1969, 1970; Steele & Pederson, 1977). We will consider these and other relevant findings to examine the types of manual adjustments that infants at different ages make for shape and texture. Representative studies are presented in Table 2.

As was the case with color, most research on manual exploration of shape and texture has been conducted within a detection of novelty framework. To determine how infants respond to each of these components separately, Steele and Pederson (1977) presented 6-month-olds with novel objects that differed from familiar ones in terms of either their shape or texture. Infants exhibited an increase in manipulation to a change in shape and an even greater increase to a change in texture.

TABLE 2
Representative Studies on Infant Manual Exploration of Texture/Shape

Study	Age range	Behaviors	Context	Findings
Steele & Pederson (1977)	6 months	Looking, manipulation	Infant-object	Shape and/or texture change—greater looking and manipulation
Pederson, Steele, & Klein (1980)	6 months	Active haptic behaviors (pulling, touching, banging, mouthing, turning); passive holding; looking	Infant-object	Shape and/or texture change—greater active exploration (and looking) to texture change; nonsignificant increase in active exploration to shape change
Ruff (1984)	6, 9, and 12 months	Looking, handling, mouthing, alternating, rotating, fingering, transferring, banging	Infant-object	Texture—greater fingering with age, less mouthing, less transferring relative to patterned objects
Ruff (1984)	9 and 12 months	Looking, fingering, rotation, transferring, mouthing, banging, dropping	Infant-object	(a) Texture change—increase looking and fingering; decrease dropping, throwing, pushing (b) Shape change—increase looking, fingering, rotating (12 mos.), transferring; decrease dropping, throwing, pushing

These findings suggest that 6-month-olds can use manipulation differentially to respond to changes in shape or texture—changes that have tactual as well as visual consequences.

The preceding studies indicate that 6-month-olds employ manipulation to explore a shape or texture change, but they do not indicate *how* infants do so. To address this issue, Pederson *et al.* (1980) used a similar novelty design, experimentally isolating shape and texture, *and* provided a much finer description of the manipulation behaviors that 6-month-olds displayed. These infants showed a significant increase in active exploration (pulling, touching, banging, mouthing, and turning) to a change in texture and a nonsignificant increase in active exploration to a change in shape. (It is not clear, however, from the Pederson *et al.* (1980) report whether each of the behaviors making up the active exploration category increased significantly.)

Ruff (1984) also provided a more detailed account of 6- to 12-month-olds' manual responses to a change in texture or shape. In one experiment, 6-, 9-, and 12-month-olds were familiarized with a series of objects in which either texture or a painted pattern was invariant across the series. In the invariant texture series, cubes of different colors shared the same surface texture, consisting of bumps or depressions. In the invariant pattern series, objects of different shapes shared the same painted pattern—either stripes or crosses. Ruff's results indicated that infants differentially manipulated the two series. In the invariant texture series, infants evidenced manual behaviors that seemed appropriate for the invariant characteristic—in this case, texture. In particular, infants exhibited more fingering of the textured series than the patterned one. For the invariant pattern series, infants seemed to be responding more to the stimulus characteristic that was changing from trial to trial—in this case, shape. Infants exhibited more mouthing and transferring of objects from one hand to another with this series, actions that appear to be more appropriate for gaining information about shape. Although fingering increased with age, the absence of reported interactions involving age and type of series suggests that infants adjusted their manual behaviors in a similar fashion at all three age levels.

In a follow-up experiment, Ruff (1984) directly examined how infants adjust their manual behaviors as a function of the object property being explored. Infants at 9 and 12 months were familiarized with an object, and then either the shape, texture, or weight of the object was changed during a test period. In general, infants displayed manual behaviors that were suited for exploring a texture or shape change. Relative to a no-change control group, the texture change elicited a marginally significant increase in fingering but not rotation; the shape change elicited a marginally significant increase in fingering and a significant increase in rotation; the weight change did not elicit a significant increase in any of the measured manual behaviors. In analyses comparing the measured manual behaviors across test trials, related findings were obtained. Most notably, infants showed the greatest hand-to-hand transferring and rotation in the shape-change condition, although the increase in rotation was only apparent at 12 months. Taken together, Ruff's results suggest that by 9 months and possibly at 6 months, infants do explore the properties of texture and shape with differential manual behaviors. Infants use fingering to explore a texture change; they also use hand transfer and somewhat later rotation to explore a shape change.

Overall, the evidence that has been reviewed suggests that there is at least a tendency for infants even by 6 months to use different patterns of manual behaviors to explore texture and shape changes. Infants primarily employ fingering to explore texture changes; they use fingering increasingly for this purpose by the end of the first year. In contrast, to explore shape changes, infants employ either hand-to-hand transfer, rotation, and/or sometimes fingering. The actual patterns of manipulation used for this purpose vary with age. Infants demonstrate hand-to-hand transfer to explore shape changes even at 6 months; however, they do not employ rotation for this purpose until sometime between 9 and 12 months.

Research on infants' manual adjustments to shape and texture can be supplemented in two important ways. First, stronger evidence concerning the use of fingering to explore texture at 6 and 9 months might be obtained by varying textures *within* an object. With texture varying this way, increased levels of rotation might also occur. Second, studies of infants' exploration of shape and texture must be expanded to situations involving joint activity with the caregiver. In all of the reviewed work, infants manipulated objects independently, by themselves. Infants might evidence different patterns and possibly more appropriate levels of manual activity when they explore objects jointly with more skilled familiar partners.

Rigidity/Flexibility

Investigators have also been concerned with the types of manual adjustments that infants make while exploring objects that are either flexible or rigid. Flexible objects in relation to rigid ones might elicit greater fingering, squeezing, pulling and so on—actions that in some way exploit the potential to deform these objects. Rigid objects, on the other hand, by virtue of not yielding to deforming motions, are perhaps better suited for striking against another surface.

Representative studies on infants' manual adjustments based on the rigidity/flexibility of an object are presented in Table 3. McCall (1974) was one of the first investigators to investigate systematically infants' manual exploration of the rigidity/flexibility dimension. Although only global measures of manipulation with visual regard were recorded, Mc-Call (1974) found that 8-, 10-, and 11½-month-olds exhibited greater amounts of manipulation with more flexible objects. No effects of age were obtained. In a related experiment, 9½-month-olds were found to manipulate a toy more often as its plasticity increased.

In later work, investigators have directed more attention to the types of manipulatory behaviors that infants use when handling rigid or flexible objects. Gibson and Walker (1984) observed that 12-month-olds exhibit more pressing of soft objects and more striking with hard ones, suggesting that by 1 year, infants are detecting these affordances and are acting appropriately. Interestingly, these differences were most pronounced when infants manipulated objects in the dark.

With younger infants, Pederson et al. (1980) conducted a longitudinal study observing infants at 6 and 8 months of age. During each testing session, infants were presented with three toys, one at a time; the toys varied in flexibility but were otherwise identical. For the most part, infants at both age levels displayed more conjoint looking and touching and pulling of the most flexible toy. Passive holding, in contrast, increased as the toys became less flexible. With somewhat different stimuli that varied in terms of flexibility (as well as sound potential), Pederson et al. (1980) also found that 6-month-olds increased their fingering as the object became more flexible.

Taken together, these findings suggest that even by 6 months, infants vary their manipulative behaviors appropriately, according to the flexibility or conversely, rigidity of an object. Depending on how flexibility has been operationalized, infants show either greater conjoint touching and looking, fingering, pulling, or pressing of more flexible objects. In contrast, rigid objects seem to elicit either passive holding or striking, at least at 12 months (Gibson & Walker, 1984). Although the available evidence suggests that there is little developmental change in the patterns of manual behaviors that infants apply when handling rigid or flexible objects, there has not really been enough work using similar definitions of flexibility/rigidity over a wide enough age range to offer a complete developmental account. Additionally, as has been the case

TABLE 3
Representative Studies on Infant Manual Exploration of Rigidity/Flexibility

Study	Age range	Behaviors	Context	Findings
McCall (1974)	8½, 10, and 11½ months 9½ months	Visually guided manipulation	Infant-object	Flexibility—greater manipulation Flexibility—greater manipulation
Pederson, Steele, & Klein (1980)	6 and 8 months	Looking, touching, conjoint looking and touching, fingering, mouthing, pulling, passive holding	Infant-object	Flexibility—greater looking, conjoint looking and touching, pulling, rigidity—greater passive holding
Gibson & Walker (1984)	12 months	Presses, throws/drops, touches, strikes, holds, holds and looks, rotates looks	Infant-object	Flexibility—greater pressing; rigidity—greater striking

with the previous object characteristics that have been reviewed, infants' handling of flexible and rigid objects has been studied by having infants explore such objects on their own. It is not clear how caregivers help infants gain such information about objects or how joint exploration affects the type of manipulation that infants display.

Sound Potential

Sound potential refers to the extent to which appropriate manipulation of an object produces a sound (McCall, 1974). Depending on the nature of the object, audible noise could be produced by striking or banging it against a surface or by shaking the object if it contains a rattle. Sometimes flexible objects also have the potential to make noise as is the case with an object on a tightly wound spring (Pederson *et al.*, 1980). In many instances, therefore, rigidity and sound potential and sometimes flexibility and sound potential are naturally confounded. Consequently, it is difficult to make conclusions about the exploration of an object's sound potential without also considering the rigidity/flexibility dimension as well. In principle, however, it is possible to unconfound these dimensions, and some attempts have been made to do so. In the following section, we consider research on how infants explore the sound potential of objects. Representative studies are presented in Table 4.

Some of the work contained in Table 4 has been previously reviewed in the rigidity/flexibility section. According to these findings, infants at 6 months spend more time actively manipulating and touching a (flexible) toy that has the potential to make noise; in contrast, they exhibit greater passive holding of a (rigid) toy without this potential (Pederson *et al.*, 1980). Also at 12 months, infants show more striking with a hard or rigid object than with a soft one (Gibson & Walker, 1984).

In these studies, sound potential was not always isolated from the rigidity/flexibility dimension. McCall (1974) attempted to isolate these dimensions from one another and found that infants at 8½ and 11½ months and boys at 10 months showed increased visually guided manipulation with sound-producing objects. Other than this research, there have been few investigations that have been directly concerned with infants' manual exploration of sound producing objects.

The research that has been reviewed highlights some of the problems in making conclusions about infants' manual exploration of an object's sound potential. Because sound potential has been operationalized in different ways, different manual behaviors become appro-

TABLE 4
Representative Studies on Infant Manual Exploration of Sound Potential

Study	Age range	Behaviors	Context	Findings
McCall (1974)	8½, 10, and 11½ months	Manipulation	Infant-object	Sound potential—greater manipulation by all infants at 8½ and 11½ months, greater manipulation by boys at 10 months
Pederson, Steele, & Klein (1980)	6 months	Touching, conjoint looking and touching, finger and hand movements, holding	Infant-object	Sound potential (flexibility)—greater touching, conjoint looking and touching, finger and hand movements
Walker & Gibson (1984)	12 months	Pressing, striking, throws/drops, touches	Infant-object	Sound potential—greater striking

priate for producing noise. A more complete developmental account might be obtained by focusing on the different types of manual actions that can be used to produce noise and asking when do infants begin to employ each of these actions for this purpose. Striking or banging might follow a different developmental course than shaking, although both are used to exploit an object's sound potential.

The present review indicates that there are gaps in our knowledge about the development of behaviors that infants use to produce noise with objects. Only a handful of studies have attempted to investigate this issue by systematically varying dimensions associated with sound potential. Additionally, work is needed that describes how these infant behaviors develop and function during the course of joint exploration with the caregiver. As has been emphasized, the studies reviewed here and in previous sections have all used a single context, that of infants exploring objects by themselves.

Summary

The preceding review yields several conclusions regarding the development of object-appropriate manipulation as well as avenues for future research. In general, investigators have moved from simply measuring amounts of manipulation to describing the types of manual behaviors that infants use to explore various object characteristics. Additionally, greater experimental control has been exercised in varying stimuli across specified dimensions. With these advances in measurement and design, conclusions about infant manual exploration of the following dimensions can be made: (1) Color: By 8 months infants use the manipulatory system to explore a color change. (2) Shape and texture: By 6 months, infants are using different patterns of manipulation to explore a change in shape and a change in texture. Fingering appears to be used to explore texture; hand-to-hand transfer is primarily used to explore shape. By 12 months, rotation is employed to explore shape as well. (3) Rigidity/flexibility: By 6 months infants also use different patterns of manipulation in exploring a flexible or rigid object. Although more pulling and fingering occurs with flexible objects, more passive holding occurs with rigid objects. By 12 months, infants are also likely to engage in pressing soft objects and striking with hard ones. (4) Sound potential: In the little work that has been conducted, the results suggest that by 8 months, possibly by 6 months, infants engage in greater manipulation of sound-producing objects. Because the rigidity/flexibility and sound potential dimensions are difficult to separate experimentally, it is not always clear which dimension(s) are guiding infants' actions.

Several avenues for future research have been identified as well. One concerns the way in which variation along a dimension has been operationalized. It was pointed out that in many studies—especially those designed to look at infants' exploration of color or texture—variation along a dimension has occurred primarily between trials and hence between objects rather than within objects. This might help explain why it has been difficult to demonstrate that infants younger than 8 months use the manipulatory system to explore color. Variation along a dimension within an object, however, might lead to earlier reports and/or more appropriate levels of manipulative activity for certain dimensions, especially color.

Future research efforts should also be concerned with describing *how* infants use the manipulatory system to explore various dimensions. Although finer descriptions of manual activities have been provided for the dimensions of texture, shape, and rigidity/flexibility, similar sorts of descriptions are needed for the dimensions of color and sound potential.

In addition to finer descriptions of these manual activities, researchers must also provide more complete descriptions of certain object dimensions. There are many ways, for example, to operationalize rigidity/flexibility or sound potential. Without considering these alternatives, we will lack a full understanding of the range of actions that infants can employ to explore these dimensions.

Finally, all the studies that have been reviewed have been restricted in one important sense. All have focused on a single behavioral context—that of infants acting independently, on their own. Little is known about the functioning of object manipulation in the context of joint activity with a caregiver, or relatedly, how such a joint context influences the level or type of exploration that infants manifest. Neglect of these contextual issues reflects a more general tradition in the object manipulation literature. Functional questions concerning the execution and operation of these manual behaviors have not often been addressed.

The preceding discussion suggests that in one way or another, the stimuli, responses, and contexts used in past work have limited the conclusions that can be drawn about the development of object appropriate manipulation. The work that we present next was designed to address some of these limitations by (1) varying objects systematically along specified perceptual dimensions, (2) describing the types of manipulative behaviors used by infants, and (3) contrasting manipulation in social and nonsocial contexts.

Infant and Maternal Manipulation of Objects

In this work, we examined how 6-, 8-, and 10-month-old infants, alone and together with their mothers, manipulate objects that systematically varied along the dimensions of either color, texture, or sound potential. The work was designed to address several of the problems that were raised after reviewing the object manipulation literature. First, in order to make statements about the appropriateness of manipulation, objects were varied systematically along salient perceptual dimensions. In addition, for some of the dimensions (color and texture), objects contained more than one value of the particular dimension. This was done to promote manual exploration of the given dimension. Second, we described the type rather than the amount of manipulation that infants displayed when exploring these dimensions. Finally, we varied the context in which infants manipulated objects—either jointly with their mothers or independently, by themselves. Our goals here were several. One was to determine how manipulation by infants actually varied in these two contexts. Another was to determine whether and how caregivers' actions were related to the objects that they explored with their infants. And finally, we were concerned with the issue of transfer. After having explored objects with their mothers, did infants show transfer of appropriate behaviors to a situation in which they explored similar objects alone? These contextual issues are of interest for a number of related reasons. They address questions about the actual functioning or operation of manipulation—that is, how situational variables influence the execution of this skill. They also are of interest because they provide an initial means of considering how social tutelage (Bruner, 1982; Kaye, 1982; Wood, 1980) contributes to the development of manipulation.

In the actual investigation, 72 infants (24 each at 6, 8, and 10 months) played with three different pairs of pyramid shaped objects: pairs with either different colors, textures, or sound potentials. The colored pyramids were constructed with alternating sides of red and green or blue and yellow; the textured pyramids with alternating sides of Velcro or different grades of sandpaper; and the sounding ones contained either a bell or grains of rice.

To investigate the contextual issues already outlined, half of each age group was assigned to a dyadic (Group D) or alone (Group A) condition. Group D infants played with their mothers with one object from each pair (Trial 1), then alone with the second object (Trial 2) for 1 minute each. This was repeated three times until infants played a minute each with the six objects. Group A infants received the same six objects but played alone on each Trial 1 and Trial 2. Sessions were videotaped, and the two observers scored infant and maternal behaviors in 5-second time-sampling intervals. Interobserver reliability was high, averaging 90% across maternal and infant behaviors.

In general the results indicated that infants as well as their mothers related their manual behaviors to the specific objects. Additionally for infants, some differential and beneficial effects of exploring objects in the context of joint activity with the caregiver were found. Each of these classes of results—infant, maternal, and contextual—is considered in more detail below.

Infant Behaviors

Infants, regardless of the context in which they participated, appropriately related their actions to the objects, in many cases even at 6 months. Different patterns of exploratory behaviors were found for the different dimensions. With the textured objects, infants at all age levels exhibited higher levels of fingering, rotation while looking, and visual regard of the object in hand. With the colored objects, infants at all age levels also exhibited higher levels of rotation while looking and visual regard of the object in hand but not fingering; in addition, they showed more sliding of these objects while looking at them. These manual behaviors all seem geared toward gaining information about the visual characteristics of the colored objects, even at 6 months. Finally, for the sounding objects, infants showed more shaking and banging. Here, however, age differences emerged. Six-month-olds did not display appropriate behaviors with the sounding objects. In contrast, 8- and 10-month-olds did show appropriate but different patterns of behaviors with these objects. Ten-month-olds shook the sounding object most frequently, whereas 8-month-olds engaged in more object-appropriate shaking than 6-month-olds. In contrast, 8-month-olds banged the sounding object more frequently than either of the other age groups or objects. In fact, neither the 10- nor 6-month-olds used banging in a differential fashion.

Taken together, these results provide some new information about the development of object-appropriate manipulation. The results suggest that by 6 months, infants display appropriate behaviors while exploring the dimensions of color and texture. Although previous studies have reported object-appropriate manipulation for texture at 6 months, the analogous achievement for color has been reported to occur around 8 months. However, in the present research, unlike previous work, variation along the color dimension occurred within stimuli. These results also provide additional information concerning how infants exploit the sound potential of objects and how this ability changes with age. Interestingly, although infants at 8 and 10 months manipulate sound-producing objects in an appropriate fashion, the patterns of actions differ at the two ages.

Maternal Behaviors

Mothers also appropriately related their behaviors to the objects, sometimes in subtle ways, even though they were simply instructed to play with their infants. With the textured objects, mothers exhibited more fingering, direction of their infants' fingers, and touching of their infants' skin. With the colored objects, they exhibited more pointing and rotation. With the sounding objects, they exhibited more shaking and mutual shaking (i.e., shaking the object jointly with their infants). These findings were consistent across mothers regardless of the infant's age. That mothers' actions are so consistently and appropriately related to the objects suggests that these behaviors may be an additional source of information about the objects for infants. Further, the fact that mothers actively engage their infants in some of these behaviors (active direction of fingers, mutual shaking) suggests that this might be an additional means by which infants can practice and perfect these skills. Some of the benefits of manipulating objects jointly with the caregiver are even more apparent when we consider the effects of context.

Context

In the present research, effects due to context can be investigated in two ways. One is to contrast how infants manipulate objects by themselves and with their caregivers. The other is to examine whether any effects due to context transfer to situations when infants subsequently explore objects alone.

Direct comparisons of infants' manipulatory behaviors during joint and independent activities can be made in the present research by contrasting infants' Trial 1 behaviors in the alone and dyad groups. These comparisons indicated that, in certain respects, the social context positively influenced infants' exploration. Infants who played with their mothers showed more focused exploration than infants who played alone. That is, they looked longer at objects while holding them. By comparison, infants playing alone exhibited more handling of the objects *without* looking at them. In addition, 8- and 10-month-old dyad infants fingered the textured object even more than similar aged infants who played alone. These findings suggest that infants benefit from jointly manipulating an object with their caregivers.

As for the issue of short-term transfer, we found little evidence that dyad infants exhibited higher levels of these behaviors when they explored objects alone on Trial 2. In fact, comparisons of dyad and alone infants on Trial 2 when they were handling similar objects revealed little difference in their manual behaviors. Thus under the present set of conditions, the benefits associated with social context were restricted to the social context itself.

To summarize, the results of this work indicate that by 6 months, infants will use the manipulatory system in appropriate ways to explore the color or texture of an object; by 8 months, they display appropriate manipulation of sounding objects. In addition, the present results also affirm the value of studying the effects of context on the functioning of manipulation. We found that mothers' behaviors while manipulating objects with their infants provide information about the objects themselves *and* ways to obtain this information. In some instances, mothers actually engage their infants in appropriate exploratory behaviors. Further, the results indicate that in certain respects, infants benefit from exploring objects in such joint situations. In these contexts, infants showed more focused exploration and more frequent use of certain appropriate behaviors.

The larger issue that this work raises concerns the contribution that social figures make to the development of object-appropriate manipulation. The present results speak only indirectly to this issue, but they do suggest some promising leads. As was noted, some theorists have suggested that social tutelage plays an important role in mastering skills having to do with objects. The mechanisms and accompanying metaphors differ from theorist to theorist—for example, from the "scaffolding" models of Bruner (1982) and Wood (1980) to the "frames" structure suggested by Kaye (1982). The models also sometimes differ in the amount of intention or goal orientation initially attributed to infants (Kaye, 1982). However, in one way or another, these models suggest that more skilled social figures structure situations so that infants may carry out the object skill in question and eventually become capable of completely executing these skills on their own (also see Rogoff & Werstch, 1984).

Demonstrating the causal chain implied by these models is likely to be difficult. More modestly, though, what can be done is to compare how certain skills function in independent and joint contexts and use these comparisons as a basis for considering how behaviors exercised in these contexts contribute to the mastery of manipulation skills. As such, the present results suggest two related contributions that joint activity might make. One deals directly with the motor actions themselves. By demonstrating or actually engaging infants in relevant motor activities, caregivers are providing opportunities whereby infants can improve, practice, or possibly even learn relevant manual behaviors. According to a Vygotskyian perspective, these behaviors would first be exercised completely during the course of joint activity, and only later would infants be able to exercise these skills on their own. Whether such a progression holds for the component actions of object manipulation is questionable. Six-month-olds in the research that we reported exhibited appropriate forms of manipulation even when they were manipulating objects on their own. The social context nevertheless may have an influence by enabling infants to refine these behaviors through observing demonstrations and by performing them with caregivers. In addition, caregivers, by modulating their infants' environments, may also promote more goal-corrected and less stereotypic forms of motor behavior (Thelen, 1981; Thelen & Fogel, Chapter 2 this volume). Research is needed that carefully examines how associated aspects of the social context—demonstrations, conjoint activity, modulation of the environment—affect the performance and development of the action classes that make up manipulation.

The second contribution that joint activity might make centers on the functions of manipulation. Through joint manipulation of an object, infants may also be able to learn or perceive what the specific object has to offer. Because caregivers' actions are uniquely tailored to the properties of an object, information about that object may be readily available to infants. The questions that these considerations raise could be examined experimentally by comparing how the context of exploration influences the information that infants register about an object or the rate at which they do so. Many investigators have suggested that parents influence their infants' exploratory and cognitive development by encouraging them to attend to and interact with objects in the environment (e.g., Belsky et al. 1980; Clarke-Stewart, 1973; Power & Parke, 1982; Vondra & Belsky, Chapter 6 this volume; Wachs & Gruen, 1982; Yarrow et al., 1975). We would like to suggest that efforts aimed at evaluating this hypothesis would be aided by investigating how exploration mediated by caregivers influences the information that infants register about objects or the rate at which they do so. Our results indicate that some benefits accrue from joint activity—at least for certain age levels and object properties. This finding suggests that any contextual effects that are found are likely to interact with the infant's developmental level and the object property being investigated. Attention to these associated variables will permit more precise descriptions of the conditions under which caregivers actually influence object exploration by their infants.

Summary and Conclusions

Object manipulation has been discussed extensively in accounts of perceptual and cognitive development, yet our understanding of its development is limited in several important ways. In this chapter, we have attempted to identify the nature of these limitations and ways to overcome them.

We have argued that a complete account of the development of object manipulation requires that it be studied for its own sake. This would have two important consequences. First, it would focus attention on the development of the individual action classes that make up manipulation. Investigators would then be more likely to consider when each of these action classes becomes used appropriately, an approach that also has been advocated for other aspects of eye–hand coordination (Lockman & Ashmead, 1983).

A second consequence of studying manipulation for its own sake would be that it would encourage investigators to adopt a functional perspective and consider variables affecting the act of manipulation and its component behaviors. As part of this functional perspective, attention would be focused on the contexts in which manipulation occurs and how these contexts influence its functioning. More generally, researchers have been suggesting that it is not possible to divorce a skill from the context(s) in which it is executed (Bruner, 1982; Rogoff, 1982). To understand the development and use of a skill, it is necessary to consider the contexts in which these achievements occur. With reference to object manipulation, it is obvious that infants frequently engage in this activity with social partners, especially parents. Yet in most investigations of object manipulation, infants have been studied handling objects on their own. The results that we presented suggest that mothers, through their actions, provide infants with a great deal of information about objects. Further, during such interactions, infants more frequently display certain forms of appropriate manipulations. Additional research is needed to specify how characteristics of the individual (e.g., developmental level) and the objects interact with context in influencing manipulation. This research may also be relevant for evaluating developmental accounts that suggest that infants master skills by first exercising them in concert with experienced partners before being able to exercise them on their own (Bruner, 1982; Kaye, 1982; Rogoff & Werstch, 1984; Vygotsky, 1978).

Because object manipulation has not often been studied for its own sake, several gaps have occurred in the object manipulation literature. Three general limitations were identified. One concerned the stimuli used in past investigations. In many instances, object properties have not been *systematically* varied within studies, preventing clear conclusions about the appropriateness of infant manipulation. In other cases, stimulus variation has been systematic but has occurred between trials and hence between objects rather than within objects. We suggested that variation along a dimension *within* an object might promote appropriate forms of exploration of that dimension. The results that we presented concerning 6-month-olds' manipulation of objects varying in color were consistent with this proposal.

A second limitation that was identified concerned the measurement of manipulation. In many studies, manipulation has often been measured in terms of the *amount* rather than the *kind* of activity that infants display. We noted that this practice stemmed from using manipulation as a means of investigating some other, usually cognitive, capacity— often sensitivity to novelty. When manipulation is broken down into its component manual behaviors, evidence can be found for appropriate activity even at 6 months (Palmer, 1985; Pederson *et al.*, 1980; Ruff, 1984). The results that we presented on infants' exploration of colored and textured objects are consistent with this conclusion as well.

Finally, we noted that in almost all investigations of object manipulation, infants have invariably been studied by having them manipulate objects on their own. We suggested that greater consideration of the act of manipulating—that is, its functioning—would in turn focus attention on the contexts in which this skill is executed. This would require studying object manipulation in the social as well as nonsocial contexts in which it naturally occurs.

Our exploration of the context variable involved contrasting infants manipulating objects by themselves and with their mothers. It is obvious, however, that the social context includes individuals besides the mother. Additionally, it should be recognized that the social/nonsocial distinction is but one way to categorize variations in context. The critical variable may concern the degree of support that a context provides for executing a skill. Social as well as nonsocial contexts vary in this way and thereby may affect the functioning of an emerging skill like manipulation. Accordingly, in discussing the influence of the social context, it would be informative to contrast how more and less experienced social partners (e.g., adult caregivers and siblings) engage infants in object manipulation and how this in turn affects the types of manipulation that infants display and the kinds of object information that infants gain from such activities. Nonsocial contexts (e.g., familiar vs. unfamiliar) may also be varied to examine how different levels of environmental support affect the functioning of manipulation.

To conclude, there is much to be learned about object manipulation during the first year. By studying manipulation for its own sake, attention would be focused on the actions that make up manipulation, how they develop and become differentially applied, and how they are executed in different contexts. With knowledge about the actual functioning of manipulation, researchers will be in a better position to examine the many other sensorimotor achievements that object manipulation is thought to reflect.

REFERENCES

Belsky, J., Goode, M. K., & Most, R. K. (1980). Maternal stimulation and infant exploratory competence: Cross-sectional, correlational, and experimental analyses. *Child Development, 51*, 1168–1178.

Bruner, J. S. (1982). The organization of action and the nature of the adult-infant transaction. In E. Z. Tronick (Ed.), *Social interchange in infancy* (pp. 23–35). Baltimore: University Park Press.

Bushnell, E. W. (1981). The ontogeny of intermodal relations: Vision and touch in infancy. In R. D. Walk & H. L. Pick, Jr. (Eds.), *Intersensory perception and sensory integration* (pp. 5–36). New York: Plenum Press.

Clarke-Stewart, K. A. (1973). Interactions between mothers and their young children: Characteristics and consequences. *Monographs of the Society for Research in Child Development, 38*, (6–7, Serial No. 153).

Fenson, L., Kagan, J., Kearsley, R. B., & Zelazo, P. R. (1976). The developmental progression of manipulative play in the first two years. *Child Development, 47*, 232–236.

Gibson, E. J. (1982). The concept of affordances in development: The renascence of functionalism. In W. A. Collins (Ed.), *The Minnesota Symposia on Child Psychology: The concept of development* (Vol. 15, pp. 55–81). Hillsdale, NJ: Erlbaum.

Gibson, E. J. (1984, April). *Perception and affordances for action*. Paper presented at the International Conference on Infant Studies, New York.

Gibson, E. J. (1985, April). *Toward a unified science of behavioral development*. Paper presented at the Society for Research in Child Development, Toronto.

Gibson, E. J., Riccio, G., Schmuckler, M. A., Stoffregen, T. A., Rosenberg, D., & Taormina, J. (1987). Detection of the traversability of surfaces by crawling and walking infants. *Journal of Experimental Psychology: Human Perception and Performance, 13*, 533–544.

Gibson, E. J., & Spelke, E. S. (1983). The development of perception. In J. H. Flavell & E. M. Markman (Eds.), P. H. Mussen (Series Ed.), *Handbook of child psychology: Vol. 3. Cognitive development* (pp. 1–76). New York: Wiley.

Gibson, E. J., & Walker, A. S. (1984). Development of knowledge of visual-tactual affordances of substances. *Child Development, 55,* 453–460.

Gibson, J. J. (1966). *The senses considered as perceptual systems.* Boston: Houghton Mifflin.

Gibson, J. J. (1979). *The ecological approach to visual perception.* Boston: Houghton Mifflin.

Hodapp, R. M., Goldfield, E. C., & Boyatzis, C. J. (1984). The use and effectiveness of maternal scaffolding in mother-infant games. *Child Development, 55,* 772–781.

Hunt, J. McV., Mohandessi, K., Ghodssi, M., & Akiyama, M. (1976). The psychological development of orphanage-reared infants: Interventions with outcomes. *Genetic Psychology Monographs, 94,* 177–226.

Kaye, K. (1982). *The mental and social life of babies.* Chicago: University of Chicago Press.

Kopp, C. B., Sigman, M., & Parmelee, A. H. (1974). Longitudinal study of sensorimotor development. *Developmental Psychology, 10,* 687–695.

Langer, J. (1980). *The origins of logic: Six to twelve months.* New York: Academic Press.

Lockman, J. J., & Ashmead, D. H. (1983). Asynchronies in the development of manual behavior. In L. P. Lipsitt (Ed.), *Advances in infancy research* (Vol. 2, pp. 113–136). Norwood, NJ: Ablex.

McCall, R. B. (1974). Exploratory manipulation and play in the human infant. *Monographs of the Society for Research in Child Development, 39*(2, Serial No. 155).

Palmer, C. F. (1985). *Infants' exploration of objects: Relations between perceiving and acting.* Unpublished doctoral dissertation, University of Minnesota, Minneapolis.

Pederson, D. R., Steele, D., & Klein, G. (1980, April). *Stimulus characteristics that determine infant's exploratory play.* Paper presented at the International Conference on Infancy Studies, New Haven, CT.

Piaget, J. (1952). *The origins of intelligence in children.* New York: International Universities Press.

Piaget, J. (1954). *The construction of reality in the child.* New York: Basic Books.

Power, T. G., & Parke, R. D. (1982). Play as a context for early learning: Lab and home analyses. In L. M. Laosa & I. E. Sigel (Eds.), *Families as learning environments for children* (pp. 147–178). New York: Plenum Press.

Ricciuti, H. N. (1965). Object grouping and selection ordering behavior in infants 12 to 24 months old. *Merrill-Palmer Quarterly, 11,* 129–148.

Rochat, P. (1985, July). *Mouthing and grasping in newborns: Cross-modal responsiveness to soft and rigid objects.* Poster presented at the International Society for the Study of Behavioural Development, Tours, France.

Rogoff, B. (1982). Integrating context and cognitive development. In M. E. Lamb & A. L. Brown (Eds.), *Advances in developmental psychology* (Vol. 2, pp. 125–170). Hillsdale, NJ: Lawrence Erlbaum Associates.

Rogoff, B. & Wertsch, J. V. (Eds.). (1984). *Children's learning in the "zone of proximal development".* San Francisco: Jossey-Bass.

Rose, S. A., Gottfried, A. W., & Bridger, W. H. (1981). Cross-modal transfer in 6-month-old infants. *Developmental Psychology, 17,* 661–669.

Rubenstein, J. (1974). A concordance of visual and manipulative responses to novel and familiar stimuli in six-month-old infants. *Child Development, 45,* 194–195.

Ruff, H. (1984). Infant's manipulative exploration of objects: Effects of age and object characteristics. *Developmental Psychology, 20,* 9–20.

Schaffer, H. R., & Parry, M. R. (1969). Perceptual-motor behavior in infancy as a function of age and stimulus familiarity. *British Journal of Psychology, 60,* 1–9.

Schaffer, H. R., & Parry, M. R. (1970). The effects of short-term familiarization on infants' perceptual motor co-ordination in a simultaneous discrimination situation. *British Journal of Psychology, 61,* 559–569.

Steele, D., & Pederson, D. R. (1977). Stimulus variables which effect the concordance of visual and manipulative exploration in six-month-olds. *Child Development, 8,* 104–111.

Thelen, E. (1981). Rhythmical behavior in infancy: An ethological perspective. *Developmental Psychology, 17,* 237–257.

Užgiris, I. C. (1967). Ordinality in the development of schemas for relating to objects. In J. Hellmuth (Ed.), *Exceptional infant* (Vol. 1, pp. 317–334). Seattle: Special Child Publications.

Užgiris, I. C. (1983). Organization of sensorimotor intelligence. In M. Lewis (Ed.), *Origins of intelligence* (2nd ed., pp. 135–189). New York: Plenum Press.

Užgiris, I. C., & Hunt, J. McV. (1975). *Assessment in infancy: Ordinal scales of psychological development.* Urbana: University of Illinois Press.

Vygotsky, L. S. (1978). *Mind in society.* Cambridge: Harvard University Press.

Wachs, T. D. (1979). Proximal experience and early cognitive-intellectual development: The physical environment. *Merrill-Palmer Quarterly, 25,* 3–41.

Wachs, T. D. (1984). Proximal experience and early cognitive-intellectual development: The social environment. In A. W. Gottfried (Ed.), *Home environment and early cognitive development.* (pp. 273–328). Orlando, FL: Academic Press.

Wachs, T. D., & Gruen, G. E. (1982). *Early experience and human development.* New York: Plenum Press.

Walker, A. S. (1982). Intermodal perception of expressive behaviors by human infants. *Journal of Experimental Child Psychology, 33,* 514–535.

Werstch, J. V. (1979). From social interaction to higher psychological processes. *Human Development, 52,* 1–22.

Wood, D. J. (1980). Teaching the young child: Some relationships between social interaction, language and thought. In D. R. Olson (Ed.), *The social foundations of language and thought* (pp. 280–298). New York: Norton.

Yarrow, L. J., Rubenstein, J. L., & Pedersen, F. A. (1975). *Infant and environment: Early cognitive and motivational development.* New York: Wiley.

PART III

Exploration and Play in Social Context
Developments from Infancy to Early Childhood

The early development of exploration and play has long been of interest to cognitive developmentalists, because exploration and play depend upon underlying cognitive capacities. As has been the case with most cognitive approaches to early skill, however, researchers interested in exploration and play as a reflection of early cognitive development have typically examined these skills in nonsocial laboratory settings, rather than within the social contexts of parent–child and peer interaction in which they develop. Although a great deal of research on parent–child and peer play has been done, most of it has been directed at understanding parent–child and peer interaction and relationships rather than understanding the development of play skills *per se*. In keeping with the spirit of this volume, the three chapters in this section all present the view that a full understanding of the development of play and exploration skills cannot be achieved without examining how these skills actually function within the social and affective contexts in which they are used in everyday life.

These three chapters deal with different periods of development and with different aspects of play and exploration skills. Vondra and Belsky examine the development of object exploration and play in infancy, from the beginnings of object manipulation at 3 months until the beginnings of symbolic play at 12 months. Hazen follows with a discussion of exploration in the toddler and preschool years, but with a primary focus on environmental exploration and its relation to developing spatial cognition. Bretherton and Beeghly discuss the development of symbolic pretense play in the toddler and preschool years. Despite these differences, all three chapters share a central concern with the issue of how social and affective contexts influence, and are influenced by, the development of play and exploration.

For Vondra and Belsky, the "social contexts" of exploratory and play skills in infancy refer essentially to the contexts of parent–infant interaction. A central point in their chapter is that the quality of parent–child relationships can affect parent–child interaction patterns, thus influencing infants' level of motivation and, consequently, their cognitive development as manifested in their exploration and play skills. Infants' motivation, or *executive capacity*, is defined as the difference between the infant's play performance, or highest level of *spontaneous* play, and play competence, or highest level of *elicited* play. Vondra and Belsky argue that the quality of the parent–child attachment relationship affects the infant's executive capacity because securely attached infants were found to have smaller gaps between spontaneous play and elicited play than insecure infants. They further argue that aspects of parent–child interaction that contribute to security of attachment also contribute to the infant's motivation to perform at close to an optimal level. Much of their chapter is devoted to presentation of a longitudinal study designed primarily to investigate how particular aspects of mother–child and father–child interactions relate to infants' executive capacity and cognitive competence in object exploration and play. Thus they present evidence linking individual differences in infants' cognitive motivation to individual differences in parents' styles of interacting with their infants.

Vondra and Belsky also stress that the social context of parent–infant interaction is a function of *both* parent and infant behaviors and characteristics. Not only were certain aspects of the infant's early temperament found to affect later parent–infant play, but parents constantly adjusted the types of object-mediated stimulation they provided as a function of the infant's developmental level. Furthermore, Vondra and Belsky point out that parents' and infants' interpretations of social contexts are critical to understanding how play and exploration function in context. For example, they found that fathers who provided more stimulation in toy play actually had infants with *lower* levels of cognitive motivation and argue that infants with more competent fathers were more inclined to view the context of playtime with father as a time for social interaction with the father, rather than as a time for object play.

Hazen, like Vondra and Belsky, focuses upon individual differences in early exploration as a function of parent–child interaction in the early years. She discusses how the parent–child relationship and interaction patterns in the early years may affect children's spatial exploration and consequently, their spatial cognition. Hazen emphasizes that parents affect the social context of their child's spatial exploration in a variety of ways, varying with the parent's and child's spatial goals and with the child's developmental level and spatial capabilities. One way might be through modulating the child's affective responses to environments and therefore their motivation to explore. Like Vondra and Belsky, Hazen suggests that individual differences in parents' ability to do this may be mediated by individual differences in the parent–child attachment relationship. In support of this, she presents evidence that security of attachment to the mother in infancy is related to higher levels of competence in exploration and cognitive mapping skills in toddlers.

The chapters by both Hazen and Vondra and Belsky emphasize that parent–child interactions involving exploration vary as a function of the child's individual needs and developmental level. Hazen suggests that parental effects on the child's motivation to explore, through modulation of child affect, may play a predominant role in the early years, with more direct parental intervention and scaffolding of spatial abilities becoming more prominent later in development. However, parents may directly intervene in their child's spatial exploration and point out object locations and spatial relationships in environments whenever they want their children to acquire specific skills for specific purposes. For example, Hazen presents data on how the mother of a young blind child provides a great deal of direct guidance of her child's exploration, matching the nature of her intervention to the particular spatial skills she wishes her child to acquire. The main theme of this chapter then is that the development of skills involved in spatial exploration and spatial cognition is a function of the interplay between the task context and the social context and that the two cannot be separated because tasks are defined by persons—the child who must complete the task and the parent who helps him or her identify the task, set goals, and achieve these goals.

Like Vondra and Belsky, Bretherton and Beeghly examine play skills as an index of early cognitive development, and like Hazen, they focus on developments in the toddler and preschool years. However, whereas Vondra and Belsky and Hazen primarily discussed how individual differences in social contexts (particularly parent–child interactions) affect differences in children's skill developments, Bretherton and Beeghly take a different approach and focus on how children's developing cognitive and play skills affect the social contexts that they understand and create. Bretherton and Beeghly argue that pretense play is an emerging skill that helps children work out their knowledge about actual social contexts, including social roles, events, and objects. Whereas very early pretense consists largely of realistic depictions of aspects of actual social contexts (i.e., familiar family roles and events), later in development, children may actually create and perform their own imaginary social contexts, including out-of-home, fictional, or counterfactual roles and events. Bretherton and Beeghly also note that with development, pretense play shifts from occurring primarily in parent–child or solitary contexts to occurring primarily in peer contexts. Pretense play with peers necessitates the development of metacommunication skills to enable children to coordinate the planning and performance of pretense.

Bretherton and Beeghly also discuss how actual social contexts can affect the imaginary contexts created in pretense play, and conversely, how pretend social contexts can affect social reality. For example, children's role assignments and enactments in pretense play often reflect their interpersonal relationships and their emotional concerns in everyday life, and enactments of pretend events can alter real-world social contexts, as when children actually become frightened of their own role enactments. Thus, not only are children's play skills critically shaped by the social contexts in which they develop, but also, as pretense play skills develop, children become capable of creating, transforming, and interpreting these social contexts according to their own wishes and needs as they play.

CHAPTER 6

Infant Play at One Year
Characteristics and Early Antecedents

JOAN VONDRA AND JAY BELSKY

INTRODUCTION

Play is a term we use to describe much of the activity of infants and young children. Despite the fact that children of all ages spend a large percentage of their waking time engaged in play, the term itself remains difficult to define and to operationalize formally. Particularly difficult are efforts to distinguish play from exploration. When is a child playing and when is a child exploring? Weisler and McCall (1976), like many others, have come to the conclusion that it is fruitless to advance formal definitions of terms like *play* and *exploration* because it is simply impossible to distinguish the two in the ongoing stream of the child's behavior.

Unfortunately, it is not only the definition of play that poses a stumbling block to scientists. Also debated is the purpose or function of this activity. Theorists such as White (1959), Garvey (1974), and Breger (1974) contend that play offers the youngster opportunities to affect and control the environment in ways that the immature organism cannot do in other contexts. Related to this perspective is Bruner's (1973) notion that play provides a forum for the development and practice of behavioral skills that are eventually integrated into more complex behavioral sequences and higher order skills in more purposeful, goal-directed activities. And, as a final example, Piaget (1952) offers a somewhat differ-

JOAN VONDRA • Department of Psychology in Education, University of Pittsburgh, Pittsburgh, Pennsylvania 15260.   JAY BELSKY • Department of Individual and Family Studies, The Pennsylvania State University, University Park, Pennsylvania 16827.

ent viewpoint, seeing play as an activity that promotes the integration of strategies from and for current use; thus play is viewed in the service of assimilation rather than accommodation.

In light of the significance accorded children's play, it is surprising that, until recently, infant exploration and play have not received the attention they seem to merit. With the exception of Piaget's (1952) early work, exploratory activity of the infant was studied primarily as a means of learning about infant attentional processes and the development of attachment relations rather than as a subject worthy of consideration in its own right. Consequently, although we have considerable knowledge about the stimulus properties of objects that attract infant interest (e.g., novelty, moderate complexity) and the manner in which infants use their mothers as "secure bases" (in focusing on the quantity of infant exploration/play), the quality and style of such activity have been largely ignored (Weisler & McCall, 1976). In recent years, researchers have given more attention to the quality of infant exploration/play (e.g., McCall, 1974a) and, in consequence, we better understand its developmental process.

In this chapter, we seek to contribute to this advance in understanding by examining several aspects of play development. We begin by summarizing the current state of knowledge about the development of infant exploration and play in order to highlight the way in which cognitive development is expressed in manipulative activity across the first 2 years of life (for a more extensive analysis of this topic, see the chapter by Bretherton and Beeghly, Chapter 8 this volume). In the second section of the chapter, we turn our attention from cognition to motivation and consider the ways in which infants' play is reflective of their curiosity and their desire to master the world about them. Further, we point out that the social context of play and exploration, and particularly the involvement of an adult, can affect the nature of children's play in a way that illuminates motivational differences between infants. From this discussion of the effect of adult involvement in children's play, we move on to consider the more general effects of variation in parent–infant interaction on infant exploratory competence. For this purpose, we review select studies that relate maternal and paternal behavior during the course of everyday interaction with children's subsequent exploratory and play behavior in an assessment situation.

These analyses of play development, motivation, and the influence of early family experience on infant exploration and play set the stage for the presentation of our most recent research, which is aimed at furthering knowledge of play development and the influence of early parent–infant interaction. Throughout the chapter, then, we shall report the results of a longitudinal study of some 57 middle- and working-class families, rearing their first infant, that we studied intensively across the infant's first year of life. Specifically, in the first section of the chapter, dealing with the development of play, we describe the methodology employed to study infant exploration at 12 and 13 months of age and examine developmental changes in play across this 1-month period. In the section devoted to discussion of motivation, we detail the procedures employed to measure this construct. Finally, in the concluding portion of the chapter concerned with the social-contextual determinants of exploratory functioning, we examine associations between parent–infant interaction observed in the home when infants were 1, 3, and 9 months of age and infant exploration and play observed in the university laboratory when infants were 12 and 13 months of age.

The Development of Play

The initial manipulative activity of the young infant through the first 6 to 8 months of life has been described as undifferentiated exploration. Casual observation suggests that materials are indiscriminately banged, mouthed, and inspected. That is, different objects appear to be treated in generally the same manner. Thus their unique properties seem not to be exploited, but rather, all objects seem to be handled in much the same way (Užgiris, 1976). During this period, "the object is what I do" (McCall, Eichorn, & Hogarty, 1977, p. 64).

Although the work reported by Lockman in this volume clearly reveals that early manipulative behavior is not as indiscriminate as thought to be the case, it is easily apparent that sometime during the second half of the first year manipulative investigation becomes increasingly tailored to particular features of the object being manipulated. A toy telephone will not simply be banged, turned over, and mouthed, but its dial may be turned and its wheels spun. As Weisler and McCall (1976, p. 493) comment, the infant seems to be guided by the question, "What is this and what can it do?"

In addition to changes involving the extraction of unique information from materials during the second half of the first year, changes also occur in the number of objects a child manipulates. Between about 7 and 8 months, activity involving single objects decreases dramatically, as infants begin to put objects together (Fein & Apfel, 1979; Fenson, Kagan, Kearsley, & Zelazo, 1976; McCall, 1974a). Initially, objects tend to be put together in an unrelated manner, a process sometimes called juxtaposition (Belsky & Most, 1981). But as exploration becomes more suited to the unique features of materials, objects are put together in ways reflective of their formal properties—so, for example, a lid is placed on a teapot, or a peg is placed in a hole. The ability to integrate objects in a functionally appropriate manner, sometimes called *functional-relational activity* (Belsky & Most, 1981), becomes evident in the play of infants sometime around 9 or 10 months of age.

Near the end of the first year of life and the beginning of the second, a major change takes place in the nature of object manipulation and exploration: pretense play emerges (Belsky & Most, 1981; Fein & Apfel, 1979; Rosenblatt, 1977). In this activity, the child seems to be less intent upon extraction of information from materials, making it seem more organism than stimulus dominated. The question posed now by the child's behaviors seems to be, "What can I do with this object?" (Weisler & McCall, 1976, p. 494). Important to note here is the fact that pretense, when it does occur, is fleeting and, relative to the entire behavior stream, takes up only a small percentage of the child's time.

The earliest form of pretend activity appears when the child produces a familiar behavior, such as drinking from a miniature toy cup or eating from an empty spoon. Often such explicit examples of pretense are preceded by more approximate forms, which Bates (1979) has labeled *enactive namings*. In such instances, a spoon may be brought to the lips or a brush may be touched to a doll's hair, but the actions that would convincingly demonstrate pretense, like lip-smacking sounds or stroking motions, are not displayed. What actually makes the activity pretense when it is accompanied by the appropriate supportive behavior is the decontextualized nature of the activity (Bates, 1979). That is, the behavior is detached from the situational context in which it ordinarily occurs—such as mealtime—and from the outcomes with which it is ordinarily associated—such as eating (Rubin, Fein, & Vandenberg, 1983).

Simple pretense acts like drinking, eating, and brushing develop in a systematic manner with respect to their referent. Initially such actions are directed toward the self, so the children first pretend to feed themselves or brush their own hair. Shortly after this, other-directed pretense emerges, in which the very same pretend actions are directed toward others (Belsky & Most, 1981; Fein & Apfel, 1979; Lowe, 1975; Watson & Fischer, 1977). In watching infant play around 13 to 15 months, then, one is likely to observe the child pretending to brush a doll's hair or to feed his or her mother with a spoon. Fenson and Ramsey (1980) discussed this shift from self to other in terms of Piaget's concept of decentration.

The next developmental change that one observes in infant play involves the use of substitute props, in which one object takes the place of another. So, for example, rather than using a cup to drink from, the child may pretend to drink from a seashell (Belsky & Most, 1981; Fein & Apfel, 1979; Lowe, 1975; Watson & Fischer, 1977). Experimental research has indicated that it is easier to use as a substitute an object with an ambiguous function than one with a clearly conflicting function. In other words, it is easier for the toddler to pretend that a stick is a spoon than to pretend that a comb is a spoon (Fein & Robertson, 1975; Jeffree & McConkey, 1976).

Through this point in play development, all pretend acts take place in isolation, one act at a time. Following the emergence of substitute actions, however, toddlers begin to join together or intercoordinate single pretend acts into sequences of pretend (Belsky & Most, 1981; Fenson & Ramsey, 1980; Nicolich, 1977). Initially, the same pretend scheme is simply applied to different agents; thus toddlers may brush their own hair and then their mothers,' or they may pretend to take a drink before pretending to give their doll a drink. Only after children have engaged in such single-scheme sequences, do we see children integrating different schemes to produce actions that have more of a story line (Fenson & Ramsey, 1980). At this point, children may first stir in a miniature cup and then feed themselves with a spoon.

What follows the emergence of sequences are more complex combinations of already existing skills. With substitutions and sequences mastered, then, sequences involving substitutions are displayed. Stirring in a cup with a stick and then feeding a doll with the stick is an example of this kind of higher order behavior. Eventually children become capable of working with more than one substitution at a time, that is, imbuing two seemingly meaningless objects with meaning in the same play act. For example, children may treat a clothespin as if it were a doll and pretend to give it a drink from a seashell.

This brief summary of the development of infant play is not meant to imply that sophisticated play acts that typically emerge during the second year of life cannot be seen earlier or that less sophisticated play acts so apparent in the first year are not also evident at later ages. In point of fact, virtually all types of play just described can be seen, though in varying frequency, by the start of the second year of life. This is evident in the results of our own study, which compared free play behavior of infants observed at 12 and 13 months of age.

Assessing Play Development

As part of our longitudinal study of infant and family development, we observed 57 firstborn infants in the university laboratory on two occasions, first accompanied by mother (12 months) and then by father (13 months). Separate, 10-minute observations of free play with each of two different sets of toys during each lab visit furnished us with indices of each child's typical and highest spontaneous level of play. We observed the frequency with which infants played at each of the 14 developmental levels of play identified by Belsky and Most (1981) as well as the highest level of free play exhibited by the infant over the entire sample of free play behavior.

During the free play session, parents were instructed to respond to their children's bids for attention with a brief comment or hug but not to initiate interaction or extend it unnecessarily or to provide the child with suggestions or directions regarding the play materials. Following a brief warmup period, infants were observed in free play with two sets of assorted toys, for a total of approximately 20 minutes. From behind a one-way mirror, a trained observer recorded a continuous narrative description of the children's play using terminology based on the developmental play scale derived by Belsky and Most (1981).

The 14 developmental levels of play identified by Belsky and Most (1981) form a valid Guttman scale, as evidenced by cross-sectional data on infants aged 7½ to 21 months. The scale is presented and described in Table 1. The first several levels of the developmental sequence describe exploratory behavior that is seen as undifferentiated ("mouthing," "simple manipulation,") or not defined by the properties of the object manipulated (Užgiris, 1976). The second set of steps describes exploration in which the child's actions are made to fit the specific properties of the object manipulated ("functional," "functional relational"). The third set of steps describes the emergence of pretense behavior, first in approximate form ("enactive naming") and then in terms of single acts directed initially toward oneself ("pretend self") and subsequently toward others ("pretend other"). The next step in the play scale involves the child's ability to use one object in place of another ("substitution"—e.g., using a stick as a spoon to feed oneself). Then, with an emphasis on increasing sophistication in symbol use, the scale describes sequence acts, first without a story line ("sequence no story"—e.g., feeding oneself with a spoon and then the doll with a spoon) and then in terms of a "logical" story line ("sequence story"— e.g., pouring from a teapot and then taking a drink from the teacup). The final set of steps involves the child's ability to combine both substitution and sequencing ("sequence substitution") as well as the capacity to use two seemingly meaningless objects to perform integrated pretend acts ("double substitution"—e.g., stirring in a seashell with a clothespin).

For purposes of some of the analyses reported in this chapter, we

TABLE 1
Belsky and Most (1981) Developmental Scale of Infant Play

Reduced-scale play levels	Full-scale play levels	Descriptions	Examples
Undifferentiated exploration	1. Mouthing	Indiscriminate mouthing of materials	Mouthing a block or plastic donut
	2. Simple manipulation	Visually guided manipulation lasting 5 seconds	Turning over an object to examine the bottom
Functional	3. Functional	Visually guided manipulation that extracts unique information	Rolling a cart on wheels; dialing a toy telephone
Transitional play	4. Juxtapose	Juxtaposing two or more objects in a random manner	Touching a shell to a ring; hitting a phone with a peg
	5. Functional relational	Integrating two objects in an "appropriate" manner	Placing a spoon in a bowl; placing a peg in a pegboard
	6. Enactive naming	Approximating pretend play	Touching a brush to one's head without making stroking motions
Simple pretend	7. Pretend self	Pretend play directed toward oneself	Bringing a toy phone receiver to one's head and vocalizing into it
	8. Pretend external	Pretend play directed toward other	Feeding a doll with a spoon; rolling a car with motor noises
Elaborated pretend	9. Substitution self	Giving a "meaningless" object meaning in the context of a "pretend self"	Bringing a peg to one's ear and vocalizing into it; feeding oneself with a stick (as spoon)
	10. Substitution external	Giving a "meaningless" object meaning in the context of a "pretend external"	Feeding a doll with a stick; pushing a block along the floor with motor noises
	11. Sequence no story	Repeating a single pretend act with a minor variation	Feeding self with spoon and feeding doll with spoon
	12. Sequence story	Linking two different pretend acts	Dialing a toy phone and talking into receiver
	13. Sequence substitution	Incorporating a substitution into a "sequence story"	Dialing a toy phone and talking into a peg
	14. Double substitution	Incorporating two substitutions into a "sequence story"	Stirring in a shell and feeding doll with a peg

summarized free play activity in terms of five molar dimensions of play. The relation between these five dimensions and the levels of play identified in the Belsky and Most (1981) scale appears in Table 1. Each child received a score for the category *Undifferentiated Exploration*, which represents mouthing and simple manipulation of toys. The category of *Functional Play*, in contrast, consists entirely of play acts that focus on unique toy properties (i.e., the definition of functional play), such as rolling wheels, dialing the toy phone, or squeezing the foam rubber. *Transitional Play* combines the kind of relational play characteristic of 8- and 9-month-olds—simple juxtaposition, as of two blocks, or context-appropriate juxtaposition, as when a peg is fitted into a pegboard—with approximations of pretense play (i.e., "enactive naming"), as when the phone receiver is brought to the head but there is no vocalization. When a child engaged in rudimentary pretend play—directed either to himself or herself, or externally to doll, mother, or examiner—she or he received credit for *Simple Pretend Play*, whereas more sophisticated substitutions and/or sequences of pretend play were recoded as *Elaborated Pretend*. By combining play acts into conceptually meaningful categories, we worked to strengthen measurement validity and, simultaneously, to minimize statistical problems arising from the infrequency of individual play acts at certain levels, particularly at the upper end of the scale.

These composite measures were based upon the frequency with which each of the 13 levels of play were coded during spontaneous exploration of the two toy sets ("substitution self" and "substitution other" were not differentiated, as they are on the 14-level Belsky and Most scale). Scores represent frequency counts of the number of 15-second play periods for which each play level was the most sophisticated behavior observed. Frequencies were prorated in cases where infants played for less than the standard 40 time-sampling periods.

As a first step in our data analysis, we examined the individual play categories for possible sex differences. Two (gender) × two (age) analyses of variance, calculated for each play level, revealed that with the single exception of functional play, more often coded for males than for females ($\bar{X}$ males = 13.50, $\bar{X}$ females = 7.45, F = 13.08, $p < .01$), there were no systematic differences between males and females in the number of periods coded for each level of play. On the basis of this general absence of sex differences, data for males and females were combined to create group means. Combined mean frequencies at 12 and at 13 months for each play level appear in Table 2.

The play level most frequently coded at both 12 and 13 months is "simple manipulation" of play materials, although "functional" (manipulation that extracts unique information), "juxtapose" (juxtaposition of

Table 2
Mean Frequency of Play Acts Coded at Each Developmental Level of Play at 12 and 13 Months of Age (20-Minute Prorated Time Sample)

Full scale	12 months	13 months	F (df = 1,55)
1. Mouthing	8.37	4.86	12.79**
2. Simple manipulation	19.56	16.54	4.52*
3. Functional	11.53	10.50	1.12
4. Juxtapose	10.42	9.16	1.26
5. Functional relational	11.78	15.77	6.73*
6. Enactive naming	3.10	3.50	2.10
7. Pretend self	3.18	3.75	1.48
8. Pretend external	1.28	2.77	8.73**
9. Substitution	0.31	1.11	9.41**
10. Sequence no story	0.17	0.50	6.89*
11. Sequence story	0.11	0.89	7.76**
12. Sequence substitution	0.09	0.56	11.94**
13. Double substitution	0.00	0.03	0.65

Reduced scale	12 months	13 months	F (df = 1,55)
1. Undifferentiated exploration	27.93	21.40	18.97**
2. Functional	11.53	10.50	1.12
3. Transitional play	25.29	28.43	3.51#
4. Simple pretend	4.45	6.52	9.05**
5. Elaborated pretend	0.67	3.09	20.41**

#$p < .10$; *$p < .05$; **$p < .01$.

two or more objects), and "functional relational" play (integrating objects in a meaningful combination) are also common. It is clear from these data that the great bulk of play at 1 year consists of mechanically oriented manipulation. All levels of pretend play, from approximations of pretense ("enactive naming") to sequences of pretense involving substitutions, occur much more infrequently, with the fewest occurrences coded for the most cognitively complex levels of play. By the time we reach simple "substitution" at 12 months and "sequence no story" at 13 months, less than one instance of play is being coded, on the average, for the entire 20-minute free-play session. This progressive decline in the observed frequency of higher level play steps is evident in the collapsed, five-level play scale as well. Mean frequencies at 12 and 13 months on this reduced scale also appear in Table 2. The pattern of results obtained here provides support for the developmental sequence operationalized in the Belsky and Most (1981) play scale. Exploratory play at 1 year of age concentrates at the lower, more mechanical end of the scale, although instances of simple pretend play and, more rarely, elaborated forms of pretend play are also observed at this developmental period.

Further evidence for the developmental sequence captured in the scale is furnished by comparisons of free play at 12 versus 13 months. The analyses of variance computed for each play level indicate developmental change in the expected direction. The results of these comparisons appear in Table 2. Play at the lowest levels of the scale—"mouthing" and "simple manipulation"—declined significantly from 12 to 13 months. In contrast, play at the upper levels of the scale—"pretend external" and most forms of elaborated pretend—substantially increased in frequency over the same time period. ("Double substitution" play, the highest level on the scale, was coded so infrequently that its occurrence remained close to zero, on the average, at both 12 and 13 months.) Play that is intermediate in cognitive sophistication, those levels toward the middle of the scale, generally did not change in frequency from 12 to 13 months. Thus no reliable differences were found across that time period for "functional," "juxtapose," "enactive naming," and "pretend self." Interestingly, "functional relational" play did increase significantly over time, the only intermediate level of play to do so. Explanation may rest in its scale status as the most developmentally advanced nonpretense (i.e., mechanical) form of play. This play level distinguishes the two adjacent lower levels of mechanical play, both of which exhibited a nonsignificant decline in frequency from 12 to 13 months, from the two adjacent upper levels of pretend play, which increased nonsignificantly over the same interval of time. The changes observed across a single month are testimony to the sensitivity of the scale in capturing what appear to be shifts in the cognitive complexity of infant free play.

Developmental change was also apparent from data on exploratory performance, that is, the highest level of play engaged in by the infant across the entire, 20-minute free play period. The mean highest level of free play at 12 months was "enactive naming" (the sixth level on the scale), but by 13 months, it had risen to "pretend external" (the eighth level on the scale). This represents a significant change in developmental level ($F = 26.11, p < .01$). "Pretend self" was the modal performance level (i.e., highest level of free play) at 12 months, whereas "sequence substitution," a full five levels higher, was the modal performance at 13 months. Thus, whether we use measures of typical play behavior (frequency counts for each play level) or of maximal play behavior (performance in free play), we observe systematic change in the expected direction of increasing developmental complexity and sophistication over time.

Final substantiation of this pattern comes from a significant correlation between the amount of simple pretend observed at 12 months and the amount of elaborated pretend observed at 13 months ($r = .39$, $p <$ .01). This relationship suggests that infants who have made the transition into pretend play at 12 months have progressed to more sophisticated forms of pretense by 13 months. Once again, there appears to be developmental progression in the cognitive sophistication of play acts that corresponds to the sequence operationalized in the Belsky and Most scale.

PLAY AS A WINDOW ON COGNITION AND MOTIVATION

It is clear that the developmental changes just described are dependent upon more general developments in the cognitive system of the infant. We can thus view infant exploration and play as a window on cognitive functioning, especially with respect to the applied or practical side of intelligence (Fein & Apfel, 1979). But it is important to recognize that play involves more than simply cognitive skills. Indeed, because it involves the application of cognitive abilities in the child's everyday behavior, it seems necessary to underscore the motivational aspect of play.

Motivation is another hard-to-define construct that is receiving increased attention from scientists whose focus is on the infancy years (Ulvand, 1980). Much of this interest grows out of the early writings of Robert White (1959) and his concept of effectance motivation, also termed *mastery* or *competence motivation*. White proposed that children have an innate motivation to exert control over their environment, to master problems, and to gain competence in dealing with the world around them. Motivational expression, however, was seen as enhanced or weakened through environmental experiences.

Individual Differences in Mastery Motivation

Recently, scientists have begun to consider the developmental origins of mastery motivation. Because it has become apparent that individual differences in measures of this construct (i.e., motivational expression) are already discernible among the youngest school children

(Harter, 1980), it has been necessary to proceed back in time in order to discover when, and how, children first exhibit such differences. For this reason, children in the toddler period and even in infancy are gaining increasing attention in investigations of mastery motivation. Leon Yarrow and his colleagues initially took principal responsibility for trying to operationalize the construct of mastery motivation during infancy (Morgan, Harmon, Gaiter, Jennings, Gist, & Yarrow, 1977; Yarrow, Morgan, Jennings, Harmon, & Gaiter, 1982). They conceptualize the construct in terms of three components: producing effects with objects, practicing emerging sensorimotor skills, and problem solving (Yarrow & Messer, 1983). To assess these dimensions of mastery, eleven specific and highly structured tasks were developed. Tasks designed to elicit effect production involve manipulating objects to secure feedback or to produce visual or auditory effects, for example, pushing a button to make an animal come out of a door. Tasks designed to assess the practice of emerging sensorimotor skills require the use of skills that are just developing, like placing objects in a container for children at 1 year of age. The problem-solving tasks involve detour problems and the use of means–end relationships. For all of these tasks, measures are taken of *persistence*, often assessed by the length of time spent in task-related behavior; *competence*, defined as the number of trials in which the infant correctly produced an effect, combined objects, or secured a goal; and *positive affect*, evaluated on a 5-point rating scale.

We have developed an alternative, less structured, approach for assessing exploratory motivation in infancy that reflects a somewhat different perspective on the construct of mastery motivation (Belsky, Garduque, & Hrncir, 1984). Our notion of motivation is founded upon the assumption that at all ages, including the early years, individuals differ in the extent to which they utilize the competencies that they possess. Some individuals function at their maximum level of ability, whereas others fail to apply themselves fully to the tasks at hand. We reasoned that, in terms of infant exploration and play, insight into the child's motivation could be gleaned by comparing what the infant does spontaneously when exploring a set of materials and what she or he can do when encouraged to engage in activities more cognitively sophisticated than those previously emitted. In essence, the difference between the infant's play performance and competence is conceptualized as a motivational construct; it is labeled *executive capacity* because it is presumed to reflect the extent to which the infant spontaneously executes the competencies she or he has available.

The assessment of executive capacity develops directly from the free play assessment described earlier. Following the 20 minutes of free play on the laboratory floor, the infant is positioned on the parent's lap, and the examiner attempts to elicit from him or her behavior that is more cognitively sophisticated than any single play act observed during free play. Using the procedures detailed by Belsky, Garduque, and Hrncir (1984), children were encouraged to play at a more advanced level through a combination of verbal suggestions and modeled play acts. The assumption on which this (elicitation) procedure is based is that infants will imitate only those behaviors that are cognitively congruent with their current level of understanding (Watson & Fischer, 1980). In other words, infants will not (actually cannot) imitate what they do not understand. This view is supported by several studies of modeling in children (Gottlieb, 1973; Harnick, 1978; McCall, Parke, & Kavanaugh, 1977; Scallon, 1976; Slobin & Welsh, 1973). Indeed, Fenson (1984) presented evidence that modeling serves to highlight individual differences in competence not detected during free play.

To increase the likelihood that infants would attempt to follow the investigator's encouragements, sessions were initiated with a simple standard activity—banging two blocks together. Once a success experience was generated (i.e., banging blocks was imitated by the child), encouragements proceeded in stepwise fashion along the scale, beginning with the level *immediately above* the highest level of spontaneous play observed.

In order to encourage children to engage in specific play acts, a three-trial strategy was employed. First a play act was encouraged verbally (e.g., "The doll is thirsty, give the doll a drink"). If the child failed to respond to the verbal suggestion or did not respond in a manner sufficient to qualify as a success at a given level of play (e.g., raised cup to lips without tilting head back or smacking lips), then the examiner modeled the desired play act (e.g., cup raised to examiner's lips, head tilted back, and drinking noises made). If the child failed to respond successfully in the second trial, then the first two elicitation strategies were combined in a third trial (verbal suggestion plus modeling).

Whenever a child successfully engaged in an elicited act, another act within the same play theme, but at the next highest level in the play scale was encouraged, first with a verbal suggestion, then a modeled act and, finally, a combination of verbal suggestion and modeled act, if necessary. Once a child failed all three trials at one level, a new play theme was employed, giving the child a second set of opportunities to succeed and, at the same time, minimizing the likelihood that failure at a given level of play was a function of a particular play theme or act. To make procedures more concrete, an illustration of a specific elicitation sequence is provided next.

Example

The Examiner notes that Erica's highest spontaneous level in the performance assessment is "pretend self." Erica pretended to drink from the miniature tea cup. The Examiner begins the competence assessment with the standard block-banging procedure. Upon successful imitation of this activity, the Examiner initiates scaled elicitation with the step immediately superceding "pretend self," which is termed "pretend other." In keeping with the play theme of drinking, and using the appropriate objects and suggestions, the Examiner first verbally suggests to Erica: "Dolly is thirsty. Give dolly something to drink." If Erica does give the doll a drink from the cup, the Examiner scores a pass. Now the Examiner proceeds to the next level of the play scale—"substitution self," and again uses a verbal instruction with Erica: "You are thirsty. Take a drink from this," offering the shell. The Examiner proceeds through the levels of the play scale in this manner as long as Erica passes each level, as demonstrated by her actions. However, if at the "substitution self" step (or any other step in the developmental progression), Erica does *not* respond or attempts but does not successfully complete the task, then the Examiner tries a modeled suggestion. The Examiner has Erica watch her pretend to drink from the shell. In so doing, the Examiner exaggerates her actions and makes "drinking" noises as she tips the shell to her mouth—to guarantee that Erica understands the intent. If Erica still does not pass on this trial, the Examiner uses both suggestions and modeling. While exaggerating taking a drink, the Examiner verbalizes to Erica: "I'm thirsty. I'm going to take a drink." If Erica still does not pass on this last trial, the Examiner stops with this play theme and tries another play theme. For example, the Examiner chooses the feeding theme, and using the appropriate objects and suggestions, verbally encourages Erica by saying: "You are hungry. Feed yourself with this" and offers her the wooden peg. If Erica passes this step, the Examiner proceeds to the next level—"substitution other"— with this new theme until Erica does not receive a pass across verbal, modeled, and verbal and modeled trials. After Erica has not received a pass across all three trials (i.e., verbal, modeled, and verbal and modeled) for the given level and for two different play themes, the assessment of competence is terminated. The Examiner works as expediently as possible so as not to lose Erica's attention but to garner from her every indication of her real competence.

Using this procedure, we obtain two distinct, but related, measures: the highest level of elicited play, which we term *competence*, and the difference between maximal scores during free versus elicited play, the competence-performance gap we label *executive capacity*. We found a significant difference, both at 12 and 13 months, between the highest level of play (performance) displayed during free play and the level of competence exhibited during elicited play. On the average, infants imitated play acts approximately two levels above their highest level of free play observed. Indeed, the high degree of competence demonstrated by these year-old infants is noteworthy. By 12 months, the typical infant in our primarily middle-class sample could not only imitate pretense acts but could direct these acts toward some external agent (doll or examiner). One month later, she or he could already employ a simple substitution in that same act of imitation (e.g., use a long, thin block as a spoon to feed self or doll). In each case—at 12 and at 13 months—the highest level of free play (performance) tended to underestimate the competence of which these infants were capable. It is this gap between competence and performance, our measure of mastery motivation, to which we now turn our attention.

Recall that we operationalized mastery motivation in terms of "executive capacity," the arithmetic difference—on an adapted version of the Belsky and Most play scale—between free play performance level and elicited play competence level. We used a transformed scale due to the undifferentiated and individualistic nature of several play levels ("simple manipulation," "juxtapose," and "enacting naming"), which the examiner neither models nor attempts to elicit. Furthermore, several adjacent play steps that are differentiated in the competence assessment may, in fact, represent parallel rather than hierarchical levels of functioning (e.g., "substitution self/other," "sequence story self/other"). For the reasons cited before, there is no distinction made between these identified play levels in the computation of executive capacity. This is taken into account in the transformed scale that appears in Table 3. Performance and competence scores are converted to transformed val-

TABLE 3
Transformations of the Belsky and Most (1981) Play Scale for Computation of Executive Capacity

Name of step	Levels for free play coding	Levels for calculating executive capacity
Mouthing	1	0
Simple manipulation	2	0
Functional	3	1
Juxtapose	4	1
Functional relational	5	2
Enactive naming	6	2
Pretend self	7	3
Pretend external	8	4
Substitution self	9	5
Substitution external	10	5
Sequence no story	11	6
Sequence story	12	7
Sequence substitution	13	8
Double substitution	14	9

ues, and the arithmetic difference is computed. The larger the computed value for executive capacity, the greater the gap between the child's competence and performance, from which we infer restricted expression of mastery motivation. On the other hand, we presume that a child readily demonstrates his or her desire to understand and be competent (his or her mastery motivation) by performing at or near his or her level of competence, in which case the score for executive capacity would be low or zero. Utilizing the 9-level transformed scale, scores on executive capacity could range, in theory, from 0 (high level of expressed mastery motivation) to 8 (low level of expressed mastery motivation).

To evaluate the validity of this index of motivation, Belsky *et al.* (1984) studied infant play and the quality of the infant–mother attachment in a sample of 1-year-olds. They hypothesized that securely attached infants would display a smaller gap between what they did spontaneously in free play and what they were able to do in elicited play than would insecurely attached infants. The reasoning was that a secure attachment relationship, indicating greater trust in the attachment figure, enables an infant to attend more easily to the environment beyond the attachment figure. Thus securely attached infants would be better able to concentrate on the exploration and play process. The Belsky and Most (1981) play scoring system was used to assess the cognitive sophistication of free play. To evaluate the child's level of competence, Belsky and his colleagues employed the elicitation procedure just described.

As initially hypothesized, they observed that variation in the child's enduring social relationships affected their exploration and play. That is, securely attached infants displayed smaller gaps between their free and elicited play behavior; they imitated fewer cognitively sophisticated acts than those that they had displayed in free play. In consequence, the insecurely attached infants appeared less skilled at deploying their competencies in free play, as compared to securely attached infants, who were significantly more likely to explore, on their own, at their highest level of ability. Clearly the social context, defined in terms of the quality of the child's emotional tie to his or her mother affects the nature of the early skilled action we observe.

The results just summarized effectively complement work initiated by others on the relationship between security of attachment and infant mastery motivation assessed through exploratory play. Harmon, Suwalsky, and Klein (1979) found that infants who display patterns of avoidance toward their mothers engage in a greater quantity of play, but poorer quality of play than their securely attached counterparts. Because evidence suggests that quality versus quantity of exploration is more intimately linked to cognitive competence, Harmon *et al.*'s data may be considered as support for the notion that security of attachment and motivation for competence are interconnected. More direct evidence is furnished by Frodi, Bridges, and Grolnick (1984) who reported that infants exhibiting the alternative pattern of insecurity—a resistant attachment—display significantly less positive and more negative affect during structured toy tasks, another proposed index of mastery motivation. These correlations were found both at 12 and at 20 months of age. In other words, there is a very small, but growing, body of evidence indicating that security of attachment and mastery motivation are linked during the infancy period.

SOCIAL-CONTEXTUAL ANTECEDENTS OF EXPLORATION AND PLAY

The fact that infants' motivation to explore, as well as the cognitive sophistication of their free play, has been found to covary with security of attachment in a theoretically predicted manner supports the notion that the nature of infants' early social experiences within the family influences their exploratory and play behavior. After all, it is widely assumed that security of attachment is itself a function of children's interactive experience with their caregivers (Ainsworth, 1979). If security of attachment is related to earlier parent–infant interaction and if attachment is related to exploratory and play behavior, then it stands to reason that early family experience ought to be related to exploratory functioning. Such a view would be compatible with White's (1959) early formulation of effectance motivation. Although he conceptualized it in terms of an innate motivating force, White considered its expression to be a function of early environmental experiences, among which parenting would certainly be prominent.

Rubenstein (1967) conducted some of the earliest research examining the influence of the social context by examining the relationship between maternal attentiveness to the baby in the home and infant performance on the "pairs test." The pairs test involves providing an infant with two toys, one familiar (a bell) and the other, novel, and evaluating the amount of time spent manipulating the novel object. Analyses revealed that mothers who were more attentive to their infants at 5 months, that is, who spent more time looking at, touching, holding, and talking to their children, had babies who spent more time at 6 months exploring the novel materials. One interpretation of these re-

sults is that mother's attentiveness serves a fueling or motivating function; that is, it helps to stimulate the child to engage the environment.

Another aspect of the social context that has been directly related to
exploratory and play behavior is maternally mediated object stimulation.
This kind of growth-promoting mothering involves deliberate attempts
to involve the infant in the environment by providing him or her with
objects to manipulate or by directing his or her attention at things to
examine. In her longitudinal study of mother–infant interaction, Clarke-
Stewart (1973) found that the best predictor of the complexity of the
child's play behavior at 18 months in a laboratory setting was the amount
of stimulation with toys and objects that the infant received from mother
at home at 9 months.

Why should such mothering promote exploration and curiosity?
One suggestion is that stimulating activity provides infants with information about the world and teaches them how to focus their attention on
objects and events so as to be able to acquire information on their own. In
an effort to evaluate this hypothesis empirically, Belsky, Goode, and
Most (1980) experimentally manipulated the social context by modifying
the frequency with which mothers of 1-year-olds directed their infants'
attention to objects and events in their homes by giving them things,
pointing out interesting events, and verbally highlighting unique properties of the world around them (e.g., "that's a big, round ball"). As
predicted, the babies of such mothers, in contrast to those assigned to a
control group, displayed more focused and cognitively sophisticated
exploratory behavior when observed several months later.

Other evidence of the motivating value of maternal attention comes
from a series of studies conducted by Yarrow and his colleagues that
highlight the potentially facilitative or fueling effect of physical contact
between mother and baby. Yarrow, Klein, Lomonaco, and Morgan
(1975; Yarrow, 1976; Yarrow, MacTurk, Vietze, McCarthy, Klein, &
McQuiston, 1984) reported strong positive associations between the frequency of kinesthetic and similar forms of sensory stimulation and infants' persistent and successful performance on items involving secondary circular reactions and goal-directed behaviors (e.g., attempting to
obtain a cube out of reach, pulling on a string to secure a ring beyond the
infant's immediate grasp, attempting to secure a toy by unwrapping the
paper around it). Moreover, follow-up assessments of these infants at 13
months indicated that mastery motivation behaviors displayed in play
situations were more systematically related to kinesthetic stimulation
than to any other category of maternal care assessed at 6 months. To
account for these data, Yarrow postulated that appropriate kinesthetic
stimulation (e.g., rocking, jiggling, moving the infant's whole body)

maintains the infant in an optimal state of arousal, which then permits the infant to attend to, respond to, and explore people, objects, and events in his or her environment. Such alertness and involvement is presumed to foster learning and thereby promote cognitive development.

Consistent with such an interpretation of the relationship between physical contact and infant functioning are Erikson's (1950) formulations concerning the development of basic trust, autonomy, initiative, and industry. As the child develops a sense of trust through physical contact and interaction, the arousal and pleasure that often accompany such contact may extend beyond the immediate exchange between infant and adult to the environment that serves as its context. Thus the child's curiosity and motivation to explore are, in a sense, fueled; "initiative" and "industry" may therefore be rooted, at least in part, in that pleasurable experience of physical contact or positive arousal.

In the Yarrow *et al.* (1982) investigation of infant persistence at tasks, kinesthetic stimulation was not the only aspect of the social context that significantly predicted infant exploratory activity. The more mothers responded contingently to distress and to infant vocalizations at 6 months, the more infants were observed to display competence in mastery tasks at 13 months. These results are consistent with data reported by Riksen-Walraven (1978) as part of an experiment designed to determine the effect of parental responsiveness on infant exploration. In this work, mothers in an experimental group were encouraged to be responsive to their infants over a 3-month period by following a curriculum of activities suggested to them. Pre-post test comparisons between the experimental and a control group revealed not only that the curriculum directives succeeded in increasing maternal responsiveness between 9 and 12 months but also that the increased responsiveness of the mother appeared to influence the infant. Specifically, infants from the experimental group engaged in more exploration of a novel stimulus when subjected to the pairs test and engaged in a greater variety of investigatory behaviors when provided with a set of objects to explore at 12 months of age.

In their investigation of correlates of mastery motivation at 12 and 20 months, Frodi and her colleagues (1984) examined several different aspects of maternal behavior, using both behavioral observations and self-report measures. These researchers discerned reliable contemporaneous associations between persistence at mastery tasks by infants and both the amount of task-directed behavior and the sensitivity exhibited by mothers during structured toy play at each of the two time periods studied. The sensitivity measure was one originally constructed by Ainsworth for her pioneering work relating maternal behavior to security of infant–parent attachment (Ainsworth, 1979). In addition to these two observational measures, maternal responses on a child-rearing attitudes questionnaire considered optimal for child development predicted infant persistence, competence, and affect during the same structured play assessments. Whether measured through observation or self-report, responsiveness of parents to infant needs and signals was one of the primary constructs being tapped in the Frodi *et al.* study, providing further evidence for the role of early social experiences—and specifically, the responsiveness of attachment figures—in the expression of mastery motivation during play.

These investigations specifically exploring the relationship between maternal responsiveness and infant exploratory behavior are consistent with the results of a variety of other correlational and experimental studies that focus on dimensions of the social context relevant to current and later competence. These have utilized a variety of different kinds of measures to assess infant functioning, including standardized infant tests, language tests, and learning tasks (see Belsky, Lerner, & Spanier, 1984, for a review). In an attempt to explain why parental responsiveness and infant competence seem to go together, it has been proposed that parental behavior that is responsive to infant behavior enables the child to discover that she or he has control over the world and, thereby, encourages the child to engage in further reinforcing activity. Lewis and Goldberg (1969) have spoken in terms of a generalized sense of efficacy that the infant develops, even in the first half of the first year, which, through the activity it encourages, generates experiences that are richly informative. It is likely, then, that it is the acquisition of such information, as well as the sense of control it affords the young child, that is responsible for the relationship between intellectual competence and responsive mothering.

When considered together, these studies highlighting experiential correlates of infant play behavior form a subset of a broader literature linking variation in parent–infant interaction and subsequent cognitive and social competence. As we have pointed out elsewhere (Belsky, 1981; Belsky, Lerner, & Spanier, 1984), this literature can be easily summarized by noting that maternal care that promotes optimal infant development can be characterized as attentive, responsive, stimulating, and positively affectionate.

Much less is known about fathers' influence on infant development, and we are aware of only a single investigation that has attempted to examine specific relations between paternal behavior and infant exploration. The results of this study are in general agreement with those of the occasional study that explore links between observed fathering and infant functioning in showing that infants whose fathers are more involved with them appear to be more intellectually and socially competent (see Belsky *et al.*, 1984, for review). In this particular study, Belsky (1980) correlated measures of fathering, obtained during naturalistic home observations at 15 months, with measure of free play behavior. Toddlers whose fathers frequently spoke to them, stimulated them, and expressed positive affection, engaged in more periods of sustained play and exhibited behavior that was considered highly creative. In contrast, toddlers whose fathers were not very responsive and who spent much time reading and watching TV spent more time in aimless activity when exposed to toys presented by the experimenter.

It must be noted that, even beyond the correlational nature of the findings just reported, it is difficult to draw conclusions regarding father influence because the assessments of fathering and infant exploration were conducted within a few days of each other. One would seem to be on much stronger ground for considering the role of fathers in promoting exploratory functioning if longitudinal data were in hand allowing correlations between early assessments of the father–infant relationship and assessments of infant functioning at a later point in time.

Fortunately, such data were available as part of our current investigation. At 1, 3, and 9 months (corrected for gestational age), two naturalistic observations of the family provided information on mother–infant and mother–father–infant interaction in the home. In the remainder of this portion of the chapter, we report the results of our attempts to link parent–infant interaction across the first year with infant exploration and play at 12 and 13 months.

Familial Antecedents of Infant Play

We structured home observations in our own investigation in such a way as to capture infants' everyday experience and to minimize the reactive effects of the observer's presence. Parents were reminded that we wished to observe the baby and his or her routine experiences and were therefore encouraged to go about their normal activities during each of the observations. No restrictions were made on individual or family activities so as to maintain naturalistic conditions for observation.

Trained observers coded preselected parent and infant behaviors as present or absent according to a 15-second time-sampling procedure for 45 minutes during each home visit, yielding frequency counts for each behavior included. Immediately after the mother–infant observations, observers rated maternal interactions with their infants on a 9-point sensitivity scale. Judgments were based upon four components of maternal behavior: (1) her awareness of her infant's behavioral cues and signals, (2) her accurate interpretation of these signals, (3) the appropriateness of her responses to them, and (4) the promptness of her responses.

From the observations of the mother–infant dyad and mother–father–infant triad at 1, 3, and 9 months, we gained measures of mothering in the dyad, mothering in the triad, and fathering in the triad. Of these we selected four categories of parental behavior as indexes of parental influence and involvement in the present study. These are: (1) responding contingently to some aspect of the infant's behavior; (2) focusing the child's attention on some object or event in the environment and/or arousing the attentional state of the infant; (3) expressing positive emotional feeling toward the baby by hugging, kissing, smiling at, or verbalizing endearments; and (4) engaging in personal leisure activity involving reading or watching television. Scores for each of these categories represent the absolute number of time-sampling units in which each behavioral function was recorded.

In all subsequent analyses, the infant free play data collected at 12 and 13 months were prorated for each 10-minute play period and then summed across all four periods (two at 12 months, two at 13 months). The two measures of maximal performance (at 12 and 13 months) were likewise summed. Only measures based on elicited play (competence and executive capacity) represent data collected at a single point in time—the 12-month assessment with mothers present or the 13-month assessment with fathers present. Because we cannot be certain how much this procedure (which involves having infants in their parents' laps) may be influenced by the particular parent present, we believed it wise to keep the two competence and executive capacity scores distinct. As will become apparent later, the presence of the parent raises the issue of competing influences on infant behavior. We must recognize that a parent's presence may either facilitate or impede a child's readiness to separate and explore as well as to engage in the examiner's elicitation "game." In other words, the choice of parent accompanying the infant creates a particular context in which infant behavior and functioning is observed and should be considered when we proceed to make interpretations about that behavior. More will be said of this later.

Maternal Behavior

Correlations linking measures of mothering and infant exploration revealed few significant associations. Those that do emerge, however, are concentrated at the 3-month observational period. At 1 month, only the maternal behavior of stimulate/arouse exhibited any systematic pat-

tern of significant correlations with 1-year infant behavior. The relationships obtained only in the triadic observations (with father present)
and predicted cognitive competence rather than motivation. None of
these findings was replicated when mothers were observed alone with
their infants. At 9 months, only a few chance associations appeared for
maternal behavior in the dyad, and none at all for maternal behavior in
the triad.

   In contrast, maternal behavior at 3 months predicted infant exploratory motivation at 1 year. Mothers who stimulated their infants more
often and who received higher ratings for sensitivity in their interactions
when alone with their infants had infants who later tended to perform at
or near their level of competence during free play ($r = -.33$, $p < .01$; $r = -.29$, $p < .05$, respectively). At the same time, mothers who spent more
time involved in personal leisure activity (reading or watching televi-
sion) when in the company of both husband and child had infants who
were *less* likely to demonstrate their competence spontaneously ($r = .26$,
$p < .05$). These mothers had infants who imitated more sophisticated
acts during the elicitation procedure than they had displayed spontaneously ($r = .32$, $p < .05$). The small, but reliable, correlations with our
index of motivation are in the direction we would predict on the basis of
hypotheses about environmental influences on motivational expression
(i.e., less maternal involvement → less motivation to deploy competencies during play).

   Although there are also correlations relating maternal behavior at 3
months to simple forms of pretend at 12 months, these are somewhat
inconsistent across observational settings. When alone with their infants, the more responsive and affectionate mothers were, the more
frequently their infants engaged in the developmentally relevant level of
simple pretend play ($r = .27$, $p < .05$; $r = .23$, $p < .10$, respectively).
Maternal stimulation in the triad, however, was associated with *fewer*
instances of simple pretend ($r = -.29$, $p < .05$).

   In summary, the pattern of correlations obtained at 3 months indicates that mothers who actively engage and sensitively respond to their
3-month-olds when alone with them but mute their interactions—without withdrawing entirely to pursue private interests—in the company of
their husbands (perhaps to give them a greater opportunity to engage
their infants) have infants who demonstrate certain cognitive competencies and express a motivation to employ their competence spontaneously when given the opportunity to do so. This pattern stands in
contrast to the 1-month data, which suggest that, at this time, mothers
who spend time stimulating their infants when in the company of their
husbands have more cognitively competent 1-year-olds.

   The concentration of results at 3 months suggests that there is particular developmental significance of this period for the measures of maternal behavior used in this study to predict later infant functioning. Furthermore, it highlights the importance of considering the situational context of measurement. In this case, the presence of the father apparently assigns different significance to the behavior of the mother during our home observations. Just as we must qualify infant play behavior according to the presence of the parent who accompanies him or her, as we will see when we examine paternal correlates, we must be prepared to interpret maternal behavior differently, depending upon the presence of the husband. When father is home, it may be more beneficial if mother reduces the amount of stimulating interaction with her infant, leaving "room" for father and baby to interact. The impact of parental behavior on the maturing infant depends on the situational setting in which it occurs.

Paternal Behavior

Unlike the observations just reported regarding maternal correlates of 1-year infant play and motivation, associations between fathering and infant functioning at 1 year occur more often at 9 months and assume a pattern that is inconsistent with expectations regarding parental influences. At 1 and 3 months, significant correlations are scattered and few, although there is some evidence that paternal affection at 1 month is associated with more competent exploration by 1-year-olds. However, given the isolated nature of these findings, the correlations may well be chance occurrences.

Active paternal involvement at 9 months, on the other hand, shows repeated but marginally significant correlations with *lower* level (functional) play at 1 year. Furthermore, involved fathers at 9 months were also more likely to have infants who demonstrated their competence only during elicited play, performing at substantially lower levels during free play. In measurement terms, the more stimulating fathers had infants with higher executive capacity scores—that is, larger competence-performance differences ($r = .38$, $p < .01$), whereas those who spent more time in personal leisure activities had infants with smaller differences between observed competence and performance ($r = -.28$, $p < .05$).

We see two separate, but related, issues here that require comment: first, the *timing* and, second, the *direction* of effects. Of relevance to both is a consistent body of research indicating that the quality of paternal involvement with infants and young children differs subtly from that of maternal involvement, with fathers typically exhibiting more active and play-oriented behaviors (Belsky, 1979; Lamb, 1981; Parke & Tinsley,

1981). Indeed, research indicates that fathers spend a disproportionately greater amount of their child-centered time devoted to play. In the present study, the quantity of paternal behaviors did not change systematically over time, remaining consistently lower than that of mothers. It is entirely possible, however, that the quality of the behaviors we recorded does change over the course of the first year. Fathers may be hesitant to engage very young infants in the kinds of active play that later typify father–child interactions. By 9 months, however, they may feel comfortable about engaging their infants in activities that are more lively and playful. In fact, regarding the direction of associations, what we may be observing in infants whose performance is below competence level at 13 months but whose fathers were less inclined to withdraw for personal leisure activities at 9 months are babies who come to associate fathers' company with active, social play (Clarke-Stewart, 1978; Lamb, 1976). This explanation is supported by work conducted by Jennings, Harmon, Morgan, Gaiter, and Yarrow (1979), who found that maternal *play* in the home with 1-year-olds was associated with less spontaneous free play and less effectance play (play that produces physical effects) in the lab. These children appear to be learning to expect social play with parents nearby, making it less likely that we will observe them in independent, object-oriented play in the company of their parents. In this case, we might expect that paternal involvement at 9 months would correlate with more low-level free exploration and a tendency not to exhibit during free play one's higher level competencies.

This pattern of results again requires that we consider the context in which we observe infant play. In a setting (father present) where social interaction and play are customary, object exploration and mastery motivation may appear diminished; in a setting (mother present) where object-mediated stimulation or independent play has predominated, exploration and motivation may appear enhanced. Our choice of (social) setting shapes the nature of the behavior we set out to study.

SUMMARY AND CONCLUSIONS

Infant play is gaining the notice of a growing coterie of developmentalists, and, we would argue, rightly so. Studies such as the one described here point to its considerable potential for learning about developmental change and individual developmental status at ages when standard developmental tests are often difficult to administer and interpret, particularly from the perspective of future functioning (McCall, 1974b). Although we are still in the initial stages of description and conceptualization, most indicators are positive regarding the theoretical and practical utility inherent in this endeavor. It is our hope that the results reported here represent a limited, but meaningful, contribution toward the effective conceptualization and operationalization of infant play as a valuable developmental assessment technique.

By making observations at two different points in time—at 12 months and then again at 13 months of age—it was possible to study infant play from a developmental perspective. We found substantial evidence to confirm the content and sequence of play operationalized in the developmental scale constructed by Belsky and Most (1981). Specifically, we found that undifferentiated exploration declines and pretend play (simple and elaborated) increases over that 1-month period. Play that is intermediate in developmental status (i.e., in the central region of the scale)—functional and transitional play—remains relatively constant over time. Moreover, developmental change is evident in measures of maximal performance as well. Both performance and competence levels changed reliably over time in the direction of increasing cognitive complexity and integration.

In other words, free and elicited play appear to be effective measures of infant developmental status. In conjunction with other research—relating play to language development (Fein, 1979; Nicolich, 1977), standardized tests of cognitive development (Hrncir, Speller, & West, 1988), and measures of cognitively enriching environmental experiences (Belsky, 1980; Rubenstein, 1967)—these data support the notion that infant play may serve as a window on cognitive development.

Using observations of maternal, paternal, and infant behavior at 1, 3, and 9 months, we found very modest relations between infants' early experiences and functioning and later play. Although correlations were limited in strength and isolated in occurrence, enough patterns were discernible to permit a developmental story line of a sort to emerge.

The major theme of that story line concerns the chronology of effects. The few significant correlations between 1-month parenting and 1-year play link early parental care with later exploratory competence, either in free or elicited play. Apparently, the very early environmental context is more relevant to later cognitive development than to motivational expression.

By 3 months of age, however, we discover many more associations with our measure of mastery motivation. Maternal stimulation when alone with her child and attentive but less active involvement when in the company of her husband each predict increased expression of infant exploratory motivation during the 12-month assessment.

The few associations that appear in the 9-month data again relate to motivation. However, these are found exclusively with measures of fathering. Fathers who are more involved with their infants at 9 months, who stimulate their infants more often at this time, have infants whose performance underestimates their competence during exploratory play. Jennings *et al.*'s (1979) hypothesis that these parents increase their infants' orientation to and expectations about parental social interaction seems particularly apt as an explanation for our findings. In many cases, fathers brought their 1-year-olds into the laboratory during times when those who were more involved with their children might typically be engaging them in lively, interactive play (shortly after supper or on weekend mornings). Preoccupation with fathers versus toys when left to their own devices would be a predictable outcome for these infants.

The fact that motivational effects do not begin to appear until 3 months of age may be taken as support for the view that motivational expression is related to environmental experiences, although we cannot rule out possible maturational effects on measurement utility. And if we focus on maternal data, we find associations consistent with research summarized earlier in the chapter regarding environmental influences on development (Clarke-Stewart, 1973; Rubenstein, 1967; Yarrow, 1976).

Although we expect that the appropriate stimulation and responsive care an infant receives from his or her parents has an important developmental impact, we would also expect that characteristics of the infant itself contribute to later behavior. Indeed, we have some data to indicate that this may, in fact, be the case.

We found that both measures of neonatal status (birthweight and gestational age), as well as observations of particular infant behaviors at 1, 3, and 9 months (aggregated into a composite measure we termed *arousal*) were of some use in predicting later exploratory competence. Specifically, infants of more robust birth status (greater birthweight and gestational age) engaged in more sophisticated free play behavior at 1 year. Similarly, infants exhibiting greater arousal at 1 and 3 months (a composite of frequency counts for exploration, responses, vocalizations, and smiles) tended to display their maximal competence during free play. Fussier 1- and 3-month-olds, on the other hand, tended to show larger competence-performance gaps in their play at 1 year, that is, lower motivational expression. In the case of these behavioral measures, the strongest correlations between early and later infant functioning again tended to occur at 3 months of age. Although limited in size (correlations ranged from .29 to .48, with an average of .32), the fact that we could find associations between global indices of newborn biological status and of early infant arousal and fussing attests to the role of constitutional factors, either directly or indirectly (through the selective experiences they engender), on early cognitive development.

It is important, however, to sound a note of caution with regard to the process of influence. Our correlational data leave this question unaddressed. Although it is possible that some infants are, in and of themselves, more motivationally expressive at 1 year, knowledge from experimental and longitudinal research on environmental effects (e.g., Belsky, Goode, & Most, 1980; Clarke-Stewart, 1973; Rubenstein, 1967) suggest that parental influences are at least as important, and probably more important, than infant characteristics in determining such developmental outcomes. Of course, the more alert, active, and content infant presumably elicits a different quality of care than the passive, lethargic, or colicky one. However, Belsky, Rovine, and Taylor (1984) found that over the course of the first 9 months of life, parental contributions were systematically greater than infant contributions to the security of later infant–parent attachment. The correlations we observe linking both infant and parent behavior, especially at 3 months, to later infant exploration probably reflect independent *and* reciprocal sources of influence on later functioning.

IMPLICATIONS FOR FUTURE RESEARCH

If there is one methodological theme that consistently emerges from our data, it is the theme of context—both social and developmental context. This theme is salient whether we focus on the different significance of maternal behavior when alone with her infant or when in the company of her husband as well, whether we try to make sense of different patterns of infant exploration in the presence of father versus mother, or whether—in developmental terms—we note that our independent variables are more informative when measured earlier in development. Indeed, we find our need to qualify findings on these bases encouraging. It encourages our belief in the very discernible impact of the social environment on both parental and infant behavior and on both infant exploration and motivation; it encourages our growing understanding of how social influences operate; and it encourages our efforts to become increasingly specific about what social factors and what developmental outcomes to look at and how best to do so.

We have already hypothesized about the "meaning" for infants of less exclusive interaction with and stimulation from mothers when fathers are home and of the presence during play assessments of a father who has been stimulating and engaging when at home. Here we will describe some methodological implications from our study for future research concerned with infant play and motivation.

When our ultimate goal is to assess cognitive sophistication and mastery motivation during play, our earlier observations of parent(s) and infant need to reflect a more refined knowledge about the timing, the setting, and the nature of the behaviors we observe. With respect to the infant, very early in development—up to 3 to 4 months—our measures of infant behavior may be relatively undifferentiated. Statelike measures of the amount of fussing or sleep, as opposed to alert and attentive periods, may suffice as predictive information. By 5 or 6 months, however, we would gain by including measures of affect, of visual versus tactile object exploration, and of social responsiveness (verbalizations, affective expressions, visual regard toward persons). From about 9 months on, we must consider the quality of the exploration observed, whether the exploration occurs in sustained bouts, whether it involves coordination of sensory modalities, whether it provides unique information about the target object, and so forth.

More differentiated measures should characterize our observations of parents as well. Recall that Yarrow's group (Yarrow *et al.*, 1982) found it was a particular kind of stimulation—physical movement of the infant—that predicted later infant functioning. Clarke-Stewart (1973) cited the unique contribution of object-mediated stimulation. Beyond global ratings of sensitivity and measures of positive affect, then, parental behavior should be classified as verbal, tactile, kinesthetic, or object-mediated stimulation versus noninvolvement. Furthermore, from 6 months or so on, it is probably increasingly important to assess the responsiveness of the parent to infant initiations. As infants gain competence in expressing their different needs and interests, we need to ask what parents are doing to encourage them. Rather than asking whether they make any kind of response, we must as whether they provide an appropriate one, defined in terms of its relevance to the signals the infant displays. Only by increasing our specificity of measurement can we identify the particular behaviors and exchanges that are linked to particular developmental outcomes. And it will require this level of specificity to refine our models of social-contextual influences on development.

But beyond the particular behaviors we choose to study and the relevant points in time we choose to study them, we can further refine our methodological approach by varying the setting of interest. Understanding the effect of setting goes beyond the expectation that behavior will differ in content and meaning when mother versus father accompanies the infant, or when both parents and/or siblings are present during an observation. It requires that we pull together knowledge from different arenas to hypothesize about and test for effects we would expect to see. An example from our own study may be instructive.

Recall the discrepant correlations we found between active father involvement at 9 months and a larger gap between performance and competence in play at 1 year. On the basis of Jennings *et al.*'s (1979) conclusion, we suspect that these infants have a competing motivation for social interaction and play that interferes with the level of toy-oriented exploration they demonstrate. We are pitting the motivation to explore objects against the motivation to interact with parents.

Consider the standard procedure used to assess the quality of infant–mother attachment. In the Ainsworth and Wittig (1969) Strange Situation, the securely attached infant is expected to be responsive to the presence of his or her parent. Thus, in the low-stress situation prior to separation, we expect such infants to explore with some thoroughness but also to share affective and exploratory pleasure with parents. When stress is introduced, in the form of a stranger's presence, or a first or second separation from the parent, the securely attached infant should respond by actively garnering the support of his or her parent, most typically by approaching for contact and physical interaction. Only after achieving the comfort of parental contact, is he or she expected to resume exploration.

If we now view the play assessment procedure from the same perspective, we see that the very fact that these infants are in unfamiliar surroundings (the lab), in the company of an unfamiliar adult (the examiner), may serve to heighten the motivation for social contact and interaction with the parent. And although contact with parent is afforded the infant, it is not encouraged. Only during the elicitation procedure are infants free to remain in their parents' laps for any extended period. The elicitation of infant competence is presumably not affected in the manner that free exploration may be.

That we do not find negative associations between exploration or motivation and maternal behavior at 9 months may be testimony to the competing interests of curiosity versus dependency. When given the choice, some securely attached infants will move off more readily to explore, whereas others will seek continued interaction with their mothers. In the case of fathers, past learning about paternal availability and opportunities for playful social interaction may tip the behavioral balance in favor of social contact as opposed to exploration.

The interpretations we offer here regarding social-contextual influences in some sense reflect the progress that has been made in the field as a whole, and the progress yet to be made. We have developed techniques to assess both infants' competence in exploration and their seeming motivation to employ that competence; we have documented the high level of cognitive skill infants can possess by the end of their first year, as well as developmental change in that skill level over the course of a single month; we have begun to etch out some interesting relationships between earlier experience and functioning and later competence and motivation. Most pertinent to future research in this field, we have begun to pose questions geared to a new level of refinement, asking about the context in which we make our play assessments, the socioemotional meaning behind the performance and the competence demonstrated, and the impact of relationships—whether between parent and infant or between mother and father—on the behavior we observe.

We have started to feel the conceptual limits of traditional approaches to early cognitive assessment; we have an opportunity to make the quantum leap to more innovative approaches with unique potential for theory testing and theory refinement. We have begun to recognize some of the contextual "confounds" of our measures; we have an opportunity to use those social and contextual factors as a rich source of knowledge about influences on behavior and development. In each case, that opportunity rests on our efforts to study infant exploration and play with a more discerning and discriminating eye.

ACKNOWLEDGMENTS. Work on this chapter and the research reported herein was supported by grants from the National Science Foundation (No. SES-8108886), the National Institute of Child Health and Human Development (No. R01HD15496-01A1), the Division of Maternal and Child Health of the Public Health Service (No. MC-R-424067-02-0), and by the March of Dimes Birth Defects Foundation (Social and Behavioral Sciences Branch, No. 12-64), Jay Belsky, Principal Investigator.

REFERENCES

Ainsworth, M. D. S. (1979). Attachment as related to mother-infant interaction. In J. S. Rosenblatt, R. H. Hinde, C. Beer, & M. C. Bushel (Eds.), *Advances in the study of behavior* (Vol. 9). New York: Academic Press, 1979.

Ainsworth, M. & Wittig, B. (1969). Attachment and exploratory behavior of one-year-olds in a strange situation. In B. M. Foss (Ed.), *Determinants of infant behavior* (Vol. 4, pp. 113–136). London: Methuen.

Bates, E. (1979). *The emergence of symbols*. New York: Academic Press.

Belsky, J. (1979). Mother–father–infant interaction: A naturalistic observational study. *Developmental Psychology, 15*, 601–607.

Belsky, J. (1980). A family analysis of parental influence on infant exploratory competence. In F. Pedersen (Ed.), *The father–infant relationship: Observational studies in a family context* (pp. 87–110). New York: Praeger.

Belsky, J. (1981). Early human experience: A family perspective. *Developmental Psychology,* 17, 3–23.

Belsky, J., & Most, R. K. (1981). From exploration to play: A cross-sectional study of infant free play behavior. *Developmental Psychology, 17,* 630–639.

Belsky, J., Garduque, L., & Hrncir, E. (1984). Assessing performance, competence, and executive capacity in infant play: Relations to home environment and security of attachment. *Developmental Psychology, 20,* 406–417.

Belsky, J., Goode, M. K., & Most, R. K. (1980). Maternal stimulation and infant exploratory competence: Cross-sectional, correlational, and experimental analyses. *Child Development, 51,* 1163–1178.

Belsky, J., Lerner, R., & Spanier, G. (1984). *The child and the family.* Reading, MA: Addison-Wesley.

Belsky, J., Rovine, M., & Taylor, D. (1984). The origins of individual differences in infant-mother attachment: Maternal and infant contributions. *Child Development, 55,* 718–728.

Breger, L. (1974). *From instinct to identity: The development of personality.* Englewood Cliffs, NJ: Prentice-Hall.

Bruner, J. S. (1973). Organization of early skilled action. *Child Development, 44,* 1–11.

Clarke-Stewart, K. A. (1973). Interactions between mothers and their young children: Characteristics and consequences. *Monographs of the Society for Research in Child Development, 38* (Serial No. 153).

Clarke-Stewart, K. A. (1978). And daddy makes three: The father's impact on mother and young child. *Child Development, 49,* 446–478.

Emde, R., Gaensbauer, T., & Harmon, R. (1976). Emotional expression in infancy: A biobehavioral study. *Psychological Issues, 10* (Monograph 37).

Erikson, E. (1950). *Childhood and society.* New York: Norton.

Fein, G. G. (1979). Echoes from the nursery: Piaget, Vygotsky, and the relationship between language and play. *New directions for child development: Fact, fiction, and fantasy in childhood, 6,* 1–14.

Fein, G. G., & Apfel, N. (1979). The development of play: Style, structure, and situations. *Genetic Psychology Monographs, 99,* 231–250.

Fenson, L., Kagan, J., Kearsley, R. B., & Zelazo, P. R. (1976). The developmental progression of manipulative play in the first two years. *Child Development, 47,* 232–236.

Fenson, L., & Ramsey, D. S. (1980). Decentration and integration of the child's play in the second year. *Child Development, 51,* 171–178.

Frodi, A., Bridges, L., & Grolnick, W. (1984). *Determinants and correlates of mastery motivation: A short-term longitudinal study of infants in their second year.* Manuscript under review, University of Rochester.

Garvey, C. (1974). Some properties of social play. *Merrill-Palmer Quarterly, 20,* 163–180.

Gottlieb, S. (1973). Modeling effects upon fantasy. In S. L. Singer (Ed.), *The child's world of make believe: Experimental studies of imaginative play.* New York: Academic Press.

Harmon, R., Suwalsky, J., & Klein, R. (1979). Infants' preferential response for mother versus an unfamiliar adult: Relationship to attachment. *Journal of the American Academy of Child Psychiatry and Psychology,* 437–449.

Harnick, F. (1978). The relationship between ability level and task difficulty in producing imitation in infants. *Child Development, 49,* 209–212.

Harter, S. (1980). A model of mastery motivation in children: Individual differences and developmental change. In A. Collins (Ed.), *Minnesota Symposium on Child Psychology* (Vol. 14). Hillsdale, NJ: Lawrence Erlbaum Associates.

Hrncir, E. J., Speller, G. M., & West, M. (1985). What are we testing? A cross-cultural comparison of infant competence. *Developmental Psychology, 21,* 226–232.

Jeffree, D., & McConkey, R. (1976). An observation scheme for recording children's imaginative doll play. *Journal of Child Psychology and Psychiatry, 17*, 189–197.

Jennings, K. D., Harmon, R. J., Morgan, G. A., Gaiter, J. L., & Yarrow, L. J. (1979). Exploratory play as an index of mastery motivation: Relationships to persistence, cognitive functioning, and environmental measures. *Developmental Psychology, 15*, 386–394.

Lamb, M. E. (1976). Interactions between two year olds and their mothers and fathers. *Psychological Reports, 38*, 447–450.

Lamb, M. E. (1981). The development of father-infant relationships. In M. Lamb (Ed.), *The role of the father in child development* (pp. 10–63). New York: Wiley.

Lewis, M. & Goldberg, S. (1969). Perceptual-cognitive development in infancy: A generalized expectancy model as a function of the mother-infant interaction. *Merrill-Palmer Quarterly, 15*, 81–100.

Lowe, M. (1975). Trends in the development of representational play in infants from one to three years: An observational study. *Journal of Child Psychology and Psychiatry, 16*, 33–47.

McCall, R. B. (1974a). The development of intellectual functioning in infancy and the prediction of later I.Q. In J. Osofsky (Ed.), *The handbook of infant development*. New York: Wiley.

McCall, R. B. (1974b). Exploratory motivation and play in the human infant. *Monographs of the Society for Research in Child Development, 39* (Serial Number 155).

McCall, R. B., Eichorn, D. H., & Hogarty, P. S. (1977). Transitions in early mental development. *Monographs of the Society for Research in Child Development, 42* (Serial No. 171).

McCall, R., Parke, R., & Kavanaugh, R. (1977). Imitation of live and televised models by children one to three years of age. *Monographs of the Society for Research in Child Development, 42* (Serial No. 173).

Morgan, G. A., Harmon, R. J., Gaiter, J. L., Jennings, K. D., Gist, N. F., & Yarrow, L. J. (1977). A method for assessing mastery motivation in one-year-old infants. *JSAS Catalog of Selected Documents in Psychology, 7*, 68.

Nicolich, L. M. (1977). Beyond sensorimotor intelligence: Assessment of symbolic maturity through analysis of pretend play. *Merrill-Palmer Quarterly, 23*, 89–99.

Parke, R., & Tinsley, B. (1981). The father's role in infancy: Determinants in caregiving and play. In M. Lamb (Ed.), *The role of the father in child development* (2nd ed., pp. 140–184). New York: Wiley.

Piaget, J. (1952). *The origins of intelligence in children* (M. Cook, Trans.). New York: International Universities Press.

Riksen-Walraven, J. M. (1978). Effects of caregiver behavior on habituation rate and self-efficacy in infants. *International Journal of Behavioral Development, 1*, 105–130.

Rosenblatt, D. (1977). Developmental trends in infant play. In B. Tizard & D. Harvey (Eds.), *Biology of play: Clinics in developmental medicine*, No. 62 (pp. 33–44). Philadelphia: J. B. Lippincott.

Rubenstein, J. (1967). Maternal attentiveness and subsequent exploratory behavior. *Child Development, 38*, 1089–1100.

Rubin, K., Fein, G., & Vandenberg, B. (1983). Play. In E. M. Hetherington (Ed.), *Handbook of child psychology: Social development* (pp. 693–774). New York: Wiley.

Scallon, R. (1976). *Conversations with a one year old*. Honolulu: University Press of Hawaii.

Slobin, D., & Welsh, C. (1973). Elicited imitation as a research tool in developmental psycholinguistics. In C. A. Ferguson & D. I. Slobin (Eds.), *Studies of child language development*. New York: Holt, Rinehart & Winston.

Ulvand, S. E. (1980). Cognition and motivation in early infancy: An interactionistic approach. *Human Development, 23*, 17–32.

Uzgiris, I. (1976). Organization of sensorimotor intelligence. In M. Lewis (Ed.), *Origins of intelligence* (pp. 123–164). New York: Plenum Press.

Watson, M., & Fischer, K. (1977). A developmental sequence of agent use in late infancy. *Child Development, 48,* 828–836.

Watson, M., & Fischer, K. (1980). Development of social roles in elicited and spontaneous behavior during the preschool years. *Developmental Psychology, 16,* 483–494.

Weisler, A., & McCall, R. B. (1976). Exploration and play: Resume and redirection. *American Psychologist, 31,* 492–508.

White, R. (1959). Motivation reconsidered: The concept of competence. *Psychological Review, 66,* 297–333.

Yarrow, L. J. (1976, October). *The origins of mastery motivation.* Paper presented at the Annual Meeting of the American Academy of Child Psychiatry, Toronto.

Yarrow, L. J., & Messer, D. J. (1983). Motivation and cognition in infancy. In M. Lewis (Ed.), *Origins of intelligence* (2nd ed., pp. 451–477). Hillsdale, NJ: Lawrence Erlbaum.

Yarrow, L. J., Klein, R. P., Lomonaco, S., & Morgan, G. A. (1975). Cognitive and motivational development in early childhood. In B. Z. Friedlander, G. M. Sterritt, & G. Kird (Eds.), *The exceptional infant, Vol. 3: Assessment and intervention.* New York: Bruner/Mazel.

Yarrow, L. J., Morgan, G. A., Jennings, K. D., Harmon, R. J., & Gaiter, J. L. (1982). Infants' persistence at tasks: Relationships to cognitive functioning and early experience. *Infant Behavior and Development, 5,* 131–141.

Yarrow, L. J., MacTurk, R. H., Vietze, P. M., McCarthy, M. E., Klein, R. P., & McQuiston, S. (1984). The developmental course of parental stimulation and its relationship to mastery motivation during infancy. *Developmental Psychology, 20,* 492–503.

CHAPTER 7

Individual Differences in Environmental Exploration and Cognitive Mapping Skills
Early Development in Social Contexts

NANCY L. HAZEN

INTRODUCTION

> [The] effective child-rearer makes the living area as safe as possible for the naive newly crawling or walking child and then provides maximum access to the living area for the child. This immediately sets the process of development off in a manner that will lead naturally to the satisfaction of and further development of the child's curiousity; the opportunity to learn about the world at large. (White, Kaban, Shapiro, & Attonucci, 1976, pp. 150–151)

> Davy's father shares the route he chooses to take and consciously develops skills of observation in his son while they journey to his work places together. Both of his parents talk with their children continually wherever they drive; they impart curiosity about places. . . . This is part of his father's educational philosophy, one which can best be termed as an apprenticeship in practical education: Davy was being trained to be competent at hunting, finding objects and using them resourcefully and finding his way about. (Hart, 1981, p. 222)

Parents can strongly influence their children's environmental experiences, as these examples illustrate. From the time infants become

---

NANCY L. HAZEN • Department of Home Economics, University of Texas at Austin, Austin, Texas 78712.

mobile, parents provide them with environments to explore, set the boundaries for exploration, structure the spatial layouts and objects provided in the home environment, encourage and discourage certain types of exploration and point out spatial locations and relationships. To the extent that they influence their children's exploration and use of environments, parents probably also influence the development of their children's cognitive mapping skills, that is, their skills for maintaining spatial orientation and solving spatial problems in large-scale environments.

Although research on the development of cognitive mapping skills has flourished during the past decade, almost nothing is known about how parents actually *do* influence the development of these skills. Perhaps this is because investigators have been concerned primarily with *structural* developments in the cognitive representations that are assumed to underlie adaptive spatial behavior, rather than with how these representations *function* in everyday contexts (Hazen & Pick, 1985). In their efforts to get at underlying spatial competence, investigators have generally tried to "decontextualize" tasks as much as possible. As Siegel (1981) stated, "The fundamental problem in understanding the aquisition and development of cognitive mapping is the externalization of cognitive maps—getting the spatial knowledge out in some public medium, unconfounded by [theoretically] 'nonspatial' task load" (p. 168).

But, as contributors to this volume have noted repeatedly, the *Zeitgeist* is changing. Investigators of the development of cognitive mapping, like investigators of cognitive development in general, are increasingly concerned that explanations of how structural cognitive competencies develop cannot be complete without reference to the everyday contexts in which they function over the course of the life span (Rogoff, 1984; Siegel, 1982; White & Siegel, 1984). Structural developments are adapted to these contexts, and in turn, contexts are altered by each new structural competence that is developed. As Thelen and Fogel (Chapter 2 this volume) have argued, "the context itself *is part of the structure of the behavior*" (p. 27). When a child performs some spatial behavior, for example takes a detour to a friend's house, it is the *context* of that behavior, not the child's structural knowledge of spatial relations, that motivates performance of that behavior. Behaviors will not develop if they are not performed.

When researchers have investigated the contexts in which spatial skills develop, they have focused almost exclusively on features of the *physical* environment (the scale of environments, the presence of landmarks, the presence of barriers, etc.). But contexts of development are also, almost without exception, social and emotional as well as physical

(White & Siegel, 1984). Although developmental changes in the children's physical environments—from relatively small, restricted, familiar spaces to increasingly large and complex spaces—no doubt play an important role in the development of children's cognitive mapping skills (Hazen & Pick, 1985), these physical environments cannot be considered in isolation from the social and affective forces that shape them and that influence children's transactions within them.

Research reported by Acredolo (1982) illustrates the importance of understanding how social and affective contexts of spatial tasks can effect children's performance. In one study (Acredolo, 1979), 9-month-old infants were given a spatial location task in their homes and in an unfamiliar laboratory. They found a toy hidden under one of two cloths on a table and were then moved to the opposite side of the table. Although 65% of the babies in the laboratory environment made the incorrect, egocentric choice, only 13% of the babies tested at home did so. Because the laboratory setting was devoid of landmarks, Acredolo (1979) at first speculated that the "home court" advantage may have been due to the presence of landmarks in the home. But further research indicated that when babies were given a 15-minute familiarization period in the lab, they performed as well in that setting as they did at home (Acredolo, 1982). Presumably, because the babies felt more comfortable and secure in the familiar surroundings of the home, they were better able to devote their attention to the task at hand.

Acredolo's study illustrates how one very small contextual change—giving the baby a few minutes to become more familiar, and thereby feel more comfortable, with some strangers in a novel setting—caused a dramatic change in the baby's spatial performance. According to Fischer (1980), "relatively minor alterations in the environmental context of action will literally change the skill being used. That is, the organism's control of a skill depends on a particular environmental context." Parents should be especially powerful influences on the developing spatial competencies of their infants and very young children because they have almost complete control over environmental contexts their young children experience (Barker & Wright, 1954) and because cognitive processing seems to have a heavier emotional component in early development (Anooshian & Siegel, 1986).

Understanding how cognitive mapping abilities develop in social contexts, and particularly in the context of parent–child interaction, may be especially critical for understanding individual differences in these abilities. Fischer (1980) has argued that individual differences in the types of skills children develop, in their rates of developing these skills, and in the developmental pathways through which skills are acquired, are all heavily dependent on contextual factors. The examples presented at the beginning of the chapter indicate some ways in which individual differences in cognitive mapping skills might develop in the context of the parent–child relationship.

The first example suggests that infants whose parents provide safe, interesting environments for them to explore and who actively encourage their exploration may develop certain cognitive mapping skills more rapidly than infants whose parents are more restrictive. For example, in fairly small, familiar environments (such as their home and yard), they may be advanced in their ability to encode spatial locations topologically (using landmarks) rather than egocentrically (using body-based cues) and to infer spatial relationships between locations that they have not directly experienced. They may also develop the ability to transfer these skills to novel environments at an earlier age. Young children with extensive environmental experience might even use an entirely different set of cognitive mapping skills than those with more limited experience when confronted with the problem of remaining oriented in unfamiliar large-scale environments. For example, they might be able to simultaneously encode the spatial relationships between several landmarks, rather than isolated relationships between one landmark and another, by mentally representing them in the form of a route or survey map (Shemyakin, 1962). Children with limited environmental experience might eventually develop the ability to construct more integrated survey-type representations through different types of experiences, for example, experience with models or maps of large-scale environments.

Parents might also contribute to individual differences in their children's cognitive mapping skills by directly guiding them to attend to spatial locations and relationships and teaching them skills for remaining oriented. Davy, the child discussed in the second example, was able to construct a model of his home town that was very accurate and well-integrated—much more so than those of children his own age (7 years old), or even 2 to 3 years older. Because Davy did not appear to be especially advanced in other domains of cognitive development, Hart (1981) attributed his advanced cognitive mapping skills to the training in large-scale spatial competency that his parents, particularly his father, had provided.

These speculations about how parents might influence their children's cognitive mapping skills need to be confirmed and extended by empirical research. To date, almost all research on how parents affect their children's exploration has focused on children's exploration of novel *objects*, rather than *environments* (see Henderson, 1984, for review).

In the remainder of this chapter, I will present recent research that indicates some ways in which individual differences in children's *environmental* exploration might develop in the context of parent–child interaction and how the development of children's cognitive mapping skills might be affected. I will then discuss different means by which parents can support their children's developing spatial competencies and argue that optimal strategies for parental intervention are adapted to the individual child's interests and capabilities in solving whatever spatial challenges are presented by the environment—from finding out where things are located in a novel environment, to learning how to read maps. Recent observations of parental guidance of visually impaired children's exploration will be presented in support of these arguments.

PARENTS' CONTRIBUTIONS TO CHILDREN'S INDIVIDUAL STYLES OF EXPLORATION

My own research has been concerned primarily with individual differences in young children's abilities to mentally represent and find their way in large-scale environments. In my first study on this topic (Hazen, 1982), my goal was to examine the relationship between young children's individual styles of spatial exploration and their spatial orientation abilities. Sixty-four children aged 20 to 28 months and 36 to 44 months explored two environments and then completed tasks designed to assess their cognitive mapping skills. In the presence of one of their parents, the children first explored in a large museum room designed to allow children to freely explore and manipulate the objects on exhibit— furs, bones, stuffed animals, and the like.

It quickly became obvious that the children's explorations could not be separated from their interactions with their parents. My original plan was to ask parents to sit on the sidelines, observing but not interacting while their child explored. This was clearly *not* a naturalistic exploration situation for the children. Children observed in pilot testing did not expect their parents to be uninvolved in the exploration and often became distressed and refused to explore when their parents resisted their attempts to involve them. The parents indicated that when they typically encountered interesting new environments like the museum room with their children, they generally walked around with the child and pointed out and discussed objects the child could explore, either throughout the whole observation period or at least until the child became accustomed to the environment. Therefore, I revised the exploration situation by asking parents to simply do whatever they would normally do to facilitate their child's exploration of a new environment.

Within 2 weeks of the museum exploration, the children and their parents returned for the second portion of the study that took place in a large laboratory room containing a mazelike "playhouse" designed to test the children's cognitive mapping skills. To examine the consistency of children's exploration styles across two different settings, half of the children in each age group explored the laboratory environment before the cognitive mapping tasks were administered. The instructions and observational techniques were the same as those used in the museum exploration. Finally, children learned a specific route to a goal in the playhouse and then were required to reverse the route and to infer new routes to the goal.

Results of this study showed a clear relationship between children's styles of exploration and their cognitive mapping skills. Children who explored *independently*, whether in the museum or the laboratory, performed better on all measures of spatial orientation ability. Independence of exploration was calculated by dividing the number of independent (self-guided) movements made through the environment by the total number of movements made (self-guided movements plus movements guided, through either physical or verbal direction, by the parent). Children's total amount of exploration, whether measured in the museum or the laboratory, was unrelated to any of the measures of spatial exploration. Also, the degree to which children explored independently was highly positively correlated across the two exploration situations, but the quantity of their exploration was not. Thus results indicated that independence of exploration may be a stable individual difference in young children that is predictive of their cognitive mapping skills.

Independent explorers were not necessarily unaccompanied by parents as they explored; in fact, more often than not, their parents followed them, or they pulled their parents along or called them to come and look at various exhibits. Children who were less independent explorers, in contrast, were more likely to rely on their parents to direct their exploration. These parents would call, lead, or even carry them to the various exhibits.

Also, whether the child was an independent explorer seemed as much a function of the parent as the child. Some parents encouraged their child to take the lead even when the child was initially reluctant. For example, when her 3-year-old son initially made no move to explore, one mother first tried to point out the general exploratory potential of the room: "Look at all the neat things to play with in here!" When he still made no move, she finally gave an explicit direction. She walked to a table containing horns and antlers, held some antlers to her head, and said, "Look, do I look like a deer?" The boy laughed and became involved himself in manipulating the antlers. From that point on, he made nearly all the decisions about where to explore.

In another case, a very wary 2-year-old boy refused to let his father put him down to explore. The father tried repeatedly to interest the boy in exploring the objects in the room, but the boy continued to cling to his father throughout the entire observation session. Interestingly, this child was only slightly more independent when exploring the laboratory room, even though he seemed much more at ease in that smaller and less stimulating environment. Although he was able to learn the initial route through the maze playhouse, he had absolutely no success in reversing the route or in inferring new routes to the goal.

In contrast to the two parents described before, some parents were consistently directive of their child's exploration. Usually children of such parents passively followed these directions and did not explore independently, but in a few cases, children with directive parents preferred to explore independently and frequently ignored their parents suggestions and directions. In fact, one 2-year-old boy with a very directive mother scored very high in independent exploration because he constantly ran away from her! At one point, she turned to the observer with exasperation and exclaimed, "He does this all the time. He's just totally out of control!"

Perhaps young children's independence of exploration is consistent across different exploration settings because of stable qualities in the parent—child relationship. Quantity of exploration, in contrast, may be more influenced by the physical qualities of environments (e.g., size of the space, amount and variety of objects to be explored, etc.) and by individual differences in children's interests in particular aspects of environments (i.e., a given child might cover less ground in one environment than in another if she or he finds something that particularly intrigues her or him and explores it extensively).

Of course, because this was a correlational study, the causal relationship between independent exploration and cognitive mapping skills is unresolved. Perhaps children who explore more independently tend to pay more attention to the environment and are thus more likely to encode aspects of its spatial layout. Results of a study by Feldman and Acredolo (1979), who manipulated independence of exploration in preschool children and examined its effect on the children's encoding of a spatial location, support this hypothesis. Children who walked to a landmark by themselves remembered the landmark's location better than children who were led to the landmark. Or, perhaps children with poor cognitive mapping skills follow their parents because they fear getting lost. Most likely, causality is bidirectional, such that children who do not explore independently acquire limited cognitive mapping skills and as a result, tend to get lost when they explore independently. Because they get lost, they continue to avoid independent exploration, thus perpetuating their poor spatial exploration skills.

Exploration, Cognitive Mapping, and Attachment

Because the child's independence of exploration seems to be largely a function of the parent–child relationship, individual differences in exploration style may have their roots in early patterns of parent–child attachment. Attachment theorists have argued that infants who are securely attached to their caregivers are able to use them as a secure base from which to explore the world (Ainsworth, Blehar, Waters, & Wall, 1978). Also, individual differences in attachment relationships between infants and their primary caregivers may relate to a variety of developmentally appropriate adaptations at later periods in development (Sroufe, 1979).

In Ainsworth's Strange Situation (Ainsworth et al., 1978), securely attached infants balance exploration of the experimental room with seeking proximity to their mothers. Infants with anxious-avoidant attachment relationships generally avoid contact with their mothers and often explore more extensively than infants in other attachment groups. Finally, anxious-resistant infants cling to their mothers but also show anger and resistance to them. This group is the most passive in exploration.

Two possible hypotheses can be made concerning the relationship between security of attachment in infancy and exploration styles and spatial skills during the toddler years. One possibility is that exploratory behavior would remain stable over time and therefore the cognitive mapping skills of anxious-avoidant children would be equal, if not superior, to those of securely attached children. Only anxious-resistant children would be less skilled in cognitive mapping. A second possibility is that continuity would not be found in the stability of exploratory behavior but rather in the general styles of adaptation to the environment. That is, children showing most competent adaptation to the environment at 1 would balance exploration with seeking proximity to their mothers, whereas competent children at age 2 seek autonomy and independent mastery of the environment. Thus securely attached children would be expected to surpass anxious-avoidant children in both independent exploration and spatial cognitive skills. Attachment theory is more consistent with the second hypothesis of continuity in developmentally appropriate adaptations, rather than in specific behaviors, and this pattern has also been found in a growing body of studies examining later effects of attachment (Sroufe, 1979).

To test these hypotheses, we examined the exploration and cognitive mapping skills of 28 children aged 30 to 34 months who had been classified at the age of 12 months for security of maternal attachment (see Hazen & Durrett, 1982, for details). The toddlers and their mothers were taken to a large experimental room containing a mazelike playhouse similar to that described in the preceding study (Hazen, 1982). After a 10-minute get-aquainted period, children were permitted to explore the entire room, including the playhouse, and mothers were told to behave as they normally would while their child explored a new environment. Observers recorded where the children went and whether each movement was self-guided or mother-guided. After the exploration period, the child's cognitive mapping skills were assessed, using a procedure similar to that used in the previously described study. Children learned a particular route through the playhouse to a goal and were then required to reverse that route and to infer new routes to the goal.

Results of this study replicated Hazen (1982) in that children's independence of exploration correlated quite highly with their cognitive mapping skills. Also, as previously found, sheer quantity of exploration, as measured by total number of movements made (both active and passive) was not correlated with measures of spatial skill.

Our most important finding was a clear relationship between early attachment and later exploration styles and cognitive mapping skills. First, the securely attached children were more likely to be independent explorers than the children in the two insecurely attached groups. Even though anxious-avoidant infants were the most active explorers at age 1, by 2½ securely attached children surpass them. Anxious-resistant infants remained the most passive explorers.

Individual differences in early attachment were also related to later differences in cognitive mapping skills. Securely attached children were better able to infer new routes to the goal than were insecurely attached children, indicating that they were able to form more accurate mental representations of the space and/or better able to use these representations to infer new routes. Somewhat surprisingly, the anxious-resistant children actually performed somewhat better on the spatial tasks than did the anxious-avoidant children.

Partial correlation procedures were used to find out more about the causal relationships between security of attachment, style of exploration, and cognitive mapping skill. Each factor was found to be correlated with each of the other two factors when the third factor was held constant. Thus the causal relationships among these three factors seem to be complex and multiply determined.

Possibly, characteristics of mother–child interaction associated with individual differences in security of attachment directly affect children's style of exploration, which in turn affects their cognitive mapping skills. One such characteristic might be the extent to which infants can use their mother as a secure base for exploration. But because anxious-avoidant infants may often explore more actively than securely attached infants (Ainsworth, Bell, & Stayton, 1971) and because anxious-resistant infants actually performed somewhat better on our cognitive mapping tasks than did anxious-avoidant infants, early individual differences in willingness to leave the mother to explore cannot fully account for the present pattern of results.

A second attachment-related characteristic might be the extent to which mothers of insecurely attached infants are more restrictive or interfering regarding their children's exploration relative to mothers of securely attached infants. Although data specifically relating to effects on exploration are unavailable, mothers of insecure infants (especially anxious-avoidant infants) have been found to be more interfering and controlling in general and to show less respect for their infant's autonomy (Ainsworth *et al.*, 1978). Again, however, this does not seem to prevent anxious-avoidant infants from being active explorers. Anecdotally, we found that a few of our subjects showed a pattern that I had observed in the previously described study, in which the mother attempts to give many directions, and the child ignores her and runs around somewhat aimlessly, as though trying to run away. Nearly all mother–child pairs showing this pattern were in the anxious-avoidant group.

Perhaps anxious-avoidant children explore actively more to avoid the mother than to investigate and learn from the environment. Connell (1974) found that avoidant infants did not show initial wariness to a novel object or habituate to it, indicating that although they appear to be actively exploring the object, they were not learning from their exploration. In contrast, securely attached infants in Connell's study were first somewhat wary of the object but habituated to it after exploring it for several minutes. Anxious-resistant infants tended to be so wary of the object that they explored it very little and did not habituate to it. If avoidant children explore primarily to avoid interaction with the mother and fail to learn from their exploration, it is not surprising that securely attached children surpass them in cognitive mapping skills. In fact, perhaps resistant children can learn more from their more limited environmental experience than avoidant children because they need to be highly motivated to explore in order to overcome their anxiety about exploration. This could explain our finding that avoidant children scored even lower than resistant children on our cognitive mapping tasks.

Individual differences in the attachment relationship might also directly affect spatial cognitive development, rather than only affecting it indirectly by influencing patterns of exploration. Presson and Ihrig (1982) demonstrated that although most research indicates that 8-month-old infants rely primarily on egocentric cues for spatial orientation, they are capable of using their mother as a geocentric landmark. Because securely attached infants are more likely to use their mother as a secure base for exploration, they may become accustomed to using her as a geocentric landmark at an earlier age than insecurely attached infants (especially anxious-avoidant infants). Moreover, the fact that this landmark is always moving around may be especially challenging to the infant's developing ability to organize spatial information. The infant must learn to update not only changes in her or his own position relative to stable environmental landmarks but changes in her or his mother's position as well.

Finally, the correlations we found between security of attachment, independence of exploration, and cognitive mapping skills may be due at least in part to maternal characteristics that contribute to general competence in infant adaptation. Characteristics such as consistency and predictability, emotional availability, sensitivity to the child's needs, and skill in helping the child adapt to environmentally imposed problems might underlie aspects of each of the three factors, as well as a variety of other cognitive and social adaptations (Arend, Gove, & Sroufe, 1979; Matas, Arend, & Sroufe, 1978; Pastor, 1981; Sroufe, 1979; Waters, Wippman, & Sroufe, 1979).

Beyond the Early Parent–Child Context

Do differences in the cognitive mapping skills of active (independent) versus passive explorers persist in contexts that do not involve the parent? In the first two studies, children were always observed in the presence of one of their parents. Because the parent–child relationship seems to directly influence exploration style and may directly or indirectly influence cognitive mapping skills, I conducted a short-term longitudinal study to examine whether individual differences in the cognitive mapping skills of active versus passive explorers are found outside the context of parent–child interaction.

A second goal of this study was to investigate more precisely how active and passive explorers differed in their cognitive mapping skills. In both the previous studies, when active and passive explorers were required to invent alternate routes to a goal, active explorers were able to find more direct routes to the goal than were passive explorers. However, the specific spatial skills that enabled them to do this were unclear. They may have been able to more effectively encode landmark locations, infer spatial relationships, or store spatial representations of the environment in a more configurational fashion.

Finally, a third goal was to examine the developmental course of individual differences in the cognitive mapping skills of active and passive explorers over the course of the preschool years (i.e., from 3 to 5 years of age). Will differences between children with these two styles of exploration disappear as the encoding and manipulation of spatial relationships shifts from being entirely sensorimotor and behavioral to being increasingly symbolic and representational, or will developmental continuity be found between acting in space and symbolically representing space?

Twenty-two 3-year-old children were observed exploring two different novel environments with their mothers—an indoor children's museum and a small outdoor zoo. Six months later, when the children were between 3½ and 4 years of age, they were given three tasks to assess different levels of their ability to manipulate their spatial knowledge of a very familiar environment—their preschool playground. I chose to use a familiar environment for these tasks so that knowledge of the environment itself would not be confounded with the particular spatial manipulation of interest. Children were also given the Peabody Picture Vocabulary Test, a test of verbal intelligence, at this time. One year later, when they were between 4½ and 5 years old, 20 of the original 22 children again completed the same three spatial tasks that they had done the previous year. At this time, their preschool teachers rated them on their attitudes toward exploring environments and materials.

The first spatial task (animal location task) was designed to assess the children's ability to use both near and distant landmarks (different types of topological information) to encode spatial locations. In this task, the child was required to replace toy animals at various locations on the playground. Half of these locations were in direct proximity to a salient landmark, and the other half were at least 6 feet from a landmark. Thus to complete the first half of the replacement tasks, the child needed to use only topological information to correctly replace the animal, whereas for the second half, some distance and direction information was needed as well.

The second task (pointer task) was designed to assess the children's ability to infer spatial relations that they could not directly experience. The child and the experimenter stood behind a door that led out to the playground. The experimenter showed the child pictures of the playground equipment and asked the child to point to each piece of equipment (which could not be seen), using a pointer mounted on a circle marked with degrees.

The third task (model reconstruction task) was presumed to be a higher order task requiring a greater degree of symbolic spatial representation. Whereas the first two tasks involved mental manipulations performed on the actual space, the third task involved performing mental manipulations on a symbolic representation of that space. Children were required to reconstruct a model of their playground using toy pieces. The toy pieces were detailed and realistic looking, so all of the children could easily identify their real-life counterparts. After identifying each piece, children were asked to put them on the model "just exactly the way they go on your real playground."

Children were classified as *active* or *passive* explorers based on the observations of their exploration that were collected when they were 3 years old. Two exploration independence scores were derived for each child by dividing the number of spatial exploration movements the child made independently by the total number of movements he or she made, for each of the two exploration settings (indoor and outdoor). Because the two exploration independence scores were highly correlated, they were averaged, and a median split was used to classify children as active or passive explorers.

Once again, individual differences in children's style of exploration were found to be stable across situations. But more importantly, they were found to be stable over time because children's average exploration independence scores were positively correlated with teacher ratings, obtained nearly 2 years later, how independently they explored, and negatively correlated with teacher ratings of their dependence on adults. This indicates that even though individual differences in styles of exploration may be rooted in the early parent–child relationship, they carry over to other social contexts, such as school, in which the parent is not directly involved.

But how did the active and passive explorers differ in their abilities to manipulate spatial information over this 2-year period? Figure 1 graphically depicts the animal location task scores of the active and passive explorers for the locations that were *directly* marked by landmarks (the first half of the task). Because scores were calculated by summing for each placement the number of feet the animal was placed from the correct location, lower scores signify more accurate perfor-

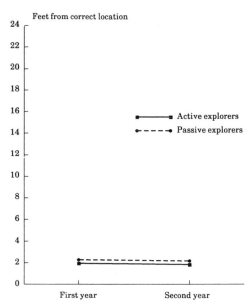

FIGURE 1. Mean number of feet from correct locations that animals were replaced when locations were directly marked by landmarks. Solid line designates mean replacement scores for active explorers; dotted line indicates mean replacement scores for passive explorers. Lower scores indicate more accurate performance.

mance. Clearly, both active and passive explorers performed extremely well in this task and did not differ, although both groups improved slightly from the first year to the second.

But a different pattern of results was found for the second half of the animal location task, in which locations were *indirectly* marked by landmarks. As shown in Figure 2, this task was clearly more difficult for both active and passive explorers. Also, the passive explorers had more difficulty than the active explorers the first year they completed this task, but by the second year, the gap between performance of the active and passive explorers had narrowed to an insignificant difference.

A similar pattern of results was found for the pointer task, as shown in Figure 3. This task was scored by giving the child 1 point for each time he or she pointed to within 10 degrees of the correct location. Because children pointed to 9 locations, scores could range from 9 to 0. Active explorers performed better than passive explorers both years, but the difference between the two groups was less pronounced the second year.

Interestingly, in the model reconstruction task, the difference be-

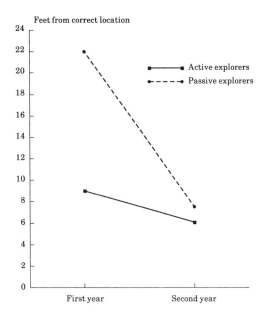

FIGURE 2. Mean number of feet from correct locations that animals were replaced when locations were indirectly marked by landmarks. Solid line designates mean replacement scores for active explorers; dotted line indicates mean replacement scores for passive explorers. Lower scores indicate more accurate performance.

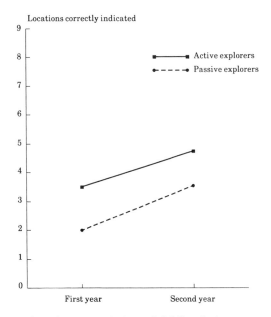

FIGURE 3. Mean number of correct pointings. Solid line designates scores for active explorers; dotted line indicates score for passive explorers. Higher scores indicate more accurate performance.

tween the active and passive explorers showed the opposite trend over time. Children were given 1 point for each of the 11 toy replicas that were placed correctly on the model (within 2 inches on the model = within 6 feet on the playground). As shown in Figure 4, active explorers scored better than passive explorers in both years, but whereas the scores for both groups were low the first year (and did not quite reach significance), the gap between active and passive explorers increased during the second year.

Overall, then, the results indicate that during the early preschool years, passive and active explorers perform equally well on tasks that assess spatial competencies that are mastered early, such as encoding locations that are directly marked by landmarks. On moderately difficult spatial tasks, such as encoding indirectly marked locations and inferring spatial relationships in a familiar environment, passive explorers perform worse than active explorers during the early preschool years but begin to catch up at around age 5. On spatial tasks that are very difficult for preschoolers, such as symbolically reconstructing spatial relationships on a reduced scale, differences between active and passive ex-

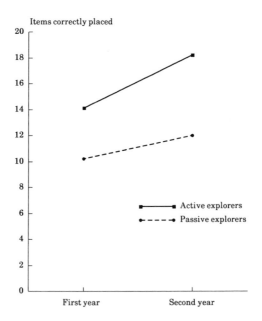

FIGURE 4. Mean number of correct placements in the model reconstruction task. Solid line designates scores for active explorers; dotted line indicates scores for passive explorers. Higher scores indicate more accurate performance.

plorers may be only slight during the early preschool years but may show up more strongly later.

Thus it appears that independent exploration of environments facilitates the development of basic spatial concepts that children first apply to the familiar environments they explore and later are able to transfer to symbolic representations of environments, such as models and maps. Independent exploration might also facilitate children's ability to apply spatial localization and inference skills to unfamiliar environments and to more extensive and complex familiar environments, such as their neighborhoods. Further research is required to examine these possibilities.

How Parents Support Children's Developing Spatial Competencies

Taken together, the results of these three studies indicate that individual differences in independence of exploration are consistent across situations and over time. Individual styles of exploration develop in the context of the early parent–child relationship, persist through the preschool years, and show up in other contexts as well. These individual differences in exploration affect performance of whatever cognitive mapping skills are currently being developed, that is, whatever skills are moderately difficult for the child.

Perhaps parents who provide an optimal context for independent exploration (and the definition of what an "optimal context" is might vary at different periods of development) are more likely to optimize their child's performance of cognitive mapping skills. According to Fischer (1983), discontinuities in skill development, defined as "sharp alterations in the curve portraying developmental change" (p. 6) are likely to occur in contexts that promote optimal performance. The idea that parents may provide contextual supports that optimize children's cognitive performance, enabling children to go beyond their normal cognitive capabilities, is reflected in Vygotsky's concept of the "zone of proximal development." This is defined as

> the distance between the (child's) actual developmental level as determined by independent problem solving and the level of potential development as determined through problem solving under adult guidance or in collaboration with more capable peers. (Vygotsky, 1978, p. 85)

Several investigators have used the metaphor of "scaffolding" originated by Wood, Bruner, and Ross (1976), to describe the nature of the process by which parents (or other more capable individuals) support and guide children to higher levels of cognitive competence. In scaffolding, parents intervene when necessary to help their children set and achieve goals that would otherwise not be possible (see volumes by Rogoff & Wertsch, 1984, and Rogoff & Lave, 1984, for examples). According to Wood (1980):

> adult tutorial interventions should be inversely related to the child's level of task competence—so, for example, the more difficulty the child had in achieving a goal, the more directive the interventions of the mother should be. (p. 284)

The results of the three studies just discussed, however, seem to conflict with the idea of scaffolded parental intervention contributing to higher levels of cognitive mapping skills. Children whose parents were more likely to direct their explorations had *poorer* cognitive mapping skills than children who explored independently. Is the development of cognitive mapping skills, then, different from the development of the many types of cognitive skills that seem to be facilitated by scaffolded parental intervention? Are these skills best developed independently, rather than in contexts of parental guidance? The example of Davy, presented at the beginning of this chapter, suggests not. Davy's parents most definitely scaffolded his developing cognitive mapping skills, probably to a greater degree than most parents, and Davy's cognitive mapping skills were very advanced for his age (Hart, 1979, 1981).

It seems unlikely that there is a single "best" way for parents to facilitate their children's spatial cognitive development. The parent's role in facilitating children's independent exploration involves more than simple nonintervention, and their role in supporting children's achievements in the zone of proximal development involves more than direct tutorial guidance. Parents can provide supportive contexts that permit children to perform higher level skills in a variety of ways. Griffen and Cole (1984) have argued that although the "scaffolding" metaphor is well adapted for describing the nature of parent–child interaction in highly structured, sequenced tasks with clear goals and subgoals, it is less effective in describing parental support in less structured situations in which goals are more divergent or ambiguous.

It is no accident, then, that studies demonstrating the value of scaffolded parental intervention have examined parent–child interaction in the context of activities such as building a pyramid, playing peek-a-boo, reading picture books, and retrieving objects from behind a barricade. Each of these activities has fairly clear goal structures and a circumscribed set of expected behaviors for each participant. Often, they also have a clearly defined end state, indicating that the goal has been achieved.

In contrast, the roles of parent and child in the context of the environmental exploration are ambiguous. Parent's goals for their children are either very general (e.g., that their children should explore), or if specific, they are highly variable (e.g., that their children should manipulate or learn about certain objects in the environment or engage in certain types of games, activities, or interactions, etc.).

When exploring the museum or laboratory rooms with their children, the parents in my studies almost never directly attempted to teach their children about relevant landmarks, routes, and spatial relations— even though they knew that their child's spatial knowledge of the laboratory environment would be tested. They did not seem to view the situation in terms of structuring a goal or getting their children spatially oriented or helping them learn the environments' spatial layout. Instead, they seemed to view each environment more in terms of its general potential to be explored. If parents had any overriding goal at all in these settings, it was to get their children to explore all parts of the environment. Perhaps they viewed this as a better way to help their children learn the spatial layouts of the environments than direct teaching would be. Parents who successfully encouraged their children to explore independently used several types of strategies, often very subtle.

Many of these interventions that seemed designed primarily to influence their children's affective reactions to the environment. Several children were very wary in the museum room, for example, and their parents generally attempted to soothe them so that they would feel comfortable about exploring. In the beginning of the exploration, these parents would stay very close to their children, sometimes holding or carrying them. They often at first directed their children to objects that were familiar and unthreatening, such as the books about animals, and steered them away from ones that might be frightening, such as the skeletons. They very frequently modeled positive affect and interest in exploration. Once children were involved in exploration, they attempted to maintain their interest and positive affect by responding to their questions and comments and by offering praise and encouragement.

If children seemed disinterested or bored, parents attempted to raise their level of interest by pointing out potentially interesting objects or interesting uses for these objects. This type of strategy was also useful for involving overly wary children, as illustrated by the example presented earlier of the mother who put deer antlers on her head to interest her child in exploring. Keeping children interested in exploration was especially problematic in the laboratory playhouse, which was devoid of objects. Parents frequently initiated hide-and-seek-type games to keep children exploring in that setting.

Thus parent's modulation of children's affective responses to environments is a critical aspect of the social contexts of their spatial cognitive development. Thelen and Fogel (Chapter 2 this volume) have argued that infants are unable to perform skilled actions if their arousal level is too high or low. By intervening to change the infant's arousal level (e.g., providing a pacifier to a crying infant), parents permit the infant to engage in actions that would not otherwise be possible. Similarly, young children will not explore if overly wary or uninterested, but parents can change their arousal level so as to encourage exploration.

Some of the same interaction processes that parents use to socialize infant affect and encourage infant object exploration may also play an important role in parental encouragement of environmental exploration by toddlers and preschool children. For example, several investigators have noted that in unfamiliar, ambiguous contexts, infants often look at their parents' emotional expressions to obtain information (Campos & Stenberg, 1981; Feinman, 1982; Klinnert, Campos, Sorce, Emde, & Svejda, 1983). Infant exploration in these ambiguous contexts may be affected by this *social referencing* behavior; for example, Klinnert (1981) and Gunnar and Stone (1983) found that infants were more likely to explore an ambiguous toy when mothers displayed positive affect than when they displayed negative affect. Similarly, parents may encourage their toddlers and preschool children to explore in uncertainty-provoking environments by promoting positive affect in their children.

Parents can encourage their preschoolers to explore environments using positive verbalizations (e.g., "Wow, look at all this great stuff!") as well as facial expressions. Parents might also induce positive affect toward environmental exploration by modeling spatial exploration, by orienting children toward interesting features of the environment, or by providing contingent positive responsiveness to children's expressions of interest and curiosity. Several studies have indicated that maternal modeling of novel object exploration increases exploration of novel objects in 5- and 6-year olds (Endsley, Hutcherson, Garner, & Martin, 1977; Johns & Endsley, 1977; Saxes & Stollack, 1971). Endsley et al. (1977) also found that maternal behaviors that orient children to novel objects and maternal contingent responsiveness were both predicitive of 5- and 6-year old's manipulation of novel objects. Because these were correlational studies, the direction of causality between these maternal behaviors and children's increased exploratory behavior cannot be determined. However, an experimental study by Belsky, Goode, and Most (1980) demonstrated that when mothers are trained to focus their infant's attention on interesting objects and events, infant exploration increases. Whether maternal behaviors designed to increase children's interest in exploration affect the spatial exploration of older children remains to be examined.

To the extent that parents have consistent effects on children's affective reactions to environments, individual differences in children's styles of exploration, and consequently, in their children's cognitive mapping skills, are likely to result. The individual differences that we found in the exploration styles and cognitive mapping skills of toddlers who differed in security of attachment might be explained on this basis. The arousal level of anxious-resistant children may often be too high to permit effective exploration because the child is overly concerned with separation from the parent and parental unpredictability. In contrast, the avoidant children's affective responses to environments may often be too "flat" to pick up information because they may be overly concerned with avoiding the parent rather than getting information about the environment.

Besides modulating their children's affect so as to permit exploration, parents can more directly influence their children's cognitive mapping skills by structuring the contexts of their exploration. Some of the ways in which they might do this —pointing out interesting objects and object uses, avoiding potentially frightening objects and places, and structuring activities such as hide-and-seek games that encourage exploration—have already been mentioned as examples of parental techniques for influencing children's affective responses to environments. But they may also be useful as indirect ways of getting children to encode salient landmarks or spatial relationships between landmarks. For example, parents that played hide-and-seek games in the playhouse tended to hide in areas that their child had not explored much, if at all.

In daily life, parents have tremendous control over the types and varieties of environments that their child may explore, and they also set limits on their child's acceptable range for exploration. Perhaps variations in the variety, complexity, and range of environments that children explore contribute to individual differences in the development of cognitive mapping capacities. This is supported by a study by Norman (1980), who found that the map-drawing skills of children who lived in an unpatterned rural environment (Appalachia) surpassed those of children living in an urban environment. Presumably, maintaining spatial orientation is much more challenging in an unpatterned environment. Also, several investigators have suggested that sex differences in spatial competence may be due at least in part to the fact that parents permit greater spatial freedom to boys (Hart, 1979; Moore & Young, 1978).

Providing an extensive, varied environment for exploration should be balanced with the need to provide safe environments for exploration. Parents who place little or no restrictions on their children's exploration may actually make their children fearful to explore because they have learned that they cannot trust their parents to establish safe limits. The parent's role in providing contexts for exploration that their children perceive as safe and secure may be more important than providing wide access to interesting environments or providing direct, scaffolded instruction to cognitive mapping skills, in terms of enhancing their children's spatial competencies.

Although modulation of affect—giving the child a feeling that exploration is safe and encouraged within certain bounds—seems in most cases to be the most optimal means of encouraging general exploration of environments; scaffolded instruction may be a very effective means of enhancing children's spatial competencies in certain contexts. The type of parental intervention used and the types of spatial skills fostered as a consequence are likely to depend upon the goals of the parent and the child in a given context.

As Soviet research on memory development has demonstrated, memory is rarely a goal in itself but rather a means to a goal, and consequently what is remembered depends upon one's purposes for remembering (Leont'ev, 1981; Smirnov & Zinchenko, 1969). The same might be said for spatial orientation skills: Children will use their spatial orientation skills pragmatically, for a particular purpose, and consequently will acquire certain types of spatial experiences and spatial knowledge. For example, Gauvain and Rogoff (1986) demonstrated that 6- to 9-year-old children's exploration and knowledge of a large-scale space was effected by their purposes for exploring the space. An experimenter told the children to either learn the fastest route through a playhouse or to learn the location of all the rooms in the playhouse. Children who were given the latter instruction remembered more layout-relevant information.

Parents may provide direct scaffolding or instruction in particular spatial skills when their children need these skills to accomplish certain goals. For example, whenever my parents took us to a large public place, such as a zoo or department store, we were first taken to a very salient landmark that was to be the place where we would meet if separated. We were then frequently instructed and quizzed about how to get to that landmark from various locations in the environment. The goal set by my parents was that we all should be able to find our way to the landmark so that we could be found if separated from the rest of the family.

In the case of families like Davy's, who participate in many outdoor activities such as hunting, fishing, and hiking, spatial orientation skills may be a more overriding concern and therefore very heavily scaffolded. Again, the particular skills that are scaffolded will depend on the specific goals set by the parent for the child. Thus a productive way of examining specific ways in which parents facilitate the development of the children's cognitive mapping skills would be to study naturally occurring situations in which way finding is likely to be a primary concern of parents and/or their children.

SCAFFOLDING OF SPATIAL EXPLORATION AND ORIENTATION IN VISUALLY IMPAIRED CHILDREN

For visually impaired children, exploring and remaining oriented in novel environments is always a challenge. Because remaining oriented while traveling through space, remembering spatial locations, and inferring spatial relationships is likely to be a primary goal for visually impaired children, parents of such children may provide much more scaffolded intervention when encountering new environments relative to parents of sighted children.

To examine these issues, Margaret Sullivan and I observed the interactions of three visually impaired preschool-aged girls and their mothers in the context of exploring an unfamiliar environment—a large preschool classroom. Two of the girls, Chris (3:11) and Sue (5:0), had some residual pattern vision. Chris's visual handicap was due to anirida, cateracts, and nystagmus; Sue's was due to cerebral palsy. The third child, Mary, was totally blind due to retrolental fibroplasia. The visual impairment for all three girls was congenital. All three were enrolled in an early childhood program for handicapped children and had been for at least 2 years, so all had received orientation and mobility training. Perhaps because of the influence of the school, all of the mothers said that they placed high priority on orientation and mobility and that they firmly believed in giving their children plenty of opportunities to explore and in encouraging their children to get around independently as much as possible.

These beliefs were clearly reflected in their interactions with their children as they explored the preschool classroom. All three mothers did encourage their daughters to explore actively and independently, and all three of the girls got around the classroom extremely well. Substantial differences were found, however, between the totally blind child and the two partially sighted children in both their exploration styles and in the types of guidance used by their mothers.

Mary, the totally blind child, made far fewer movements through the environment that did Chris and Sue (31 movements versus 114 and 56, respectively). Also, Mary made a lower proportion of independent movements than the other two girls (49% independent versus 100%

independent for Chris and 97% independent for Sue). Because the average proportion of independent movements for 3-year-old girls' exploration in the Hazen (1982) study is 65%, Chris and Sue are very active explorers indeed, and in fact Chris is much more active than sighted girls her age. Although Mary would be considered a passive explorer if she were a sighted child, it is remarkable that her independence of exploration is well within the range of (slightly younger) sighted children. (A 3-year-old girl one standard deviation below the mean would have 44% independent explorations.)

The mothers of the partially sighted girls almost never used any sort of direct intervention to get their child from place to place. They never led the child, pointed her in a certain direction, or gave her directions. These types of guidance were unnecessary because both girls felt very comfortable in the environment from the first and immediately involved themselves in independent exploration.

The main type of guidance these mothers did use was contingent positive attention to their children's questions, comments, and explorations, for example:

CHRIS: (Walks to toy shelf, pick up a "Happy Apple" that jingles to show her mother.)

MOTHER: Oh, music.

CHRIS: (Walks to crib, picks up baby doll and carries it to mother, making crying sounds.)

MOTHER: Okay, I'll hold the baby.

CHRIS: (Walks to sink, finds a feather, walks back toward mother, blowing on the feather to keep it aloft.)

MOTHER: Look at that!

Essentially, the guidance used by the mothers of the partially sighted children was no different from the guidance used by the mothers of young, emotionally secure sighted children who are very independent explorers. No direct intervention or scaffolding of spatial orientation was observed.

As expected, however, Mary's mother used much more scaffolded intervention in the exploration situation. Typically, to encourage Mary to explore, she would offer some suggestions about what Mary might do, or would simply say, "Let's experiment, okay?" She often related objects and events in the environment to Mary's past experiences. If Mary had not been to a particular location, her mother would first take Mary's hand, then step behind Mary to subtly guide her in the correct direction. If Mary began to veer from the correct direction, her mother usually gave her verbal directions; for example, "To the left." She almost always praised Mary when she reached her goal. In this example, Mary and her mother have just entered the room and are sitting at a table:

MOTHER: Want to find some blocks?

MARY: Yeah. (Pushes her chair back and stands up.)

MOTHER: Okay, let's go find some blocks. (Stands up behind Mary, pats her back twice to guide her in the right direction. Mary stops walking and stoops down to inspect some masking tape on the floor, which she apparently felt with her feet.)

MARY: Why's there tape here?

MOTHER: Mmmm (with intonation like "I don't know"), Want to find the toys?

MARY: Yeah. (Stands up, continues to walk forward in the same direction without guidance.) Where's daddy?

MOTHER: Go to the right. (Mary does.) Walk straight; there's a shelf in front of you and blocks on the other side of it, like the toy shelves in your school. (Mary touches the top of the shelf.) Good girl!

Her mother's goal orientation is obvious; she repeatedly directed Mary back to her goal of reaching the shelf when she begins to get distracted. She gave Mary whatever support she needs to reach the goal—telling her that blocks are available, referring to Mary's familiar school to help her picture their location on the shelf, giving her the minimum physical guidance needed, and replacing physical with verbal guidance when possible. To encourage her positive feelings about exploring independently, she also praised her when she achieves her goal.

When Mary's mother believed that Mary knew something about the spatial layout, she increased her demands for independent and correct spatial behavior. For example, she insisted that Mary replace objects on the shelf in the same location, and after Mary bumped her head on the top shelf once, she expected that Mary should know to be careful of it in the future:

MARY: (Sitting at the table, stringing beads.) I'm done.

MOTHER: Okay, put 'em back.

MARY: (Holding her arm in front of her, walks to the shelf independently with the basket of beads but begins to put the beads on the wrong side of the shelf.)

MOTHER: No, the other side. Is that where we got 'em from?

MARY: Yeah.

MOTHER: We got 'em from the top shelf, remember? (Mary stands up and bumps her head on the top shelf for the second time.)

MOTHER: Mary, what did Mama tell you about reaching up? You stand back a little and then you can.

All of Mary's mother's guidance was delivered in a warm, positive tone and despite its corrective intentions did not sound like criticism. The next time Mary replaced an object on the shelf, her mother noticed immediately that she reached up to touch the shelf while starting to stand in order to keep from bumping her head, and she immediately praised her for remembering. Besides using a great deal of scaffolded intervention, Mary's mother also kept Mary interested and involved by providing praise, encouragement, and contingent positive responsiveness through the exploration sessions.

Mary's mother used many of the same scaffolding strategies that other investigators have observed parents use in structured teaching tasks. For example, she transferred responsibilities for achieving the goal to Mary whenever she thought Mary may be able to handle it successfully on her own but intervened again when Mary had difficulty (e.g., when Mary bumped her head for the second time, her mother reminded her about the previous incident and gave verbal instructions for how she could avoid bumping her head again; when Mary started to veer from the correct direction when moving independently, her mother provided verbal correction). She tried to use minimal direct intervention at all times. This closely conforms to Rogoff and Gardner's (1984) description of parental guidance of children's learning:

> They jointly manage the transfer of responsibility for the task so that the novice is participating at a comfortable yet challenging level in the problem's solution. The expert revises the scaffolding for learning as the novice's capabilities develop, adjusting the support for the novice's performance to a level just beyond that which the novice could independently manage. In this manner, adults routinely guide children's growth in understanding problems and ways to solve them. (p. 116)

Mary's mother also frequently related aspects of the unfamiliar environment, or of particular spatial problems in that environment, to Mary's past experiences. Rogoff and Gardner (1984) have suggested that one important function of adult intervention and guidance of children's problem solving is helping the child to generalize relevant problem-solving skills from one situation to another. Adults do this by pointing out similarities between the current problem situation and problems of the same type that the adult knows are familiar to the child.

Finally, Mary's mother helped her both to set up goals and to achieve these goals. The goals her mother set were progressively more general and higher order, and her interventions to help her achieve them were progressively less directive, as Mary became more familiar with the environment and moved more independently. For example, Mary's mother at first would set a very specific goal (e.g., to have Mary travel to a particular location where she could play with toys) and then a more general goal of simply encouraging exploration (e.g., "Want to experiment?"). Her means of guiding Mary began with physical direction (taking her hand, pointing her in the right direction, patting her back as she walked), progressed to verbal directions (e.g., "Go straight", "Turn left") and finally moved to hints and reminders (e.g., "Remember where those were?"). In contrast, the mothers of the partially sighted girls almost never used any direct intervention because, at most, they needed only to set the highest level goal of simply encouraging exploration. (And even this was not really needed because both girls were such active, enthusiastic explorers.) Similarly, Saxe, Gearhart, and Guberman (1984) found that the parents of less skilled children set lower-order subgoals for their children in helping them solve a number reproduction task as compared to the parents of more skilled children.

These observations indicate that there is no one "best" way for parents to facilitate their children's spatial cognitive development. Instead, the optimal parental strategy depends on the abilities of the child, the nature of the particular task or problem situation, the child's goals in the situation, and the parents' goals for the child. In the case of the three visually impaired girls, the problem situation and the children's goals were about the same for all three: They were all in the same classroom, and they all wanted to explore and play. The differences in parental guidance were due primarily to differences in the children's abilities, which resulted in the parents' setting up different types of goal structures.

Conclusions

Clearly, parents can create and support contexts to help their children develop competent environmental behavior in a variety of ways. First, they can provide, alter, and structure the environments themselves. Examples of this include exposing children to a variety of environments, setting up safe environments for exploration (e.g., baby proofing, setting free-range boundaries), and structuring children's activities within environments (e.g., pointing out objects and places to explore).

Second, they can modulate children's affective responses to environments such that children will feel secure and enthusiastic about exploration, neither too wary nor too disinterested. This can be done by modeling positive affect and enthusiasm for exploration, orienting children toward objects and events of interest and away from those that might be frightening, and providing general positive support through the use of contingent positive responses and praise.

Finally, they can provide direct guidance about the environmental features and spatial relationships found in environments. This may sometimes take the form of physical guidance, particularly with very young children (or blind children like Mary) but more often probably takes the form of verbal explanations. In providing direct intervention or teaching, parents may relate environmental settings or tasks to children's past experiences in similar types of situations. Direct teaching is also likely to involve transmission of the culture's tools for spatial problem solving, as Vygotsky (1978) has suggested. This may include instructing children in the use of maps, compasses, and the like, to navigate through space.

In general, structuring safe, interesting environments for exploration and helping children feel secure about exploration may be most important in children's early development, whereas direct teaching of spatial relationships, concepts, and cultural tools for solving spatial problems may become more critical later. (Social networks outside the family context, such as peers and school, will also play increasingly critical roles in the child's later development.) However, if certain children are likely to encounter difficult spatial problems early in life, either because of the environments they inhabit and their ways of using these environments (as is the case with Davy and with Appalachian children), or because of limits in their own abilities (as is the case with Mary), direct intervention may be an optimal strategy for parents to use at an earlier point in their child's development. Researchers must begin to look beyond correlations between parent behaviors and child outcomes and to look more at how parents' strategies are adapted to the needs of the child and the task at hand.

References

Acredolo, L. P. (1979). Laboratory versus home: The effect of environment on the 9-month-old infant's choice of spatial reference system. *Developmental Psychology, 15,* 666–667.

Acredolo, L. P. (1982). The familiarity factor in spatial research. In R. Cohen (Ed.), *Children's conceptions of spatial relationships* (pp. 19–30). San Francisco: Jossey-Bass.

Ainsworth, M.D.S., Bell, S. M., & Stayton, D. J. (1971). Individual differences in the strange situation behavior of one-year-olds. In H. R. Schaffer (Ed.), *The origins of human social relations* (pp. 17–57). London: Academic Press.

Ainsworth, M.D.S., Blehar, M. C., Waters, E., & Wall, S. (1978). *Patterns of attachment: A psychological study of the Strange Situation.* Hillsdale, NJ: Erlbaum.

Anooshian, L. J., & Siegel, A. W. (1986). From cognitive to procedural mapping. In C. J. Brainard & M. Pressley (Eds.), *Basic processes in memory development* (pp. 47–101). New York: Springer-Verlag.

Arend, R., Gove, F., & Sroufe, L. A. (1979). Continuity of individual adaptation from infancy to kindergarten: A predictive study of ego-resiliency and curiosity in preschoolers. *Child Development, 50,* 950–959.

Barker, R. G., & Wright, H. F. (1954). *Midwest and its children: The psychological ecology of an American town.* Evanston, IL: Peterson.

Belsky, J., Goode, M. K., & Most, R. K. (1980). Maternal stimulation and infant exploratory competence: Cross-sectional, correlational, and experimental analyses. *Child Development, 51,* 1163–1178.

Campos, J., & Stenberg, C. (1981). Perception, appraisal, and emotion: The onset of social referencing. In M. Lamb & L. Sherrod (Eds.), *Infant social cognition: Empirical and theoretical considerations* (pp. 273–309). Hillsdale, NJ: Erlbaum.

Connell, D. B. (1974). *Individual differences in infant attachment related to habituation to a redundant stimulus.* Unpublished master's thesis, Syracuse University.

Endsley, R. C., Hutcherson, M. A., Garner, A. P., & Martin, M. J. (1979). Interrelationships among selected maternal behaviors, authoritarianism, and preschool children's verbal and nonverbal curiosity. *Child Development, 50,* 331–339.

Feinman, S. (1982). Social referencing in infancy. *Merrill Palmer Quarterly, 28,* 445–470.

Feldman, A., & Acredolo, L. P. (1979). The effect of active versus passive exploration on memory for spatial location in children. *Child Development, 49,* 623–636.

Fischer, K. W. (1980). A theory of cognitive development: The control and construction of hierarchies of skills. *Psychological Review, 87,* 477–531.

Fischer, K. W. (1983). Developmental levels as periods of discontinuity. In K. W. Fischer (Ed.), *Levels and transitions in children's development* (pp. 5–20). San Francisco: Jossey-Bass.

Gauvain, M., & Rogoff, B. (1986). Influence of the goal on children's exploration and memory of large-scale space. *Developmental Psychology, 22,* 72–77.

Griffen, P. & Cole, M. (1984). Current activity for the future: The Zo-ped. In J. Wertsch & B. Rogoff (Eds.), *Children's learning in the "zone of proximal development"* (pp. 45–64). San Francisco: Jossey-Bass.

Gunnar, M. R., & Stone, C. (1983). *The effects of positive maternal affect on infant responses to pleasant, ambiguous, and fear-provoking toys.* Paper presented at the meeting of the Society for Research in Child Development, Detroit, MI.

Hart, R. A. (1979). *Children's experience of place.* New York: Irvington.

Hart, R. A. (1981). Children's spatial representation of the landscape: Lessons and questions from a field study. In L. S. Liben, A. H. Patterson, and N. Newcombe (Eds.), *Spatial representation and behavior across the life span* (pp. 195–236). New York: Academic Press.

Hazen, N. L. (1982). Spatial exploration and spatial knowledge: Individual and developmental differences in very young children. *Child Development, 53,* 826–833.

Hazen, N. L., & Durrett, M. E. (1982). Relationship of security of attachment to exploration and cognitive mapping abilities in 2-year-olds. *Developmental Psychology, 18,* 751–759.

Hazen, N. L., & Pick, H. L., Jr. (1985). An ecological approach to the development of spatial orientation. In T. Johnson & A. Pietrewicz (Eds.), *Issues in the ecological study of learning.* (pp. 201–243). Hillsdale, NJ: Lawrence Erlbaum Associates.

Henderson, B. B. (1984). The social context of exploratory play. In T. D. Yawkey & A. D. Pelligrini (Eds.), *Child's play: Developmental and applied* (pp. 171–201). Hillsdale, N.J.: Erlbaum.

Johns, C., & Endsley, R. C. (1977). The effects of a maternal model on young children's tactual curiosity. *Journal of Genetic Psychology, 131,* 21–28.

Klinnert, M. D. (1984). The regulation of infant behavior by maternal facial expression. *Infant Behavior and Development, 7,* 447–465.

Klinnert, M., Campos, J., Sorce, J., Emde, R., & Svejda, M. (1983). Social referencing: Emotional expressions as behavior regulators. *Emotion: Theory, research and experience* (Vol. 2). *Emotions in early development* (pp. 57–86). Orlando, FL: Academic.

Leont'ev, A. N. (1981). The problem of activity in psychology. In J. V. Wertsch (Ed.), *The concept of activity in Soviet psychology* (pp. 37–71). Armonk, NY: Sharpe.

Matas, L., Arend, R. A., & Sroufe, L. A. (1978). Continuity of adaptation in the second year: The relationship between quality of attachment and later competence. *Child Development, 49,* 547–556.

Moore, R., & Young, D. (1978). Childhood outdoors: Toward a social ecology of the landscape. In I. Altman & J. F. Wohlwill (Eds.), *Children and the environment* (pp. 83–130). New York: Plenum Press.

Norman, D. K. (1980). A comparison of children's spatial reasoning: Rural Appalachia, suburban, and urban New England. *Child Development, 51,* 288–291.

Pastor, D. L. (1981). The quality of mother-infant attachment and its relationship to toddler's initial sociability with peers. *Developmental Psychology, 17,* 323–335.

Presson, C. C., & Ihrig, L. H. (1982). Using mother as a spatial landmark: Evidence against egocentric coding in infancy. *Developmental Psychology, 18,* 699–703.

Rogoff, B. (1984). Introduction: Thinking and learning in social context. In B. Rogoff & J. Lave (Eds.), *Everyday cognition: Its development in social context* (pp. 1–8). Cambridge, MA: Harvard University Press.

Rogoff, B., & Gardner, W. (1984). Adult guidance of cognitive development. In B. Rogoff & J. Lave (Eds.), *Everyday cognition: Its development in social context* (pp. 95–116). Cambridge, MA: Harvard University Press.

Rogoff, B., & Lave, J. (Eds.). (1984). *Everyday cognition: Its development in social context.* Cambridge, MA: Harvard University Press.

Rogoff, B., & Wertsch, J. (Eds.). (1984). *Children's learning in the "zone of proximal development."* San Francisco: Jossey-Bass.

Saxe, R. M., & Stollak, G. (1971). Curiosity and the parent-child relationship. *Child Development, 42,* 373–384.

Shemyakin, F. N. (1962). Orientation in space. In B. G. Ananyev *et al.* (Eds.), *Psychological science in the U.S.S.R.* (Vol. I, pp. 186–247). Washington, DC: Office of Technical Services.

Siegel, A. W. (1981). The externalization of cognitive maps by children and adults: In search of ways to ask better questions. In L. S. Liben, A. H. Patterson, N. Newcombe (Eds.), *Spatial representation and behavior across the life span* (pp. 167–194). New York: Academic Press.

Siegel, A. W. (1982). Toward a social ecology of cognitive mapping. In R. Cohen (Ed.), *Children's conceptions of spatial relationships* (pp. 83–94). San Francisco: Jossey-Bass.

Smirnov, A. A., & Zinchenko, P. I. (1969). Problems in the psychology of memory. In M. Cole & I. Maltzman (Eds.), *A handbook of contemporary Soviet psychology* (pp. 452–502). New York: Basic Books.

Sroufe, L. A. (1979). The coherence of individual development. *American Psychologist, 43,* 834–841.

Vygotsky, L. S. (1978). *Mind in society: The development of higher psychological processes.* Cambridge: Harvard University Press.

Waters, E., Wippman, J., & Sroufe, L. A. (1979). Attachment, positive affect, and competence in the peer group: Two studies in construct validation. *Child Development, 50,* 821–829.

White, B. L., Kaban, B., Shapiro, B., & Attonucci, J. (1976). Competence and experience. In I. C. Uzgiris & F. Weizmann (Eds.), *The structuring of experience* (pp. 115–152). New York: Plenum Press.

White, S. H., & Siegel, A. W. (1984). Cognitive development in time and space. In B. Rogoff & J. Lave (Eds.), *Everyday cognition: Its development in social context* (pp. 238–278). Cambridge, MA: Harvard University Press.

Wood, D. J. (1980). Teaching the young child: Some relationships between social interaction, language, and thought. In D. R. Olson (Ed.), *The social foundations of language and thought.* New York: Norton.

Wood, D. J., Bruner, J. S., & Ross, G. (1976). The role of tutoring in problem solving. *Journal of Child Psychology and Psychiatry, 17,* 89–100.

CHAPTER 8

Pretense
Acting "As If"

INGE BRETHERTON AND MARJORIE BEEGHLY

INTRODUCTION: CREATING ALTERNATIVE REALITIES IN PRETENSE

In pretense, children perform actions not to achieve everyday objectives but to create alternative social and physical realities. This ability to operate in the subjunctive mode is acquired surprisingly early in development. True, 1-year-olds are limited to pretending that they are asleep or are drinking juice when, in reality, they are not. But soon children can playfully assume family or occupational roles that they do not have to perform in everyday life until adulthood, and later still they can create impossible worlds through enactments in which physical and social causality as well as natural laws are suspended or turned upside down.

Most recent studies of pretense have been closely tied to Piaget's name and work, but in this chapter we would like to take a somewhat different approach. Piaget's interest lay in play as an aspect of symbol use (one person can stand for another; a shell can stand for a cup), not in play as representation of the possible and impossible. Admittedly, Piaget (1962) was quite aware that pretense allows the child to go be-

This chapter is based on a paper that was presented at the SRCD workshop, "Action in Social Context," in New Orleans.

INGE BRETHERTON • Department of Child and Family Studies, University of Wisconsin-Madison, Madison, Wisconsin, 53706. MARJORIE J. BEEGHLY • Child Development Unit, Children's Hospital and Harvard Medical School, Boston, Massachusetts 02115.

yond the perceptual field, to rearrange reality in line with momentary desires, in short, to subordinate reality to the ego. But, he said, as soon as thought processes become more coherent, the child no longer needs to distort reality in play. Hence, as soon as the child can adapt to the natural and social world, "wild" pretense fades away, collaborative pretending becomes more reality oriented, and is finally replaced by games with rules. The process whereby the child becomes able to entertain the possibility of alternatives to reality is written off as "assimilation of the world to the ego":

> But why is there assimilation of reality to the ego instead of immediate assimilation of the universe to experimental and logical thought? It is simply because in early childhood this thought has not yet been constructed, and during its development it is inadequate to supply the needs of daily life. (Piaget, 1962, p. 166)

Piaget fails to explain in what sense wishful thinking or correction of reality through play constitutes assimilation. What is the origin of the assimilatory schemata that permit a toddler to state: "I a daddy?" (example from Dunn & Dale, 1984). In our view, the subjunctive capacity exercised in play is closely related to the toddler's concurrently emerging ability to engage in "serious" mental trial and error through mental or imagined action. The onset of this "serious" representational ability has been described by Piaget (1954, 1963), but its further development was of interest to him only inasmuch as it led to the acquisition of logicomathematical thought. To understand the development of subjunctive thought about the social world, both serious and not serious, we must therefore turn elsewhere.

In what follows, we will argue that early pretense can be understood and studied in terms of an emerging ability to create and perform subjunctive and counterfactual event representations, alone and with others. To explain this capacity, we will draw on recent schema-based theories of representation by Mandler (1979), Nelson and Gruendel (1981), and Schank and Abelson (1977) that depart in important ways from Piaget's (1962) formulations. This work has been primarily concerned with the representation of actual, repeatedly experienced everyday events such as "having dinner" or "going to a birthday party," not with the invention of new events. To consider how event schemata derived from real-world experiences can form the basis for counterfactual event representations, we will therefore rely on Schank's more recent work (1982). In his reformulation of script theory, Schank proposes that episodic or autobiographical event memories are summarized, partitioned, and abstracted in a variety of ways to form a hierarchical framework of schemata from which new event representations (including representations of impossible events) can be constructed. We will then go on to discuss the organizational devices of make-believe play through which children learn to mark the boundary between here-and-now reality and the subjunctive worlds of pretense, as well as the boundary between planning/directing and actually performing make-believe plots (Bateson, 1955; Garvey & Berndt, 1977; Giffin, 1984). Without such organizational devices, the communal creation of pretend plots would be impossible. Finally we will consider the reason why children engage in acting "as if": sometimes just for fun, to play with the representational system, but often to make sense of and master hoped-for, feared, and puzzling experiences. We will suggest that the dramatic and narrative arts fulfill much the same function for adults and that pretense might fruitfully be studied as an early form of these artistic functions.

SUBJUNCTIVE EVENT REPRESENTATION IN PRETENSE: DEVELOPMENTAL SEQUENCES

In pretending, children initially perform very simple "as-if" enactments of routine events of family life such as eating or going to bed. Later they draw on events that they have only vicariously experienced. However, the ability to reenact and transform these familiar events in the make-believe play undergoes a long process of development: 1-year-olds perform simple pretend actions with realistic objects, 3-year-olds perform long action sequences with several interacting agents and recipients, using transformed objects in imaginary settings. We have chosen to discuss the development of early pretense not primarily in terms of its specific content (always initially derived from familiar events) but in terms of three structural dimensions of events: roles, plots, and props. Despite the fact that roles (agents and recipients), plots, and props are interdependent aspects of performing make-believe events, separate consideration of each dimension makes sense because each contributes to the creation of the dramatic play in different ways.

The Development of Roles

Piaget (1962) was the first investigator to outline a systematic developmental progression from self-representation to the representation of multirole networks. This progression has been replicated and elaborated in many studies of both normally developing children (e.g., Fenson & Ramsay, 1980; Kagan, 1981; Nicolich, 1977; Watson & Fischer, 1980;

Wolf, 1982) and developmentally delayed children (e.g., Beeghly & Cicchetti, 1987; Weiss, Beeghly, & Cicchetti, 1985). There are some dis-
agreements about the finer distinctions that ought to be made in describing the development of role-representation, but the general level of
agreement among investigators is impressive.

Self as Pretend Agent

To begin with, babies play at being themselves. They reproduce
simple activities from their own everyday repertoire, such as lying down
to sleep, but outside of the bedtime context and without being tired.
Mere functional acts (lifting a cup to lips, putting the head on a pillow)
are not enough. To count as pretense, infants must metacommunicate
their awareness that "this is play" (see Bateson, 1955; Nicolich, 1977;
Piaget, 1962). A very clear example is Jacqueline's behavior at the age of
15 months:

> She saw a cloth whose fringed edges vaguely recalled those of her pillow; she
> seized it, held a fold of it in her right hand, sucked the thumb of the same
> hand, and lay down on her side, laughing hard. She kept her eyes open, but
> blinked them from time to time as if she were alluding to closed eyes. Finally,
> laughing more and more, she cried "nene" [no no]. (Piaget, 1962, Obs. 64a,
> p. 96)

In this example, laughing and blinking metacommunicate "I am
only pretending to sleep," and this is further emphasized by the subsequent statement "no no." Interestingly, it is very much later in development that children become able to express the same idea linguistically as
a counterfactual conditional: "If I were tired and this were a pillow, I
could go to sleep" (Bates, 1975), or that they can provide explicit verbal
explanations of the distinction between appearance and reality (Flavell,
1985).

Pretending at Another Person's Behavior

The difference between pretending at one's own behavior and simulation of actions normally associated with other people's roles is not
recognized as a separate developmental step by all investigators (Fenson
& Ramsay, 1980; Largo & Howard, 1979; Jeffree & McConkey, 1976;
Kagan, 1981; Lowe, 1975; Watson & Fischer, 1977). However, because
playful reproduction of another person's actions can be regarded as a
rudimentary form of role taking (or trying out the world from another
vantage point), we believe that it is important to draw this distinction.
True, when infants lift a toy telephone receiver to the ear and say "hi,"

they are not necessarily pretending at parental behavior. They may just be doing what they have been shown to do with a toy telephone. However, there are unambiguous instances of pretense at an adult's behavior. An example is Piaget's (1962, Obs. 76a) description of Lucienne, at the age of 19 months, sitting in an armchair, "reading" the newspaper, pointing, and muttering to herself.

Persons and Replicas as Passive Recipients of Pretend Action

Simulation of another person's behavior seems to emerge at about the same time as pretend activities with dolls and stuffed animals (Nicolich, 1977), but is the child who holds a spoon to the mother's or to a doll's mouth merely projecting his or her own behavior onto the person or the doll, or is the child actually pretending at caregiving. Piaget clearly assumed the former:

> In projecting his own behavior onto others (making dolls cry, eat, drink or sleep) the child himself is imitating the actions they do when they reproduce his own actions! (Piaget, 1962, p. 123)

This statement sounds remarkably like a description of role taking or seeing oneself from the viewpoint of the other (Mead, 1934), doubly surprising because of Piaget's belief in the profound egocentrism of toddlers.

Although the distinction between projection of one's own behavior on a doll and pretend caregiving is not always easy, some early doll-directed behaviors do seem to constitute unambiguous simulations of caregiving (putting a doll to bed and tucking in its blankets), and this is important. If the adult or doll is not merely a symbolic representation of the self but a passive partner, we are dealing with a two-role plot or agent and recipient in interaction (see also Fein & Apfel, 1979).

Parallel Roles: Self as Pretend Agent and Other as Passive Pretend Recipient

The earliest unambiguous pretend activities with two roles are simple parallel actions. The child "feeds" him- or herself, then the partner or vice versa (Nicolich, 1977), as the following example from Wolf's (1982) case study shows:

> O. presents a bag of toy implements to J. at 1:4. Each one that he tries, he tries first on himself, and then on a big doll. He takes out a comb and combs the back and then the front of his hair, then the doll's. He takes toy scissors, clipping at the hair around his and then the doll's ears. (p. 314)

Reciprocal Roles: Self as Pretend Agent and Replica or Person as Active Pretend Recipient

Mere holding of a bottle to the mouth of a doll or live partner (as passive recipient or alter ego) differs from "feeding" a doll, talking to it, and ascribing feelings to it (see also Wolf, 1982). Again, Piaget (1962) provides a striking example:

> At 2; 1(13) she (Jacqueline) fed it (her doll) for a long time in the way we used to encourage her to eat her own meals: "a little drop more, to please Jacqueline. Just eat this little bit." (Piaget, 1962, Obs. 81, p. 127)

Jacqueline here enacts maternal behavior toward a doll to whom she imputes sensations and wishes. However, the child is not yet vicariously acting *for* a doll. This constitutes the next step in role development.

A Doll as Pretend Agent: Assuming a Vicarious Role

When the child pretends that a doll can act on its own (e.g., feed itself, look at itself in the mirror), the child becomes a vicarious actor (for relevant studies, see Fenson & Ramsay, 1980; Fenson, 1984; Inhelder, Lezine, Sinclair, & Stambak, 1972; Lowe, 1975; and Watson & Fischer, 1980). Curiously, the act of talking for the doll is seldom discussed in this connection, perhaps because of a desire to consider enactive and verbal representation in terms of separate symbol systems. Again, Piaget provides an instructive example:

> At 1; 6(30) J. said "cry, cry" to her dog and herself imitated the sound of crying. On the following day, she made her bear, duck, etc. cry. (Piaget, 1962, Obs. 75a, p. 121)

Assuming a Pretend Role

Both the ability to confer independent agency on a doll and the ability to assume another person's identity constitute role play: In the case of animating a doll, role play is vicarious; in assuming another person's role, it is direct. Piaget describes several early examples of direct role play that he terms "assimilation of the ego to others":

> At 1; 9(20) J. rubbed the floor with a shell, then with a cardboard lid, saying: "Brush Abebert" (like the charwoman). The same day she pulled her hair back as she looked at herself in the mirror, and said, laughing "Daddy." (Piaget, 1962, Obs. 76a, p. 122)

As Piaget (1962) notes, such behavior transcends imitation because the child does not merely copy the behavior of others while continuing to be him- or herself but identifies completely with others. Some (e.g., Huttenlocher & Higgins, 1978) require that the child make a verbal statement indicating identification with the other in order to categorize the activity as role play. It may, however, be possible to create nonverbal criteria for role play.

Simple Replica Play: Self and Replica as Active Reciprocal Pretend Partners

A more complex form of role structure than either activation of a doll or assumption of another person's role is to combine both activities (e.g., assume the role of caregiver and vicariously act the role of baby for the doll). A striking instance of this type of behavior at a relatively early age appears in a case study by Wolf (1982):

> J. at 1:9 develops a new pattern of interaction with his jack-in-the-box. If, when he presses down the lid on top of the box, its hand is poking out of the corner of the lid, J. calls out "ouch, ouch. Boo-boo" (his word for a hurt). He then quickly cranks the lid so that it pops open, rubs down the clown's hand and kisses it, before careful stuffing it back down into the hole, hand and all. (p. 319)

Miller and Garvey (1984) provide several additional illustrations of this ability around 30 months (a child mothers a baby doll but also speaks and cries for it).

Simple Reciprocal Role Play with a Familiar Pretend Partner

In joint pretense with a liver partner, a child need only enact one role, not two (as is necessary when a doll becomes the self's active reciprocal partner). On the other hand, joint role play requires that the child coordinate his or her pretend plans with those of another person, an equivalent ability. Coordination of plans is easiest when one of the partners is more experienced and both partners are familiar with each other. Joint pretense with reciprocal roles therefore tends to emerge earliest in play with an older sibling or the parent (see Dunn & Dale, 1984; Dunn, 1985; Miller & Garvey, 1984).

Complex Pretend Interaction among Replicas with Self as Narrator

The development of spontaneous and prompted play with small figures (replica play) has been extensively studied by Wolf and her colleagues (Rubin & Wolf, 1979; Scarlett & Wolf, 1979; Wolf, 1982; Wolf, Goldfield, Beeghly, Warner, & Cardona, 1985; Wolf, Rygh, & Altshuler, 1984). Watson and Fischer (1980) independently covered some of the same ground. Rubin and Wolf emphasize that it is only in the later part of the third year that children come to animate several small figures without injecting themselves into the plot as actor. The earliest attempts at activating two figures tend to cast them in parallel roles: Instead of making a lion chase a boy, the child makes both lion and boy run away. The subsequent mastery of doll play with several interacting figures *about whom* the child talks as narrator and *for whom* the child talks as vicarious actor marks a great step forward (see also Bretherton, O'Connell, Shore, & Bates, 1984). An example of this simple form of story telling can be found in Wolf's case study (1982):

> J. at 2:0 has a parent figure and a child figure. O. has also given him some doll furniture. He lays the child in bed, making the parent walk over and kiss the child. Then he makes the child hop out of bed and run off to under the table. He makes the parent figure chase after the child, calling out "Get you."
> (Wolf, 1982, p. 320)

With development, the roles assigned to the replicas tend to become more differentiated (a nasty lion may chase a frightened boy but is also capable of feeling lonely; see Rubin & Wolf, 1979). In addition, each replica can be made to assume more than one social role; that is, a pretend mother can also be a pretend doctor, and a pretend child can be her daughter as well as her patient (Watson & Fischer, 1980).

Complex Joint Pretend Play with Several Complementary Roles

When several players collaborate in sociodramatic play, each has to coordinate his or her role with that of one or more partners. Hence, some knowledge of complementary role structures is as necessary for collaborative pretense as for complex replica play. Miller and Garvey (1984) describe an early instance of this ability: A 39-month-old girl plays "mother" to "baby" and "wife" to her 30-month-old "husband," while simultaneously coaching "husband" in how to perform the role of "father."

Content of Roles

With development, the role repertoire widens from the performance of family roles to occupational roles (doctor, nurse, police officer) and fictive roles (Superman, Snow White). Younger children tend to pretend mostly at those family roles with which they have direct experience (baby or child, father, mother). Older preschoolers continue to enact family roles but add the roles of husband and wife to their repertoire. They also take on occupational roles and fictive roles such as Superwoman (Garvey & Berndt, 1977).

In sum, it is evident that some forms of role taking and playing emerge as soon as the infant can go beyond self-representation. At the end of the third year, children are capable of much more. In performing a drama that includes several interacting dolls, the child engages in role play at multiple levels. On one level, he or she plays reciprocal pretend roles; on another level, he or she takes the perspective of narrator, that is steps outside the acting frame, talking *about* the protagonists' actions. In joint make-believe the situation is comparable. The child coordinates his or her viewpoint of the make-believe event with that of other children, both at the level of planning and negotiating *about* the plot and, at another level, in actually performing it with coplayers.

The Development of Plots

A baby's initial make-believe plots consist of single behaviors or schemes. Later, in the second year, toddlers begin to produce more complicated dramas. There is a large measure of agreement among investigators regarding the development of plot structures, but—as with role play—some definitional problems remain.

Single Action Plots

One question to arise in conjunction with single pretend behaviors, such as drinking from an empty cup, is whether the child is merely performing the appropriate action with a familiar object or actually pretending at the function (drinking pretend liquid). As noted earlier, there are certain indexes (e.g., "knowing" looks and smiles, or sound effects such as lip smacking and slurping when drinking pretend liquid) on which this distinction can be based. However, even when children signal "this is play," the level of understanding that the child brings to make-believe actions varies from object to object. For example, 1-year-old infants do not seem to understand the function of the telephone receiver (communication), even though they know how to perform the ritual of holding it somewhere near the neck/face area and saying something like "hi." On the other hand, it is likely that when infants are pretend drinking with sound effects (slurping, saying "yumm"), they are pretending at the consumption of liquid.

Plots with Action Sequences

Most investigators (Fenson & Ramsay, 1980; Nicolich, 1977) have reported that children begin to combine pretend acts late in the second year. However, Bretherton, Bates, McNew, Shore, Williamson, and Beeghly-Smith (1981) noticed very simple combinations in 13-month-olds (hugging and kissing a bear, rocking a doll and cooing to it, lifting a telephone receiver to the neck/face area and saying "hi"). These were admittedly simpler combinations than some of the examples described in the literature (but see Belsky & Most, 1981), yet they undeniably constituted two separate behaviors because each could also be shown singly. In studying the plot structure of early pretense, it may therefore be useful to make finer qualitative distinctions among various forms of action sequencing. In addition, as the previously mentioned examples indicate, the combination of manual and vocal behaviors in the performance of pretend actions must be taken into account in the study of make-believe plots.

Parallel Pretend Action Sequences

The first pretend action sequences described by Nicolich (1977) consisted of one and the same behavior applied to several objects in turn, such as stirring in a cup, then stirring in a pitcher (single-scheme combinations in Nicolich's framework). Interestingly, most infants acquired the component actions and performed them separately before they could combine them into a sequence (Fenson & Ramsay, 1981). It is therefore not paucity of the child's pretend action repertoire that delays the onset of these simple sequences without obligatory order.

Ordered Action Sequences

Ordered sequences are those in which each action has a meaningful relation to the preceding one. Fenson and Ramsay (1980, 1981) hypothesized that the execution of unordered sequences should precede the reproduction of ordered sequences. Examples of ordered sequences were pouring "tea" into a cup, then "drinking" from it, or placing a pillow on the doll bed, then laying the head on the pillow as if to go to sleep. To count as ordered, the scheme sequence had to reflect a logical or ecological order. Unordered sequences consisted of behaviors such as placing the doll in bed and then combing its hair. Fenson and Ramsay (1981) were surprised to find very few nonordered sequences, even at 15 months, though presentation of the toys in organized sets may have facilitated the behavior (personal communication, 1984). Experimental studies by Gerard (1984) and O'Connell (O'Connell & Gerard, 1984; O'Connell, 1984), using more stringent criteria, contend that plots in which all actions are ordered are mastered only in the course of the third year.

Plots with Longer Action Sequences

There are few systematic studies describing the subsequent development of action sequencing. Yet it is surely necessary to distinguish a mere two-action sequence from the following richly elaborated example provided by Inhelder *et al.*:

> Thus Pierre, at 22 months, imitates in detail how his mother feeds her baby as he puts the nipple of the bottle to the baby-doll's mouth with a well-coordinated movement, lifts up the baby's head which is resting in the crook of his arm, then holds up the bottle and pulls on the nipple as if it had collapsed, looks at the bottle, shakes it like an adult feeding a baby and "checks" the level of formula in the bottle, then returns the bottle to the baby's mouth, pushing the nipple forcefully against its mouth. (Inhelder *et al.*, 1972, p. 217)

Fenson (personal communication) who studied spontaneous action sequences in 20- to 31-month-olds, found that half of his sample performed two-act sequences at 20 months. At 26 and 31 months, this percentage had risen to 71%. In addition, 33% of the 31-month-olds enacted three-act sequences and 17% four-act sequences. Bretherton *et al.* (1984) also report a significant increase in spontaneous and elicited ordered action sequences from around two schemes at 20 months to about three separate actions at 28 months. Rheingold and Emery (1986) observed more complex action sequences somewhat earlier. In their study, all 18-month-olds achieved two-act sequences and, by 30 months, all of the children performed meaningful five-act sequences. The cause for this discrepancy may lie in the prolonged observation period (30 minutes) used by Rheingold and Emery.

Episode Sequences: Hierarchical Structure of Pretend Plots

Inhelder *et al.* (1972) briefly mention the emergence of multiepisode play in the third year, where two episodes are linked a meaningful order (e.g. a multiaction episode of feeding the baby doll, followed by a multi-action episode of giving it a bath). Unfortunately, no detailed examples are given. However, Wolf's case study (1982) illustrates an early instance of episode combinations. In this example, there are two episodes, an accident followed by medical treatment:

> J., at 1;8, had a minor accident in which he cut his forehead. For several weeks thereafter he re-enacts the specific details of falling, crying, being stitched up, wearing a bike helmet to protect the cut using a large doll. (Wolf, 1982, p. 314)

Many of the longer sequences performed by 28-month-olds in the study by Bretherton *et al.* (1984) consisted of several subepisodes (bathing a baby, then giving it a ride in a stroller), although such episode combinations were rare at 20 months (information about episode structure was not available for studies by Fenson, 1984, and Rheingold & Emery, 1986). Much more work is necessary to study the development of hierarchical episode structure in pretend plots.

Content of Pretense

Throughout the infant and toddler period, the content of pretense revolves around familiar everyday events, either directly experienced or observed. The initial developmental changes have to do with increased plot complexity, not their basic thematic content. In a study of collaborative play between 24-month-olds and their mothers or older siblings, mealtimes, cooking/ironing, shopping/going to the park, and bedtime accounted for the majority of play content (Dunn, 1985). Even the 3- to 5-year-olds studied by Garvey (1977) focused much of their sociodramatic play on family life, although the older children also incorporated more and more out-of-home and fictional material into their joint pretense. Similar findings were obtained for children with Down's syndrome at comparable developmental ages (Beeghly & Cicchetti, 1987). A few general themes accounted for the greater proportion of make-believe plots in Garvey's preschoolers: treating/healing, averting threat, packing/taking a trip, going to the store, cooking and having a meal, as well as repairing. A theme, as defined by Garvey, is an abstract, rather general action plan that can be linked to a variety of contents. For example, in enacting the theme *averting threat,* the threat can be a monster, a fire, or abandonment.

The Development of Prop Use

Infants' first efforts at pretending appear to require the presence of prototypical props such as realistic spoons, telephones, or baby dolls (Nicolich, 1977; Piaget, 1962; Vygotsky, 1967). Later such realism is less and less necessary to sustain make-believe enactments, although many children still seem to need tangible place holders to stand for the imagined objects. Empty-handed miming tends to be infrequent in spontaneous play until at least the middle of the third year (Fenson, 1984).

Realistic Props

The presence of realistic objects provides perceptual/tactile/spatial support for the performance of simple behaviors such as sleeping or eating. Without such support, 12-month-olds are unlikely to engage in pretending at all. However, complete realism is *not* required. Abstract (pared-down) versions of the "real thing" also elicit spontaneous pretend play. This weak form of substitution is possible even for 13-month-olds (Bretherton *et al.*, 1981). Most of these infants spontaneously performed some pretend behaviors with abstract but recognizable versions of cups, spoons, telephones, dolls, and cars. But note that 13-month-olds did produce significantly fewer symbolic schemes with pared-down than with fully realistic props.

Nonrealistic Props: Object Substitution

Later in the second year, children substitute blocks for cars and spoons for telephones, thus freeing the content of their make-believe plots from environmental constraints. Vygotsky (1967) pointed out that substitute objects serve as "pivots" whose function, in symbolic terms, is to sever the intended pretend meaning of an object from its actual appearance. Nicolich (1977) said much the same thing when she categorized object substitution as a planful pretend behavior, along with verbal announcement of the theme, and search for toys relevant to the intended theme. Substitution or transformation in these cases was driven by the need for a tangible—but not necessarily veridical—prop to support enactment of the plan.

Several investigators have compared toddlers' spontaneous and elicited play with meaningful (realistic) and nonmeaningful object sets. Jeffree and McConkey (1976) observed 10 children in a play-house situation at six-monthly intervals, beginning at 18 and ending at 42 months. Two sets of toys, one prototypical and the other consisting of "junk" materials (cans, boxes, rags) were given to the children for 5 minutes of spontaneous play. The children played significantly less with the junk materials but reached the same level of play with both types of objects. Unfortunately, the findings were not broken down by age and thus cannot be compared with results obtained in a more recent study by

Kagan (1981) that also examined spontaneous play with realistic and unrealistic objects in 13- to 25-month-olds. Again children engaged in more symbolic acts with the realistic toys at all ages, but at 25 months, the difference in the proportion of time they spent playing with each type of toy was not significant.

In both of the proceeding studies, multiple substitutions were necessary. The children played either with a whole set of realistic or a whole set of abstract toys. There is only one investigation in which the effect of single and multiple substitutions was compared. Fein (1975) invited 26-month-old children to play with prototypical and abstract versions of a horse and egg cup. Almost all children spontaneously fed the prototypical horse with the prototypical cup. Seventy-nine percent of the toddlers "fed" the prototypical horse with the abstract cup (a clam shell), whereas 61% fed the abstract horse (a metal horse shape) with the realistic egg cup. Double substitutions (feeding the abstract horse with the shell) were much rarer. Only 33% of the toddlers performed them.

Counterconventional Props versus Placeholders

Several recent experimental studies have attempted to identify those features of the substitute object (appearance, conventional function) that facilitate or interfere with substitution (Bretherton et al., 1984; Fein, 1975; Jackowitz & Watson, 1980; Kagan, 1981; Killen & Užgiris, 1981; Largo & Howard, 1979; Ungerer, Zelazo, Kearsley, & O'Leary, 1981; Watson & Fischer, 1980). It appears that object substitution is easier when the substitute object is a relatively meaningless placeholder such as a block, than when it is a highly meaningful familiar object that must be used in a "counterconventional" manner (Bretherton et al., 1984; Ungerer et al., 1981). One plausible reason for this may be that the counterconventional object (a comb serving the function of spoon) already has strong object-associated meanings for the child that interfere with the act of substitution. At the younger ages, a placeholder object such as a stick or a block may be more easily imbued with imaginary qualities than a meaningful object such as a cup or comb, although these conclusions must be qualified by noting that most object substitution studies are not based on observations of spontaneous behavior but on attempts at eliciting substitution by modeling it.

Miming

Empty-handed miming, unsupported by perceptual/tactile cues from an object appears to be uncommon in early pretense (though not in communication, see Acredolo & Goodwyn, 1985). Fenson (1984) saw virtually no miming in the spontaneous play of 21- to 31-month-olds. It is therefore surprising that Piaget (1962) reports an instance of miming at 12 months:

> At 1; (20) J. scratched at the wall paper in the bedroom where there was the design of a bird, then shut her hand as if it held the bird and went to her mother: "Look (she opened her hand and pretended to be giving some thing). -What have you brought me?- a birdie." (Obs. 74)

Other examples occurred after the age of 2 years. At 2; 0(2), Jacqueline moved her finger along the edge of a table, saying: "finger walking, horse trotting." Note that she actually described the transformation (finger to horse) and that she used a body part (the finger) to stand for agent action (horse trotting). At 2; 3(8), Jacqueline made a circular movement with her fingers, saying "bicycle spoilt," followed by another circular gesture, accompanied by "bicycle mended." Here the gesture appeared to depict the object (the wheel or perhaps the rolling of the wheel as well), whereas the event representation (breakage/repair) was purely verbal. At 2; 5(25), Jacqueline, in preparation for giving her sister a make-believe bath, mimed an undressing sequence without ever touching Lucienne's clothes. At 2; 6(22), she pretended to have a baby in her arms and put it down on an imaginary bed. What is noteworthy about the latter two examples is that they were pure pantomime, in the sense that the child did not depict the object but merely the action on the object. Work by Overton and Jackson (1973) suggests that pure pantomime is more difficult than use of a body part to depict object and action simultaneously, but their results are based on a verbal prompting paradigm, not observation of spontaneous play. In the course of our own studies, we have observed a 13-month-old boy build a tower consisting of several blocks and then construct alongside it an imaginary tower of equal height. This child also played tossing games with imaginary pebbles. These examples, taken together with Piaget's observations of Jacqueline's early miming, suggest that it might be useful to look for instances of spontaneous miming at earlier ages. We may also need to make finer distinctions in our descriptions of miming. Fenson (1984) points out that "pouring" from an empty pitcher is a form of miming with object support, especially when the child shakes the pitcher to "get out the last drop."

Miming is not the only way in which an imaginary object can be introduced into pretense. Sometimes invented substances are merely specified by verbal naming (Bretherton et al., 1984; Fenson, 1984; Matthews, 1977). Verbal invention in the presence of perceptual support becomes very frequent during the third year and deserves further study.

Although play with nonveridical objects and miming become more common with age, realistic objects continue to be important. In a study of collaborative pretending, Garvey and Berndt (1977) found that the presence of a realistic prop often seemed to inspire a particular theme. However, once make-believe was underway, it was most often the on-going theme that determined subsequent object transformations. In their study of 3- to 5-year-olds, a three-legged stool with a magnifying glass in its center was transformed into a telescope (to spot a fire), a toilet (to take care of baby), a workchair (while performing a household task), a trailer (packing for a trip) and a milk carton (while shopping for provisions). It is difficult to see how the last two substitutions could have been inspired by the perceptual properties of the transformed object. In this connection, Wolf and Grollmann (1982) present interesting findings regarding individual differences in children's willingness to transform objects in pretense. Some children insist on "good" substitutes (only red beads are transformed into cherries), other children can easily do without tangible objects or are not particularly concerned with the appearance of the substitute, provided it still affords the desired action (a small cube can function as a bath towel because it still permits the necessary rubbing action). So far, it is not clear whether the willingness to do without "good" substitutes is closely linked to the ability to invent original make-believe plots or whether these two propensities are independent.

SUBJUNCTIVE EVENT REPRESENTATION IN PRETENSE: THEORETICAL CONSIDERATIONS

We have suggested that pretense is one facet of the human ability to create alternative realities, and we have shown that young children's ability to do so in make-believe play develops from performing single-role, single-act plots supported by realistic props, to enactment of complex role structures with intricate plots supported by nonveridical and imaginary props. Likewise, the content of play is at first restricted to reproduction of familiar themes from everyday life but followed by make-believe plots that increasingly incorporate themes from the world outside the home, from storybooks and television programs or films (older children become "firemen" and "Superwomen"). The sequences described for role performance, for plot development, and for prop use have been replicated in many studies, including studies with atypical children. For example, Beeghly and Cicchetti (1987) and Weiss et al. (1985) found that children with Down's syndrome seem to progress

through the same developmental sequences of role play, plot enactment, and prop use as nonhandicapped children, although the pace of
their development is delayed in comparison to normal children matched
for mental age.

What developments make the ability to engage in make-believe
possible? We believe that the reemergence of schema-based theories of
representation (inspired by Bartlett's, 1932, work on memory) can offer
useful new insights. According to such theories (Mandler, 1979; Nelson
& Gruendel, 1981; Schank & Abelson, 1977), symbolic activity is based
on event schemata. Event schemata are dynamic mental structures that
represent the interaction of agents and recipients in terms of their goals,
feelings, and actions, within a temporal-spatial-causal framework. Although the structure of event schemata can be described in general
terms (who does what to whom, when, where, how, and why), event
schemata always have a content because individuals construct these
skeletal frameworks out of repeated encounters with similar events.
Once constructed, event schemata serve to guide a person's interpretation of reality (akin to Piaget's assimilation), but they are also subject to
change through new input (akin to Piaget's accommodation). In serious
planning, these schemata are internally manipulated to yield a variety of
possible courses of action; in pretense, these schemata are playfully
reproduced and transformed for a variety of purposes that we will discuss later.

Until recently, studies of event representation have focused on 3- to
5-year-olds (Nelson & Gruendel, 1981; Stein, 1978). For example, Nelson
and her colleagues (see Nelson & Gruendel, 1981) discovered that 3-
year-olds can report the correct sequence of events in response to questions such as: "What happens when you have a birthday party, . . .
when you go to McDonald's, . . . when you go to the store . . ."
(Nelson & Gruendel, 1981). Older children add more details to their
accounts (Stein, 1978), but the reports given by younger children are
certainly not chaotic, and few repetitions of an event are sufficient to set
up a schema (Price & Goodman, 1985). Although these studies did not
directly look at children's ability to consider alternative courses of action, they show that young children can represent the spatiotemporal
and causal order of routine events in a fairly coherent way. Furthermore, we would argue that the development of pretense from 1 to 3
years of age documents the presence of simple event schemata at an
even earlier age.

A number of criticisms have been raised against explaining pretense
in terms of play with an event-based representational system (Fein,
1985). Fein points out that pretense is not a documentary of everyday

experience (we agree) and that event representations constructed on the basis of real-world experience could not therefore be used to invent and enact unlikely events (we do not agree).

Fein (1985) contends that play is an expressive activity that requires a separate affective representational system, restricted to use in pretense. This hypothesized affective symbol system represents real or imagined affective experiences of pleasure, abandonment, or fear at a fairly general level, allowing the child to fill in particulars of persons, events, and occasions (p. 44). Details do not matter as long as they fit with the affective meaning to be expressed (pleasant, nasty, satisfying, confusing). Fein's view justly emphasizes that the events represented in play tend to be highly significant to the child (and are hence frequently accompanied by strong emotions), but it neglects to specify where the particular contents of affective events originate.

We believe, in contrast, that one representational system used in different ways can account for both serious and playful subjunctive thought. Fein's objections to basing explanations of pretense on theories of event representation derive from the fact that earlier versions of these theories placed little emphasis on the representation of emotion and did not explain how event schemata could yield the transformations of reality that we actually find in symbolic play. In a revision of one version (Schank & Abelson, 1977) of this theory, Schank (1982) points out that the event structures (scripts) that were earlier proposed as basic building blocks of representation were much too long and unwieldy, making cross-referencing of part scripts impossible (see Schank & Abelson, 1977). Second, there was little consideration of how scripts change with new contradictory input and how scripts are related to autobiographical memories. Third, there was too little emphasis on the emotional aspect of represented experience. The revised theory (Schank, 1982) provides a much more adequate conceptual basis for pretense.

Schank now argues that information derived from episodic or autobiographical memories (including affect and motivation) is reprocessed, partitioned, cross-indexed but also summarized and abstracted in a variety of ways. All of the resulting mental structures are said to preserve a spatiotemporal-causal relation structure that simulates event structures in the world. Some of the structures order mini-event representations into coordinated longer event sequences (generating the former scripts), others generalize across mini-event categories (feeding situations regardless of context; all sad events), and yet others generalize across different event sequences (e.g., across all caregiving events, all aggression-punishment events, etc.). Schank's conceptualization deliberately blurs the distinction between episodic and semantic memory proposed by Tulving (1972, 1983) and substitutes instead a multiply interconnected hierarchy of schemata that are graded from very experience-near to very general or abstract. This hierarchy is continually reconstructed and revised on the basis of new input.

How are event schemata revised? Event schemata ensure that past encodings (memory) determine how the next similar experience is decoded (processing). Thus event schemata lend a certain conservatism to mental functioning. When a quite unexpected turn of events is encountered, the new episode is first registered as an exception. Only if the one-time unexpected event recurs will a new schema will be constructed. In addition, each new episodic memory will be parsed and information fed into many other structures that represent generalized information about agents, actions, intentions, goals, and emotions. These parsing and ordering processes can therefore explain how generalized knowledge structures are built from memory structures.

If the representational system has the capacity to parse and generalize event information in the way just described, it is easy to see how it could be used in the generation of make-believe events. At first, children use their event schemata of interaction with mother to substitute themselves into the maternal role, acting "as if" they were mommy and sometimes asking mother to act "as if" she was baby. Even if the child plays adult roles, these tend initially to represent familiar people in familiar contexts, though behaviors and feelings may be somewhat exaggerated. However, toddlers do not yet deliberately toy with the laws of time, space, and causality; they do not yet engage in "what-if" play. Such play becomes much more prominent in preschoolers, probably because skillful play with representational systems is difficult until representational schemata at all levels in the hierarchy have been fairly well consolidated. Scarlett and Wolf's (1979) case study supports the contention that, whereas older preschoolers are able to generate "impossible" fictive worlds with their own natural laws, toddlers cannot. As these researchers put it, the ability to engage in fantasy (not only real-world understanding) undergoes development, although even fantastic pretense is not always original but often adapted from stories and television programs (Watson, personal communication).

An as yet-unsolved problem, as Leslie (1987) and Fein (1985) have pointed out, is how playful representations are marked or "decoupled" so that they do not interfere with real-world understanding. Whatever the solution to that problem will turn out to be, note that it also holds for representations of rejected, nonworkable solutions to real-world problems. Moreover, as we will discuss later, some of these exaggerated, transposed, and transformed pretend plots may lead to deeper understandings of actual experience. As Bruner (1986) has recently stated, "life informs fiction, but fiction in turn informs life."

Multiple Conceptual Levels of Representation in Pretense

Because acts of pretense can look and sound quite "real," it is necessary to identify them as simulation or fiction to avoid misunderstandings. Bateson (1955) first drew attention to the fact that pretense must be framed by the metacommunicative message *this is play*. Such metacommunicative statements are logically paradoxical, saying in effect that "these actions in which we now engage do not denote what the actions for which they stand would denote" or to put it more concretely: "This nip is not a bite."

Early instances of metacommunication in pretense are described in Piaget (1962). For example, Jacqueline at 15 months "alluded" to closed eyes by blinking as she put her head on a blanket in pretend sleep (Obs. 64a). At 28 months, she announced her transformed identity to her father ("It's mommy"), assuming a third-person bystander role, before requesting that Piaget give "mommy" a kiss (Obs. 79). Yet when she transformed herself into a cat at 32 months (Obs. 79), she merely crawled into the room on all fours saying "Miouw." Perhaps overt metacommunication is less necessary when the pretend act is not likely to be confused with real-world action. Several further illustrations of metacommunication during the third year can be found in Miller and Garvey (1984), and Dunn and Dale (1984). Very early comprehension, as opposed to production, of metacommunicative signals is suggested by Fein and Moorin's (1984) case study of a 15-month-old girl who responded appropriately to verbal pretend invitations (to "feed" a doll, or adults) as well as other studies in which infants are invited to engage in pretense with an adult (e.g., Bretherton *et al.*, 1981).

Notwithstanding early precursors, the ability to manage make-believe play at multiple conceptual levels (entering the pretend frame, communicating about what is to be pretended, and actual pretend performance) comes truly into its own during the preschool years (Göncü & Kessel, 1984). We will focus here on four of the several studies that have examined the development of metacommunication in pretense: Two are concerned with the conduct of collaborative make-believe (Garvey & Berndt, 1977; Giffin, 1984), and two describe stage management techniques in replica play (Wolf *et al.*, 1985; Scarlett & Wolf, 1979). Each of these studies approached the topic of pretense management from a somewhat different angle.

Garvey and Berndt (1977) emphasize that the joint creation of a make-believe reality requires more than the simple message that "this is play." In order to pretend with companions, children need stage-management techniques for negotiating about content: what theme or script is to be played and where as well as how the theme is to be realized. Garvey and Berndt studied 48 acquainted dyads in which the two partners were of similar age, but the ages of children varied from 34 to 67 months. The children were observed during 8 minutes of spontaneous, joint make-believe play in a laboratory playroom. From this material, Garvey and Berndt developed a system for categorizing metacommunicative behaviors (mostly verbal statements) by which children coordinate sociodramatic play:

1. Mention role	Other's	"Are you going to be a bride?"
	Own	"I'm a lady at work."
	Joint	"We can both be wives."
2. Mention plan	Other's	"Pretend you hated baby fish."
	Own	"I gotta drive to the shopping center."
	Joint	"We have to eat. Our dinner's ready."
3. Mention object	Transform	"This is the train," putting suitcase on sofa.
	Invent	"Now this is cheese," pointing to empty plate.
4. Mention setting	Transform	"This is a cave," pointing to wooden structure.
	Invent	"We're there," about imaginary picnic site.

Garvey and Berndt also point out that exits from the pretend world were explicitly marked. Children negated make-believe roles by statements like: "I'm not the Dad," actions by: "I'm not dead," props' identities by: "that's not a car," and settings by: "we're not at the beach." Especially interesting were back transformations ("It's not a cake anymore"; "Please don't push me 'cause I'm not the dragon anymore"). Similar exit statements were analyzed by Matthews (1978).

Giffin's study (1984), in contrast to Garvey and Berndt's, focused not so much on the content of metacommunication but on *how* children used a variety of metacommunicative options to create and coordinate shared meanings. Her analysis of 31 play episodes produced by 38 previously acquainted preschool children in groups of two to five players identified a variety of metacommunicative devices that lie on a continuum from explicit to implicit stage managing. She noted that the children's play seemed to be guided by an unspoken rule not to expose the pretend illusion unnecessarily.

Giffin discovered that the children in her study were masters at the task of combining metacommunication (or stage managing) with acting. One category of metacommunication, *ulterior conversation*, looked like enactment but was in reality a surreptitious way of suggesting a change in the ongoing plot. For example, the question, "Is it lunchtime?", was considered ulterior conversation, if the children were not at that point playing at having lunch. A somewhat more overt form of stage management was *underscoring*, or statements such as "I'll pour the milk," spoken as a pitcher was tipped over an empty cup. These statements serve to inform the playmate that the pitcher "contains" milk as opposed to juice. At a real breakfast table, such statements of the obvious would sound peculiar. Other underscoring remarks, such as "I'm crying" said in a wailing tone of voice, disturb the pretend illusion somewhat more obviously but do not require that the actor step explicitly into the stage-directing mode. Even more ambiguous is *magicking* that consists of rhythmically chanted statements (e.g., "wash wash wash" accompanied by brief rubbing of clothes; "cooky cooky cooky" accompanied by a few stirring motions above a pot). Giffin interprets magicking as a theatrical device where chanting explains the otherwise perhaps incomprehensible abbreviated action.

A special sing-song cadence also characterized *storytelling*. This sophisticated form of verbal make-believe allowed children to develop more elaborate plots without acting them out ("and you went to bed right after supper . . . I went to bed later than you . . . I went to bed 3 hours later than you . . . and the kitty went to bed even before you"; from Giffin, 1981). Interestingly, the children tended to couch their "storytelling" in the past tense.

On occasion, a player must step out of the pretend role and engage in overt stage management even during ongoing pretense. *Prompting* is one such device. The prompter "drops" the play voice to whisper: "You didn't talk like that, you say (modeling in a honeyed voice) 'What's the matter, mother'?" (from Giffin, 1984). One of Garvey and Berndt's (1977) protocols provides an early example: A girl of 3;3 prompted a boy of 2;9 how to play daddy!

Formal pretend proposals are the most direct forms of stage management (e.g., "Let's pretend [say, play] we were monsters"). In Giffin's study, formal pretend proposals were quite rare and were most likely to occur at the beginning of play. Once a play episode was under way, players tended to resort to more indirect forms of managing the pretend reality (e.g., ulterior conversation, storytelling, magicking). Skilled players knew when they could afford to engage in implicit stage-managing and when it was necessary to step out of the actor role into the director role, even though this broke the "Illusion Conservation

Rule." An example was the command, "Pretend that I was dead, but you thought I was alive" (made by a child of 3;9). It is difficult to see how the suggestion to pretend at a false belief could have been conveyed by mere acting (lying still) or ulterior conversation. Further studies are now needed to find out in what order the various metacommunicative options are acquired and to pinpoint developmental changes in the skill with which they are used (for further examples of surreptitious metacommunication, see Fein, 1985).

Independently of the work on collaborative pretense, Scarlett and Wolf (1979) and Wolf et al. (1985) examined how children manage the boundary between make-believe and reality in replica play. Interestingly, they found in replica play many of the same stage management devices that children also employ in sociodramatic play. Instead of switching between the roles of director and actor, the child who animates small figures switches between the roles of narrator ("Once upon a time, the baby and the mommy, and the daddy walked through the forest to find a house . . . and then the baby said: . . .) and vicarious actor ("there's not enough room"). Out-of-frame formal pretend proposals in sociodramatic play were paralleled in replica play by the narrator's proposals to the adult onlooker: "There's not enough room in this house. Can you make the porch bigger? People won't fit on the porch." An analysis of the linguistic features of the three strands of play discourse revealed marked syntactic and lexical differences. For example, the narrative voice was characterized by a higher ratio of nouns to pronouns, more connective words ("and then," "so"), predominant use of declaratives couched in present and past tenses, and the occasional use of narrative markers ("once upon a time"). The character voice, in contrast, was marked by a lower ratio of nouns to pronouns, fewer connective words, a mix of declaratives, imperatives, and questions, more internal state words, and an almost exclusive use of present tense. With increasing age, children's skill at distinguishing each strand became more consistent and reliable. Intensive case studies of four children observed from 28 to 60 months revealed that all had mastered the ability to use each strand of play discourse by 32 months. Examination of thirty 28-month-olds' play with small replicas showed that 55% were able to use all three strands of play discourse, though at this early age much of the story is told through enactment as well as speech. By the end of the preschool period, the bulk of fictive meaning in replica play— as in sociodramatic play—tends to be carried by what children say about or for the characters, including descriptions of the characters' plans, and motives (Wolf, 1984; Wolf et al., 1984; Wolf et al., 1985).

In sociodramatic and replica play (as well as hybrids thereof), children operate on several conceptual levels of representation (planning the theme and acting it out; narrating the story and performing it vicariously with small figures). Because they weave back and forth between conceptual levels quite effortlessly, it has been easy to overlook the continuous perspective switching that takes place in pretense. Rarely do children get confused about whether they are operating in the actor or director mode or whether they are being themselves. This is true whether, as in prompting, stepping from the character role into the director role is brief and intermittent or, as in ulterior conversation or narration, only implicit.

BLURRING OF REPRESENTATIONAL CONCEPTUAL LEVELS OR GETTING CAUGHT IN TANGLED HIERARCHIES

Despite the logically clear distinction between real-world and pretend action and between stage managing the plots and acting them out, the boundaries between these domains are sometimes unwittingly and sometimes deliberately blurred.

As Bateson (1955) has so aptly stated: "The map is not the territory." Pretend action is not real action, and yet map and territory (pretense and reality) have a strange way of becoming tangled in the same way as levels are tangled in the well-known Escher print in which each of two hands appears to rise out of the paper to draw the other (Hoffstadter, 1979). Map-territory confusions may make "scary" make-believe themes so "real" that a player feels compelled to step outside the play frame or may refuse to enter it, as the following conversation between two preschoolers, taken from Garvey and Berndt's (1977) protocols, illustrates:

—Pretend there is a monster coming, o.k.?
—No, let's don't pretend that.
—Okay, why?
—Cause it's too scarey, that's why.

The earlier example of Jacqueline Piaget's make-believe bedtime illustrates that even 13-month-olds can clearly communicate their awareness of the difference between pretense and reality. Nevertheless, when the pretense is about highly charged emotional themes, map and territory are not so easily kept apart. Scarlett and Wolf (1979) noticed that 2-year-olds frequently backed away with genuine fear when the adult observer animated a small toy alligator in a threatening way. Toddlers, unlike older children, were unable to cope with the pretend danger on its own terms (for example, by making a lion chase the observer's alligator). Similarly, toddlers tended to "drop" the narrator role and intervene in the story scene as deus ex machina to rescue a figure "endangered" by the adult's pretense. Wolf and Scarlett point out that boundary management of reality and pretense becomes more controlled with age. However, transitions remain problematic when the thematic content of pretense is highly emotional. This is not so surprising. After all, even adults weep during dramatic presentations, and adults, not merely children, sometimes treat symbolic objects (a flag, a cross) as if they were that for which they stand (Bateson, 1955). Fictive reality does arouse genuine emotional participation. It is never completely detached except in the logical sense. Indeed, it would carry little meaning if it were.

Not only does pretense sometimes become "too real," real-world concerns intrude into the make-believe world through the way in which roles are distributed or external reality incorporated into ongoing themes. Schwartzman's (1978) detailed study of collaborative play in a day-care center illustrates the intrusion of everyday reality into role assignments. In observations of a group of working-class preschoolers over a period of 18 months, she found that the relationship that the players had to each other outside the play context (friendships, dominance) affected the content and process of their sociodramatic play. Schwartzman discovered that high-status children could join ongoing pretend episodes by imperiously adopting a role or defining an activity. Low-status children had to ask for permission to join the group or play particular roles ("Can I be the witch?"). Thus the roles children played and how they entered play tended to reflect the actual authority structure of the group. Those who frequently played mothers and fathers were the most popular children in the classroom. By contrast, the role of pet (kitty or doggy) was often assumed by one of the less popular children, although there were exceptions to this rule. The leading child in the day-care center sometimes paradoxically defined herself in a submissive role even as she continued to direct activities of her coplayers.

These findings persuaded Schwartzman that play should be regarded as text and context. Play as text is the creation of make-believe plots within the real-world context of the day-care center. Play as context is the creation of the plot as a commentary on the everyday relationships of the players as children in a day-care center:

> In order to be a successful player, one must be able to communicate information that simultaneously (and paradoxically) defines one as a player *subject* (e.g., adopting the play role of witch, mother, etc.) and as a person in the

> defining social context (e.g., the daycare center) and therefore a play *object*. For example, a child (Linda) must be able to communicate to other players that she is both Linda (i.e., a person who leads, dominates, and directs activities, as she is known for this in the general classroom setting) and not-Linda (i.e. a witch or mother) in a play situation. (Schwartzman, 1978, p. 236)

Along similar lines, Garvey and Berndt (1977) found that preschool boys appeared far more willing to transform their generational status than their gender (Garvey & Berndt, 1977; see also Greif, 1975). In mixed-sex dyads, boys vehemently refused the role of mother but willingly accepted the role of father. In single-sex, dyads boys did sometimes assume functional roles normally played by females (server of food) but refrained from overtly identifying with a female role. When mixed-sex dyads played "averting threat," the boy, true to stereotype, was usually cast in the role of defender and the girl in the role of victim.

The everyday world also intrudes into the play world in other, less emotionally charged ways. Some of the plot changes (retransformations) described by Giffin (1984) were precipitated by the wish to admit new players to the group. When a "car" to be taken on an imaginary journey became too small to hold all the players who were eager to join, a "camper" was added to accommodate them. In one case, two children created the synthetic role of doctor-mommy to play the family and doctor script simultaneously, thus satisfying both children's desires. In addition, out-of-frame events (a child falls over) are often taken into the frame by adjusting the plot (the child is taken to "hospital"). This phenomenon was also noticed by Schwartzman (1978) and by Wolf and Pusch (1982). The latter observed that such incorporations are not produced by toddlers but become frequent in the play of older preschoolers.

The tendency to blur map and territory is probably one reason why many parents feel some ambivalence about pretense, indeed equate it with lying as the following statements by two mothers of 4-year-olds show:

> 1. It got so bad, I tried to stop him because I didn't want him to go from an imaginary story to an outright lie—because there's not much difference between the two.
> 2. It worries me sometimes; he has a vivid imagination; and it goes on and on until he *lives* it; and sometimes, these imaginary people you have to feed them with him, you see what I mean? It worries me. (Newson & Newson, 1978, cited in Dunn, 1985, p. 149)

Subtly, by claiming that an aggressive act "is only pretend," children can make the real parade as make-believe and surreptitiously act out real-world antagonisms under the guise of "it's only pretend," as illustrated in the following example from Piaget (1962, p. 174):

Obs. 96. At 5; 8(5), being for the moment on bad terms with her father, X. charged one of her imaginary characters with the task of avenging her: "Zoubab cut off her daddy's head. But she has some very strong glue, and partly stuck it on again. But it's not very firm now."

This process can also work in the reverse direction. What started as deliciously thrilling make-believe can become frighteningly or distressingly real, making it necessary to step out of pretense. In one of Fein's (1985) protocols, a child who is chasing her pretend father with a pretend knife becomes anxious upon hearing one of the coplayers comment: "She picked up a knife. Was trying to kill her dad." The child hastily stepped out of the acting frame, saying: "No I didn't. I just maked a play one." In Piaget's example, X. is able to stay within the play frame by making reparations (sticking the father's head back on with glue).

CONCLUDING REMARKS: THE FUNCTION OF PRETENSE AND THE DRAMATIC ARTS

We have suggested that pretense is play with the representational system, play with the subjunctive ability, but toward what end? Erikson (1963, 1977) proposed that play with small objects is the infantile form of the adult human ability to deal with experience by creating model situations and to master reality by experiment and planning, but what Erikson had in mind was mastery of emotional conflict, not logical problem solving. Through play, children can relive, correct, and recreate reality, enact pervasive uncertainties and wished-for solutions in increasingly more complex ways. Piaget (1962) said much the same thing but claimed that this ability was important only for very young children. Pretense, he pointed out, allows the child to reproduce a modified version of reality for pleasure or to correct unpleasant reality:

At 2; 4(8)., J., not being allowed to play with the water being used for washing, took an empty cup, went and stood by the forbidden tub and went through the actions saying: "I'm pouring out water." At 2; 6(28), she wanted to carry Nonette (i.e., L. who had been born shortly before). Her mother told her she could try later on. J. folded her arms and said: "Nonette's in there. There are two Nonettes." She then talked to the imaginary Nonette, rocked her etc. (Piaget, 1962, Obs. 84, p. 131)

Piaget also illustrated children's use of pretense to "liquidate" disagreeable events by "reproducing scenes in which the ego ran the risk of failure, thereby enabling it to assimilate them and emerge victorious"

(Piaget, 1962, p. 134). In the following example, Jacqueline accepts the unpleasant reality but projects it onto another recipient:

> J., at 2; 1(7), was afraid when sitting on a new chair at table. In the afternoon she put her dolls in uncomfortable positions and said to them: "It doesn't matter. It will be all right," repeating what had been said to her. (Piaget, 1962; Obs. 86, p. 133)

Curiously, Piaget did not feel that these uses of play were early versions of a continuing human ability to create subjunctive worlds. Compensatory and liquidating forms of pretense, he claimed, are a sort of holding strategy, necessary only until the child can engage in adaptive problem solving through realistic coping (see also Sutton-Smith, 1966, for further discussion of this point). "In reality," Piaget says, "the child has no imagination, and what we ascribe to him as such is no more than lack of coherence . . . and still more, subjective assimilation" (Piaget, 1962, p. 131). Only later, at the end of the preschool period, can symbolic play become a source of creative imagination and then only, provided that it is reintegrated with adapted thought. But the question that needs to be answered is whether this account is correct, whether there were ever two separate strands of representation?

From studies of play we now know that the pretense of older preschoolers is actually more, not less fantastic than that of infants (for examples, see Fein, 1985; Giffin, 1984; Watson, personal communication). With a firmer grip on reality, children can afford to turn their event-based representational system topsy-turvy, not only to create a fictive world that depicts their fears, desires, or hopes (see Vandenberg, 1985), but, as Sutton-Smith has pointed out, to mock and make fun of powerful figures (Sutton-Smith, 1979).

In sum, we believe that the ability to create symbolic alternatives to reality and to play with that ability is as deeply part of human experience as the ability to construct an adapted model of everyday reality. Indeed, the successful building of useful representational models may often involve prior play with a number of alternative possibilities some of which are eventually discarded. Conversely, the complexity and quality of subjunctive thought (whether in symbolic play or other contexts) is likely to draw on already existing representational structures. This is why creativity, cognitive flexibility, and divergent thinking have frequently been linked to a fantasy predisposition (Dansky & Silverman, 1973; Liebermann, 1977; Singer, 1973; Sutton-Smith, 1979).

In play, the subjunctive ability is used not for serious reflection on future plans but to act out stories that are of special significance for a variety of reasons (stories of caring and aggression, of obedience and naughtiness, of danger and power, of pain, of puzzlement, and of fun).

It has often been said that the ability to reinvent and correct reality continues into adult life in the form of daydreams. This seems intuitively true but does not go far enough. It is in the theatre and other dramatic and narrative art forms that the subjunctive ability reaches its most sophisticated adult development. Moreover, the work of playwrights and novelists seems to have objectives that are quite similar to the objectives pursued by children in their pretend play.

Even the metacommunicative or stage management techniques we see in children's make-believe play have their counterparts in the dramatic arts, but mature artists, in their fictive plots, toy much more consciously with potential map/territory confusions and distinctions and with the paradoxes of metacommunication than young children. Some try to pack as many layers of meaning into a literary work as possible; others tease an audience with inappropriate or omitted metacommunication (an actor suddenly complains about the role he has to play); and yet others explore the paradox of levels by creating plays within plays and stories within stories (see Shakespeare's *Midsummernight's Dream* for a veritable firework of such devices). Preschoolers do not yet exploit the possibilities of pretense with the conscious artfulness of a writer or playwright, but even during the preschool period, one can find occasional glimpses of play with the paradoxes of pretense. Giffin's (1981) protocols describe a small boy holding up a match-box car while warning his companion, "this is a real fire, this car is burning up." He intensifies pretense by claiming it is real. Likewise, one of the preschoolers in Garvey and Berndt's (1977) study teased her playmate by claiming she had "stealed" her nonexistent cake. The partner turned the tables on the other child by nonchalantly retorting that it was not cake anymore. Finally, one of the children in Schwartzman's study "invented" the technique of the play within the play by designating a brief episode during which the plot went off track as "well, I guess it was just a dream."

In light of the striking similarities in function, content, and technique between childhood pretense and the dramatic and narrative arts, it may be fruitful at this point to go beyond the study of children's make-believe play as related to the development of physical and social cognition on which we have tended to focus. Let us examine it as a precursor to the subsequent development of play writing, dramatic performance, and storytelling, the developed adult forms of acting "as if."

ACKNOWLEDGMENT. During the writing of this chapter both authors received support from the John D. and Catherine T. MacArthur Research Network for the Transition from Infancy to Early Childhood.

INGE BRETHERTON AND MARJORIE BEEGHLY

REFERENCES

Acredolo, L. P., & Goodwyn, S. W. (1985). Symbolic gesturing in language development: A case study. *Human Development, 28,* 40–49.

Bartlett, F. C. (1932). *Remembering: A study in experimental and social psychology.* Cambridge: Cambridge University Press.

Bates, E. (1976). *Language and context: The acquisition of pragmatics.* New York: Academic Press.

Bateson, G. (1955). A theory of play and fantasy. *American Psychiatric Association Research Reports II:* 39–51. Reprinted in G. Bateson, *Steps to an ecology of mind.* New York: Chandler.

Beeghly, M., & Cicchetti, D. (1987). An organizational approach to symbolic development in children with Down syndrome. In D. Cicchetti & M. Beeghly (Eds.), *Symbol development in atypical children* (pp. 5–29). San Francisco: Jossey-Bass.

Belsky, J., & Most, R. K. (1981). From exploration to play: A cross-sectional study of infant free play behavior. *Developmental Psychology, 17,* 630–639.

Bretherton, I., Bates, E., McNew, S., Shore, C., Williamson, C., & Beeghly-Smith, M. (1981). Comprehension and production of symbols in infancy: An experimental study. *Developmental Psychology, 17,* 728–736.

Bretherton, I., O'Connell, B., Shore, C., & Bates, E. (1984). The effect of contextual variation on symbolic play: Development from 20 to 28 months. In I. Bretherton (Ed.), *Symbolic play: The development of social understanding* (pp. 271–298). New York: Academic Press.

Bruner, J. S. (1986, May). *Fact and fiction.* Invited address given at the International Conference on Developing Theories of Mind, Toronto.

Dansky, J. L., & Silverman, W. I. (1973). Effects of play on associative fluency in preschool-aged children. *Developmental Psychology, 9,* 38–44.

Dunn, J. (1985). Pretend play in the family. In A. W. Gottfried & C. C. Brown (Eds.), *Play interactions: The contribution of play material and parental involvement to children's play development* (pp. 149–162). Lexington, MA: Lexington Press.

Dunn, J., & Dale, N. (1984). I a daddy: 2-year-olds' collaboration in joint pretend with sibling and with mother. In I. Bretherton (Ed.), *Symbolic play: The development of social understanding* (pp. 131–158). New York: Academic Press.

Erikson, E. H. (1963). *Childhood and society.* New York: Norton.

Erikson, E. H. (1977). *Toys and reasons.* New York: Norton.

Fein, G. G. (1975). A transformational analysis of pretending. *Developmental Psychology, 11,* 291–296.

Fein, G. G. (1985). The affective psychology of play. In A. W. Gottfried & C. C. Brown (Eds.), *Play interactions: The contribution of play material and parental involvement to children's development* (pp. 31–49). Lexington, MA: Lexington Books.

Fein, G. G., & Apfel, N. (1979). Some preliminary observations on knowing and pretending. In M. Smith & M. B. Franklin (Eds.), *Symbolic functioning in childhood* (pp. 87–100). Hillsdale, NJ: Erlbaum.

Fein, G. G., & Moorin, E. R. (1984). Confusion, substitution, and mastery: Pretend play during the second year of life. In K. Nelson (Ed.), *Children's language* (Vol. 5, pp. 61–76). New York: Gardner Press.

Fenson, L. (1984). Developmental trends for action and speech in pretend play. In I. Bretherton (Ed.), *Symbolic play: The development of social understanding* (pp. 249–270). New York: Academic Press.

Fenson, L., & Ramsay, D. S. (1980). Decentration and integration of the child's play in the second year. *Child Development, 51*, 171–178.

Fenson, L., & Ramsay, D. S. (1981). Effects of modeling action sequences on the play of twelve-, fifteen-, and nineteen-month-old children. *Child Development, 52*, 1028–1036.

Flavell, J. (1985, August). *The development of children's knowledge about the appearance-reality distinction.* Address presented at the meeting of the American Psychological Association, Los Angeles.

Garvey, C., & Berndt, R. (1977). Organization of pretend play. Catalogue of *Selected Documents in Psychology, 7*, Manuscript 1589.

Gerard, A. B. (1984). *Imitation and sequencing in early childhood.* Unpublished doctoral dissertation, University of California, San Diego.

Giffin, H. (1981). *The metacommunicative process in collective make-believe play.* Unpublished doctoral dissertation, University of Colorado, Boulder.

Giffin, H. (1984). The coordination of meaning in the creation of a shared make-believe reality. In I. Bretherton (Ed.), *Symbolic play: The development of social understanding* (pp. 73–100). New York: Academic Press.

Goncu, A., & Kessel, F. (1984). Children's play: A contextual-functional perspective. In F. Kessel & A. Goncu (Eds.), *Analyzing children's play dialogues* (pp. 5–22). San Francisco: Jossey-Bass.

Greif, E. B. (1975). Sex-role playing in pre-school children. In J. S. Bruner, A. Jolly, & K. Sylva (Eds.), *Play—Its role in development and evolution* (pp. 385–391). New York: Basic Books.

Hoffstadter, D. R. (1979). *Goedel, Escher, Bach: An eternal golden braid.* New York: Basic Books.

Huttenlocher, J., & Higgins, E. T. (1978). Issues in the study of symbolic development. In W. A. Collins (Ed.), *Minnesota Symposia on Child Psychology* (Vol. 11, pp. 98–140). Hillsdale, NJ: Erlbaum.

Inhelder, B., Lezine, I., Sinclair, H., & Stambak, G. (1972). Les debuts de la fonction symbolique. *Archives de Psychologie, 163*, 187–243.

Jackowitz, E. R., & Watson, M. W. (1980). *Developmental Psychology, 16*, 543–549.

Jeffree, D., & McConkey, R. (1976). An observation scheme for recording children's imaginative doll play. *Journal of Child Psychology and Psychiatry, 17*, 189–197.

Kagan, J. (1981). *The second year: The emergence of self-awareness.* Cambridge, MA: Harvard University Press.

Killen, M., & Užgiris, I. (1981). Imitation of actions with objects. *Journal of Genetic Psychology, 138*, 219–229.

Largo, R., & Howard, J. (1979). Developmental progression in play behavior in children between 9 and 30 months. *Developmental Medicine and Child Neurology, 21*, 299–310.

Leslie, A. (1987). Pretense and representation in infancy: The origins of theory of mind." *Psychological Review, 94*, 412–426.

Liebermann, J. N. (1977). *Playfulness: Its relation to imagination and creativity.* New York: Academic Press.

Lowe, H. (1975). Trends in the development of representational play in infants from one to three years: An observational study. *Psychology and Psychiatry, 16*, 33–47.

Mandler, J. H. (1979). Categorical and schematic organization in memory. In C. K. Puff (Ed.), *Memory organization and structure* (pp. 259–299). New York: Academic Press.

Matthews, W. S. (1977). Modes of transformation in the initiation of fantasy play. *Developmental Psychology, 13*, 211–216.

Miller, P., & Garvey, K. (1984). Mother-baby role play: Its origin in social support. In I.

Bretherton (Ed.), *Symbolic play: The development of social understanding* (pp. 101–130). New York: Academic Press.

Nelson, K., & Gruendel, J. (1981). Generalized event representations: Basic building blocks of cognitive development. In A. Brown & M. Lamb (Eds.), *Advances in developmental psychology* (Vol. 1, pp. 131–158). Hillsdale, NJ: Erlbaum.

Newson, J., & Newson, E. (1968). *Four year olds in an urban community.* Harmondsworth, England: Pelican Books.

Nicolich, L. M. (1977). Beyond sensorimotor intelligence: Assessment of symbolic maturity through analysis of pretend play. *Merrill-Palmer Quarterly, 23,* 88–99.

O'Connell, B. (1984). *The development of sequential understanding revisited: The role of meaning and familiarity.* Unpublished doctoral dissertation, University of California, San Diego.

O'Connell, B., & Gerard, R. (1985). The development of sequential understanding: Scripts and scraps. *Child Development, 56,* 671–681.

Overton, W. F., & Jackson, J. P. (1973). The representation of imaged objects in action sequences: A developmental study. *Child Development, 44,* 309–314.

Piaget, J. (1954). *The child's construction of reality.* New York: Basic Books.

Piaget, J. (1962). *Play, dreams and imitation in childhood.* New York: Norton.

Piaget, J. (1963). *The origins of intelligence in children.* New York: Norton.

Price, D., & Goodman, G. S. (1985, April). *Preschool children's comprehension of a recurring episode.* Paper presented at the biennial meeting of the Society for research in Child Development, Toronto, Canada.

Rheingold, H. L., & Emery, G. N. (1986). The nurturant acts of very young children. In J. Black, D. Olweus, & M. Radke-Yarrow (Eds.), *Aggression and socially valued behavior: Biological and cultural perspectives* (pp. 74–94). New York: Academic Press.

Rubin, S., & Wolf, D. (1979). The development of maybe: The evolution of social roles into narrative roles. In D. Wolf (Ed.), *New Directions for Child Development, 6,* 15–28.

Scarlett, W. G., & Wolf, D. (1979). When it's only make-believe: The construction of a boundary between fantasy and reality. In D. Wolf (Ed.), *New Directions for Child Development, 3,* 29–40.

Schank, R. C. (1982). *Dynamic memory: A theory of reminding and learning in computers and people.* New York: Cambridge University Press.

Schank, R. C., & Abelson, R. P. (1977). *Scripts, plans, goals and understanding.* Hillsdale, NJ: Erlbaum.

Schwartzman, H. B. (1978). *Transformations: The anthropology of children's play.* New York: Plenum Press.

Singer, J. L. (Ed.). (1973). *The child's world of make-believe: Experimental studies of imaginative play.* New York: Academic Press.

Stein, N. (1978). The comprehension and appreciation of stories: A developmental analysis. In S. Madeja (Ed.), *The arts and cognition* (Vol. 2, pp. 231–249). St. Louis: Cemrel.

Sutton-Smith, B. (1966). Piaget on play: A critique. *Psychological Review, 73,* 104–110.

Sutton-Smith, B. (1979). *Play and learning.* New York: Gardner.

Tulving, E. (1972). Episodic and semantic memory. In E. Tulving & W. Donaldson (Eds.), *Organization of memory* (pp. 382–403). New York: Academic Press.

Tulving, E. (1983). *Elements of episodic memory.* New York: Oxford University Press.

Ungerer, J. A., Zelazo, P. R., Kearsley, R. B., & O'Leary, K. (1981). Developmental changes in the representation of objects from 18–34 months of age. *Child Development, 52,* 186–195.

Vandenberg, B. R. (1985). Beyond the ethology of play. In A. W. Gottfried and C. C. Brown (Eds.), *Play interactions: The contribution of play material and parental involvement to children's development* (pp. 3–11). Lexington, MA: Lexington Press.

Vygotsky, L. S. (1967). Play and its role in the mental development of the child. *Soviet Psychology, 5,* 6–18.

Watson, M. W., & Fischer, K. W. (1977). A developmental sequence of agent use in late infancy. *Child Development, 48,* 828–836.

Watson, M. W., & Fischer, K. W. (1980). Development of social roles in elicited and spontaneous behavior during the preschool years. *Child Development, 18,* 483–494.

Weiss, B., Beeghly, M., & Cicchetti, D. (1985, April). *Symbolic play development in children with Down syndrome and nonhandicapped children.* Paper presented at the biennial meeting of the Society for Research in Child Development, Toronto.

Wolf, D. (1982). Understanding others: A longitudinal case study of the concept of independent agency. In G. Forman (Ed.), *Action and thought: From sensorimotor schemes to symbol use* (pp. 297–327). New York: Academic Press.

Wolf, D., & Grollmann, S. (1982). Ways of playing: Individual differences in imaginative play. In K. Rubin & D. Pepler (Eds.), *The play of children: Current theory and research* (pp. 46–63). New York: Karger.

Wolf, D., & Pusch, J. (1982). The origins of autonomous texts in play boundaries. In L. Galda & A. Pellegrini (Eds.), *Play, language and stories* (pp. 63–77). Norwood, NJ: Ablex.

Wolf, D., Rygh, J., & Altshuler, J. (1984). Agency and experience: Actions and states in play narratives. In I. Bretherton (Ed.), *Symbolic play: The development of social understanding* (pp. 195–217). New York: Academic Press.

Wolf, D., Goldfield, B., Beeghly, M., Waner, D., & Cardona, L. (1985, October). *"There's not room enough," the baby said: A study of intertextuality in young children's discourse.* Paper presented at the Tenth Annual Boston University Conference on Language Development.

PART IV

Conclusion

CHAPTER 9

The Big Picture for Infant Development
Levels and Variations

KURT W. FISCHER AND ANNE E. HOGAN

INTRODUCTION

Infant behavior varies enormously; that is obvious from the chapters in this volume. Research clearly indicates that the maturity or sophistication of infant behavior varies widely from moment to moment and across contexts.

In a quiet, alert state with her eyes wide open, a 1-month-old infant girl moves her hand clumsily in the general direction of a red ball she sees moving in front of her. Ten minutes later, when she is drowsy, she seems to ignore the ball, not relating to it at all (Als, Chapter 3 this volume; von Hofsten, 1984, in press). Is she capable of looking at the ball and reaching toward it, or is she not?

Similarly, a 4-year-old boy watches his mother acting out a pretend story with dolls: The patient doll tells the doctor doll he has a cold, and the doctor examines him and gives him medicine to make him feel better. The boy promptly acts out a similar story. Then, 10 minutes later, the mother asks him to show her the best story he can about a doctor and a patient, just like the one he did before. Instead of producing the

KURT W. FISCHER • Department of Human Development, Harvard University, Cambridge, Massachusetts 02138. ANNE E. HOGAN • Department of Psychology, University of Miami, Coral Gables, Florida 33124.

complex story he did 10 minutes earlier, he produces a much simpler story: He makes the doctor doll simply walk around the doctor's office carrying a thermometer, with no interaction between doctor and patient (Watson & Fischer, 1980). Is the boy capable of acting out a doctor–patient interaction, or is he not?

As these examples demonstrate, the developmental stage or level of behaviors varies with state of arousal, assessment situation, emotional state, and task, just to name a few of the most obvious sources of variation. Piaget (1941) himself acknowledged that these variations were common and called them by the name *decalage*. Vygotsky (1978) also described variations of this kind. Most of the chapters in this volume deal directly or indirectly with such variations.

With so many factors producing variations in behavior, is there any order to be found? Or is behavior simply so tied to the particular situation and child that there is no big developmental picture behind the variations?

Some researchers argue that the variations demonstrate that there is little developmental order. They argue that the variations call into question the existence of general cognitive-developmental stages (Flavell, 1982; Fogel & Thelen, 1987; Lockman & McHale, Chapter 5 this volume; Thelen & Fogel, Chapter 2 this volume). If infants' developmental stage changes as a function of basic factors such as task, assessment situation, and state of arousal, they say, then stages cannot be real. Of course, we have stated the argument baldly to highlight the problem with it.

Such arguments do not hold because there is no simple dichotomy between stage and variation. The organization of behavior develops systematically, as reflected by many stage descriptions, and it also varies from moment to moment. These facts are contradictory only for overly simple concepts of stage and variation.

If behavior is adaptive, then its organization should vary not only with development but also with factors such as task, situation, and state. Likewise, if developmental scales are sensitive measures of behavioral organization, then they should show changes as a function of these factors. The occurrence of such systematic variation in "developmental stage" does not necessarily reflect a defect of either the scales or the stages hypothesized. Instead it shows that developmental scales gauge both the increases in complexity that occur with development and the variations that occur as a function of these factors.

What is needed is to move beyond the dichotomy between stage and variation to build an explanatory system that subsumes both. Only a framework that integrates organization with variation can specify the processes that produce cognitive development (Als, Chapter 3 this volume; Fogel & Thelen, 1987; Thelen & Fogel, Chapter 2 this volume;

Užgiris *et al.*, Chapter 4 this volume). Understanding these processes requires tools for describing both behavioral structures and functional mechanisms. The tools for describing behavioral structures provide a metric for relating behaviors within and across domains. The tools for describing functional mechanisms specify how behaviors vary.

We will suggest a framework for integrating developmental and short-term variations in infant behavioral development. Based on the concept of skill, the theory is intended to show how these structures and functional mechanisms work together as a coherent set of developmental processes. In the presentation here, we are focusing on infancy, but skill theory applies in general to later periods of development as well (Fischer, 1980; Fischer & Farrar, 1987; Fischer & Pipp, 1984; Fischer & Lamborn, in press).

SKILLS ARE CHARACTERISTICS OF THE INFANT IN A CONTEXT

The concept of skill in English usage suggests an ability to carry out a set of actions in a particular type of task (Bruner, 1973; Fischer, 1980). A skill for driving a car is tied to cars and does not apply to boats, airplanes, or bicycles. It may not even generalize effectively to driving a car with a different sort of gearshift from the one the driver is accustomed to, nor to driving a car on mud and snow instead of paved roads. A skill is a characteristic neither of a person nor of a context, but of a person in a context.

In using a skill, an infant or young child controls variations in his or her actions (including thoughts) in a context. Thus a skill is a control structure or an operant (Skinner, 1969). The skill level of a particular behavior derives from not just characteristics of a child or a brain but also the context that supports the child's actions. (The chapters in this volume by Hazen and Thelen & Fogel make similar arguments.) Some of the most important sources of variations in skill level are the task, the infant's state, the familiarity of the task, and the degree of environmental support for performance provided by the immediate context, especially the social context.

Because skill development is relatively context-specific, skills differ from the structures hypothesized by Piaget (1957, 1936/1952), where a stage such as tertiary circular reactions is supposed to be a general characteristic of the infant across contexts. Skills develop through *levels*, not stages, and infants function at different skill levels for different tasks, states, and situations. This is how *decalage* is the rule in cognitive development (Fischer, 1980).

Amid these variations, there is order showing the existence of developmental levels. Within a task domain, the *sequence of development* for a particular assessment situation follows predicted levels (see also Flavell, 1982; Wohlwill, 1973). And across domains, the infant's skills show an upper limit on complexity, his or her *optimal level*. This limit specifies the most complex skills that the infant can consistently produce, which is hypothesized to reflect a central information-processing limit. At certain times in development, the optimal level shifts abruptly higher, producing stagelike changes in optimal performance. At the same time, ordinary behavior below optimum may show continuous, nonstagelike growth (Fischer & Pipp, 1984).

The structures of levels specify how infants progress through developmental sequences, and the functional mechanisms stipulate when these sequences obtain and how various factors produce variations in level. Because the two sorts of mechanisms work together, it should be obvious that the levels cannot be considered to be merely maturational in any simple sense. After carefully reviewing the diverse developmental data presented in the chapters of this book, we believe that they all fit within this skill-development framework.

Multiple Levels of Early Development

Research findings have shown an impressive convergence with regard to developmental levels in infancy. Data from a number of different laboratories have reported evidence for at least four periods of rapid behavioral change in infant development (Corrigan, 1983; Emde, Gaensbauer, & Harmon, 1976; Kagan, 1982; McCall, 1983; Seibert & Hogan, 1982; Seibert, Hogan, & Mundy, 1984; Užgiris, 1976; Zelazo & Leonard, 1983). Using longitudinal assessments with standardized infant intelligence tests, McCall, Eichorn, and Hogarty (1977) found these rapid changes at 2 to 4 months, 7 to 8 months, 12 to 13 months, and 18 to 21 months.

There is also some evidence that major changes in brain-growth patterns may be associated with these transition periods. Changes in brain-activity patterns have been documented for each of the predicted ages in human infants (Chugani & Phelps, 1986; Dreyfus-Brisac, 1978; Emde & Robinson, 1980; Woodruff, 1978) and for some of them in rhesus monkeys (Caveness, 1962). Changes in synaptogentic growth and even in global brain growth may also relate to the infant levels (Fischer, 1987; Goldman-Rakic, 1987).

Finally, several independent theories of infant development have posited similar developmental levels (Case, 1985; Fischer, 1980; McCall *et al.*, 1977; Seibert & Hogan, 1982; Užgiris, 1976). Additional levels between those already identified seem unlikely because careful investigations have uncovered no evidence for additional discontinuities (for example, Corrigan, 1983; McCall *et al.*, 1977).

Developments in the first 4 months and between 2 and 5 years have not been as carefully charted. Based on theory and evidence, we posit that infants develop through three additional levels in the first 4 months and one additional level at about 4 years of age.

Table 1 shows the resulting eight developmental levels for the first 5 years of life. The ages given for each level are for its emergence, when the infant can first control a number of skills at that level. Of course, many skills will not immediately reflect the new level because it takes time for the infant to master skills at the new level. Also, more precise research is required to determine how much individual infants vary in the exact age of emergence of each level.

The levels in Table 1 provide a characterization of the structure of developing skills in any domain. At the early levels, the infant controls, combines, and differentiates action components called reflexes. Gradually these combinations and differentiations produce a new type of cognitive unit, flexible sensorimotor actions, which in turn are combined and differentiated. Finally, at the last two levels in early childhood, the child controls a third type of unit, representations, and relations between them. The changes to a new type of cognitive unit are larger than the moves to a new level involving a more complex combination of the same type of cognitive unit. Consequently the levels are organized into tiers—the reflex tier, the sensorimotor tier, and the representational tier in Table 1. In our descriptions of the levels, we will focus not only on traditional cognitive tasks such as eye–hand coordination but also on social interaction.

The structures of the levels specify how skills relate to each other developmentally, especially which skills will develop in sequence and which in approximate synchrony. Skill theory also describes processes for predicting smaller developmental steps within levels and thus devising more detailed developmental scales for specific task domains. For information about those microdevelopmental processes, see Fischer (1980) and Fischer and Pipp (1984).

Levels of Reflex Development

Many investigators have emphasized the dramatic nature of the developments in biology and behavior during the first few months of life

TABLE 1
Levels of Cognitive Development in Infancy and Early Childhood

Level	Age of emergence	Examples of skills
Rf1: single reflexes[a]	3 to 4 weeks	Single, simple species-specific action-components: With fixed posture—Infant looks at ball moving in front of face. Infant grasps cloth placed in hand.
Rf2: reflex mappings[a]	7 to 8 weeks	Simple relations of a few action components: Hearing voice leads to looking at eyes. Infant extends arm toward seen ball.
Rf3: reflex systems[a]	10 to 11 weeks	Complex relations of subsets of action-components: Looking at face and hearing voice evokes co-ordinated smiling, cooing, and nodding of head (greeting response). Infant opens hand while extending arm toward ball.
Rf4/S1: systems of reflex systems, which are single sensorimotor actions	15 to 17 weeks	Relations of reflex systems to produce a single, flexible sensorimotor action: Infant looks at ball as it moves through a complex trajectory. Infant opens hand while extending arm toward seen ball and in middle of reach sometimes adjusts hand to changes in trajectory of ball, but coordination is still unstable.
S2: sensorimotor mappings	7 to 8 months	Simple relations of a few sensorimotor actions: Infant grasps a ball in order to bring it in front of face to look at it. Infant uses looking at ball to finely guide reaching for it.
S3: sensorimotor systems	11 to 13 months	Complex relations of subsets of sensorimotor actions: Infant moves a rattle in different ways to see different parts of it. Infant imitates pronunciation of many single words.
S4/Rpl: systems of sensorimotor systems, which are single representations	18 to 24 months	Coordination of action systems to produce concrete representations of objects, people, or events: Child pretends that a doll is walking. Child says, "Doll walk."

TABLE 1   (*Continued*)

Level	Age of emergence	Examples of skills
Rp2: representational mappings	3.5 to 4.5 years	Simple relations of concrete representations: Child pretends that two dolls are Mom and Dad interacting appropriately in terms of parental roles. Child understands that self knows a secret and Dad does not know it.

*a*These levels are hypothesized, but to date there are too few data to test their existence unequivocally.
Note: Ages given are modal ages at which a level first appears based on research with middle-class European and American children. They may differ across cultures and other social groups.

(Dreyfus-Brisac, 1978; Emde & Robinson, 1980; Ilg & Ames, 1955; Mounoud, 1976). Careful descriptions of early behaviors have demonstrated major changes in behavioral organization in both human infants (McGraw, 1943; Peiper, 1963; Touwen, 1976) and macaque monkeys (Goldman-Rakic, 1987; Parker, 1977). Indeed, the magnitude of the documented changes seems to have led some scholars to assume that there is no relation between early behaviors and later skills (see discussion by Rovee-Collier, 1987). According to our analysis, the changes are indeed large, and at the same time the skills of later infancy are built directly upon those of early infancy. The magnitude of the changes reflects the occurrence of a rapid-fire series of developmental levels, not an absence of connection between behaviors in early and late infancy.

Recent research and theory have helped to spell out what seem to be a series of major qualitative changes in early infancy. We hypothesize that human infants move through four developmental levels in the first 4 months after birth (Fischer, 1980). The last of these levels is the same as the first of those reported for later infancy, as seen in Table 1.

Emerging at approximately 3 to 4, 7 to 8, 10 to 11, and 15 to 17 weeks in human infants, the early levels involve action components that have traditionally been called "reflexes" (Piaget, 1937/1954). These are primarily innate, species-specific behaviors, probably numbering in the hundreds, including looking, grasping, smiling, protoimitation, listening, postural responses, and most of the developmental reflexes described in standard assessments of newborn behavior (Peiper, 1963; Touwen, 1976). Despite the traditional name *reflex*, these are not the same as the involuntary, subcortical reflexes, such as the eyeblink and knee jerk. Unlike the involuntary reflexes, the voluntary ones are controlled by the infant, who gradually combines and differentiates them to form flexible, voluntary actions.

At the first reflex level, emerging at approximately 3 to 4 weeks of age, infants can control single reflexes. For example, they can look at or look away from a ball moving in front of their face so long as its motions are limited and the situation is controlled to prevent interfering action components such as the tonic neck reflex (Bullinger, 1981; Pipp & Haith, 1977; von Hofsten, 1984). Likewise, they can "voluntarily" grasp a ball placed in their hand, or they can kick their legs (Thelen & Fogel, Chapter 2 this volume). In general, at this and the next level, specific postures or body positions must be appropriate for a particular reflex. Inappropriate posture can easily prevent the infant from producing a reflex. Also, the 1-month-old infant must generally be in an alert state (Als, Chapter 3 this volume; Prechtl & O'Brien, 1982; Wolff, 1966) to show these organized behaviors.

At the second level, emerging at approximately 7 to 8 weeks, infants can coordinate and differentiate two action components in a single reflex mapping. When seated comfortably in front of their mothers face to face, for instance, they can look at their mother's face (Maurer & Salapatek, 1976) or respond to her voice by looking at her eyes (Haith, Bergman, & Moore, 1977). They can also smile or coo to their mother's face or voice (Kaye & Fogel, 1980; Legerstee, Pomerleau, Malcuit, & Feider, 1987). When facing a screen where objects appear in regular alternation on left and right, they can sometimes anticipate which side the object will appear at next (Canfield, 1988).

Research by von Hofsten (1984) indicates that at this age children start to coordinate looking at a ball with reaching for it. Earlier, infants may reach and look simultaneously but without any evidence that the two behaviors are coordinated. At this level, when they reach and look, they seem to try, in an initial, coarse way, to grasp what they see. For example, they look at a ball, and they close their hand in a grasp as they reach toward it. Of course, this behavior makes their grasping attempt unsuccessful because the hand is closed before it reaches the ball. But it also shows a first coordination of looking and grasping, and the beginning of movement beyond the limitations of the initial species-specific action components.

Another apparently negative result of emergence of the first coordination of reflexes seems to be a temporary decrease in the frequency of some single action components when the situation naturally elicits two or more of them simultaneously (Field, Muir, Pilon, Sinclair, & Dodwell,

1980; von Hofsten, 1984; Maratos, 1982; Zelazo, Zelazo, & Kolb, 1972). It is as if the effort to control two behaviors leads to the temporary suppression of one of them. For looking and reaching, infants are less likely to reach while looking; but when they do reach, they seem to be relating reaching to looking, as when they close their hand. Once the infant gains control of one or more relations among the reflexes, the behavior returns to a higher frequency.

With the third reflex level, emerging at 10 to 11 weeks, infants can coordinate several action components in a reflex system. That is, the related mappings of reflexes from the previous level are combined into clusters of coordinated behaviors, with considerable independence from interference among components. For example, infants can simultaneously coordinate looking at their mother's face, listening to her voice, and smiling at her, in what is often called a greeting response (Kaye & Fogel, 1980; Papousek & Papousek, 1979). Similarly, they can extend their hand toward a person or ball they see in front of them and open their hand as they reach (Legerstee et al., 1987; von Hofsten, 1984).

In perceptual skills, when facing a screen where objects regularly alternate, they can reliably anticipate which side the object will appear on (Haith, Hazan, & Goodman, 1988), and they even give evidence of being able to anticipate more complex alternations, where one object on one side is followed by two on the other (Canfield, 1988). They can coordinate seeing two lines to form a perception of an angle across variations in orientation (Cohen & Younger, 1984), and apparently they can also learn to discriminate some other simple visual categories (Hayne, Rovee-Collier, & Perris, 1987).

Levels of Sensorimotor Development

The fourth reflex level, which emerges at 15 to 17 weeks, is also the first level of sensorimotor development, marking the full realization of the independent action that is the basis of what Piaget (1936/1952) called "sensorimotor intelligence." It brings the coordination of two or more systems of reflexes from the previous level to form a single action.

This flexible control structure is mostly free of interference from the constraints of posture and reflex evident in the first two levels. To elicit a behavior, there is much less need for the tester to carefully control infants' posture. From most ordinary positions, they can skillfully turn their head from side to side and visually follow a ball that is moving or making a sound (Bullinger, 1981; Bullinger & Chatillon, 1983; Touwen,

1976). They can use their hand to pursue a ball lying on the bed beside them until they grasp it (without looking at it). And in eye–hand coordination, they can not only extend their hand toward a ball that they see and open their hand as they reach, but they can also make some adjustment in their movement in midreach to follow the ball's movement.

Although the infant has made enormous progress in eye–hand coordination, it is important to realize that he or she is still not capable of smooth, flexible, visually guided reaching across a wide range of situations. They skills of the 4-month-old are still a long way from the flexible coordination of eye and hand that will come later in the first year (von Hofsten, in press; Piaget, 1936/1952).

Even when infants of this age seem to have a coordinated skill relating eye and hand, it is fragile. At 5 months, Seth Fischer would look at some familiar beads tied to the front of his walker and reach directly to them, showing considerable skill. But when his father placed a new rattle on top of the beads in virtually the same place that Seth normally grasped skillfully, he reached for it awkwardly, flailing and groping with his hands and not succeeding in getting hold of it. A little later, after the rattle had been removed, he again reached skillfully for the beads. The change from beads to rattle apparently disrupted his skill, even though the situation was nearly identical to the one where he grasped skillfully.

At 7 to 8 months, with the second sensorimotor level, infants develop the ability to consistently relate two actions in a single sensorimotor mapping. An 8-month-old girl can skillfully use looking at a ball in many different positions to guide how she reaches for the ball. Likewise, she can examine the ball carefully, holding it in front of her face and turning it with her hand to look at some part of it or touching it with just her index finger (Thelen & Fogel, Chapter 2 this volume). By traditional Piagetian criteria, this is when the child finally has skilled eye–hand coordination and can find hidden objects under screens in the standard object-permanence tasks (Corrigan & Fischer, 1985; Hazen, Chapter 7 this volume).

This coordination of manipulation with perception extends beyond vision (Vondra & Belsky, Chapter 6 this volume; Lockman & McHale, Chapter 5 this volume). By 6 to 8 months, infants use manipulation to explore many types of changes in the perceived characteristics of objects, including texture, color, and sound, and more generally they begin to use manipulation to explore objects in play.

Other types of mappings include the coordination of vocalizing with hearing to repeat simple wordlike sounds such as "mamama"

(Ramsey, 1984) and the coordination of looking acts to produce perception of a complex visual pattern such as the subjective-contour illusion for a square (Bertenthal, Campos, & Haith, 1980). Thelen and Fogel (Chapter 2 this volume) describe a study of how infants can control a mapping relating the action of crying to that of sucking their thumb. Infants of about 9 months of age could consistently put their hand in their mouth to calm themselves when they were crying. At earlier ages, babies could sometimes get their hand into their mouth to calm themselves, but the skill was less consistent and seemed more haphazard.

Research on the 8-month transition is extensive, and the existence of a cluster of developmental spurts at this point is thoroughly documented. At the same time, research on this transition has also uncovered the complexity of the functional mechanism leading to spurts in performance. Campos and his collaborators have demonstrated in an elegant series of studies that the emergence of crawling induces spurts in a wide range of spatial skills associated with this transition (Campos & Bertenthal, 1987). That is, experience with crawling seems to be a major catalyst for the development of a cluster of spatial skills. Similar mechanisms are almost certainly involved in the development of all the levels. The emergence of a new level involves a complex interplay of forces, not a simple maturational unfolding.

By 12 to 13 months, babies develop the capacity to relate a number of actions in a complex system of actions, which marks the third sensorimotor level. A 13-month-old can facilely move a ball around, using what she sees to guide what she does with it and anticipating many of the consequences of moving the ball a particular way. When she does not know how to accomplish some desired goal, such as dropping the ball so that it falls into a small hole in a box, she experiments with different ways of holding and dropping it until she finds one that works (Piaget, 1936/1952).

At this level, infants also begin to carry out simple pretending with stereotyped actions, such as pretending to drink from an empty cup (Vondra & Belsky, Chapter 6 this volume; Bretherton & Beeghly, Chapter 8 this volume; Fischer, Hand, Watson, Van Parys, & Tucker, 1984). And they produce a few dozen single words, which require coordinating vocalizing with hearing several specific sounds in a combination to produce the sound of the specific word (Fischer & Corrigan, 1981). Although these single words involve primitive symbolization, genuine representation does not emerge until the next level, when the child can produce simple sentences describing actions or pretend that other people can carry out such actions.

From Action to Representation

In the middle of the second year, at 18 to 21 months, toddlers develop to the fourth sensorimotor level, which is also the first level of representations. Coordinating two sensorimotor action systems, they can cognitively evoke an object, event, or person that is not actually present. The prototype for such a representation is that they evoke the person or thing carrying out an action or having a characteristic, as in a simple sentence. For example, in pretending, they make a doll pretend to walk across the table by coordinating a system for manipulating the doll with a system for walking (Bretherton & Beeghly, Chapter 8 this volume; Fischer et al., 1984). The pretending is analogous to saying, "Doll walk." More generally, infants show spurts in a wide array of skills that involve the coordination of two sensorimotor systems into a single unit (Fischer & Jennings, 1981). Many of these skills involve representation or symbolization as originally described by Piaget (1946/1951). Along with a rapid increase in pretending comes a spurt in vocabulary and in the production of sentences (Bates, Benigni, Bretherton, Camaioni, & Volterra, 1979; Bloom, 1973; Corrigan, 1983; Fischer & Corrigan, 1981).

The final level in early childhood, representational mappings, emerges at 3½ to 4½ years of age, when preschool children can relate one representation to another. In pretending, they can make two dolls interact appropriately in terms of reciprocal, concrete social roles, such as mother and father, mother and child, or doctor and patient (Fischer et al., 1984). In perspective taking, they can relate a representation of knowing a secret themselves to their representation of their father not knowing it (Marvin, Greenberg, & Mossler, 1976). Although most of the work in this book does not deal with behavior at such a late age, a few of the contributions do deal with the middle preschool years. The most complex pretend stories discussed by Bretherton and Beeghley (Chapter 8 this volume) seem to involve this level, and the oldest children studied by Hazen (Chapter 7 this volume) were in the age range where this level emerges.

Skill theory and Case's (1985) information-processing theory, among others, predict additional levels after those of early childhood. Empirical evidence supports at least three periods of rapid behavorial change—at approximately 6 to 7 years, 10 to 12 years, and 14 to 16 years (Fischer & Silvern, 1985). As always, the exact ages vary with the particular tasks and assessment criteria.

FUNCTIONAL MECHANISMS OF SHORT-TERM VARIATIONS IN LEVEL

Skills develop through the levels in Table 1, and they also show smaller microdevelopmental steps between levels. However, these developmental scales are not merely simple, linear descriptions of how behavior develops step by step and level by level. Skill or competence for a child at a given time in a domain is not fixed at a particular point on a developmental scale. Skill, like behavior, is fluid, constantly varying in complexity with changes in task, situation, and state (Fischer & Bullock, 1984). Certainly some short-term variations in behavior do not reflect changes in skill or competence, but many do. Skills are characteristics of the child in a context, not of the child independent of context. Consequently, factors such as task, assessment condition, and state are actually a part of the child's skill. (See Fogel & Thelen, 1987, Thelen & Fogel, Chapter 2 this volume, and Hazen, Chapter 7 this volume, for related arguments.) Developmental scales can be used to assess not only developmental sequence and level but also the variations in children's skills.

The functional mechanisms of skill development specify how variations in level occur, including the conditions under which a simple, linear developmental sequence will obtain (Fischer, Pipp, & Bullock, 1984; Fischer & Farrar, 1987). Of the many different functional mechanisms potentially relating to variation (Fogel & Thelen, 1987; Thelen & Fogel, Chapter 2 this volume), only a few have been specified in any detail. We will focus on those mechanisms that have been explicated and that have the most direct links to early development. Some of the mechanisms—task, optimal level, and functional level—relate directly to the procedures that the observer controls in assessing developmental levels. Other mechanisms—state, emotions, and the role of the body— are also relevant to assessment, especially in infancy, although the experimenter has less control over them. Of course, all these mechanisms work together in the infant, as we will try to show.

Task Effects and Generalization

Tasks are one of the primary organizers of behavior. A change in the task an infant is performing normally produces a change in behavior. Within Piaget's (1983) theory, as well as many other cognitive-developmental approaches, the importance of task effects is neglected because the child's stage is used as the main explanation of behavioral change. For skill theory, however, a change in task necessarily produces a change in skill. This mechanism is consistent with Gibson's (1979) argument that the environment provides the person with highly structured perceptual information that powerfully affects behavior. It also fits the role of perceptual input in neural organization, according to recent theories of the formation of neural networks in learning and development (Grossberg, 1980). Much of the task structure comes from the environment; it is not all imposed by processes in the brain.

An analysis of the structure of a task includes specification of the important perceptual information in the task. Such analysis cannot be captured by a simple list of perceptual dimensions such as color, shape, and texture. Although these dimensions do contribute to infant behavior (Lockman and McHale, Chapter 5 this volume), they capture only a portion of the information in the task. The researcher must go beyond a catalog of perceptual dimensions to provide an analysis of the organization of the particular task.

The skill approach provides a system for analyzing the structures of tasks and a method for dealing with the variations produced by tasks. The organizing influence of tasks is central to the analysis of developmental order. Because an infant builds individual skills in particular tasks, developmental order is greatest when task is held constant, or as nearly constant as possible. When the infant performs highly similar tasks, the skills used share many components; they are all in the same *task domain*. Because task factors are held approximately constant, the levels and transformations of skill theory can be used to produce a structural analysis of a task domain and to precisely predict developmental sequences based on variations in complexity in that domain. These variations specify how skills are generalized and differentiated within the domain. On the other hand, when tasks differ not only in complexity but also in content and procedure, the skills used in those tasks vary in important ways. Consequently, the structure of development is harder to analyze, and sequences are much less predictable.

Generalization across task domains can occur when skills developed in one domain can be used directly in a second one. The skills from the first domain make up a subset of the skills required for successful performance in the second one. Such specific generalization occurs when there are close links in the skills required in the two domains (Fischer & Farrar, 1987).

For example, in language development, the emergence of specific words at the level of single representations is tied to the development of closely related types of understandings. Toddlers learn to say words encoding disappearance such as *more* and *gone*, shortly after they demonstrate an understanding of invisible (hidden) displacements in object-permanence tasks (Corrigan, 1977; Gopnik & Meltzoff, 1986, 1987; McCune-Nicolich, 1981; Tomasello & Farrar, 1984). The relation with understanding of invisible displacements is specific to words encoding disappearance. There is no relation between understanding such displacements and using other types of words, such as those for colors or mistakes (*uh oh*).

In an elegant demonstration of this relation, Tomasello and Farrar (1986) attempted to train toddlers to use nonsense words referring to the identity, visible movement, or invisible movement of an object. The learning of the words proved to be specific to the children's understandings. When they could not yet understand visible movements, they could only learn the words dealing with identity and visible movements. When they had achieved an understanding of invisible movements, they could learn that type of word as well.

A child's skill for using a word encoding disappearance includes many of the same skill components she or he uses in searching for an invisibly displaced object. When there is no such sharing of components, there will be no systematic generalization across domains. Predicting such connections between domains requires careful task analysis to determine when skill components are shared.

In rare but important cases, the development of a particular skill can act as a general catalyst, changing the infant's experience in many task domains and thus leading the infant to learn many new skills. In those cases, the relation between skills is less locally specific, as with the far-reaching effects of the emergence of crawling at about 8 months of age (Campos & Bertenthal, 1987). Crawling affects the acquisition of a broad range of spatial skills at the level of sensorimotor mappings. Apparently crawling produces developmental spurts in diverse spatial skills, including simple object permanence (search for objects the infant sees hidden), wariness of heights, and social referencing (using the mother's facial expression to interpret the significance of a novel event).

The broad array of skills affected by these catalysts belong to a different type of domain, a *skill domain*. These skills normally show only a small amount of overlap because they share only a component here or there. At rare times in development, such skills are all affected similarly the way that crawling affects spatial skills. In statistical tests of association such as factor analysis, the tasks in a skill domain are correlated: They show a loose, statistical connection even though they do not usually form reliable developmental sequences. Within a skill domain, many different organizing effects of tasks produce wide variations in performance, but the weak relations between tasks can be detected statistically with large samples (see Horn, 1976; McCall *et al.*, 1977). Many of the correlations among tasks discussed in this volume, as in the chapters by Bretherton and Beegly and Belsky and Vondra, involve such skill domains. It is important that these relations not be interpreted as demonstrating strong connections among tasks, like those within a task domain.

Optimal Level

Although tasks and other factors produce wide variations in developmental level, the mechanism of optimal level sets a limit on how high in any developmental sequence an infant's performance can go. Even under the best testing conditions, the baby's performance does not move beyond his or her optimal level, the upper limit on the complexity of skills he or she can control.

This upper limit seems to develop in spurts—rapid changes in behavior at certain age periods, as indicated in the right-hand column of Table 1 (Fischer, Pipp, & Bullock, 1984). For each level in that table, the baby shows a cluster of spurts in optimal performance (Fischer, 1983; Fischer & Silvern, 1985). For example, for sensorimotor mappings, there are spurts at approximately 8 months of age in object permanence, crawling, fear of heights, detection of subjective contours, and many other skills (Bertenthal *et al.*, 1980; Campos & Bertenthal, 1987; McCall *et al.*, 1977; Seibert *et al.*, 1984; Užgiris, 1976). For single representations, there are spurts late in the second year in vocabulary, multiword utterances, pretend play, object permanence, and many other skills (Anisfeld, 1984; Corrigan, 1983; McCall *et al.*, 1977; Užgiris, 1976).

The hypothesized mechanism inducing these synchronous spurts is the development of a new capacity to build skills with the type of structure specified by the respective level. This capacity is not to be confused with the powerful, general competencies hypothesized by Piaget (1957) and Chomsky (1965). Unlike those competencies, the change in capacity does not automatically eventuate in skill changes. Instead, the infant must take time and effort to use the capacity to actually build the changed skills, and factors such as state and task contribute to the actual skill the baby produces. That is the main reason that only some behaviors show spurts for each level.

Babies do not automatically perform at optimal level. Optimal performance requires optimal conditions, including a familiar context, practice with the task, environmental support for high-level performance, optimal state, and the absence of interfering conditions, such as conflicting postures in early infancy.

Functional Level and Environmental Support

Outside optimal contexts, infants usually perform at lower steps in a developmental scale. In nonoptimal contexts, the developmental level of behavior often varies, but there still seems to be a highest step beyond which a baby's performance does not go. This highest level of performance is called the baby's functional level for that context (Lamborn & Fischer, 1988).

Environmental support is an important determinant of whether people produce optimal- or functional-level performance. High-support conditions include the clear definition of task demands and the presence of aids or cues that minimize memory demands. Such conditions make it easier for the person to use environmental information about the structure of the task to sustain the components of the necessary skill. High support does not include scaffolding, which involves direct intervention by an adult in the infant's performance (Bruner, 1982; Vygotsky, 1978; Wood, 1980). Direct intervention certainly can improve task performance, but for purposes of skill analysis, it is difficult to separate the infant's contribution to the behavior from the adult's.

Other factors relevant to learning, such as the use of familiar materials and the opportunity for practice, are also central to optimal performance. Indeed, for the first few years of life, they seem to be more important than environmental support. In children and adolescents, the removal of environmental support for high-level performance often produces an immediate drop to a lower functional level, as in our example at the beginning of this chapter of the 4-year-old telling stories about a doctor. Infants, on the other hand, appear to typically perform at optimum so long as they are carrying out well-practiced skills in familiar domains. That is, infants show a functional level lower than optimum as a result of unfamiliarity, insufficient practice, and other factors, but apparently not as a result of absence of explicit environmental support.

Explicit environmental support seems to emerge suddenly as an important factor during the preschool years. In studies of imitative pretend play in the Cognitive Development Laboratory, the inclusion of high support was more important for children older than 3½ than for infants (Fischer, Hand, Watson, Van Parys, & Tucker, 1984; Watson & Fischer, 1980). Initially, children were tested under a high-support, elic-ited-imitation condition: They were shown a series of stories in a familiar domain, and immediately after each story they were asked to make up a similar story. A few minutes later, infants were tested under two low-support assessments, with no immediate modeling of stories: In one, they were asked to play for several minutes, making up stores like the ones they had been shown earlier. In the second, they were asked to show the experimenter the best story they could.

The sudden emergence of a gap between high- and low-support conditions occurred with the emergence of representational mappings between 3 and 4 years. When performance under the high-support condition was at levels up to single representations, the degree of support had little effect. Almost all children produced stories in the low-support conditions at the same functional level as they had shown in the high-support condition. However, when performance under high support was at representational mappings or beyond, the removal of support led to a sharp drop in developmental level. Shift to the low-support conditions led to an abrupt drop in level.

We expect these findings reflect a much more general phenomenon: Before the emergence of representational mappings, infants tend naturally to function near their optimal level so long as they are in a good arousal state and a familiar environment. They do not need environmental support specifically geared to elicit high-level performance. One reason for this effect is probably that the infant's skills are so closely tied to the environment that familiar environments naturally provide support. After the emergence of representational mappings, high-level functioning becomes much more dependent on explicit environmental support, and the importance of this support probably becomes even greater at levels that emerge later in childhood and adolescence.

Consequently, in an important sense, it is easier to detect the emergence of developmental levels in infancy than in childhood and adolescence. Many studies using standard assessment conditions give evidence of spurts in early development (e.g., Corrigan, 1983; McCall et al., 1977; Seibert et al., 1984; Zelazo, 1983). In later development, however, standard assessments tend to evoke a functional level far below optimum. As a result, developmental curves after the first few years show slow, continuous change rather than discontinuities. To detect the underlying descontinuities in the preschool years and beyond, re-searchers need to use assessments that provide environmental support for high-level performance (Fischer, Pipp, & Bullock, 1984).

State of Arousal

Unlike environmental support, some factors seem to be more important in infancy than at later ages. Three factors that are obviously important as organizers of infant behavior are state, emotions, and the organization of the body.

The baby's state or degree of arousal is crucial to learning and performance, especially in early infancy (Als, Chapter 3 this volume; Prechtl & O'Brien, 1982; Wolff, 1966), as illustrated in the example at the beginning of the chapter of the 1-month-old reaching toward a ball. The state of "quiet alert"—eyes open and bright, accompanied by little diffuse motor activity—is the optimal state for assessing skill. Other states, such as drowsiness or fretting and crying, typically preclude skill assessments because the infant does not seem to be capable of producing the sorts of complex behaviors that investigators, physicians, or parents wish to examine. The younger the infant, the larger role the tester must assume in monitoring and facilitating the baby's degree of arousal, as Als (Chapter 3 this volume) demonstrates.

After infancy, investigators typically ignore state, except to make sure that the person they are assessing is in a state that allows engagement in the task. Older children and adults—at least the well-functioning ones that most behavioral scientists study—seem to be capable of controlling their state in such a way as to substantially reduce interference with performance. Thelen and Fogel (Chapter 2 this volume) describe how infants late in the first year show reliable skills for quieting themselves when they are distressed. By 5 or 6 years of age, most middle class children can regulate their own state well enough to follow the demands of an assessment procedure.

The development of this control is not well understood despite its obvious importance (Kessen & Mandler, 1961). Early in the history of psychology, researchers formulated the Yerkes–Dodson law relating arousal to task performance. In general, an intermediate degree of arousal is necessary for optimal performance, and more complex tasks require slightly lower amounts of arousal than simpler ones (Yerkes & Dodson, 1908). Also, classic neurological research has established the centrality of arousal for brain functioning (Hebb, 1955; Lindsley, 1951). Yet for development beyond early infancy, scholars have not integrated these concepts into their research or theory.

Despite the general neglect of arousal as a factor in assessments beyond infancy, state of arousal does seem to be central in performance in older children, as shown by the phenomenon of attention deficit disorder or hyperactivity. Children with this disorder are described as either being chronically underaroused or having difficulty regulating arousal (Campbell & Werry, 1986). In what might be called a psycho-pharmacological adjustment of state, stimulant medication often improves their performance by increasing their arousal or assisting in arousal regulation.

Even normal children and adults may respond to stimulants with an improvement in state and performance. In one study, three different groups were given a single dose of stimulant medication: hyperactive boys, normal boys, and normal adult males (Rapoport, Buchsbaum, Weingartner, Zahn, Ludlow, & Mikkelsen, 1980). For all three groups, the stimulant produced increased attention and decreased motor activity, reminiscent of the infant's quiet, alert state. At the same time, all three showed improvement in memory performance, with the largest effect occurring for the hyperactive group.

In general, state of arousal seems to be one of the most basic functional mechanisms affecting developmental level, although most studies of children and adults have ignored it. The most plausible generalization about arousal follows the Yerkes–Dodson law: The developmental level of behavior is optimal at an intermediate degree of arousal, and it falls as arousal moves either higher or lower (Fischer & Elmendorf, 1986). Ultimately, this law may prove to be a special case of a more general model of the role of emotions in development.

Emotions and Prototypical Scripts

Emotions are one of the most potent organizers of behavior, and they have powerful effects on variation in developmental level. The activation of an emotion specifies a particular organization for the person's behavior, with different emotions specifying different organizations. The effect is analogous in some ways to that of tasks, in that emotions specify what might be called the organismic context. Recent breakthroughs in emotion theory and research provide a framework for defining the organizations activated by emotions and analyzing their effects.

The preemptive effect of emotions is illustrated by an example of how fear affected the behavior of Seth Fischer at 3½ years of age (Fischer & Elmendorf, 1986). The Will Rogers Museum on Cheyenne Mountain in Colorado is an eerie stone building that is entered through a narrow, winding set of stairs in a tower. As soon as he and his father (Kurt Fischer) approached the entrance, Seth became afraid and asked if there were any monsters inside. Of course, I assured him that there were none. Entering the door, he asked me to carry him. As I carried him up the stairwell, he paused at each door and asked about monsters or bad guys behind it. Will Roger's speeches were playing over the loud-speaker, and Seth misheard Rogers's words in ways that fit his fear. When Rogers said "try," Seth asked, "Who's dying?" When Rogers said, "got," Seth asked, "Who's getting shot?" Only when we left the building did he stop acting afraid and asking about monsters and injury.

This example shows how an emotion evokes a particular organization that facilitates some behaviors and interferes with others, as a task facilitates behaviors relevant to it and interferes with those unrelated. Fear biased Seth toward detecting potential threats and made him less able to explore the tower or learn about Rogers. The effect was so strong that it even led him to mishear Rogers' speech. There was still a strong element of voluntary control in his actions, but the fear strongly constrained or biased their organization in the direction of wariness and defensiveness.

By several months of age, infants possess a set of half a dozen or more basic, species-specific emotions, including anger, fear, sadness, joy, love, perhaps interest, and a few others (Ekman & Oster, 1979; Izard, 1977, 1978; Sroufe, 1979; Tomkins, 1962-1963). For example, Campos's studies of anger have shown that by 4 months of age, infants show a well-organized anger response when their arms are held to prevent movement, and at 7 months, they become angry when a cookie is taken from them as they are about to eat it (Campos, Barrett, Lamb, Goldsmith, & Stenberg, 1983; Stenberg, Campos, & Emde, 1983). Even at 1 month, many of the components of anger are present when the infants' arms are held, but the complete species-specific response pattern is not present.

In general, these basic emotions form species-specific behavioral organizations that arise when the person's goal is promoted (producing a positive emotion) or impeded (producing a negative emotion). By a few months of age, infants show the fundamental behaviors for each of these emotions, but the emotion components can be elaborated and differentiated to form much more complex emotional organizations, such as jealousy, resentment, pride, and guilt (Fischer, Shaver, & Carnochan, 1988).

Anger develops through the reflex levels and gradually becomes an action, a sensorimotor control structure, as shown in Table 1. The finding of a full-blown anger response in 4-month-olds reflects this level of single sensorimotor actions. The anger action is then gradually differentiated and integrated with other actions during the later sensorimotor levels. At approximately 2 years of age, this process eventuates in single representations for anger, in which the child represents anger as occurring both in the self and independently in others. The emotions continue to develop in many ways at later levels, as representations are combined to form more complex skills, beginning with the representational mappings in Table 1.

One of the important breakthroughs in emotion theory is the specification for each basic emotion of a prototypical behavioral script that defines the organization of behavior for that emotion. Researchers have described these scripts for adults based on accounts of emotional experiences or episodes (Shaver, Schwartz, Kirson, & O'Connor, 1987; see also de Rivera, 1981; Scherer, Walbott, & Summerfield, 1986).

Table 2 presents a recasting and simplification of the adult script for anger to fit infant behavior (Fischer *et al.*, 1988). This script is intended to describe the anger reactions of infants in general, and it clearly fits the reactions of those whose arms are being held or who have had a cookie taken from them. Something has interfered with the infants' goal of moving their arms or eating the cookie. They have therefore become activated to focus on the distressing situation, look angry, and remove the interference, although their capacities for removing it are not yet very effective. In addition, they show no evidence of several other adult components of anger: imagining attacking the obstacle, trying to hide their anger, and mentally redefining the situation to eliminate their anger. These components will develop later in childhood.

The organization of behavior produced by such an emotion partially determines the infant's developmental level in a task. If a task demands,

TABLE 2

Prototypic Script for Anger in Infancy[a]

Antecedents
 Something interferes with the infant's plans or goals or threatens to harm him or her.

Responses
 The infant becomes energized to fight or attack the agent causing the anger.
 The infant looks angry and moves in a heavy, tight, or exaggerated way.
 The infant focuses on the anger-inducing situation and is persistent or obstinate in his or her effort to do something about it.

Self-control procedures
 By the end of the first year, the infant may try to inhibit his or her anger.

[a]Adapted from the prototypic scripts for adults presented by Shaver, Schwartz, Kirson, and O'Connor (1987) and Fischer, Shaver, and Carnochan (1988).

for example, aggressive efforts to remove an obstacle, then anger will facilitate performance. On most other sorts of tasks, anger will interfere with infants' behaviors, just as fear interferes with behaviors other than wariness and defensiveness.

The effects of infant state on developmental level may partially result from this interference and facilitation of specific emotions. For example, the emotions of distress (anger, fear, or sadness) undoubtedly produce the wrong scripts for performance on the sorts of tasks used to assess cognitive development. On the other hand, as Demos (1988) has pointed out, the mood or emotion called *interest* facilitates those performances. The curvilinear effects of arousal, leading to worse performance at both high and low arousal, may stem at least partially from these specific effects of emotion scripts, where the distress emotions also produce high or low arousal and interest produces intermediate arousal.

Role of the Body

Somehow, researchers have neglected the role that the body plays in organizing development in childhood and adulthood. For infancy, there has been more investigation of its role, perhaps because the importance of the body is especially obvious then. During the first months of life, the baby's posture has large effects on the baby's behavior, as described for the early levels of the development of reflex skills. But the role of the body is much broader than the effects of posture on reflexes.

Over recent decades, cognitive approaches have dominated psychology and the study of development. Theorists have routinely assumed that development of behavior must arise from changes in the brain. Recent work on dynamic motor theory (Bullock & Grossberg, 1988; Fogel & Thelen, 1987; Kelso & Scholz, 1986; Thelen & Fogel, Chapter 2 this volume; Turvey, 1977) has documented how the structures of the limbs and muscles have direct potent effects on how behavior is organized and how it develops. Many of the phenomena that were previously assumed to arise from brain processes have been shown to depend fundamentally on the organization of parts of the body. For example, the organization and development of eye–hand coordination and of walking both depend in important ways on the body. During these behaviors, the brain plays an important role, but it does not process or specify nearly as much information as was generally assumed.

Thelen's research on the early development of the stepping reflex illustrates how bodily changes can account for some important developmental phenomena (Thelen & Fischer, 1982). The stepping reflex can be easily observed in the first weeks of life. When babies are placed in the right position with their body weight supported, they will take steps with their legs as if walking, but by 1 to 4 months of age, this reflex seems to disappear (Touwen, 1976). The standard interpretation has been that the brain's cortex inhibits this primitive reflex. Thelen has shown that the reflex reappears if babies are tested with their legs in water. Apparently, the legs become fat during the early months of life, and this increased mass makes it difficult for the baby to produce the stepping reflex. Placing the legs in water effectively lightens their mass, and the reflex reappears.

Research by Pipp, Fischer, and Jennings (1987) shows another approach to specifying the influence of the body in development. They hypothesized that the architecture of the body affects the patterns of early development of knowledge of self and mother. Because the sense organs point outward to the world, infants generally learn about their mothers' features before their own. On the other hand, because infants control their own actions more directly than their mothers, they generally learn about their own agency before their mothers'. In developmental sequences designed to assess both features and agency, the hypothesis was supported. On average, infants understood their mothers' features before their own, and they understood their own agency before their mothers. Interestingly, the bias based on the body's architecture seemed to become more complex with the emergence of single representations at about 2 years of age. Then the bias toward mother in features seemed to disappear, and the bias toward self in agency was sometimes overridden by a bias toward positive representation of the self.

In general, the emphasis on the role of the body fits well with the orientation toward acknowledging that the developmental level varies as a result of a number of functional mechanisms. Just as with emotions, much more research is needed to specify the many ways that the body affects development, but enough research has been done to clearly show that the body plays a fundamental role. Just as there is no such thing as a child without a context, there is no such thing as a brain without a body.

SUMMARY AND CONCLUSION

Infants develop through a series of cognitive levels or reorganizations, and at the same time their behavior varies dramatically as a result of various functional mechanisms. There is no opposition between the organization of behavior by developmental levels and the variations in behavior across contexts and states. Indeed, the same developmental scales can be used to gauge both levels and variations.

Recent theoretical advances support this integrative approach, treating the child as using a highly structured set of bodily tools to act in a dynamic world. The world and the body, as well as the brain, contribute to children's developing behavior.

We present a framework for integrating organization with functional mechanisms. Development proceeds through a series of cognitive levels (Table 1). In the first months of life, infants establish control over inborn action components called reflexes, recombining and differentiating them to gradually construct flexible sensorimotor actions. During most of infancy, they recombine and differentiate the actions to gradually construct single concrete representations, which are elaborated during childhood.

On any given day, however, infants do not produce behavior at only one of these levels. To the contrary, their behavior varies widely across levels. A set of functional mechanisms produce short-term variations along developmental scales. Tasks provide one of the most powerful mechanisms of variation, defining domains of skill acquisition and generalization. Even within a given task domain, however, behavior varies in level. Under optimal conditions, behavior occurs at infants' optimal or highest level, which develops in a stagelike pattern of spurts and growth plateaus. Under ordinary conditions, behavior occurs below optimum, at infants' various functional levels. Functional levels vary dramatically as a function of task, assessment condition, arousal state, and many other factors.

Several major functional mechanisms that are generally ignored in research on children and adolescents are especially obvious from research on infancy. Arousal state affects developmental level, with an intermediate arousal state producing the best performance. More broadly, a number of emotions affect level, specifying the kind of behavioral script that infants will follow when they are experiencing a particular emotion. The organization of the body also plays a major role in development, with the structure of the limbs and sense organs making important contributions to the pattern of development. Until recently, the structures of the body have been neglected in most developmental explanations.

Only by integrating these functional mechanisms with the structural analysis of developmental levels will scholars be able to provide an adequate, accurate portrait of infant development.

ACKNOWLEDGMENTS. The authors would like to thank Bennett Bertenthal, Daniel Bullock, John Byers, Andre Bullinger, Joseph Campos, Richard Canfield, Roberta Corrigan, Seth and Johanna Fischer, Marshall Haith, Jeffrey Seibert, and Malcolm Watson for their contributions to the ideas in this chapter. The research on which the chapter is based was supported by grants from the Cattell Fund, the Spencer Foundation, and the Carnegie Corporation.

REFERENCES

Anisfeld, M. (1984). *Language development from birth to three.* Hillsdale, N. J.: Erlbaum.

Bates, E., Benigni, L. Bretherton, I., Camaioni, L., & Volterra, V. (1979). *The emergence of symbols.* New York: Academic Press.

Bertenthal, B. I., Campos, J. J., & Haith, M. M. (1980). Development of visual organization: The perception of subjective contours. *Child Development, 51,* 1072–1080.

Bloom, L. (1973). *One word at a time.* The Hague: Mouton.

Bruner, J. S. (1973). *Beyond the information given: Studies in the psychology of knowing.* New York: Norton

Bruner, J. S. (1982). The organization of action and the nature of adult-infant transaction. In M. Cranach & R. Harre (Eds.), *The analysis of action.* New York: Cambridge University Press.

Bullinger, A. (1981). Cognitive elaboration of sensorimotor behavior. In G. Butterworth (Ed.), *Infancy and epistemology.* Hassocks, England: Harvester Press.

Bullinger, A., & Chatillon, J.-F. (1983). Recent theory and research of the Genevan school. In P. H. Mussen (Ed.), *Handbook of child psychology.* Vol. 3: *Cognitive development* (J. H. Flavell & E. M. Markman, Eds., pp. 231–262). New York: Wiley.

Bullock, D., & Grossberg, S. (1988). Neural dynamics of planned arm movements: Emergent invariants and speed-accuracy properties during trajectory formation. *Psychological Review, 95,* 49–90.

Campbell, S. B., & Werry, J. S. (1986). Attention deficit disorder (hyperactivity). In H. C. Quay & J. S. Werry (Eds.), *Psychopathological disorders in children* (3rd ed., pp. 111–155). New York: Wiley.

Campos, J. J., & Bertenthal, B. I. (1987). Locomotion and psychological development in infancy. In F. Morrison, K. Lord, & D. Keating (Eds.), *Advances in applied developmental psychology.* New York: Academic Press.

Campos, J. J., Barrett, K. C., Lamb, M. E., Goldsmith, H. H., & Stenberg, C. (1983). Socioemotional development. In P. H. Mussen (Ed.), *Handbook of child psychology.* Vol. 2: *Infancy and developmental psychobiology* (M. M. Haith & J. J. Campos, Eds., pp. 783–915). New York: Wiley.

Canfield, R. (1988). *Visual anticipation in infancy.* Unpublished doctoral dissertation, University of Denver.

Case, R. (1985). *Intellectual development: Birth to adulthood.* New York: Academic Press.

Caveness, W. F. (1962). *Atlas of electroencephalography in the developing monkey (Macaca Mulatta).* Reading, MA: Addison-Wesley.

Chomsky, N. (1965). *Aspects of the theory of syntax.* Cambridge: M. I. T. Press.

Chugani, H. T., & Phelps, M. E. (1986). Maturational changes in cerebral function in infants determined by [18]FDG Positron Emission Tomography. *Science, 231,* 840–843.

Cohen, L. B., & Younger, B. A. (1984). Infant perception of angular relations. *Infant behavior and development, 7,* 37–47.

Corrigan, R. (1977). Patterns of individual communication and cognitive development. (Unpublished doctoral dissertation, University of Denver, 1976). *Dissertation Abstracts International, 37*(10), 5393B. (University Microfilms No. 77-7400).

Corrigan, R. (1983). The development of representational skills. In K. W. Fischer (Ed.), *Levels and transitions in children's development. New Directions for Child Development* (No. 21, pp. 51–64). San Francisco: Jossey-Bass.

Corrigan, R., & Fischer, K. W. (1985). Controlling sources of variation in search tasks: A skill theory approach. In H. Wellman (Ed.), *Children's searching: The development of search skill and spatial representation* (pp. 287–318). Hillsdale, NJ: Erlbaum.

de Rivera, J. (1981). The structure of anger. In J. de Rivera (Ed.), *Conceptual encounter: A method for the exploration of human experience* (pp. 35–81). Washington, DC: University Press of America.

Demos, E. V. (1988). Affect and the development of the self: New frontiers. In A. Goldberg (Ed.), *Frontiers in self psychology: Progress in self psychology* (Vol. 3, pp. 27–53). Hillsdale, NJ: Analytic Press.

Dreyfus-Brisac, C. (1978). Ontogenesis of brain bioelectrical activity and sleep organization in neonates and infants. In F. Falkner & J. M. Tanner (Eds.), *Human growth 3: Neurobiology and nutrition* (pp. 157–182). New York: Plenum Press.

Ekman, P., & Oster, H. (1979). Facial expressions of emotion. *Annual Review of Psychology, 30,* 527–554.

Emde, R., & Robinson, J. (1980). The first two months: Recent research in developmental psychobiology and the changing view of the newborn. In J. Call & R. Noshpitz (Eds.), *Basic handbook of child psychiatry* (pp. 72–105). New York: Academic Press.

Emde, R., Gaensbauer, T., & Harmon, R. (1976). Emotional expression in infancy: A biobehavioral study. *Psychological Issues (10,* no. 37). New York: International Universities Press.

Field, J., Muir, D., Pilon, R., Sinclair, M. & Dodwell, P.C. (1980). Infants' orientation to lateral sound from birth to three months. *Child Development, 51,* 195–298.

Fischer, K. W. (1980). A theory of cognitive development: The control and construction of hierarchies of skills. *Psychological Review, 87,* 477–531.

Fischer, K. W. (1983). Developmental levels as periods of discontinuity. In K. W. Fischer (Ed.), *Levels and transitions in children's development. New Directions for Child Development* (No. 21, pp. 5–20). San Francisco: Jossey-Bass.

Fischer, K. W. (1987). Relations between brain and cognitive development. *Child Development, 57,* 623–632.

Fischer, K. W., & Bullock, D. (1984). Cognitive development in school-age children: Conclusions and new directions. In W. A. Collins (Ed.), *The years from six to twelve: Cognitive development during middle childhood* (pp. 70–146). Washington, DC: National Academy Press.

Fischer, K. W., & Corrigan, R. (1981). A skill approach to language development. In R. Stark (Ed.), *Language behavior in infancy and early childhood* (pp. 245–273). Amsterdam: Elsevier.

Fischer, K. W., & Elmendorf, D. (1986). Becoming a different person: Transformations in personality and social behavior. In M. Perlmutter (Ed.), *Minnesota symposium on child psychology* (Vol. 18, pp. 137–178). Hillsdale, NJ: Erlbaum.

Fischer, K. W., & Farrar, M. J. (1987). Generalizations about generalization: How a theory of skill development explains both generality and specificity. *International Journal of Psychology, 22,* 643–677.

Fischer, K. W., Hand, H. H., Watson, M. W., Van Parys, M., & Tucker, J. (1984). Putting the child into socialization: The development of social categories in preschool children. In L. Katz (Ed.), *Current topics in early childhood education* (Vol. 5, pp. 27–72). Norwood, NJ: Ablex.

Fischer, K. W., & Jennings, S. (1981). The emergence of representation in search. *Developmental Review, 1,* 18–30.

Fischer, K. W., & Lamborn, S. (in press). Sources of variations in developmental levels: Cognitive and emotional transitions during adolescence. To be published in A. de Ribaupierre (Ed.), *Mechanisms of transition in cognitive and emotional development*. New York: Cambridge University Press.

Fischer, K. W., & Pipp, S. L. (1984). Processes of cognitive development: Optimal level and skill acquisition. In R. J. Sternberg (Ed.), *Mechanisms of cognitive development* (pp. 45–80). New York: W. H. Freeman.

Fischer, K. W., Pipp, S. L., & Bullock, D. (1984). Detecting developmental discontinuities: Methods and measurement. In R. Emde & R. Harmon (Eds.), *Continuities and discontinuities in development* (pp. 95–121). New York: Plenum Press.

Fischer, K. W., Shaver, P., & Carnochan, P. (1988). From basic- to subordinate-category emotions: A skill approach to emotional development. In W. Damon (Ed.), *Child development today and tomorrow*. (pp. 107–136). San Francisco: Jossey-Bass.

Fischer, K. W., & Silvern, L. (1985). Stages and individual differences in cognitive development. *Annual Review of Psychology, 36,* 613–648.

Flavell, J. (1982). Structures, stages, and sequences in cognitive development. In W.A. Collins (Eds.), *The concept of development*. Minnesota Symposium on Child Psychology (Vol. 15). Hillsdale, NJ: Erlbaum.

Fogel, A., & Thelen, E. (1987). Development of early expressive and communicative action: Reinterpreting the evidence from a dynamic systems perspective. *Developmental Psychology, 23,* 747–761.

Gibson, J. J. (1979). *The ecological approach to visual perception*. Boston: Houghton-Mifflin.

Goldman-Rakic, P. (1987). Connectionist theory and the biological basis of cognitive development. *Child Development, 58,* 601–622.

Gopnik, A., & Meltzoff, A. N. (1986). Relations between semantic and cognitive development in the one-word stage. *Child Development, 57,* 1040–1053.

Gopnik, A., & Meltzoff, A. N. (1987). The development of categorization in the second year and its relation to other cognitive and linguistic developments. *Child Development, 58,* 1523–1531.

Grossberg, S. (1980). How does a brain build a cognitive code? *Psychological Review, 87,* 1–57.

Haith, M. M., Bergman, T., & Moore, M. J. (1977). Eye contact and face scanning in early infancy. *Science, 198,* 853–855.

Haith, M. M., Hazan, C., & Goodman, G. S. (1988). Expectation and anticipation of dynamic visual events by 3.5-month-old babies. *Child Development, 59,* 467–479.

Hayne, H., Rovee-Collier, C., & Perris, E. E. (1987). Categorization and memory retrieval by three-month-olds. *Child Development, 58,* 750–767.

Hebb, D. O. (1955). Drives and the C. N. S. *Psychological Review, 62,* 243–254.

Hofsten, C. von (in press). Transition mechanisms in sensorimotor development. In A. de Ribaupierre (Ed.), *Transition mechanisms in child development*. New York: Cambridge University Press.

Horn, J. L. (1976). Human abilities. *Annual Review of Psychology, 27,* 437–486.

Ilg, F. L., & Ames, L. B. (1955). *Child behavior from birth to ten*. New York: Harper & Row.

Izard, C. E. (1977). *Human Emotions*. New York: Plenum Press.

Izard, C. E. (1978). On the ontogenesis of emotions and emotion-cognition relationships in infancy. In M. Lewis & L. Rosenblum (Eds.), *The development of affect*. New York: Plenum Press.

Kagan, J. (1982). *Psychological research on the human infant: An evaluative summary*. New York: W. T. Grant Foundation.

Kaye, K., & Fogel, A. (1980). The temporal structure of face-to-face communication between mothers and infants. *Developmental Psychology, 16,* 454–464.

Kelso, J. A. S., & Scholz, J. P. (1986). Cooperative phenomena in biological motion. In J. Haken (Ed.), *Synergetics of complex systems in physics, chemistry, and biology*. New York: Springer-Verlag.

Kessen, W., & Mandler, J. (1961). Anxiety, pain, and the inhibition of distress. *Psychological Review*, 68, 396–404.

Lamborn, S. E., & Fischer, K. W. (1988). Optimal and functional levels in cognitive development: The individual's developmental range, *Newsletter of the International Society for the Study of Behavioral Development*, No. 2 (Serial No. 14), 1–4.

Legerstee, M., Pomerleau, A., Malcuit, G., & Feider, H. (1987). The development of infants' responses to people and a doll: Implications for research in communication. *Infant Behavior and Development*, 10, 81–96.

Lindsley, D. B. (1951). Emotion. In S. S. Stevens (Ed.), *Handbook of experimental psychology*. New York: Wiley.

Maratos, O. (1982). Trends in the development of imitation in early infancy. In T. G. Bever (Ed.), *Regressions in mental development: Basic phenomena and theories* (pp. 81–101). Hillsdale, NJ: Erlbaum.

Marvin, R. S., Greenberg, M. T., & Mossler, D. G. (1976). The early development of conceptual perspective taking: Distinguising among multiple perspectives. *Child Development*, 47, 511–514.

Maurer, D., & Salapatek, P. (1976). Developmental changes in the scanning of faces by young infants. *Child Development*, 46, 523–527.

McCall, R. B. (1983). Exploring developmental transitions in mental performance. In K. W. Fischer (Ed.), *Levels and transitions in children's development. New Directions for Child Development* (No. 21, pp. 65–80). San Francisco: Jossey-Bass.

McCall, R. B., Eichorn, D. H., & Hogarty, P. S. (1977). Transitions in early mental development. *Monographs of the Society for Research in Development*, 42, (3, Serial No. 171).

McCune-Nicolich, L. (1981). Toward symbolic functioning: Structure of early pretend games and potential parallels with language. *Child Development*, 52, 785–797.

McGraw, M. B. (1943). *The neuromuscular maturation of human infant*. New York: Columbia University Press.

Mounoud, P. (1976). Les revolutions psychologiques de l'enfant. *Archives de Psychologie*, 44, 103–114.

Papousek, H., & Papousek, M. (1979). The infant's fundamental adaptive response system in social interaction. In E. B. Thoman (Ed.), *Origins of the infant's social responsiveness*. Hillsdale, NJ: Erlbaum, 1979.

Parker, S. T. (1977). Piaget's sensorimotor series in an infant macaque: A model for comparing unstereotyped behavior and intelligence in human and nonhuman primates. In S. Chevalier-Skolnikoff & F. E. Poirier (Eds.) *Primate bio-social development: Biological, social, and ecological determinants* (pp. 43–112). New York: Garland.

Peiper, A. (1963). *Cerebral function in infancy and childhood*. New York: Consultants Bureau, 1963.

Piaget, J. (1941). Le mécanisme du devèloppement mental et les lois du groupement des opérations. *Archives de Psychologie, Genève*, 28, 215–285.

Piaget, J. (1951). *Play, dreams, and imitation in childhood* (C. Gattegno & F. M. Hodgson, Trans.). New York: Harcourt Brace. (Originally published 1946)

Piaget, J. (1952). *The origins of intelligence in children* (M. Cook, Trans.). New York: International Universities Press (Originally published 1936)

Piaget, J. (1954). *The construction of reality in the child* (M. Cook, Trans.). New York, Basic Books. (Originally published 1937)

Piaget, J. (1957). Logique et équilibre dans les comportements du sujet. *Études d'Épistémologie Génétique*, 2, 27–118.

304   KURT W. FISCHER AND ANNE E. HOGAN

Piaget, J. (1983). Piaget's theory. In P. H. Mussen (Ed.), *Handbook of child psychology*, Vol. 1: *History, theory, and methods*. (W. Kessen, Ed., pp. 103–126). New York: Wiley.

Pipp, S. L., & Haith, M. M. (1977). Infant visual scanning of two- and three-dimension forms. *Child Development, 48*, 1640–1644.

Pipp, S. L., Fischer, K. W. & Jennings, S. L. (1987). The acquisition of self and mother knowledge in infancy. *Developmental Psychology. 22*, 86–96.

Prechtl, H. F. R., & O'Brien, M. J. (1982). Behavioral states of the full-term newborn: The emergence of a concept. In P. Stratton (Ed.), *Psychobiology of the human newborn* (pp. 53–73). New York: Wiley.

Ramsay, D. S. (1984). Onset of duplicated syllable babbling and unimanual handedness in infancy: Evidence for developmental change in hemispheric specialization? *Developmental Psychology, 20*, 64–71.

Rapaport, J. L., Buchsbaum, M. S., Weingartner, J. L., Zahn, T. P., Ludlow, C., & Mikkelsen, E. J. (1980). Dextroamphetamine: Its cognitive and behavioral effects in normal and hyperactive boys and normal men. *Archives of General Psychiatry, 37*, 933–943.

Rovee-Collier, C. (1987). Learning and memory in infancy. In J. D. Osofsky (Ed.), *Handbook of infant development* (2nd ed., pp. 98–148). New York: Wiley.

Scherer, K. R., Walbott, H. G., & Summerfield, A. B. (Eds.). (1986). *Experiencing emotions: A cross-cultural study*. Cambridge, England: Cambridge University Press.

Seibert, J., & Hogan, A. (1982). A model for assessing social and object skills and planning intervention. In D. P. McClowry, A. M. Guilford, & S. O. Richardson (Eds.), *Infant communication* (pp. 21–51). New York: Grune & Stratton.

Seibert, J. M., Hogan, A. F., & Mundy, P. C. (1984). Mental age and cognitive stage in young handicapped and at-risk children. *Intelligence, 8*, 11–29.

Shaver, P., Schwartz, J., Kirson, D., & O'Connor, C. (1987). Emotion knowledge: Further exploration of a prototype approach. *Journal of Personality and Social Psychology, 52*, 1061–1086.

Skinner, B. F. (1969). *Contingencies of reinforcement: A theoretical analysis*. New York: Appleton-Century-Crofts.

Sroufe, L. A. (1979). Socioemotional development. In J. Osofsky (Ed.), *Handbook of infant development* (pp. 462–516). New York: Wiley, 1979.

Stenberg, C., Campos, J., & Emde, R. (1983). The facial expression of anger in seven-month-old infants. *Child Development, 54*, 178–184.

Thelen, E., & Fisher, D. M. (1982). Newborn stepping: An explanation for the "disappearing reflex." *Developmental Psychology, 18*, 760–775.

Tomasello, M., & Farrar, M. J. (1984). Cognitive bases of lexical development: Object permanence and relational words. *Journal of Child Language, 11*, 477–493.

Tomasello, M., & Farrar, M. J. (1986). Object permanence and relational words: A lexical training study. *Journal of Child Language, 13*, 495–505.

Tomkins, S. (1962–1963). *Affect, imagery, consciousness*. New York: Springer.

Touwen, B. C. L. (1976). *Neurological development in infancy* (Clinics in developmental medicine, No. 58). London: Spastics International.

Turvey, M. T. (1977). Preliminaries to a theory of action with reference to vision. In R. Shaw & J. Bradsford (Eds.), *Perceiving, acting, and knowing: Toward an ecological psychology* (pp. 211–267). Hillsdale, NJ: Erlbaum.

Uzgiris, I. C. (1976). Organization of sensorimotor intelligence. In M. Lewis (Ed.), *Origins of intelligence: Infancy and early childhood* (pp. 123–164). New York: Plenum Press.

von Hofsten, C. (1984). Developmental changes in the organization of prereaching movements. *Developmental Psychology, 20*, 378–388.

Vygotsky, L. (1978). *Mind in society: The development of higher psychological processes* (M. Cole,

V. John-Steiner, S. Scribner, & Ellen Souberman, Trans.). Cambridge, MA: Harvard University Press.

Watson, M. W., & Fischer, K. W. (1980). Development of social roles in elicited and spontaneous behavior during the preschool years. *Developmental Psychology, 16*, 484–494.

Wohlwill, J. F. (1973). *The study of behavioral development.* New York: Academic Press.

Wolff, P. H. (1966). The causes, controls, and organization of behavior in the neonate. *Psychological Issues, 5*(17).

Wood, D. J. (1980). Teaching the young child: Some relationships between social interaction, language, and thought. In D. R. Olson (Ed.), *The social foundations of language and thought* (pp. 280–296). New York: Norton.

Woodruff, D. S. (1978). Brain electrical activity and behavior relationships over the life-span. In P. B. Baltes (Ed.), *Life-span development and behavior* (Vol. 1, pp. 111–179). New York: Academic Press.

Yerkes, R. M., & Dodson, J. D. (1908). The relation of strength of stimulus to rapidity of habit formation. *Journal of Comparative Neurology and Psychology, 18*, 459–482.

Zelazo, P. R., & Leonard, E. L. (1983). The dawn of active thought. In K. W. Fischer (Ed.), *Levels and transitions in children's development. New Directions for Child Development* (No. 21, pp. 37–50). San Francisco: Jossey-Bass.

Zelazo, P. R., Zelazo, N. A., & Kolb, S. (1972). "Walking" in the newborn. *Science, 176*, 314–315.

Index